Language Variation

Editors: Elena Anagnostopoulou, Mark Baker,) Roberta D'Alessandro, David Pesetsky, Susi Wurmbrand

In this series:

1. Bailey, Laura R. & Michelle Sheehan. Order and structure in syntax I: Word order and syntactic structure.

2. Sheehan, Michelle & Laura R. Bailey. Order and structure in syntax II: Subjecthood and argument structure.

Order and structure in syntax I

Word order and syntactic structure

Edited by

Laura R. Bailey

Michelle Sheehan

language
science
press

Laura R. Bailey & Michelle Sheehan (ed.). 2017. *Order and structure in syntax I: Word order and syntactic structure* (Open Generative Syntax 1). Berlin: Language Science Press.

This title can be downloaded at:
http://langsci-press.org/catalog/book/159
© 2017, the authors
Published under the Creative Commons Attribution 4.0 Licence (CC BY 4.0):
http://creativecommons.org/licenses/by/4.0/
ISBN: 978-3-96110-026-2 (Digital)
    978-3-96110-027-9 (Hardcover)
DOI:10.5281/zenodo.1117686
Source code available from www.github.com/langsci/159
Collaborative reading: paperhive.org/documents/remote?type=langsci&id=159

Cover and concept of design: Ulrike Harbort
Typesetting: Felix Kopecky, Sebastian Nordhoff
Proofreading: Waldfried Premper, Eran Asoulin, Esther Yap, Andreas Hölzl, Shannon Bischoff, Prisca Jerono, Ikmi Nur Oktavianti, Gerald Delahunty, Bev Erasmus, Alec Shaw, George Walkden, Eitan Grossman, Amr Zawawy, Matthew Czuba, Kleanthes Grohmann, Maria Isabel Maldonado, Annie Zaenen, Timm Lichte
Fonts: Linux Libertine, Arimo, DejaVu Sans Mono
Typesetting software: XƎLATEX

Language Science Press
Unter den Linden 6
10099 Berlin, Germany
langsci-press.org

Storage and cataloguing done by FU Berlin

Freie Universität Berlin

This book is dedicated to Anders Holmberg in recognition not only of his significant contribution to the field of syntax, but also of his support, guidance and friendship to the editors and the contributors to this volume.

Contents

Introduction: Order and structure in syntax

Michelle Sheehan
Anglia Ruskin University

Laura R. Bailey
University of Kent

Hierarchical structure and argument structure are two of the most pervasive and widely studied properties of natural language.[1] The papers in this set of two volumes further explore these aspects of language from a range of perspectives, touching on a number of fundamental issues, notably the relationship between linear order and hierarchical structure and variation in subjecthood properties across languages. The first volume focuses on issues of word order and its relationship to structure, while the second turns to argument structure and subjecthood in particular. In this introduction, we provide a brief overview of the content of this first volume, drawing out important threads and questions which they raise.

This first volume, consisting of 12 papers and six squibs, addresses the important question of what word order can tell us about syntactic structure and by implication the syntax/semantics interface. In some cases, the claim is that (some aspects of) word order should not be encoded in the narrow syntax (Zwart; Haddican & Extepare; Julien; and Erteschik-Shir & Josefsson) because PF-based explanations are sufficient or even more explanatory. In other cases, it is claimed that word order gaps are best explained by a theory in which word order is encoded narrow syntactically (Biberauer), and the implications of this for the narrow syntax or syntax/semantics interface are explored.

The first three papers (by Djärv, Heycock & Rohde; Zwart; and Poole) focus on the verb second property (henceforth V2), which is characteristic of most of the Germanic language family as well as certain diachronic and synchronic Romance varieties, whereby the finite verb in matrix (and a subset of embedded) clauses occupies the second position and is (usually) preceded by a single constituent (see Holmberg 2015b for an

---

[1] All of the papers in this volume were written on the occasion of Anders Holmberg's 65th birthday in recognition of the enormous contribution he has made to these issues.

Michelle Sheehan & Laura R. Bailey. 2017. Introduction: Order and structure in syntax. In Laura R. Bailey & Michelle Sheehan (eds.), *Order and structure in syntax I: Word order and syntactic structure*, vii–x. Berlin: Language Science Press. DOI:10.5281/zenodo.1117704

overview). The papers address either how V2 is derived (Poole, Zwart) or its seman-tic/discourse function (Djärv, Heycock & Rohde), providing novel observations and anal-yses on a much studied topic. On one hand, Zwart argues that V2 must be a PF phenom-enon, based on the fact that auxiliary verbs undergo V2 movement and yet periphrastic tenses must be inserted late in the morphology. Poole, on the other hand, argues that V2 in Old Spanish is derived in the syntactic manner proposed by Holmberg (2012) for the Germanic family: via head and XP movement to the same phrase. Djärv, Heycock & Rohde focus on the semantics/pragmatics of V2 rather than its syntax and are concerned with establishing the precise distribution of V2 clauses and embedded root phenomena more generally, based on novel survey data from Swedish and English. These three pa-pers touch on different aspects of the well-studied V2 phenomenon, highlighting very clearly that the connection between order and structure cannot be taken for granted and nor can the mapping between syntactic and semantic/pragmatic structure. The is-sues addressed in Djärv, Heycock & Rohde's paper are taken up again in Nikanne's paper (chapter 4), which sketches a new way of thinking about word order in Finnish, a language that displays complex word order patterns, depending on both morphology and information structure. Finally, Sulaiman's squib on verb movement in Syrian Arabic argues that although this language is not generally held to be V2, certain word order pat-terns are best explained if a similar mechanism to that found in V2 languages is present in this Arabic variety.

The next pair of papers (by Erteschik-Shir & Josefsson and Woolford) and the squib by Vikner, Christensen & Nyvad all focus on another curious word order phenomenon: object shift, a process by which some subset of objects undergoes obligatory or optional movement to the left of adverbs/negation in certain contexts. This phenomenon was studied at length by Anders Holmberg, who observed a curious connection between ob-ject shift and verb movement in the Scandinavian languages (Holmberg's Generalization; Holmberg 1986, 1999). Once again, while one paper argues, based on prosodic evidence, that this is a PF operation (Erteschik-Shir & Josefsson), the other takes it to be syntactic and active in languages well beyond those Germanic languages in which it was first ob-served (Woolford). Woolford's paper argues that in Aleut, ergative case occurs wherever the object of V is null because these null pronouns undergo obligatory object shift out of VP, triggering ergative case (see Woolford 2015).

Chapter 7–9 focus on a peculiar word order gap (the Final-over-Final Condition, hence-forth FOFC), which was first discovered by Holmberg (2000) and then developed by Bib-erauer et al. (2014); Sheehan et al. (2017). FOFC is based on the observation that a head final phrase cannot dominate a head-initial phrase in the same domain (where different definitions of the relevant notion of domain have been offered). Haddican & Extepare consider certain word order gaps in Basque verb clusters, showing that the repairs which occur raise challenges for a narrow syntactic view of FOFC. Biberauer and Julien both discuss the relevance of FOFC to the adpositional domain. Biberauer considers the com-plex adpositional system of Afrikaans in the contexts of broader cross-linguistic patterns and defends a narrow syntactic view of FOFC. Julien, on the other hand, focuses on data from Sámi, a language which also has both prepositions and postpositions, but argues for a PF-based account, departing from previous approaches.

Finally, chapters 10–12 and the squibs by Rizzi, Platzack and Kayne focus on word order and other issues connected to the left periphery of the clause. Wiltschko's and Tsoulas' contributions focus on questions, answers and responses, showing that complex structures lie behind simple response particles such as *yes* and *no* (see also Holmberg 2015a). While Wiltschko adopts the idea that particles are simplex and their complex meaning arises from the clausal structures into which they are inserted, Tsoulas argues that particles themselves contain internal structure.

Rizzi's squib considers the uniqueness condition on focus and whether this effect should be explained by locality or interface conditions. He argues, based on the fact that the uniqueness condition is preserved even in complex sentences containing multiple clauses, that locality based explanations are insufficient. He further shows, however, that locality may be required to rule out word order restrictions between foci and interrogative complementisers, the conclusion being that both kinds of explanations may be necessary in order to explain cartographic generalisations. Kayne's squib adopts an explanation for the different landing sites of wh-movement in questions vs. relative clauses, in terms of locality. He goes on to show, however, that the derivation of relative clauses is more complex than previously thought as it is possible to form relative clauses containing multiple wh-phrases. Such examples, he argues, can be accounted for if relative pronouns are actually determiners which get stranded when their NP complement moves to a higher position. Platzack's squib turns to word order effects in a different kind of wh-clause: wh-root-infinitive clauses in Swedish. He proposes, based on word order facts and the unavailability of overt subjects, that these kinds of clauses lack a T projection.

Richards' paper focuses on movement operations and how they contribute to syntactic structure building, bringing together several different strands of research to argue for two distinct kinds of A-bar movement: one which leaves a null pronoun and another which leaves a null definite description.

Lastly, Emonds' paper uses word order differences between Old and Middle English amongst other grammatical differences to further defend Emonds & Faarlund's (2014) proposal that Modern English is a North Germanic language. While Old English was an OV language (with some complications), Middle English has umarked VO order in both main and dependent clauses. It also has preposition stranding, parasitic gaps, subject+tense tag questions, all features which it shares with North Germanic but not West Germanic.

The papers in this first volume address different word order-related issues and focus on data from a wide range of languages including Afrikaans, Aleut, Basque, Danish, Dutch, English, Finnish, German, Greek, North Sámi, Norwegian, Old Spanish, and Swedish. They all share the desire to better understand the relationship between linear order, syntax and semantics, using intricate data from the detailed study of individual languages informed by broader cross-linguistic patterns. Anders Holmberg has been a pioneer of this kind of careful syntactic investigation for the past 30 years, and continues to be so to this day.

References

Biberauer, Theresa, Anders Holmberg & Ian Roberts. 2014. A syntactic universal and its consequences. *Linguistic Inquiry* 45. 169–225.

Emonds, Joseph & Jan Terje Faarlund. 2014. *English: The language of the Vikings.* Olomouc: Palacky University Press.

Holmberg, Anders. 1986. *Word order and syntactic features in the Scandinavian languages and English.* Stockholm: Stockholm University dissertation.

Holmberg, Anders. 1999. Remarks on Holmberg's Generalization. *Studia Linguistica* 53(1). 1–39.

Holmberg, Anders. 2000. Deriving OV order in Finnish. In Peter Svenonius (ed.), *The derivation of VO and OV*, 123–152. Amsterdam: John Benjamins.

Holmberg, Anders. 2012. Verb second. In Tibor Kiss & Artemis Alexiadou (eds.), *Syntax – an international handbook of contemporary syntactic research*, 343–384. Berlin: Walter de Gruyter Verlag.

Holmberg, Anders. 2015a. *The syntax of yes and no.* Oxford: Oxford University Press.

Holmberg, Anders. 2015b. Verb second. In Tibor Kiss & Artemis Alexiadou (eds.), *Syntax – Theory and analysis: An international handbook*, 2nd edn., 342–382. Berlin: de Gruyter.

Sheehan, Michelle, Theresa Biberauer, Ian Roberts & Anders Holmberg (eds.). 2017. *The Final-over-Final condition.* Cambridge, MA: MIT Press.

Woolford, Ellen. 2015. Ergativity and transitivity. *Linguistic Inquiry* 46(3). 489–531.

Part I

Word order and syntactic structure

Chapter 1

Assertion and factivity: Towards explaining restrictions on embedded V2 in Scandinavian

Kajsa Djärv
University of Pennsylvania

Caroline Heycock
University of Edinburgh

Hannah Rohde
University of Edinburgh

Since Hooper & Thompson (1973), many researchers have pursued the insight that V2 is licensed by assertion. H&T categorise predicates depending on whether their complement can be asserted: e.g. communication verbs (*say*) permit the assertion of their complement, in contrast to factives (*be happy*). Simons (2007) proposes distinguishing between embedded propositions that do or do not constitute the Main Point of Utterance (MPU) – a sharpening of the notion of assertion: in question/response-sequences, the proposition answering the question is the MPU. Given this definition/diagnostic for assertion, factives *can*, given the appropriate discourse context, embed MPU and thus should allow embedded V2 (EV2). This paper presents two experiments testing whether factives can embed MPU and whether MPU licenses EV2 in Swedish. The results support both Simons's (2007) contention that factives can embed MPU, while providing new evidence that MPU does not correlate with EV2.

1 Introduction

The study of "Verb Second" (V2) has a long history in the literature on Scandinavian syntax (see review in Holmberg 2013). Although as a first approximation V2 is a phenomenon that is characteristic of root clauses, it has long been known that it occurs also in a restricted set of embedded clauses. What remains unresolved is a precise characterisation – and a fortiori a theoretical account – of this restricted distribution in embedded contexts. In this paper we present new experimental results concerning one aspect of

Kajsa Djärv, Caroline Heycock & Hannah Rohde. 2017. Assertion and factivity: Towards explaining restrictions on embedded V2 in Scandinavian. In Laura R. Bailey & Michelle Sheehan (eds.), *Order and structure in syntax I: Word order and syntactic structure*, 3–28. Berlin: Language Science Press. DOI:10.5281/zenodo.1117696

the distribution of embedded V2, namely the constraints on where it can appear in the complement to various types of verb. At issue is whether such cases of V2 are sensitive primarily to local lexical constraints or are reflective of pragmatic factors concerning the status of the embedded clause in the larger discourse context.

All the Scandinavian languages exhibit V2 robustly in root clauses. Unlike German and Dutch, they are SVO languages and hence in many subject-initial clauses the V2 property is not unambiguously manifested. If a non-subject occurs in first position in a root clause, however, the finite verb must immediately follow it: hence (1) is an unambiguous example of a V2 clause in Swedish.

(1) Den här boken   läste han inte.
    this here book.DEF read he   not
    'This book, he didn't read.'

In the standard varieties of the Mainland Scandinavian languages there is an additional diagnostic. In contexts in which V2 is expected not to be found, such as embedded interrogatives or relative clauses, sentential negation precedes the finite verb.[1] In root clauses, however, the finite verb obligatorily precedes negation. This contrast is illustrated in (2).

(2) a. Det här är boken   som han **inte läste**.
       this here is book.DEF that he   not read
       'This is the book that he didn't read.'

    b. Han **läste inte** den här boken.
       he   read not   this here book.DEF
       'He didn't read this book.'

It is standardly assumed, then, that negation in these languages occupies a position above that of the finite verb in a non-V2 sentence, but that part of the derivation of V2 involves movement of the verb to a higher position in the left periphery. Hence the V_{fin}<Neg order is standardly used as a diagnostic for a clause exhibiting V2.

As just stated, root clauses in Mainland Scandinavian contrast with relatives or embedded interrogatives in that these latter contexts disallow V2. However, as is well-known, in some cases V2 appears to be possible in embedded clauses, as in (3b):

(3) a. Han sa   att han **inte hade** läst den här boken.
       he   said that he   not had   read this here book.DEF
       'He said that he hadn't read this book.'

    b. Han sa   att han **hade inte** läst den här boken.
       he   said that he   had not   read this here book.DEF
       'He said that he hadn't read this book.'

---

[1] The difference in this respect between these varieties and Icelandic in particular has been intensively researched in a series of independent and collaborative works by Anders Holmberg and Christer Platzack, see e.g. Platzack (1987); Platzack & Holmberg (1989); Holmberg & Platzack (1991; 1995); Holmberg (2010).

Such examples of embedded Verb Second (EV2) constitute a classic case of an "Embedded Root Phenomenon," and much of the discussion of the distribution of EV2 has relied heavily on the insights of Hooper & Thompson (1973) (H&T) – although H&T discussed only English. On the one hand, H&T established five different classes of predicates taking clausal complements, noting in particular that **factive** predicates did not license root phenomena in their complements.[2] On the other, H&T argued that this constraint on factive complements derived ultimately from the impossibility of such complements being **asserted**; the fundamental claim being that root phenomena in general are only possible in assertions, for reasons which H&T took to be essentially pragmatic.

In work on EV2 in Scandinavian ever since Andersson's (1975) classic dissertation, both of these aspects of H&T's analysis have been invoked. One important question is whether H&T were correct in their argument – revisited in recent corpus work by Jensen & Christensen (2013) – that the (claimed) ungrammaticality of root phenomena in factive complements is in fact an epiphenomenon, with the ultimate explanation being tied rather to assertion.

In this paper we discuss how the work of Simons (2007) gives us a way to address this question. Simons' concept of "Main Point of Utterance" (MPU) can be seen as a more precise characterisation of what H&T refer to as the "main assertion." We first provide experimental evidence, using Simons' Question-Answer paradigm, that manipulations of the discourse context can indeed influence what comprehenders take to be the MPU. We also confirm that embedded clauses, even under factives, can be the MPU (Experiment 1). Then we test whether that type of manipulation of the discourse context influences the acceptability of EV2 in Swedish or whether the acceptability of EV2 is determined solely by the class of the embedding predicate (Experiment 2). The results show that the acceptability of EV2 is sensitive only to predicate type, with no evidence for pragmatic variation dependent on MPU. The implications of these results are discussed in the final section.

2 The licensing of embedded verb second in Scandinavian

2.1 Factivity, presupposition, and assertion

The observation that embedded clauses can have the syntactic properties of root clauses goes back at least to Emonds (1970), but a central article that has inspired much subsequent work is Hooper & Thompson (1973). In this study of embedded root phenomena in English, H&T distinguish between five classes of predicates that take clausal complements, as summarised below. The acceptability of embedded root phenomena is argued to reflect these predicate classes, deriving ultimately from the extent to which material in the complement clause can be **asserted**.

---

[2]Here we follow H&T in our use of "factive" and "semifactive"; these two classes are now commonly referred to as "emotive factives" and "cognitive factives" respectively.

Class A predicates e.g. *say, report, be true, be obvious.* The verbs in this group are – with the possible exception of *vow* – all verbs of communication, while the adjectives express high degrees of certainty. These predicates can function "parenthetically", in which case the subordinate clause has been said to constitute the "main assertion" of the sentence. H&T maintain that root transformations are available *iff* the embedded clause consitutes the main assertion (p. 477).

Class B predicates e.g. *suppose, expect, it seems, it appears.* This group contains only verbs, which seem to fall into two subsets: verbs of thought, and impersonals. In this group also the predicates can function parenthetically, in which case the subordinate clause is likewise asserted. Class B predicates in English allow "Neg raising" and tag questions based on the subordinate clause.

Class C predicates e.g. *be (un)likely, be (im)possible, doubt, deny.* H&T do not offer a general characterization of this class of predicates, but comment that their complements are neither asserted nor presupposed, and that these predicates cannot be used parenthetically.

Class D predicates e.g. *resent, regret, be sorry, be surprised, be interesting.* These are the (emotive) factive predicates. Given H&T's assumptions about the relation between factivity, presupposition, and assertion, the use of these verbs entails that the complement of these verbs is presupposed, and cannot be asserted.

Class E predicates e.g. *realize, learn, discover, know.*[3] This group constitutes the semi-factives, which presuppose/entail the truth of their complements only in some environments – in particular, this presupposition can be lost in questions and conditionals (Kiparsky & Kiparsky 1970).

H&T make the empirical claim that embedded root phenomena in English are impossible in the complements of Class C and Class D predicates. They then argue that this follows from the fact that in neither case can the complement be asserted; assertion is, on their assumptions, incompatible with presupposition (and hence with factivity, since factives presuppose the truth of their complements). Problematically for H&T's analysis, but as they themselves observe, root phenomena in English can occur in the complement to semifactive verbs even in the environments in which they behave like factives (e.g. when they occur in non-modal, declarative contexts). As pointed out in Wiklund et al. (2009), and as will be discussed further below, the same holds for embedded V2 in Scandinavian. H&T also claim that for non-factive predicates in classes A and B, embedded root phenomena are possible if and only if the embedded clause constitutes the **main assertion** of the sentence. H&T then argue that assertion licenses the root phenomena they are investigating in English because all these phenomena involve emphasis, and "emphasis would be unacceptable in clauses that are not asserted" (p. 472). There are problems for this last link in their argument (for some discussion see e.g. Heycock

---

[3]Whether *know* should be grouped together with the semifactives is highly contentious; here we take no position on this.

2006). However, their observation about the absence of root phenomena from factive complements in particular, and, conversely, the association of such phenomena with some notion of "assertion" has had a lasting influence.

Despite this, the term "assertion" itself has largely been abandoned in recent literature. As Simons et al. (2010: 1041) points out, the point of clause embedding is often precisely to indicate the weakness of the speaker's commitment to the proposition expressed, whereas assertion is generally taken to involve a strong commitment. Observe, for example, the lower speaker commitment conveyed in (4) compared to (5):

(4)   I believe that it will rain tomorrow.

(5)   It will rain tomorrow.

Still, we want to capture the intuition that in (4), the main proposition conveyed by the speaker is typically the proposition that it will rain tomorrow (and not that the speaker has a belief about the rain tomorrow). Simons (2007) introduces the concept "Main Point of Utterance" (MPU) for this purpose.[4] She provides the following working definition of MPU:

> [T]he main point of an utterance U of a declarative sentence S is the proposition p, communicated by U, which renders U relevant. [...] To sharpen intuitive judgments, we will utilize question/response sequences as a diagnostic for main point content. I assume that whatever proposition communicated by the response constitutes an answer (complete or partial) to the question is the main point of the response. (Simons 2007: 1035–1036)

This definition provides a useful tool for identifying the MPU in an utterance. Importantly, it makes MPU a property relative to a discourse, rather than to a sentence, as illustrated in (6) and (7):

(6)   Q.   Why didn't Kate come to the party?
       A.   John thinks that she's left town.

(7)   Q.   Why didn't John invite Kate to the party?
       A.   He thinks that she's left town.

(6-A) and (7-A) are formally identical, expressing the proposition that John thinks that Kate has left town. Where they differ is precisely at the level of MPU. Following Simons (2007: 1037) (6-A) can be paraphrased as "The answer to your question why Kate didn't come to the party may be that she has left town. I'm saying this based on what John told me that he believes to be the case.", and (7-A) as "The answer to your question why John

---

[4]We will keep to the convention of referring to verbs of communication and cognition such as *say*, *claim* and *think*, which generally accept MPU-complements, as "assertive". However, we will use the term MPU, rather than "assertion", when referring to the discourse status of the proposition expressed by the embedded clause.

didn't invite Kate to the party is that he thinks that she was out of town and therefore would be unable to attend." In (6-A), the root clause *John thinks* has a parenthetical, essentially evidential use, qualifying the speaker's claim that Kate is out of town.[5]

We now return to the question of why some, but not other predicates appear to be felicitous when used with this discourse function. Compare, for example, (8) and (9):

(8)   a. When does the game start?

      b. I think that it starts at 10.

(9)   a. When does the game start?

      b. I know that it starts at 10.

      c. I'm happy that it starts at 10.

      d. I regret that it starts at 10.

As discussed above, according to Hooper & Thompson (1973) and Hooper (1975), clause-embedding factives (such as *be happy* and possibly *know*) cannot be used parenthetically in this way, that is, with the main assertion being the embedded clause. They take this to be because the factive predicate **presupposes** the embedded proposition. That is, the embedded proposition is taken to be part of the conversational common ground, and therefore cannot be used to update the common ground (by adding propositions to it, in the sense of Stalnaker 1974, 2002). In essence, this is to claim that a factive complement cannot be the MPU. Interestingly however, as already mentioned, Hooper & Thompson (1973) note that semifactives, which can lose their factivity in questions and in the antecedents of conditionals, *can* be used parenthetically even in contexts where their factivity is retained. H&T demonstrate this by showing that, for example, a tag question can be formed from the complement to such a verb, which they take to indicate that this complement is the main assertion; they contrast this with the behaviour of a true factive. The following examples are H&T's examples (129) and (131):

(10)   (Hooper & Thompson 1973: 481)
      I see that Harry drank all the beer, didn't he?

(11)   (Hooper & Thompson 1973: 481)
      *I am sorry that Suzanne isn't here, is she?

Simons (2007) makes the same point by demonstrating that the complement to a semifactive like *discover* can constitute the MPU. The following is her example (21a):

---

[5]The observation that embedding verbs can be used parenthetically is originally due to Urmson (1952: 484) who explains the parenthetical use as "priming the hearer to the emotional significance, the logical relevance, and the reliability of our statements."

(12)   (Simons 2007: 1045)

> Q: Where did Louise go last week?
>
> A: Henry discovered that she had a job interview at Princeton.

Simons' conclusion is that semifactives show us that presupposition and factivity must be disassociated. Presuppositions are treated by the speaker as part of the conversational common ground. In contrast, factivity is the entailment of the truth of the embedded proposition. For parenthetical assertives, like *think* or *say*, the complement is neither presupposed nor entailed. In (12-A) on the other hand, the complement is entailed (Henry could not have discovered that Louise had a job interview at Princeton unless she did in fact have such an interview), but it is not presupposed. That is, it provides discourse-new information, serving the function of updating the conversational common ground (it is the MPU).

A question that naturally arises from this observation is the following: if factivity does not block MPU (that is, if factivity does not entail presupposition), why is it that *true* factives (like *know*, *regret* and *be happy*), unlike semifactives (like *discover* and *realize*) resist MPU-complements, as exemplified by the infelicity of (9d)? In other words, what is it about factives, that is not the property of factivity itself, that render these infelicitous as parentheticals? A plausible answer to this question comes from Simons (2007). She appeals to what is an essentially Gricean reasoning process to explain how parenthetical uses of embedding predicates come about. In (13) we sketch an outline of the pragmatic process which, according to these authors, underlies the parenthetical use of *think* in (6) above.

(13)   • The response to the question "Why didn't Kate come to the party?" in (6) contains two propositions, *p*: *John thinks q*, and *q*: *Kate has left town*. Only *q* directly answers this question.
       • Assuming that the speaker is being cooperative, and intends to answer the question in a conversationally appropriate manner (given Quantity, Relevance etc.), the hearer infers that the speaker must have some reason for not directly asserting *q*. Such a reason could be that she does not have sufficient evidence for directly asserting *q*. However, *p*, indicating that John is the source of *q*, allows the speaker to offer *q* as a possible answer to the question.

The restriction on factives as parentheticals now follows quite naturally (Simons 2007: 1049-1050). The following is from her example (37):

(14)   (Simons 2007: 1050)

a. Where did Louise go yesterday?

b. Henry forgot that she went to Princeton.

c. Henry remembered that she went to Princeton.

As shown in (14), these matrix clauses are problematic as parentheticals. It is not clear how Henry's forgetting or remembering that Kate has left town is relevant to the question just asked (though see example (18) for a question that makes such information relevant). The responses thus present a violation of Grice's (1975) Maxim of Quantity, in that they provide the hearer with considerably more information than the question asked for. Further, consider the case of *know*. The following is from Simons's (2007) example (35):

(15) (Simons 2007: 1049)

  a. Where was Louise yesterday?

  b. ??Henry knows that she was in Princeton.

The meaning of *know* is essentially to express a strong commitment to the truth of its complement. However, this is also the function of directly asserting the proposition. Hence, it is not clear what non-redundant discourse function would be achieved by embedding the proposition under *know*. In effect then, it is not the factivity *per se* that renders the utterance bad, but rather the lack of relevant communicative content contributed by the matrix clause.

This point can be further illustrated with an "assertive" matrix predicate. Imagine someone blurting out, out of the blue:

(16) I say that I will go and get a coffee.

A hearer might wonder what the purpose of the embedding is, given that the matrix clause does not fill any clear conversational purpose beyond what would be accomplished simply by asserting "I will go and get a coffee." However, given an appropriate discourse context, factives like *know* and *forget* can be assigned felicitous parenthetical readings. The following examples are Simons's (2007) (36) and (39):[6]

(17) (Simons 2007: 1050)

  Q: Where was Louise yesterday?

  A: Y'know she had to go to Princeton.

(18) (Simons 2007: 1050)

  Sorry, we're going to have to change our plans for dinner tonight.

  a. Henry forgot that he has an evening appointment.

  b. Henry just realized/remembered that he has an evening appointment.

In (17), *know* fills a non-evidential parenthetical function. Roughly, the answer can be paraphrased as "Louise had to go to Princeton yesterday, and you know that already (so

---

[6]Note also that with appropriate stress placement, a sentence like "I know that she's in *Princeton*" and a continuation like "...but I don't know if that answers your question?", would render *know* much more natural in answering a question like (15) (see Simons 2007: 1049).

you shouldn't be asking)." (Compare with a slightly modified version of (16): "I said that I will go and get a coffee!" whereby the embedding is understandable and non-redundant if the speaker is trying to highlight that the hearer was not listening.) In (18a,b) on the other hand, the speaker is citing Henry's evening appointment as the reason for changing the dinner plans. Here, *forget/realize/remember* fill the relevant discourse function of informing the hearer of the reason for not telling her earlier. Simons uses examples like (17) and (18) to support her claim that a factive can function parenthetically in an appropriate discourse context, such that its embedded clause acts as the main assertion. Our first study tests this claim experimentally.

2.2 (Non)factivity or MPU as a factor for embedded verb second

We have summarised above aspects of the proposal in Simons (2007), according to which H&T's concept of "main assertion" is replaced by that of "Main Point of Utterance," and MPU in turn is argued to be a conversational property of utterances in context, sensitive both to properties of the discourse, as well as to a number of linguistic factors that we have not discussed here. As shown above, under this view – in contrast to that of H&T – factivity is not incompatible with MPU status. While neither H&T nor Simons discuss data from any language other than English, there is a tradition that dates back at least as far as Andersson (1975) of taking Embedded Verb Second (EV2) in Scandinavian to be another type of "Embedded Root Phenomenon". EV2 is known to be sensitive to a variety of factors (see e.g., Zwart 1997), but of interest here is how its distribution can be analysed along the lines set out in H&T. Given Simons' argument that the lexical semantic property of (non-)factivity can be teased apart from the discourse pragmatic property of being the MPU, the question evidently arises as to which of these is relevant to the licensing of EV2.

Clearly, one possible hypothesis is that the crucial concept for the distribution of EV2 in Scandinavian is MPU, and that any apparent association with non-factivity is due to the greater ease – given the interaction between lexical meaning and discourse contexts – with which non-factive verbs can embed the MPU. This hypothesis is put forward explicitly in Jensen & Christensen (2013), a corpus study of EV2 in Danish. Jensen & Christensen (2013) state as their hypothesis that "V>Adv [EV2 order] signals foregrounding of the subordinate clause, i.e. that its content is the main point of the utterance." However, they do not code for MPU in any direct way, while they do code for (among other factors) the "type of the matrix predicate," described as an operationalization of H&T's five classes of predicates, with the addition of a class of "Causatives" and a residual "Other" class.[7] They discover a clear effect of predicate type, but interpret it as supporting their MPU hypothesis (note that they intend their use of "foreground" to mean the same as MPU (p. 40)):

> [...] both FACTIVE and CAUSATIVE matrix predicates, *as expected from the hypothesis of V>Adv as a foregrounding signal* [our emphasis], clearly disfavour V>Adv

---

[7]H&T's Class C was not coded for as it turned out there were virtually no tokens of this class in their corpus (p. 50).

> word order [...] Subclauses governed by communicative predicates [Class A] are significantly more disposed to V>Adv word order than subclauses governed by cognitive predicates [Class B], which are again significantly more disposed to V>Adv than OTHER predicates. *This, again, supports the hypothesis of V>Adv as a foregrounding signal, since we would expect communicative predicates to frequently govern subclauses that are foregrounded,* [our emphasis] even when they do not contain any explicit signals of being quotes [...] Cognitive predicates will often introduce something important that the speaker or some other person knows or has learned, *and these would then be foregrounded* [our emphasis]. (Jensen & Christensen 2013: 50)

So while their hypothesis is clearly that EV2 (or at least, the V>Adv order that we take to be one manifestation of this structure) is a signal of MPU, they in fact have only indirect evidence for this (essentially as was the case also for H&T).

Another author who could be read as adopting the hypothesis that MPU is the crucial concept for licensing EV2 in Scandinavian is Julien (2009; 2015), although this is less clear. In both papers Julien argues that EV2 signals assertion, but it is not always clear how assertion is defined (and hence diagnosed). As a result the extent to which her understanding of this might differ from Simon's definition of MPU is not always clear. In Julien (2009) the term MPU is never used, and Simons' work is not referenced; in Julien (2015) she argues explicitly against the relevance of MPU, although her argument mainly bears on the particular use of the concept in Wiklund et al. (2009), to be discussed shortly.[8]

One possible hypothesis, then, is that EV2 is directly licensed by, or signals, MPU status – a status that under the account of Simons (2007) is determined relative to a discourse. The alternative is that lexical semantic properties of the embedding predicates – (non)-factivity being at least one such property – are directly responsible for the possibility of EV2 in the embedded clause. A version of this alternative hypothesis can be found in Wiklund et al. (2009). Using the predicate classes identified by H&T, and taking as their data their own judgments (supplemented in some cases with those of a small number of other linguists), rather than a corpus, Wiklund et al. (2009) argue that EV2 is grammatical under assertives (Classes A and B) and semifactives (Class E), but not under

---

[8]One important aspect of Julien's proposal which does clearly distinguish it from one which links EV2 exclusively to MPU status (as for example is the case in Jensen & Christensen 2013) is that she essentially allows for two ways in which EV2 might be licensed. On the one hand, a clause with EV2 may be a "direct assertion," that is, one attributed to the speaker. This comes very close to – or is perhaps identical to – the concept of the embedding predicate having an evidential, parenthetical interpretation (see the discussion in Section 2.1 above). On the other, a clause with EV2 may be the report of an assertion made by the person denoted by the subject of the embedding verb. This predicts that EV2 would be possible in a context like the following, for example, where the Jensen & Christensen (2013) hypothesis would exclude it, since the embedded proposition – that the world is not round – can be taken to be an assertion of Jasper's, but is clearly not intended to be added to the common ground by the speaker:

    Q: Why do you think Jasper isn't so bright?

    A: He said that the world is not round. What an idiot!

factives (Class D) or the class of non-assertive, non-presuppositional predicates (Class C). Examples below are from Wiklund et al. (2009: 1918–1921).

(19) (Wiklund et al. 2009: 1918–1921)
   Han sa   att han **kunde inte** sjunga på bröllopet.
   he said that he   could not sing   at wedding.DEF
   'He said that he could not sing at the wedding.'   Assertive Class A

(20) (Wiklund et al. 2009: 1918-1921)
   Han trodde att vi **hade inte** sett den här   filmen.
   he   believed that we had   not seen this here film.DEF
   'He believed that we hadn't seen this film.'   Assertive Class B

(21) (Wiklund et al. 2009: 1918-1921)
   *Han tvivlar på att   hon **har inte** träffat den här   mannen.
   he   doubts on that she has not   met   this here man.DEF
   'He doubts that she hasn't met this man.'   Non-assertive Class C

(22) (Wiklund et al. 2009: 1918-1921)
   *Han ångrade att han **hade inte** sjungit.
   he   regretted that he had   not sung.
   'He regretted that he hadn't sung.'   Factive Class D

(23) (Wiklund et al. 2009: 1918-1921)
   Jag upptäckte att jag **hade inte** läst den.
   I   discovered that I   had   not read it.
   'I discovered that I hadn't read it.'   Semifactive Class E

Given that EV2 is possible under semifactives – crucially, even in contexts where their factivity is preserved – factivity cannot be what restricts the availability of EV2. Wiklund et al. (2009: 14) invoke instead the concept of MPU from Simons' work. However, this does not mean that they claim that MPU status is what licenses or is signalled by EV2. First, while they follow Simons (2007) in that they take MPU to be the proposition in an utterance which is used to update the common ground, and which can be diagnosed by the question/answer-pairs discussed above, their understanding of MPU is in fact crucially different from that of Simons (2007). They state:

> Those *predicate classes* [our emphasis] which may not embed an MPU are exactly those that impose restrictions on V2 in the embedded clause (Class C and D). In other words, MPU-compatible environments correspond to environments where V2 is unrestricted in all four varieties of Scandinavian investigated here. (Wiklund et al. 2009: 1927)

That is to say, whereas Simons argues that MPU is a property of utterances, not predicates, Wiklund et al. take possible environments for MPU to be lexically defined, in that MPU is licensed by assertives and semifactives, but not by factives.

The second way in which the approach of Wiklund et al. (2009) departs from an account that really depends on the notion of MPU is that they state clearly that the relation between MPU and EV2 is only indirect. That is, EV2 and MPU are licensed in the same structural domain – ForceP – that is selected by assertives and semifactives, but not by factives, which select a smaller clause, incompatible with both EV2 and MPU (2009: 1930). However, they argue that verb-movement and interpretation as MPU are both optional, and independent, properties of ForceP: hence it is possible for an MPU-clause to be V-in situ (EV3), and for an EV2-clause to not be the MPU. This much weaker linkage between the two is motivated by the following type of judgments (Wiklund et al. 2009: 1927):

(24)   Varför kom han inte på mötet igår?
       'Why didn't he come to the meeting yesterday?'

     a. Vi upptäckte att han **hade** tyvärr **inte** fått på vinterdäcken ännu.
       we discovered that he had unfortunately not put on winter-tires.DEF yet

     b. Vi upptäckte att han tyvärr **inte hade** fått på vinterdäcken ännu.
       we discovered that he unfortunately not had put on winter-tires.DEF yet
       'We discovered that he unfortunately hadn't changed to winter tires yet.'
       (Wiklund et al. 2009: 1927)

They argue that since both (24a) and (24b) are possible in response to the question – which provides a context that makes the embedded clause in the answer the most plausible MPU – it must be the case that MPU does not require EV2 syntax. Conversely, they also cite examples where the MPU is *not* the embedded clause, but EV2 is still possible, so there is not even a one-way implication:

(25)   a. Varför kom han inte på festen?
       why came he not to party.DEF
       'Why didn't he come to the party?'

     b. Kristine sa att han **fick inte**.
       Kristine said that he was-allowed not
       'Kristine said that he wasn't allowed to.'
       (Wiklund et al. 2009: 1929)

According to Wiklund et al. (2009: 1929), the answer in (25b) is ambiguous; crucially, it can have the interpretation that one reason for the person in question not coming to the party was that Kristine said something – that is, a reading where the MPU is not the embedded clause, even though this unambiguously displays EV2 word order.

For these reasons, even though Wiklund et al. (2009) explicitly invoke Simons´ work, in fact the concept of MPU as presented there plays no explanatory role within their hypothesis; rather, their approach predicts that the possibility – but not the presence in any given example – of EV2 is determined by the lexical class of the embedding predicate.

The hypothesis that MPU, as described in Simons (2007), is directly responsible for the occurrence of EV2 in Scandinavian has been put forward most unambiguously in Jensen & Christensen (2013), referred to above. However, as they did not code their corpus data for the kind of contextual cues that might enable us to determine whether any given example of EV2/EV3 is in fact an instance of embedded MPU or not, their evidence for this hypothesis is at best indirect. Since contexts in which the status of an embedded or root clause as MPU is unambiguous are likely to be hard to find in a corpus, Experiment 2 aims to test this hypothesis with an experimental paradigm in which we manipulate MPU and class of embedding predicate independently, making use of the Question–Answer paradigm proposed in Simons (2007).[9]

3 Experiment 1: Factivity & MPU in English

This experiment tests whether it is possible to manipulate the discourse in order to 'coerce' an embedded-MPU interpretation of sentences that typically strongly disfavour this reading, that is, where the clause-embedding predicate is factive. In other words, given an appropriate discourse context, can factives be used parenthetically, as Simons claimed? Following the above authors, we identify the MPU as the proposition in an answer that provides the most direct answer to the question, as illustrated in (6) and (7) above, repeated here:

(26) Q. Why didn't Kate come to the party?
      A. John thinks that she's left town.

(27) Q. Why didn't John invite Kate to the party?
      A. He thinks that she's left town.

As there is no reason to expect that Swedish speakers and English speakers should differ in their pragmatic (by hypothesis, Gricean) reasoning, we conducted this experiment with English-speaking participants, who were easier to recruit given their greater numbers. The experiment asked participants to make a judgment about how directly a particular response answered a preceding question. We manipulated both the question posed in the preceding discourse context as well as properties of the response. When the response contained an embedded clause, the embedding verb was either factive or non-factive. The question-response pairs thus created conditions that favoured a reading in which the response's embedded clause served as the MPU under a factive verb.

---

[9]In essence, what we do in Experiment 2 is to systematically gather judgment data of the kind reported in the few examples of such question-answer pairs discussed in Wiklund et al. (2009).

3.1 Methodology

3.1.1 Participants

Forty seven native speakers of English participated in the study. The participants were recruited on Amazon's Mechanical Turk, a crowd-sourcing tool for recruiting workers who can be paid anonymously for small amounts of work (for review of Mechanical Turk in cognitive science research, see Munro et al. 2010). Participants were paid 8 USD per hour for their participation.

3.1.2 Materials

All items consisted of short dialogues between two speakers. Each experimental item occurred in 6 conditions: 2 question types × 3 response types.

(28)   **Background:**
         I hear that you went to Paris last summer.
         Question: specific content condition:
         What was the city like?
         Question: general experience condition:
         How was it?
         Response: Unembedded:
         The city was really great.
         Response: Non-factive embedding verb:
         I got the impression that the city was really great.
         Response: Factive embedding verb:
         I was surprised that the city was really great.

By varying the question, we can see whether participants are sensitive to the discourse context in assessing an utterance. Taking the unembedded condition as a baseline, participants are expected to rate that response (*The city was really great* in (28)) as a more direct answer to the specific content question than to the general experience question because the content of the response directly matches the wording of the former question but not the latter. Likewise in the responses with embedding, the match between the wording of the specific question and the content of the embedded clause in the response is expected to yield higher directness ratings for the specific question than the general experience question.

By varying the response type, specifically the embedding verb, we can test Simons' claims about how participants treat the information embedded under factives by comparing the factive response to the other two response types. The non-factive condition contained predicates that detract from the speaker's commitment to the embedded content (either *I got the impression* or *it seemed to me*). This hedging is predicted to yield lower directness ratings because the speaker is not committed to their answer to the question posed. This condition contrasts with the unembedded response in which the speaker strongly commits to an answer. The question then is how participants will assess responses that contain a factive embedding verb (here, *be happy, be disappointed, be relieved* or *be surprised*). If factives can be used parenthetically, then a response like *I was surprised that the city was really great* should constitute a direct answer to the question about what the city was like, similar to an unembedded response. If factives resist embedded MPU, the factive responses are predicted to receive lower directness ratings, similar to those assigned in the non-factive response condition.

The experiment included 24 experimental items and 24 fillers. The fillers were of the same general format as the experimental items: 6 of the fillers involved a relevance violation, 6 involved a presupposition violation, and the remaining half were equal parts acceptable Factives and acceptable Non-Factives. The 48 items were pseudo-randomized across lists, such that each participant saw each item only once, and all conditions were equally represented in each list.

3.1.3 Procedure

Participants viewed each dialogue and then were prompted with "The response addressed the preceding question:". They were given the alternatives "Not at all", "Somewhat Indirectly", "Indirectly", "Somewhat Directly" and "Directly". The participants were told that there was no correct answer, and instructed to choose the option that corresponded best to their intuition about the answer. Participants were further instructed to read the entire dialogue before providing their rating, and not to go back and revise their answers to previous questions.

3.1.4 Analysis

In order to establish which manipulated factor most strongly impacts participant ratings, directly or in conjunction with another factor, the raw scores were analyzed with lincar mixed effects models in R. The full model contained fixed effects of question type, response type, and their interaction, with participants and items as random effects. This type of mixed-effect modeling for statistical analysis is standard in psycholinguistics, as is the recasting of the qualitative scale as numeric scores ("Not at all"=1... "Directly"=5). Question type was centered. For the 3-level factor of response type, the factive condition was coded as the baseline in order to test whether the factive responses yield ratings that are more like the unembedded responses or the non-factive responses. Each fixed effect is tested for significance comparing a model which lacks that fixed effect to the full model. For the 3-level fixed effect and its interaction, p-values are derived from a subset model comparing factives with either non-factive or unembedded responses.

3.2 Results

The ratings for the 6 conditions are illustrated in Figure 1. The three lines show the three response types (factive predicates vs. non-factive predicates vs. unembedded responses).

All receive higher directness scores when the question is specific rather than general (confirmed as a main effect of question type in the statistical analysis: p<0.001).

Of primary interest is how the responses containing factive predicates compare with other response types. The results show that these responses pattern with the direct unembedded responses (in a model of the subset of the data excluding non-factives, the directness ratings for unembedded responses are not significantly higher than for factive responses: p=0.54) and differ from the hedged indirect responses (same modeling technique, significant difference between factive and non-factive: p<0.001). This lends experimental support to Simons' claim that factives can be used parenthetically in a sufficiently supportive discourse context.

We did not specifically predict an interaction between question type and response type, but the effect of question type is bigger for unembedded responses (p<0.05) and for non-factives (p<0.05), compared with factive responses. This pattern appears to arise because of the relatively high directness ratings assigned to the factive responses in the general question condition (making the difference between the two question types smaller for the factive condition than for the other two conditions). This may reflect an interpretation of the general question 'How was it?' as seeking information about the speakers' own experience, in which case reporting that one was surprised (or happy or disappointed or relieved) adds to the relevance (and hence directness) of that response for that question.

Given that discourse contexts can be manipulated such that factives do appear to license MPU, the next experiment tests whether a discourse context manipulation that shifts MPU can also influence the acceptability of EV2 in Swedish.

4 Experiment 2: Swedish embedded V2

Acceptability judgments were elicited from native Swedish speakers in a $4 \times 2 \times 2$ design that manipulated MPU (main vs. embedded clause), verb class (communicative assertive, epistemic assertive, (emotive) factive, (cognitive) semifactive), and word order (EV2 vs. EV3).[10] Since the consensus among researchers appears to be that EV2 is optional even when it is permitted, EV3 word order is predicted to be generally more acceptable than EV2. If MPU is lexically defined, we predict a word order × predicate class interaction whereby EV2 is acceptable only under assertives and under semifactives (see Wiklund et al. 2009). Alternatively, if MPU is a property of utterances in context, we predict a word order × MPU interaction whereby EV2 is more acceptable when the context signals that the embedded clause is the MPU (see Jensen & Christensen 2013).

---

[10]In order to keep the questionnaire to a manageable length, we did not include examples of Class C predicates (e.g. *deny*, *doubt*, etc).

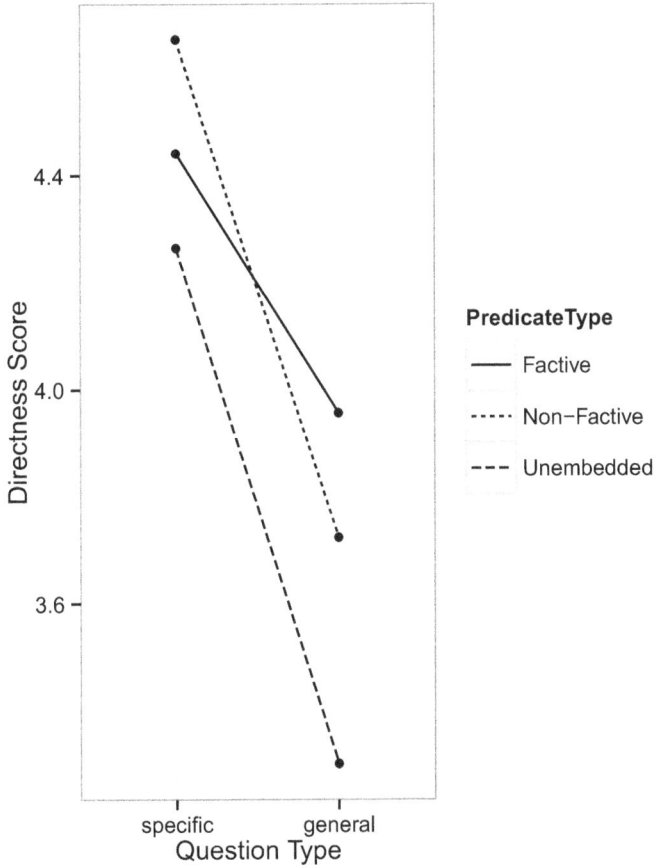

Figure 1: Directness ratings in Experiment 1 by question type (general vs. specific) and response type (factive vs. non-factive vs. unembedded)

4.1 Methodology

4.1.1 Participants

A group of 118 Swedish-speaking students (age 18–19) from a senior high school in the northern Swedish city of Umeå participated in the study. All participants were volunteers.

4.1.2 Materials

Each item consisted of a 3-utterance passage. For the 16 experimental items, these passages contained a background sentence, a question to establish MPU for the target sentence, and the target sentence itself, as in (29). The background sentence introduced two individuals. The second utterance posed a question about one of those two individuals. The target sentence mentioned one individual as the subject of the matrix clause and one as the subject of the embedded clause.

The MPU manipulation was achieved via the combination of the question posed and the positions of mention of the two individuals in the target sentence. In (29), the target sentence mentions Carina as the matrix clause subject and Albin as the embedded clause subject. The question to trigger main clause MPU therefore asks about Carina; the embedded clause MPU trigger asks about Albin. The word order manipulation was indicated via the position of negation relative to the verb. Both MPU and word order were manipulated within items. With this design, each passage could be minimally varied to construct 4 conditions (MPU-matrix:EV2, MPU-embedded:EV2, MPU-matrix:EV3, MPU-embedded:EV3).

(29)   **Background:**
Lille Albin och hans mamma Carina gick och såg en film på bio.
'Little Albin and his mother Carina went to see a movie in the cinema.'
Embedded Clause MPU Trigger:
Hur upplevde Albin biobesöket?
'How did Albin find the visit to the cinema?'
Main Clause MPU Trigger:
Hur upplevde Carina biobesöket?
'How did Carina find the visit to the cinema?'
Target:
Carina gissade att han **(hade)** nog   inte **(hade)** väntat   sig så mycket
Carina guessed that he (had) maybe not (had) expected self so much
action.
action

'Carina guessed that he probably hadn't expected that much action.'

The remaining manipulation of predicate class of the embedding verb was between items (4 items for each of 4 predicate classes). The predicates were classified according to Hooper & Thompson's scheme, omitting their Class C: (communicative) assertive, (epistemic) assertive, factive (emotive), semifactive (cognitive).[11] The predicates we used for each group are listed in Table 1.

The experiment consisted of 16 experimental items mixed with 16 fillers. Fillers consisted of passages in the same 3-utterance format and their complexity roughly matched the experimental items, with embedded complement clauses and relative clauses. The fillers varied as to whether they were fully grammatical (n=8), fully ungrammatical (n=4), or pragmatically infelicitous (n=4).

---

[11]Communicative and epistemic assertives are sometimes labeled "weak" and "strong" assertive Wiklund et al. (2009). However, it is not at all clear to us that strength of assertion, in any straightforward understanding of the concept, is the relevant variable: rather the verbs in Class A are verbs of communication, while those in Class B are verbs of thought or cognition.

Table 1: The clause-embedding predicates used in the experiment, by predicate-type.

	Assertive (communicative)	Assertive (Epistemic)	Factive	Semifactive
Group 1	*säga* say	*anta* suppose	*vara lättad* be relieved	*upptäcka* discover
Group 2	*berätta* tell	*förmoda* assume	*vara glad* be happy	*märka* notice
Group 3	*förklara* explain	*gissa* guess	*vara ledsen* be sad/sorry	*komma fram till* arrive at
Group 4	*hävda* claim	*vara säker* be sure	*vara förvånad* be surprised	*få veta* come to know

So as not to repeat verbs across items, only 16 experimental items were constructed. Each participant saw all 16 items and therefore saw each of the 16 conditions only once. Because of this, a large number of participants were recruited. The 16 experimental items were assigned to conditions in a Latin Square design such that, across 4 lists, each item was presented in each MPU × word order condition once and each participant saw each condition once.

4.1.3 Procedure

The experiment was conducted as a pen and paper task in a classroom setting. The experimenter provided participants with a booklet containing the instructions and passages (all in Swedish). Participants were instructed to judge the acceptability of the passages on a scale from 1 to 6, where 1 represented **unacceptable**, and 6 represented **fully acceptable**. Each passage appeared on a page by itself with a question asking participants to "Indicate how natural you consider the answers to the questions to be." The task took roughly 20 minutes.

4.1.4 Analysis

The raw scores were analyzed with linear mixed effects models in R, with participants and items as random effects. Maximum random effect structure was used (Barr et al. 2013). The word order and MPU conditions were centered, and predicate class was contrast coded. We conducted likelihood-ratio tests between mixed-effects models differing only in the presence or absence of a fixed main effect or interaction. We report the p-values derived from the model comparisons.

4.2 Results

Judgments from 6 non-native Swedish speakers were removed. In addition, 8 participants whose judgments failed to distinguish the grammatical and ungrammatical fillers were excluded. 20 requested judgments (1%) were left blank. The remaining dataset consisted of 1644 judgments on experimental items from 104 native speakers.

The results from Experiment 2 are illustrated in Figure 2. As predicted, EV3 receiving higher ratings than EV2 (main effect of word order: $p<0.001$). In addition, higher ratings were assigned to passages that contained semifactive and communicative assertive embedding verbs (main effect of predicate class: $p<0.001$). This main effect of predicate class was driven by a word order × predicate class interaction ($p<0.001$): As predicted under an account in which MPU is lexically defined and the embedding verb directly influences the acceptability of EV2, ratings for EV2 were almost as high as for EV3 for the class of communicative assertives and the class of semifactives. There was no main effect of MPU ($p=0.88$), and contrary to a context-driven account of the role of MPU in EV2, there was no interaction with MPU ($p's>0.75$).

Given Julien´s claim that – regardless of the MPU – a speaker can use EV2 when reporting a 3rd party's assertion, and the higher frequency of EV2 reported by Jensen & Christensen for communicative assertives over epistemic assertives in their Danish corpus, we tested whether the acceptability of EV2 is higher for communicative assertives than epistemic assertives. A model of the data across those two predicate classes shows a word order × predicate class interaction ($p<0.001$) whereby the acceptability of EV2 is indeed much higher for communicative assertives than epistemic assertives. This interaction appears alongside a main effect of word order ($p<0.001$), a main effect of predicate class ($p<0.001$) and non-significant effects and interactions for MPU ($p's>0.68$). This result, which matches the frequencies of EV2 in Danish reported by Jensen & Christensen, lends support to Julien´s claim.

These results support the claim that Swedish EV2 is possible under semi-factive (*discover/realize*) and non-factive (*think/claim*) clause-embedding predicates, but not under purely factive ones (*be happy/be surprised*) (Wiklund et al. 2009). However, the results show no interaction between word order and MPU. That is, our data suggest, contra Jensen & Christensen (2013), that the low acceptability of V2 under factives cannot be explained by the twin hypotheses that MPU licenses EV2 and that factives cannot embed MPU. Even if we set aside the factives, there was no effect of MPU when the embedding predicate was a non-factive or a semi-factive. There is no controversy in the literature about the ability of these predicates to embed the MPU. But even in these contexts, participants did not rate the use of EV2 any higher in the embedded-MPU condition. Our results therefore suggest that MPU is not relevant, and a different account is needed to explain the unavailability of EV2 under factives.

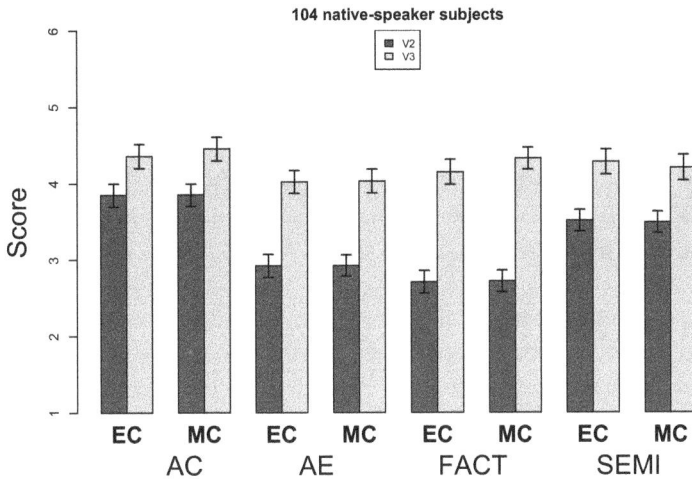

Figure 2: Acceptability judgments of target sentences in Experiment 2, broken down by MPU (Main Clause (MC), Embedded Clause (EC)), Predicate Class (communicative assertive (AC), epistemic assertive (AE), factive (FACT), semi-factive (SEMI)), and Word Order (V2, V3).

5 Discussion and conclusion

In this paper we have described two experiments that bear on the relation between "assertion," factivity, and the distribution of one classic case of an embedded root phenomenon: embedded Verb Second (EV2) in Swedish. As discussed in Section 2.1, although Hooper & Thompson (1973) classified complement clauses licensing or disallowing root phenomena in terms of the semantic properties of the embedding predicates, and the lexical classes that they set up have been extensively referred to in the subsequent literature, their explanation for the effect of these embedding predicates was a functional/pragmatic one. For example, factives were argued to disallow root phenomena in their complements because their complements were presupposed, and hence could not be **asserted**. Indeed, H&T argued that even predicates in classes that allow embedded root phenomena only do so when their complement is in fact the "main assertion" of the utterance, and the embedding predicate is being used parenthetically – see for example their discussion of the contrast between (30a) and (30b), their (67) and (68).

(30)   (Hooper & Thompson 1973: 476)

    a. *That never in his life has he had to borrow money is true.

    b. It's true that never in his life has he had to borrow money.

In their recent corpus work, Jensen & Christensen (2013) have essentially adopted this explanation for the distribution of EV2 in Danish.

As discussed in the same section, the work of Simons (2007) has provided a way to test whether indeed the effect of the embedding predicate is only epiphenomenal, as argued by Jensen & Christensen, since we should be able to manipulate MPU independently of the class of the embedding predicate. In Experiment 1 we tested Simons' claim that factives can be used parenthetically. As reported in Section 3.2, our experiment supports Simons' claim. First, the contrast in participants' judgments on the directness of the answer depending on the question type shows that we were successful in manipulating the discourse context to change what they took to be the MPU. Second, the fact that participants readily judged the complements of factives to constitute direct answers, in the relevant context, bears out Simons' view that factives need not necessarily resist "assertion": that is, in the right context, factives *can* indeed embed MPU clauses.

Having established that participants can show sensitivity to the experimental manipulation of the MPU by a preceding question, and that factives can embed the MPU, in Experiment 2 we then tested whether the same type of manipulation of the MPU affects the acceptability of EV2 in Swedish. In contrast to the robust effects of MPU in Experiment 1, the MPU manipulations in Experiment 2 yielded no differences in the acceptability of EV2. Rather, the acceptability of EV2 was shown to be driven entirely by predicate class. EV2 was most acceptable for semifactives and communicative assertives. Compared with assertive predicates that explicitly convey a communicative act, epistemic (or cognitive) assertives yielded much lower ratings for EV2. And finally, EV2 was least acceptable under factives. These EV2 preferences match the data reported by Jensen & Christensen and Wiklund et al., but an account of such data that relies on MPU was not supported. Lastly, we observed an overall preference for EV3 across all predicate classes. This is in keeping with prior work suggesting that EV2, even when permitted, is never required.

These results clearly raise the question: if the deeper explanation for the effect of the different predicates is not a correlation with MPU, what is the alternative? The proposal in Wiklund et al. (2009) is that certain classes of verb (H&T's Classes A, B, and E – the "strongly and weakly assertive" predicates and the semifactives) syntactically select for a particular "size" of complement clause (specifically ForceP), while the other classes (C and D, the non-assertive, non-presuppositional predicates, and the factives) select a smaller clausal constituent that lacks this projection; V2 is syntactically possible within ForceP but not in the smaller structure. A variant of this kind of account would be to adopt the "intervention" approach put forward in Haegeman (2010; 2012), among other works, according to which A'-movement inside clauses may be blocked by other (often covert) operations of A'-movement. Thus for example Haegeman argues that English argument topicalisation inside conditionals is blocked by the A'-movement of a world operator; similarly, factives have been argued to involve movement of a factive operator, which would also interfere with other A' movement (see for example Zanuttini & Portner 2003). If we were to assume that V2 always involves A'-movement of some phrase to the left periphery (in the examples we have been citing, this is always the subject, but its high position is evidenced indirectly by the high position of the verb, to the left of negation), this type of account gives an essentially syntactic explanation for the low acceptability of V2 in the complement to factives that we observed in our data.

What prevents such accounts from being circular is that the smaller clause size (in a "truncation" account such as the one sketched in Wiklund et al. 2009) or the operator movement (in an intervention account along the lines of Zanuttini & Portner 2003; Haegeman 2010; 2012) has semantic/pragmatic effects. Wiklund et al. propose that "MPU and the possibility of non-subject-topicalization (including unrestricted V2) are licensed by the same structural domain [...], ForceP"; Zanuttini & Portner derive the factive interpretation from the presence of the factive operator.

But the results of Experiment 2 are problematic for both of these variants, for different reasons. Taking the clause-truncation explanation first: as discussed above in §2.2, and as suggested by the quote just above, Wiklund et al. appear to take the view that factives (for example) cannot embed the MPU. But as argued by Simons, and now supported also by the results of Experiment 1, it appears that speakers *are* able to treat the complement of a factive as the MPU. Nevertheless, Experiment 2 showed that EV2 is always given low ratings in the complements of factives – *even when the context sets this up as the MPU*. In consequence, the analysis sketched in Wiklund et al. (2009) does not in fact avoid a circular account of possible environments for EV2. The independent evidence for the distribution of ForceP – the syntactic environment in which V2 is licensed, by hypothesis – was to be the possibility for an MPU interpretation. But as we have just seen, MPU interpretation *is* possible for the complement of factives, but our results show that this is not an environment in which speakers accept EV2. So now it appears to be just a lexical idiosyncrasy that factives do not readily license EV2 in their complements.

Our results are also problematic for an intervention approach to the blocking effect of factivity. Here the problem is the finding that semifactives constitute one of the most favourable environments for EV2. This finding confirms what has already been claimed on the basis of speaker judgments and corpus work (e.g. Wiklund et al. 2009; Jensen & Christensen 2013; Julien 2015) and what H&T observed for embedded root phenomena in English. But if factivity is the result of the presence of a factive operator, this operator ought also to be present in the complement to semi-factives in those environments in which the factive interpretation is not cancelled – and all the semifactive environments in our experiment were of this type (declarative non-modal sentences). Clearly a better understanding of the exact nature of the distinction between factives and semifactives is crucial here, and this is one topic that merits future investigation.

A sceptical reader may wonder whether the participants in Experiment 2 were paying sufficient attention to the discourse context manipulation and, if they were, whether the manipulation successfully established embedded MPU interpretations. We know from the first study that participants in experimental paradigms like this are capable of attending to the discourse context in evaluating a target sentence. However, the relationship between the two paradigms is indirect – in Experiment 1, the task asks participants to pay attention to how the target sentence responds to the posed question, whereas in Experiment 2, the task asks for an acceptability judgment. The tasks differ because Experiment 1 was probing factivity and MPU, whereas Experiment 2 was designed to determine the status of EV2 across different contexts. If participants in Experiment 2 effectively ignored the question context, then it might still be possible to give an explanation for the effect of verb class on the acceptability of EV2 that appeals to MPU as a crucial factor. For example, since it is at least plausible that the frequency of embedded MPU in the complement of factives is low compared to its occurrence in other contexts, it could be that speakers draw on this knowledge when assessing the acceptability of sentences considered out of context. Finding a single task that could overcome this potential problem is tricky, but future work should look to address the indirect relationship between the two experiments just described, perhaps by including in the acceptability ratings a measure of participants' assessment of a target sentence as an appropriate answer to the posed question.

Acknowledgments

Thanks to participants at the Experimental Study of Meaning Lab at the University of Pennsylvania for helpful feedback and comments. Likewise to audiences at MACSIM V at the University of Delaware, CSI Lisbon (2014), LEL Syntax and Semantics seminar at the University of Edinburgh, and the ULAB/LEL undergraduate conferences. Thanks to Hezekiah Akiva Bacovcin for help with the statistical analysis of Experiment 1 and to research assistant Ivana Žetko for help with data processing for Experiment 2. Particular thanks to Florian Schwarz for guidance, feedback, and help with statistical analysis of Experiment 1. Part of this work was supported by NSF grant BCS-1349009 to Florian Schwarz.

Like so much work on the syntax of Scandinavian, the inspiration for this study can be traced back to Anders Holmberg's research (going all the way back to his dissertation, in fact). We are grateful to have the opportunity to contribute to this volume in his honour.

References

Andersson, Lars-Gunnar. 1975. *Form and function of subordinate clauses*. University of Göteborg dissertation.

Barr, Dale J., Roger Levy, Christoph Scheepers & Harry L. Tily. 2013. Random effects structure of confirmatory hypothesis testing: Keep it maximal. *Journal of Memory and Language* 68(3). 255–278.

Emonds, Joseph. 1970. *Root and structure-preserving transformations*. MIT dissertation.

Grice, H. Paul. 1975. Logic and conversation. In Peter Cole & Jerry L. Morgan (eds.), *Syntax and semantics*, vol. 3, 41–58. New York, NY: Academic Press.

Haegeman, Liliane. 2010. The movement derivation of conditional clauses. *Linguistic Inquiry* 41(4). 595–621.

Haegeman, Liliane. 2012. The syntax of MCP: Deriving the truncation account. In Lobke Aelbrecht, Liliane Haegeman & Rachel Nye (eds.), *Main clause phenomena: New horizons*, vol. 190 (Linguistik Aktuell / Linguistics Today), 113–134. Amsterdam: John Benjamins.

Heycock, Caroline. 2006. Embedded root phenomena. In Martin Everaert & Henk van Riemsdijk (eds.), *The Blackwell companion to syntax*, vol. II, chap. 23, 174–209. Oxford: Blackwell.

Holmberg, Anders. 2010. Parameters in Minimalist Theory: The case of Scandinavian. *Theoretical Linguistics* 36. 1–48.

Holmberg, Anders. 2013. The syntax of answers to polar questions in English and Swedish. *Lingua* 128. 31–50.

Holmberg, Anders & Christer Platzack. 1991. On the role of inflection in Scandinavian syntax. In Werner Abraham, Wim Kosmeijer & Eric Reuland (eds.), *Issues in Germanic syntax*, 93–118. Berlin: Mouton de Gruyter.

Holmberg, Anders & Christer Platzack. 1995. *The role of inflection in Scandinavian syntax*. Oxford: Oxford University Press.

Hooper, Joan B. 1975. On assertive predicates. In John P. Kimball (ed.), *Syntax and semantics*, 91–124. New York, NY: Academic Press.

Hooper, Joan B. & Sandra Thompson. 1973. On the applicability of root transformations. *Linguistic Inquiry* 4(4). 465–497.

Jensen, Torben Juel & Tanya Karoli Christensen. 2013. Promoting the demoted: The distribution and semantics of "main clause word order" in spoken Danish complement clauses. *Lingua* 137. 38–58.

Julien, Marit. 2009. *Embedded clauses with main clause word order in Mainland Scandinavian*. http://ling.auf.net/lingBuzz/000475.

Julien, Marit. 2015. The force of V2 revisited. *Journal of Comparative Germanic Linguistics* 18(2). 139–181.

Kiparsky, Paul & Carol Kiparsky. 1970. Fact. In Michael Bierwisch & Karl Erich Heidolph (eds.), *Progress in linguistics*, 143–173. The Hague: Mouton.

Munro, Robert, Steven Bethard, Victor Kuperman, Vicky Tzuyin Lai, Robert Melnick, Christopher Potts, Tylor Schnoebelen & Harry Tily. 2010. Crowdsourcing and language studies: The new generation of linguistic data. In *Proceedings of the NAACL HLT 2010 workshop on creating speech and language data with Amazon's Mechanical Turk*, 122–130. Association for Computational Linguistics.

Platzack, Christer. 1987. The Scandinavian languages and the null subject parameter. *Natural Language and Linguistic Theory* 5. 377–401.

Platzack, Christer & Anders Holmberg. 1989. The role of Agr and finiteness in Germanic VO languages. *Working Papers in Scandinavian Syntax* 43. 51–76.

Simons, Mandy. 2007. Observations on embedding verbs, evidentiality, and presupposition. *Lingua* 117. 1034–1056.

Simons, Mandy, Judith Tonhauser, David Beaver & Craige Roberts. 2010. What projects and why. In Nan Li & David Lutz (eds.), *Proceedings of SALT 20*, 309–327. Ithaca, NY: CLC Publications.

Stalnaker, Robert. 1974. Pragmatic presuppositions. In Milton K. Munitz & Peter K. Unger (eds.), *Semantics and philosophy*, 197–213. New York, NY: New York University Press.

Stalnaker, Robert. 2002. Common Ground. *Linguistics and Philosophy* 25. 701–721.

Urmson, James Opie. 1952. Parenthetical verbs. *Mind* 61. 480–496.

Wiklund, Anna-Lena, Kristine Bentzen, Gunnar Hrafn Hrafnbjargarson & Þorbjörg Hróarsdóttir. 2009. On the distribution and illocution of V2 in Scandinavian that-clauses. *Lingua* 119(12). 1914–1938.

Zanuttini, Raffaela & Paul P. Portner. 2003. Exclamative clauses: At the syntax-semantics interface. *Language* 79(1). 39–81.

Zwart, Jan-Wouter. 1997. Morphosyntax of verb movement: A minimalist approach to the syntax of Dutch. In Marcel den Dikken, Joan Maling, Liliane Haegeman & Maria Polinsky (eds.), *Morphosyntax of verb movement: A minimalist approach to the syntax of Dutch* (Studies in Natural Language and Linguistic Theory 39). Dordrecht: Kluwer Academic Publications.

Chapter 2

An argument against the syntactic nature of verb movement

Jan-Wouter Zwart
University of Groningen

Recent research into the nature of periphrasis converges on the view that periphrastic forms occupy cells in morphological paradigms. This paper argues that the relative past ("perfect") in Dutch should be understood as periphrastic in this sense. Adopting the current minimalist view on the relation between morphology and syntax, in which inflectional morphemes are not generated in syntax but realized postsyntactically in a morphological component, the analysis leads to the conclusion that the relative past's auxiliary is not an element of narrow syntax either. The paper argues that this approach simplifies the syntactic analysis of Dutch verb clusters. The upshot of the analysis is that since auxiliaries undergo verb-second, verb movement must be a postsyntactic operation, as suggested by Chomsky (2001).

1 Introduction

Like many languages, Dutch has two ways of expressing that an event took place in the past, a simple (synthetic) past and a periphrastic past, often mistakenly associated with perfective aspect. These are illustrated in (1), where it can be observed that the periphrastic tense involves an auxiliary (*hebben* 'have' or *zijn* 'be') and a past participle, typically marked by a prefix *ge-*.[1]

(1)

		VERB		SIMPLE PAST	PERIPHRASTIC PAST	
a.		wandel-t	'walk'	wandel-de	heeft	ge-wandel-d
		walk-3SG		walk-PAST.SG	AUX.3SG	GE-walk-PART
b.		loop-t	'walk'	liep	heeft	ge-lop-en
		walk-3SG		walk:PAST.SG	AUX.3SG	GE-walk-PART
c.		gebeur-t	'happen'	gebeur-de	is	ge-beur-d
					AUX.3SG	
d.		kom-t	'come'	kwam	is	ge-kom-en
e.		ontdek-t	'discover'	ontdek-te	heeft	ontdek-t

---

[1]The examples in (1) and (2) are all third person singular.

Jan-Wouter Zwart. 2017. An argument against the syntactic nature of verb movement. In Laura R. Bailey & Michelle Sheehan (eds.), *Order and structure in syntax I: Word order and syntactic structure*, 29–47. Berlin: Language Science Press. DOI:10.5281/zenodo.1117746

The periphrastic past's auxiliary itself may express the present tense, as in (1), or the (simple) past, yielding the opposition in (2).

(2)

		PERIPHRASTIC PAST (PRESENT)		PERIPHRASTIC PAST (PAST)	
a.	heeft	ge-wandel-d	had	ge-wandel-d
	AUX.3SG	GE-walk-PART	AUX.PAST.3SG	GE-walk-PART
b.	heeft	ge-lop-en	had	gelopen
c.	is	ge-beur-d	was	gebeurd
	AUX.3SG		AUX.PAST.3SG	
d.	is	ge-kom-en	was	gekomen
e.	heeft	ontdek-t	had	ontdekt

The periphrastic past tense locates the event in the past relative to a reference point, which may be in the present or in the past, and the tense of the auxiliary refers to the position of the reference point on the time axis. The choice of the synthetic or periphrastic past is independent of the telicity or the progressive/completed nature of the verb/event, showing that the distinction is one of (relative) tense, not aspect.[2]

The simple past must be used to express cotemporaneity with a reference point in the past. Making a cotemporaneous reference point in the past explicit forces the use of the simple past, to the exclusion of all other tenses:

(3)

		[	Toen	ik	binnen kwam] ...			(Dutch)
			when	I	in come.PAST.SG			
a.				...	sliep	hij		
					sleep.PAST.SG	he		
b.	*			...	slaap-t	hij		
					sleep.3SG	he		
c.	*			...	heeft	hij	ge-slap-en	
					AUX.3SG	he	GE-sleep-PART	

'When I came in, he was asleep.'

We want to recall this as a test for a) the syntactic presence of a feature PAST and b) a morphological effect correlated with the presence of the feature PAST. Assuming, as is common in current minimalism, that the morphological component is fed by the syntactic derivation, the morphological effect can be described as the selection of a particular form from the relevant paradigm, based on the features associated with the root SLEEP (cf. Halle 1997: 428). In this example, the root SLEEP activates the paradigm of the Dutch verb *slapen* 'sleep', and the features PAST and SINGULAR associated with the root SLEEP serve to select the unique form *sliep* from that paradigm.

The question how tense and agreement features come to be associated with a verb root has been approached in various ways throughout the history of generative grammar. I

---

[2]For further discussion see Vendryes (1937: 89), Kiparsky (2002: 117), Verkuyl (2008: 20f), Zwart (2011: 12), and Broekhuis et al. (2015: 108).

will assume a simple, minimalist approach in which a syntactic structure contains a range of *controllers* sharing their feature values with the verb (or, more exactly, with their sister constituents dominating the verb), where the feature sharing process is taken to be a function of Merge (as defined in Chomsky 2001: 3). Relevant controllers include the subject (for person and number features) and the tense operator (typically described as a functional head T, but I will remain agnostic as to its syntactic status). It helps to think of the control relation as c-command (where α c-commands β iff α is merged with β or a constituent dominating β), itself a function of Merge.[3]

The advantage of this approach to inflectional morphology is that no special mechanisms, such as Affix Hopping, verb raising, or the operations proposed in the context of Distributed Morphology (Halle & Marantz 1993; Embick 2000), need to be invoked to get the functional features to be associated with the verb. Feature sharing (Koster 1987) as a function of asymmetric Merge (Zwart 2005) is all that is needed.

None of this brings us any closer to an understanding of the nature of the periphrastic tense. In particular, it is not clear what the syntactic status of the auxiliary is, and as far as I am aware, this question has not often been explicitly addressed, at least not for Dutch. I think most analyses implicitly take the auxiliary to be a defective verb, generated inside a more layered VP (following the lead of Akmajian et al. 1979: 20 for English). Let us call this the SYNTACTIC approach (which allows for a range of variants, most notably generating the auxiliary in a functional head position), in which the auxiliary is an independently merged member of the Numeration (the set of elements feeding the syntactic derivation).

I can see at least two potential alternative approaches, which we might call PRESYN-TACTIC and POSTSYNTACTIC. In the presyntactic approach, the auxiliary and the participle would be syntactically merged in a separate derivation, yielding a cluster to be inserted as a Root into the Numeration for another derivation (the derivation generating the clause in which the periphrastic tense features). In the postsyntactic approach, the derivation would contain just a single verb Root, and the auxiliary will not appear in the syntactic derivation at all; rather, the cluster would happen to fill a cell in the morphological paradigm, in opposition to other (synthetic or periphrastic) members of the paradigm.

The postsyntactic approach is supported by research of the past fifteen years on the relation between inflection and periphrasis, as I will show below. What I want to argue here is that this postsyntactic approach is also supported in that it yields the simplest syntactic derivation, needing no ad hoc mechanisms to complicate the general minimalist procedure sketched above.

If so, I submit that this state of affairs provides an argument in support of Chomsky's (2001: 37) conjecture that "a substantial core of head-raising processes (...) may fall within the phonological component". In particular, since auxiliaries undergo verb-second in Dutch, and auxiliaries are only introduced in the morphological component, verb-second must be a postsyntactic process as well.

---

[3]Epstein (1999). Note that the concept of feature sharing between a controller and its sister is different from the probe-goal Agree mechanism of Chomsky (2000: 122). See Zwart (2006) for more discussion.

The discussion is organized as follows. §2 discusses recent research in theoretical morphology on the status of periphrastic expressions. §3 addresses the question of the division of labor between syntax and morphology in periphrasis. §4 argues that deriving the periphrastic past in morphology sheds new light on a range of syntactic problems associated with verb clusters in Dutch. §5 concludes.

2 Periphrasis and postsyntactic morphology

Let us continue to assume that morphology is postsyntactic, i.e. inflectional affixes do not exist in syntax (neither in functional heads nor on lexical roots). Inflected words exist only in morphological paradigms, which are accessed postsyntactically to find a spell-out for a syntactic terminal. What exists in syntax are roots and grammatical features, the latter instrumental in picking the right form from the paradigm.

The question to be asked here is the following: given that affixes do not exist in syntax, what evidence is there that the auxiliaries featuring in periphrastic tenses exist in syntax? Until recently, the fact that auxiliaries undergo movements like verb-second could be taken as evidence that auxiliaries are syntactically present (cf. Embick 2000: 203, Kiparsky 2005: 132). But since verb movement is at issue here (it might also be postsyntactic), we need evidence of a different kind.[4]

Recent research into the nature of periphrasis leans heavily towards the alternative position, in which periphrastic forms occupy cells in morphological paradigms (see Chumakina 2013 and Spencer & Popova 2015 for a survey). The construction of a periphrastic expression, on this view, is not a matter of syntactic derivation any more than the formation of inflected word forms.

In the three following subsections, we discuss the key issues figuring in the discussion of periphrasis in theoretical morphology: the status of periphrasis vis-à-vis morphological paradigms, the compositionality of periphrastic expressions, and the process of auxiliation.

2.1 Periphrasis and paradigms

The idea that paradigms may include periphrastic formations appears to have been commonplace in structuralist linguistics (see e.g. Robins 1959: 124, Benveniste 1965: 130). The thinking here is that paradigms "represent interlocking systems of grammatical oppositions" and where periphrastic expressions are "comparable to single words in the corresponding places of a different paradigm they are obviously to be included in paradigms themselves" (Robins 1959: 124).[5]

---

[4]This is where Chomsky's observation that verb movements do not seem to feed the postsyntactic component dealing with interpretation becomes relevant; I will not address this line of argumentation, but see Holmberg (2015) for discussion.

[5]Robins says "syntactically comparable", the context suggesting that he has syntactic category and syntactic dependency in mind rather than syntactic position.

This position was (silently) abandoned in the weak-lexicalist approach of early generative grammar, where even inflectional affixes constituted independent syntactic elements, generated in functional heads (e.g. Chomsky 1981: 52). But in a strong-lexicalist approach (as adopted in minimalism, where inflected words are not created in syntax but introduced pre- or postsyntactically in fully inflected form), the question of paradigm structure resurfaces, and the idea that periphrasis is part of the inflectional paradigm can be entertained once more.

This is reflected in the survey article by Spencer & Popova (2015: 202f), referring to recent work by Börjars et al. (1997), Stump (2001), and Ackerman & Stump (2004), among others, in which we find versions of the original structuralist position again. As before, the central idea is that paradigms are structured by the intersection of features expressed in the forms (e.g. combinations of person, number, tense, voice, etc.). Each feature intersection defines a cell in the paradigm, which may be filled by a specific inflectional form, or, in its absence, by a periphrastic expression (Stump 2001: 14).

This may be exemplified by Latin, where the features tense and voice intersect to yield the paradigm in Table 1. As is well-known, the cell where perfect tense and passive voice intersect cannot be filled by a synthetic form (forms in third person singular, from the verb *laudāre* 'praise').

Table 1: Latin tense/voice paradigm

TENSE	VOICE	
	ACTIVE	PASSIVE
PRESENT	laudat	laudātur
IMPERFECT	laudābat	laudabātur
PERFECT	laudāvit	laudātus est

Another example is provided by Burushaski (Lorimer 1935: 243f), where even a single tense paradigm can show a mix of synthetic and periphrastic forms, involving the verb *ɛtʌs* 'to do, to make' and a form of the copula (Table 2; see also Chumakina 2013: 9 and references cited there).

If periphrastic expressions are not allowed to fill the relevant cells in the Latin and Burushaski paradigms, these paradigms would be randomly defective. Moreover, we would have to explain why syntax provides a periphrastic construction precisely there where these gaps in the paradigm happen to exist. Assuming that periphrasis is syntactic and inflectional morphology postsyntactic would lead us to the conclusion that periphrasis somehow causes the gaps in the paradigm observed in Tables 1–2 (i.e. periphrasis blocks inflection), the converse of what we typically find in blocking relations (Kiparsky 2005).[6]

In Dutch, the relevant features are TENSE and some feature responsible for the relative tense interpretation (anteriority). We may follow Wiltschko (2014: 75) in identifying

---

[6]Kiparsky solves this problem by assuming morphology before syntax.

Table 2: Burushaski present tense paradigm (Lorimer 1935: 245)

PERSON	NUMBER	
	SINGULAR	PLURAL
1.	ɛča ba	ɛča baːn
2.	ɛča	ɛčaːn
3. HUM.M	ɛčaii	ɛčaːn
3. HUM.F	ɛču bo	ɛčaːn
3. ANIMATE	ɛči bi	ɛčiɛ(n)
3. INANIMATE	ɛči biːla / ɛčiːla	ɛčitsʌn

this feature as POINT OF VIEW. Wiltschko calls the tense feature ANCHORING and locates both ANCHORING and POINT OF VIEW as particular areas in the clausal spine, comparable with TP (IP) and AspP in current minimalist analyses. Using the terminology introduced above, we may say that both TENSE and POINT OF VIEW (POV) are potential controllers that may share features with the verbal root. The paradigm, then, is as in Table 3 (cf. 1).

Table 3: Dutch finite paradigm (3SG)

TENSE	POV	
	UNMARKED	ANTERIOR
PRESENT	wandelt	heeft gewandeld
PAST	wandelde	had gewandeld

The "anterior present" is what we described above as the relative past: it locates the event prior to the here and now. The "anterior past", marked by the past tense on the auxiliary, locates the event prior to a reference point in the past (i.e. a past-shifted relative past). As can be seen, the periphrastic expressions fill the cells where the tense feature interacts with the anterior point of view feature.

A simple way to describe the situation in Dutch would be to say that the operators TENSE and POV control the corresponding features on the verb, assigning them certain values pointing to particular cells in the paradigm in Table 3. That some of these cells are filled by periphrastic expressions is not a matter of syntax, but of morphology.

2.2 Compositionality

There is a long tradition, going back to at least Benveniste (1965), that treats the Indo-European periphrastic perfect, exemplified here by Dutch, as non-compositional, in the sense that "the construction as a whole might be associated with morphosyntactic properties that do not arise from any of the component parts" (Spencer & Popova 2015: 211).

To Ackerman & Stump (2004), this is one of the diagnostic criteria for periphrasis (for which they refer to Mirra Gukhman).

As Benveniste (1965: 184) argues, the auxiliary-participle construction shows a clear division of labor (the auxiliary carrying inflection and the participle conveying lexical meaning), but the grammatical property of anteriority arises only as a function of the combination of the auxiliary and the participle.

In contrast, Kiparsky (2005: 123) argues that the periphrastic (relative) past *is* compositionally derived from the meaning of its parts. This assumes that the past participle contributes the meaning PAST (i.e. anteriority), and the auxiliary (through its tense features) the location of the reference point relative to which the anteriority is to be interpreted.

I am not convinced that the participle denotes the past, as Kiparsky contends. In many languages, the same participle appears in the passive (with a different auxiliary), without a hint of anteriority (cf. Wackernagel 1920: 288–289). Moreover, Kiparsky's suggestion that the periphrastic tense is compositional fails to specify the contribution made by the (possessive) auxiliary, since the reference point relative to which the anteriority is to be interpreted is not derived from the presence and nature of the auxiliary, but from the tense feature of the clause (spelled out by the auxiliary's tense morphology).

More seriously, we can show that any compositionality that may have existed originally in the formation of the periphrastic past is very often lost as the periphrastic past became enshrined in the temporal/aspectual system of the language. As a result, closely related languages like Dutch, German and English show subtle differences in the grammatical properties of the auxiliary-participle combination.

In English, unlike Dutch, the "perfect time span" in which the event is situated is not fully anterior, running up to and including the here and now (Iatridou et al. 2001). This can be seen from the incompatibility of the periphrastic past ("perfect") with time adverbials locating the event squarely in the past, like *yesterday* (cf. Klein 1992; Zwart 2008):

(4) a. John (*has) read the book yesterday.

    b. Jan heeft het boek gisteren ge-lez-en.　　　　　　　　　　(Dutch)
        John AUX.3SG the book yesterday GE-read-PART

      'John read the book yesterday.'

It is not so clear where this subtle but high-impact distinction between Dutch and English participles originates, or what this instance of variation tells us about the core meaning of the past participle.

German is like Dutch in this respect, but in large parts of the German speaking area, the periphrastic past tense has completely replaced the simple past, so that it can now be used to express cotemporaneity with a reference point in the past ("Präteritumschwund", cf. Abraham & Conradie 2001). Compare German (5) with Dutch (3c):

(5) Als ich herein kam　　　　　　hat　　er ge-schlaf-en.　　　　　　　(German)
    when I　 in　　come.PAST.SG AUX.3SG he GE-sleep-PART

    'When I came in he was asleep.'

This additional shift in interpretation indicates that anteriority is not an inherent or stable property of the periphrastic tense, casting doubt on the suggestion that the particular semantics of the Dutch relative past derive compositionally from its morphological component parts.

Moreover, as already observed for English in Hoffmann (1966: 8), the forced anteriority reading of the periphrastic tense disappears in Dutch nonfinite clauses (Zwart 2014). This can be seen in (6), applying the past tense diagnostics of (3).

(6) Hij beweer-t ...
    he claim-3SG

    'He claims ...

     a.   ... te   slap-en.
              INF sleep-INF

              ... to be asleep.'

     b.   ... te   heb-ben ge-slap-en   toen ik binnen kwam.
              INF AUX-INF GE-sleep-PART when I in   come:PAST.SG

              ... to have been asleep when I came in.'

     c. * ... te   slap-en   toen ik binnen kwam.
              INF sleep-INF when I in   come:PAST.SG

In (6b), making the reference point in the past explicit (by *toen ik binnen kwam* 'when I came in') forces a shift from the unmarked infinitive *te slapen* 'to sleep' to an infinitive marked for past tense *te hebben geslapen* 'to have been asleep'. But since Dutch lacks a synthetic past tense infinitive, once again the periphrastic expression appears. If the periphrastic past's anteriority reading were compositional, (6b) should have a forced anteriority reading as well, contrary to fact.[7]

We can now supplement Table 3 with its nonfinite counterpart in Table 4.

Table 4: Dutch nonfinite paradigm

TENSE	POV	
	UNMARKED	ANTERIOR
PRESENT	te wandelen	te hebben gewandeld
PAST	te hebben gewandeld	te hebben gewandeld

Like in southern German, the periphrastic expression encroaches on the synthetic form, apparently ignoring whatever compositionality (if any) gave rise to its formation in the first place.

The non-compositionality of the periphrastic past in Dutch is consistent with the idea that the periphrastic past is a morphological rather than a syntactic creation.

---

[7]The infinitival periphrastic construction can also be used to express present and past anteriority.

2.3 Auxiliation

The development of the periphrastic past tense of the type discussed here is a textbook example of the process of grammaticalization (e.g. Hopper & Traugott 1993: 57, Harris & Campbell 1995: 182f, Kuteva 2001: 40f). In the course of this process, a lexical verb of possession becomes an auxiliary, and what was initially a secondary predicate is reanalyzed as a participial main verb. A detailed discussion of this development is beyond the scope of this article, so we will assume our understanding of it to be by and large correct, noting the important refinements by Benveniste (1968: 86f).

What is striking is that the same development took place in many languages, and that its distribution can certainly not be explained as contact-induced propagation (Vendryes 1937: 87–88). Moreover, what we find repeatedly is a push chain effect, shaking up the temporal/aspectual system of the language. Thus, Benveniste (1968: 88) notes that the development of the periphrastic perfect in Latin leads to a reinterpretation of the original synthetic perfect as an aorist. In other languages, the synthetic perfect has disappeared completely (Vendryes 1937: 90, Meillet 1921: 149f).

What these changes seem to indicate is that periphrasis and synthesis are competing for the same turf. This follows naturally if periphrasis is morphological, but is somewhat unexpected if both processes, periphrasis and synthesis, are in the different leagues of syntax and morphology.

3 Division of labor between syntax and morphology in periphrasis

Periphrasis is analyzed as a mix of morphology and syntax in Brown et al. (2012), with the aim of identifying a set of criteria to be employed for the proper characterization of apparent periphrastic phenomena in (ideally) any language. Using these criteria, we may decide where the Dutch periphrastic tense may be located in this morphosyntactic spectrum.

Criteria favoring morphological character are (i) obligatoriness: the inevitable need to use a particular form in a particular morphosyntactic environment, (ii) expression of contextual rather than inherent features, (iii) the creation of a word *form* rather than a (new) lexeme, and (iv) the expression of a paradigmatic opposition. All these criteria apply to the periphrastic past tense in Dutch: it (i) must be used to express relative past, (ii) expresses tense, a clausal feature, (iii) creates a (periphrastic) form of a word rather than a new lexeme, which (iv) enters into paradigmatic oppositions (see Tables 3 and 4).

A fifth criterium listed by Brown et al. (2012), that of (v) being complex, applies to both morphological and syntactic formations, and indeed to the Dutch periphrastic past as well.

Criteria favoring syntactic character are (vi) word order flexibility and (vii) allowing inflected subparts. These both apply to the Dutch periphrastic tense: the auxiliary (vi) need not be adjacent to the participle, and appears on either side of the participle (see below), and (vii) carries the clausal tense and agreement inflections. There is, however, a problem with these two criteria, as they serve to demarcate syntax from word formation, but not (necessarily) syntax from the formation of periphrasis. Being composed of more than one word is in the very nature of periphrasis, and it is not clear what would block the component words from undergoing processes of postsyntactic movement or inflection marking.

It seems, then, that the set of criteria identified in Brown et al. (2012) overwhelmingly points to periphrasis being morphological.

This is not to deny that periphrasis is complex and structured. A useful starting point is to assume that anything complex and structured is derived by Merge, i.e. syntactically. But many complex and structured items are clearly morphological, such as compounds and the products of derivational morphology. Evidently, the morphological inventory contains elements that are produced syntactically (see Ackema & Neeleman 2004), just like lexical items (roots) can be produced syntactically (Hale & Keyser 2002).

However, when we say that a periphrastic item [α β] is syntactic, as opposed to morphological, we mean that α and β, along with a range of other elements {γ, ..., ω}, are members of a single Numeration feeding a single derivation that yields the sentence composed of α, β, γ, etc. and ω. In other words, there is no separate syntactic subderivation in which [α β] is created, either before syntax (feeding the Numeration) or after syntax (feeding the morphological paradigms), but the periphrastic expression is created "on the fly", during the derivation that yields the clause in which it appears. When I deny the syntactic status of periphrasis, it is in this particular sense, in which levels of derivation that should be kept apart have been mixed.

This approach to the division of labor between syntax and morphology is close to that of Börjars et al. (1997), which drew a sharp critique in Embick (2000: 223–224). Embick's point seems to be that if cells in the morphological paradigm can be filled by phrases created in a separate derivation, no predictions can be made about the nature and structure of those phrases. His own proposal holds that both the synthetic and the periphrastic perfect of Latin are created in clausal syntax (thus mixing the levels of syntax and word formation in the tradition of weak lexicalism and Distributed Morphology; cf. Halle & Marantz 1993; Halle 1997). It seems to me that the interesting part of this analysis can be made compatible with the Börjars et al. approach quite easily, whereas the part involving the syntactic derivation is considerably less compelling, as shown by Kiparsky (2005: 129f).[8]

---

[8]Embick (2000) argues that the synthetic and the periphrastic perfect in Latin involve the same sets of features, distributed across identical syntactic structures, and that word formation is a function of syntactic movement, which is blocked in the periphrastic present by an opacity factor. The blocking is stipulated, but let us assume it to be correct. As far as I can tell, the generalizations of the analysis are not lost if the syntactic structure in fact describes a subderivation feeding into the morphological paradigm, separate from the sentential syntactic derivation. Since the elements in the morphological paradigm serve to express the features in the (sentential) syntactic terminals, some parallelism between the sentential syntactic and morpho-syntactic derivations is to be expected. This also answers Embick's objection that in a Börjars et al. (1997) type approach, anything goes. Clearly, for a phrase to obtain a position in an inflectional paradigm, some commonality in morphosyntactic features has to exist, which arguably requires some structural parallelism between the phrasal and inflectional elements as well (perhaps along the lines of Williams's (2003) *shape conservation*). Embick's analysis goes a long way towards bringing such parallelisms to light, strengthening rather than weakening the lexicalist approach.

4 Further arguments

So far we have seen that there are reasons to consider the periphrastic past as a morphological phenomenon, occupying a cell in the morphological paradigm. Assuming postsyntactic morphology, this entails that the auxiliary is only introduced after the narrow syntactic derivation has run its course.

It is important to note that this conclusion does not necessarily carry over to the other types of verb clusters in Dutch, involving modal auxiliaries (7a) or lexical verbs selecting infinitival complements (7b).

(7)   a. modal auxiliaries
      ... dat   Tasman het   Zuidland   wil   ontdek-ken
      COMP Tasman DEF.NTR South.Land AUX.VOLITION.SG discover-INF

      '... that Tasman wants to discover the South Land.'

      b. infinitival complements
      ... dat   Tasman het probeer-t te   ontdek-ken
      COMP Tasman it   try-3SG   INF discover-INF

      '... that Tasman is trying to discover it.'

Clusters with modal auxiliaries or infinitival complement taking verbs are straightforwardly compositional and cannot be analyzed as occupying a cell in an otherwise inflectional morphological paradigm. These clusters, therefore, must be thought of as being created either in narrow syntax or before that (i.e. in a separate derivation feeding the Numeration rather than the morphological paradigms).

With this out of the way, we can briefly discuss a number of additional observations supporting the morphological (postsyntactic) nature of the periphrastic past in Dutch.

4.1 Variability

The verb cluster expressing the periphrastic past (i.e. consisting of a temporal auxiliary *hebben* 'have' or *zijn* 'be' and a past participle) shows a remarkable variability in the order of its elements, both across dialects and within the standard language. Marking the auxiliary 1 and the participle 2, both ascending (*1-2*, auxiliary—participle) and descending (*2-1*, participle—auxiliary) orders occur. This is different from the clusters featuring modal auxiliaries and infinitive-taking lexical verbs, which are predominantly ascending (*1-2*) across dialects and almost invariably ascending (*1-2*) in the standard language (see Stroop 1970; Zwart 1996, and more recently Barbiers et al. 2008: 14–25).

Deriving the variable orders in the cluster syntactically poses a range of problems, giving rise to a diversity of analyses too wide to discuss here (but see Wurmbrand 2005). Suffice it to say that existing proposals often must resort to ad hoc devices, such as optional movement, rightward movement, movement of intermediate projections, verb incorporation ("verb raising") and excorporation, reanalysis, and roll-up movement. None of this is necessary if the periphrastic past is a product of postsyntactic morphology.

More particularly, the fact that the verb cluster in the periphrastic past behaves differently from the verb clusters headed by modal auxiliaries and lexical verbs taking infinitives can now be ascribed to the circumstance that the periphrastic past is created postsyntactically, and the other verb clusters are not.

To some extent, the problem of how to account for variability in the order of the auxiliary and the participle remains, but a large part of that problem, namely to describe the phenomena in terms of syntactic processes, has disappeared. And perhaps we may even ascribe the variation in linear order to the externalization process ("spell out"), reducing the problem of cluster generation simply to the merger of an auxiliary and a participle in a separate derivation feeding morphological paradigms.

4.2 The IPP-effect

In three-verb clusters, where the highest verb is a temporal auxiliary, the second verb is realized as an infinitive instead of as a past participle (the Infinitivus Pro Participio or IPP effect; Lange 1981; Zwart 2007; Schallert 2014, among many others):

(8) a. two-verb cluster, auxiliary selects participle
         heeft   { ge-wil-d   / *wil-len }
         AUX.3SG   GE-want-PART / want-INF
         'wanted'

     b. three-verb cluster, auxiliary selects infinitive
         heeft   { *ge-wil-d   / wil-len   } ontdek-ken
         AUX.3SG   GE-want-PART / want-INF   discover-INF
         'wanted to discover'

While much about the IPP-effect remains unclear, the present approach suggests a new angle. Recall that we assume that the periphrastic past is created postsyntactically: in syntax, (8a) is just the verb *willen* 'want' with relative past (present anterior) features. In (8b), however, the syntactic element to be replaced in morphology is not a single verb but a cluster *willen ontdekken* 'want discover'. The generalization, then, would be as in (9):[9]

(9) *IPP-effect*
     The relative past of x is marked with *ge*- only if x is not a verb cluster.

This is a morphological generalization, referring to the inventory of forms and the processes generating them, and not to syntax.

One generalization about the IPP-effect follows immediately, namely the generalization that the IPP-effect is absent in dialects not marking the relative past with *ge*- (Hoeksema 1980; Lange 1981). More problematic, however, is the generalization that the IPP-effect is sensitive to linear order, clusters with strictly descending orders (*3-2-1*) typically

---

[9]I am assuming that the replacement of the participial ending by the infinitival ending is a secondary effect, see Zwart (2007: 85) following Paul (1920: 128).

not showing the IPP-effect (though exceptions do exist, cf. Zwart 2007: 78f). The following example is from Achterhoeks Dutch (Blom & Hoekstra 1996: 76).

(10) ... dat ik schriev-m e-wil-d   had   (Achterhoeks Dutch)
      COMP I write-INF GE-want-PART AUX.PAST.SG

   '... that I had wanted to write.'

Further refinement of (9), then, would still be needed, but it is not clear that this would put the entire approach in any kind of jeopardy. One possibility would be that in (10), *schrievm* 'write' and *willn* 'want' are separate terminals in syntax (so there is no presyntactic cluster formation), with only *willn* marked with the present anterior features triggering periphrastic tense formation in morphology.[10]

4.3 Mixed cluster orders

It has been observed that not all mixed cluster orders (*1-3-2, 2-1-3, 2-3-1, 3-1-2*) are equally frequent across Continental West Germanic dialects, though all are attested (see Zwart 2007 and Salzmann 2016 on the rare *2-1-3* type). The question is whether this is what we expect to find if periphrastic tense formation is postsyntactic.

If the temporal auxiliary (*have* or *be*) is the highest verb in the cluster, there are two possibilities. First, the *2-3* verbs form a cluster, created presyntactically; in that case the cluster is transfered as a single terminal after completion of the narrow syntactic derivation, which is turned into a three-verb cluster in morphology. The IPP-effect (9) applies, and we expect the mixed orders *1-3-2* and *2-3-1* to occur (in addition to the consistent ascending *1-2-3* and descending *3-2-1* orders). The other possibility, hinted at in section 4.2, is that the *2* and *3* verbs are independent elements in the syntactic derivation, only one of which (the *2* verb) is turned into a periphrastic past in morphology. The IPP-effect does not apply, as the relevant verb is not a cluster, and we expect the orders *2-1-3* and *3-1-2* to occur (*2-1/1-2* being the periphrastic element produced by morphology).

This is indeed what we find. Interestingly, all attested *2-1-3* cases show no IPP-effect (Zwart 2007; Salzmann 2016). An example is given in (11) from Luxemburgish (Bruch 1973: 95).

(11) ... ob-s   de hollänesch ge-leier-t   hues   schwätz-en   (Luxemburgish)
      comp.INT-2SG you Dutch   GE-learn-PART AUX.2SG speak-INF

   '... whether you learned to speak Dutch.'

On the other hand, the *3-1-2* order does show the IPP-effect (example from Austrian Bavarian, Patocka 1997: 278; the IPP-verb is *soin*, the modal infinitive):

(12) ... da   ma wås   lean-a   hett-n   soi-n   (Austrian Bavarian)
      COMP we something learn-INF AUX.PAST-PL MOD-INF

   '... that we should have learned something.'

---

[10] The IPP-variant is optional in (10). This variant would then differ in involving presyntactic cluster formation, so that (9) applies.

On our approach, this can only be explained if the position of the *3* verb *leana* 'learn' is due to a postsyntactic leftward shift process, breaking up the cluster *soin leana*.

If the temporal auxiliary is the number *2* verb, we again have to consider the two possibilities of presyntactic cluster formation, yielding a single terminal at the end of the narrow syntactic derivation, and the alternative derivation in which both verbs are independent syntactic elements. Let us assume that the number *1* verb is a modal auxiliary selecting an infinitive (ultimately the number *3* verb). Then assuming presyntactic cluster formation, the periphrastic past can only occur if the infinitive has an independent tense feature (present anterior), not a straightforward possibility, but let us proceed. This yields a cluster *2-3* after syntax, which we predict to have to stay together, barring the postsyntactic leftward shift of the number *3* verb needed for (12). This gives us *1-3-2*, *2-3-1* and *3-1-2* (after leftward shift), but not *2-1-3*. If the modal and the infinitive are both independently present in syntax, and the infinitive gets an independent tense feature (present anterior), the result is the same.

It is interesting, then, to note that all the *2-1-3* orders I have seen in dialect descriptions and in the theoretical literature involve a number *1* temporal auxiliary, none involving a number *1* modal auxiliary and a number *2* temporal auxiliary (see also Schallert 2014: 271). This follows from the analysis contemplated here, where the periphrastic past is produced in postsyntactic morphology, assuming that the cluster thus created can only be broken up by postsyntactic leftward shift of the participle (itself a generalization in need of explanation).[11]

4.4 Auxiliary selection

A well-known property of the periphrastic past is that the nature of the temporal auxiliary may vary, with verbs "selecting" as the auxiliary to be used either a copula (*be*, Dutch *zijn*) or a possessive verb (*have*, Dutch *hebben*). Basically, auxiliary *be* is selected by unaccusative and passive verbs, and *have* is selected by active transitive and unergative verbs. Some verbs may select both *have* and *be*, but as Hoekstra (1984) has shown, the variation is not random, as these verbs can be construed in different ways, featuring either unaccusative or unergative syntax.

I am assuming here that the discussion in Hoekstra (1999) is essentially correct, showing that auxiliary selection is not a function of a lexical mutativity feature (Kern 1912), but of syntactic structure. But not assuming postsyntactic morphology, Hoekstra describes the auxiliary *have* as being created in syntax through movement of a functional head specific to transitive and unergative structures into Infl (see Kayne 1993 for a related proposal).

Assuming postsyntactic morphology, this analysis can be simplified in that we may adopt the syntactic structures without the hypothesized movements. The more complex

---

[11]Three-verb clusters in which the number *1* verb is not an auxiliary show the same pattern as the three-verb clusters with a modal auxiliary in the number *1* position, with *3-1-2* allowed but *2-1-3* excluded, and I would suggest an explanation along similar lines, except that the pattern also applies where the number *2* verb is not a temporal but a modal auxiliary. These patterns, then, do not bear directly on the proposed analysis of periphrastic tense.

structure associated with transitivity (including unergative constructions) may involve controllers imparting additional features on the verb, to be spelled out in morphology.

The advantage of this approach would be that it leaves room for morphological idiosyncrasies, which we know are quite frequent in this domain. For example, languages featuring the periphrastic past do not always show the same auxiliary selection pattern, as is immediately clear from the example of English (using *have* systematically). Realization of the auxiliary, then, cannot be an automatic function of syntactic structure.

This is nowhere more apparent than in the selection of the auxiliary for the copular verb itself. The syntactic analysis of Hoekstra (1999) here predicts the auxiliary to have to be *be*, as it is in Dutch, but many languages employ *have* instead. The crosslinguistic pattern has been studied in Postma (1993), who derives the surprising generalization that selection of the auxiliary *be* in this domain is determined by the presence of suppletive morphology in the participial form of the copula. This is exemplified in Table 5 for the closely related languages Dutch and Frisian.[12]

Table 5: Auxiliary selection

LANGUAGE	COPULA (INFINITIVE)	PERIPHRASTIC TENSE	AUXILIARY	SUPPLETION
Dutch	zij-n	is ge-wees-t	be	+
Frisian	wêz-e	ha wes-t	have	–

Postma proposes a syntactic analysis of this generalization, which space does not permit me to discuss more fully here. But if suppletion, a hallmark of inflectional morphology, determines auxiliary selection, then auxiliary selection must be morphological too. And if morphology is postsyntactic, as we have been assuming throughout, then auxiliary selection must be postsyntactic, too.

5 Conclusion

In this article, I have argued that if morphology is postsyntactic, as in current minimalism, the periphrastic tense must be thought of as a product of morphology rather than syntax.

We have seen that the periphrastic past in Dutch occupies a cell in the verbal paradigm, as illustrated in Table 3 for the finite paradigm and in Table 4 for the nonfinite paradigm. The "meaning" of the periphrastic tense is not compositionally derived from its component parts (following Benveniste 1965, *pace* Kiparsky 2005), witness the shifts in interpretation that the periphrastic tense displays across languages and dialects, sometimes even replacing the simple past, as in Southern German dialects and in nonfinite contexts more generally. While the auxiliation process giving rise to the periphrastic tense has been described as syntactic reanalysis, the fact that the periphrastic tense effectuates

---

[12]Postma bases his generalization on 19 Indo-European languages.

a reorganization of a language's temporal/aspectual system shows that the process is really morphological.

We have applied the diagnostic criteria of Brown et al. (2012) to show that the periphrastic tense of Dutch is a morphological, rather than a syntactic phenomenon. This is not to deny that the fine structure of the periphrastic tense formation may parallel the structure of the clause in which the periphrastic tense appears, as observed by Embick (2000), but rather than taking the (imperfect) parallel as evidence for a syntactic derivation of the periphrastic tense, the similarity must be ascribed to the need for the products of morphology to externalize the features accrued in the syntactic derivation.

We have shown that taking this perspective on the periphrastic tense casts new light on several curious aspects of Dutch verbal syntax, including the IPP-effect, generalizations about the order of elements in the verb clusters, and auxiliary selection.

The upshot of the discussion is this. If the periphrastic tense is a product of postsyntactic morphology, the auxiliary that we observe in the periphrastic tense does not exist in syntax. Yet the auxiliary, when finite, invariably undergoes verb movement ('verb-second') to the position to the immediate right of the first clausal constituent in Dutch main clauses. This movement, then, cannot take place in narrow syntax, but must be postsyntactic. Since all finite verbs in main clauses are subject to the same linearization restriction, all of verb-second must be postsyntactic. And since verb-second represents a core case of head movement, a case can be made for the postsyntactic nature of head movement more generally.

References

Abraham, Werner & C. Jac. Conradie. 2001. *Präteritumschwund und Diskurs-Grammatik.* Amsterdam: John Benjamins.

Ackema, Peter & Ad Neeleman. 2004. *Beyond morphology: Interface conditions on word formation.* Oxford: Oxford University Press.

Ackerman, Farrell & Gregory Stump. 2004. Paradigms and periphrastic expression: A study in realization-based lexicalism. In Andrew Spencer & Louisa Sadler (eds.), *Projecting morphology*, 111–158. Stanford: CSLI Publications.

Akmajian, Adrian, Susan M. Steele & Thomas Wasow. 1979. The category AUX in Universal Grammar. *Linguistic Inquiry* 10. 1–64.

Barbiers, Sjef, Johan van der Auwera, Hans Bennis, Eefje Boef, Gunther De Vogelaer & Margreet van der Ham. 2008. *Syntactic atlas of the Dutch dialects.* Vol. 2. Amsterdam: Amsterdam University Press.

Benveniste, Émile. 1965. Structure des relations de l'auxiliarité. *Acta Linguistica Hafniensia* 9. 1–15. Reproduced in *Problèmes de linguistique générale*, vol 2, 177–193 (Paris: Gallimard, 1974).

Benveniste, Émile. 1968. Mutations of linguistic categories. In Winfred P. Lehmann & Yakov Malkiel (eds.), *Directions for historical linguistics: A symposium*, 83–94. Austin: University of Texas Press.

Blom, Elma & Eric Hoekstra. 1996. IPP en werkwoordsvolgorde in het Achterhoeks. *Taal en Tongval* 48. 72–83.

Börjars, Kersti, Nigel Vincent & Carol Chapman. 1997. Paradigms, periphrases and pronominal inflection: A feature-based account. In Geert Booij & Jaap van Marle (eds.), *Paradigms, periphrases and pronominal inflection: A feature-based account*, vol. 1996, 155–180. Dordrecht: Kluwer Academic Publishers.

Broekhuis, Hans, Norbert Corver & Riet Vos. 2015. *Syntax of Dutch: Verbs and verb phrases*. Amsterdam: Amsterdam University Press.

Brown, Dunstan, Marina Chumakina, Greville Corbett, Gergana Popova & Andrew Spencer. 2012. Defining 'periphrasis': Key notions. *Morphology* 22. 233–275.

Bruch, Robert. 1973. *Luxemburger Grammatik in volkstümlichem Abriss*. Luxembourg: Éditions de la Section de Linguistique de l'Institut gr.-d.

Chomsky, Noam. 1981. *Lectures on government and binding*. Dordrecht: Foris.

Chomsky, Noam. 2000. Minimalist inquiries: The framework. In Roger Martin, David Michaels & Juan Uriagereka (eds.), *Step by step: Essays on minimalist syntax in honor of Howard Lasnik*, 89–155. Cambridge: MIT Press.

Chomsky, Noam. 2001. Derivation by phase. In Michael Kenstowicz (ed.), *Ken Hale: A life in language*, 1–52. Cambridge: MIT Press.

Chumakina, Marina. 2013. Introduction. In Marina Chumakina & Greville G. Corbett (eds.), *Periphrasis: The role of syntax and morphology in paradigms*, 1–23. Oxford: Oxford University Press.

Embick, David. 2000. Features, syntax, and categories in the Latin perfect. *Linguistic Inquiry* 31. 185–230.

Epstein, Samuel D. 1999. Un-principled syntax: The derivation of syntactic relations. In Samuel D. Epstein & Norbert Hornstein (eds.), *Working minimalism*, 317–345. Cambridge: MIT Press.

Hale, Kenneth L. & Samuel J. Keyser. 2002. *Prolegomenon to the theory of argument structure*. Cambridge: MIT Press.

Halle, Morris. 1997. Distributed morphology: Impoverishment and fission. *MIT Working Papers in Linguistics* 30. 425–449.

Halle, Morris & Alec Marantz. 1993. Distributed morphology and the pieces of inflection. In Kenneth L. Hale & Samuel J. Keyser (eds.), *The view from Building 20: Essays in linguistics in honor of Sylvain Bromberger*, 111–176. Cambridge: MIT Press.

Harris, Alice & Lyle Campbell. 1995. *Historical syntax in cross-linguistic perspective*. Cambridge: Cambridge University Press.

Hoeksema, Jack. 1980. Verbale verstrengeling ontstrengeld. *Spektator* 10. 221–249.

Hoekstra, Teun. 1984. *Transitivity: Grammatical relations in Government-Binding theory*. Dordrecht: Foris.

Hoekstra, Teun. 1999. Auxiliary selection in Dutch. *Natural Language and Linguistic Theory* 17. 67–84.

Hoffmann, T. Ronald. 1966. Past tense replacement and the modal system. In Anthony G. Oettinger (ed.), *Mathematical linguistics and automatic translation*, 1–21. Cambridge: Harvard Computational Laboratory.

Holmberg, Anders. 2015. Verb second. In Tibor Kiss & Artemis Alexiadou (eds.), *Syntax – Theory and analysis: An international handbook*, 2nd edn., 342–382. Berlin: de Gruyter.

Hopper, Paul J. & Elizabeth Closs Traugott. 1993. *Grammaticalization*. Cambridge: Cambridge University Press.

Iatridou, Sabine, Elena Anagnostopoulou & Roumyana Izvorski. 2001. Observations about the form and meaning of the perfect. In Michael Kenstowicz (ed.), *Ken Hale: A life in language*, 189–238. Cambridge: MIT Press.

Kayne, Richard S. 1993. Towards a modular theory of auxiliary selection. *Studia Linguistica* 47. 3–31.

Kern, Johan Hendrik. 1912. *De met het Participium Praeteriti omschreven werkwoordsvormen in 't Nederlands*. Amsterdam: Johannes Mulder.

Kiparsky, Paul. 2002. Event structure and the perfect. In David I. Beaver, Luis D. Casillas, Brady Z. Clark & Stefan Kaufmann (eds.), *The construction of meaning*, 113–135. Stanford: CSLI Publications.

Kiparsky, Paul. 2005. Blocking and periphrasis in inflectional paradigms. In Geert Booij (ed.), *Yearbook of Morphology 2004*, 113–135. Dordrecht: Springer.

Klein, Wolfgang. 1992. The present perfect puzzle. *Language* 68. 525–552.

Koster, Jan. 1987. *Domains and dynasties: The radical autonomy of syntax*. Dordrecht: Foris.

Kuteva, Tania. 2001. *Auxiliation: An inquiry into the nature of grammaticalization*. Oxford: Oxford University Press.

Lange, Klaus-Peter. 1981. Warum Ersatzinfinitiv? *Groninger Arbeiten zur germanistischen Linguistik* 19. 62–81.

Lorimer, David L. R. 1935. *The Burushaski language: Introduction and grammar*. Vol. 1. Oslo: Aschehoug.

Meillet, Antoine. 1921. *Linguistique historique et linguistique générale*. Paris: Champion.

Patocka, Franz. 1997. *Satzgliedstellung in den bairischen Dialekten österreichs*. Frankfurt: Peter Lang.

Paul, Hermann. 1920. *Deutsche Grammatik*. Vol. 4: Syntax (2. Hälfte). Halle: Max Niemeyer.

Postma, Gertjan. 1993. The syntax of the morphological defectivity of *be*. *HIL Manuscripts* 3. 31–67.

Robins, G. H. 1959. In defense of WP. *Transactions of the Philological Society* 58. 116–144.

Salzmann, Martin. 2016. *On the limits of variation in West-Germanic verb clusters: Evidence from displaced morphology and extraposition for the existence of clusters with 213 order*. Ms., University of Leipzig.

Schallert, Oliver. 2014. *Zur Syntax der Ersatzinfinitivkonstruktion: Typologie und Variation*. Tübingen: Stauffenburg Verlag.

Spencer, Andrew & Gergana Popova. 2015. Periphrasis and inflection. In Matthew Baerman (ed.), *The Oxford handbook of inflection*, 197–232. Oxford: Oxford University Press.

Stroop, Jan. 1970. Systeem in gesproken werkwoordsgroepen. In Jan Stroop (ed.), *Nederlands dialectonderzoek*, 247–264. Amsterdam: Huis aan de drie grachten.

Stump, Gregory. 2001. *Inflectional morphology*. Cambridge: Cambridge University Press.

Vendryes, Joseph. 1937. Sur l'emploi de l'auxiliaire avoir pour marquer le passé. In Jan Wils, Rob. Meesters & W. Slijpen (eds.), *Mélanges de linguistique et de philologie offerts à Jacq. Van Ginneken à l'occasion du soixantième anniversaire de sa naissance*, 85–92. Paris: Klincksieck.

Verkuyl, Henk. 2008. *Binary tense*. Stanford: CSLI Publications.

Wackernagel, Jacob. 1920. *Vorlesungen über Syntax mit besonderer Berücksichtigung von Griechisch, Lateinisch und Deutsch*. Basel: Birkhäuser.

Williams, Edwin. 2003. *Representation theory*. Cambridge, MA: MIT Press.

Wiltschko, Martina. 2014. *The universal structure of categories: Towards a formal typology*. Cambridge: Cambridge University Press.

Wurmbrand, Susi. 2005. Verb clusters, verb raising, and restructuring. In Martin Everaert & Henk van Riemsdijk (eds.), *The Blackwell companion to syntax*, vol. 5, 227–341. Oxford: Blackwell.

Zwart, Jan-Wouter. 1996. Verb clusters in West Germanic dialects. In James R. Black & Virginia Motapanyane (eds.), *Microparametric syntax and dialect variation*, 229–258. Amsterdam: John Benjamins.

Zwart, Jan-Wouter. 2005. Verb-second as a function of merge. In Marcel den Dikken & Christina M. Tortora (eds.), *The function of function words and functional categories*, 11–40. Amsterdam: John Benjamins.

Zwart, Jan-Wouter. 2006. Local agreement. In Cédric Boeckx (ed.), *Agreement systems*, 317–339. Amsterdam: John Benjamins.

Zwart, Jan-Wouter. 2007. Some notes on the origin and distribution of the IPP-effect. *Groninger Arbeiten zur germanistischen Linguistik* 45. 77–99.

Zwart, Jan-Wouter. 2008. Almost perfect: Some notes on the present perfect puzzle. In Cees Dekker, Alasdair MacDonald & Hermann Niebaum (eds.), *Northern voices: Essays on Old Germanic and related topics offered to Professor Tette Hofstra*, 399–404. Leuven: Peeters.

Zwart, Jan-Wouter. 2011. *The syntax of Dutch*. Cambridge: Cambridge University Press.

Zwart, Jan-Wouter. 2014. The tense of infinitives in Dutch. In Jack Hoeksema & Dicky Gilbers (eds.), *Black book: A festschrift in honor of Frans Zwarts*, 376–387. Groningen: University of Groningen.

Chapter 3

Feature inheritance in Old Spanish: (re)visiting V2

Geoffrey Poole
Newcastle University

On the basis of an extensive overview of verb-second languages and data, Holmberg (2015: 376) arrives at the following general characterization of the V2 property: (a) a functional head in the left periphery attracts the finite verb and (b) this functional head requires that a constituent move to its specifier position. In this paper I argue that this view of the V2 property, together with Salvi's (2012) observations concerning the syntactic positions which precede the finite verb in medieval Romance, suggest that Old Spanish was indeed a verb-second language. More specifically, I argue that the existence and nature of the features which effect (a) and (b) in Old Spanish find a natural motivation/explanation within Biberauer & Roberts's (2010) feature-inheritance approach to typology, in which languages differ with respect to whether EPP- and Tense-features are retained by C, donated to T or shared between the two (cf. Ouali 2008). While I assume, following Biberauer & Roberts (2010), that EPP- and T-features are donated to T in Modern Romance (including Modern Spanish), I suggest that these features were retained by C in Old Spanish.

1 Introduction

As noted by Salvi (2012), there is a long-standing observation regarding medieval Romance to the effect that there are two syntactic positions which precede the finite verb: one which immediately precedes the finite verb, which Salvi calls P2, and one which precedes *that* position, which Salvi calls P1. With respect to information structure, the P1 position hosts "thematic material", while P2 can host either thematic or focal material. This traditional observation would seem to be expressible naturally within a standard version of an articulated left-periphery (in the sense of Rizzi 1997 and much subsequent work).

(1)　[ForceP [TopicP [FocusP [TopicP [FinP [TP]]]]]]

　　　　　　　 P1　　　　　　 P2

Geoffrey Poole. 2017. Feature inheritance in Old Spanish: (re)visiting V2. In Laura R. Bailey & Michelle Sheehan (eds.), *Order and structure in syntax I: Word order and syntactic structure*, 49–68. Berlin: Language Science Press. DOI:10.5281/zenodo.1117714

The P1 position would seem to straightforwardly map on to the high Topic position, while the lower Focus and Topic projections are a natural locus for Salvi's P2 position.[1]

In §2, I argue that Salvi's generalization does descriptively characterize Spanish during the pre-Golden Age period (i.e., prior to the 16th century), taking P2 to refer to the cluster of low left peripheral positions as in (1). These positions could contain only *one* XP, but it could be either topical or focal. Furthermore, the finite verb must be right-adjacent to the left-peripheral element. However, I then "extend" Salvi's generalization, primarily by considering wide-focus fronting in Old Spanish (Mackenzie 2010). This phenomenon is of particular interest in this context because it indicates that the lone XP occupying P2, in addition to being topical or focal, could be *neither*. In other words, this construction (and others) appear to show that Salvi's P2 position in the low left periphery can, in some cases, be occupied by an element which cannot be interpreted *either* as topical *or* as focal.

In §3, I suggest that Salvi's extended generalization is naturally captured under the assumption that elements are attracted to the low left periphery during this period by a purely formal EPP feature present in the low left periphery (rather than via syntactic features encoding specific discourse interpretations such as [+focus]). In addition, the requirement that the verb be immediately adjacent to the fronted element suggests that Tense features were also retained in this low area of the C-domain. Diachronically, it appears that *certain* left-peripheral displacements, including wide focus fronting and interpolation (see below), decline to extinction in parallel with verb-raising to a high position during the Golden Age period, suggesting a close connection between the EPP- and T-features.

§4 observes that Salvi's descriptive generalization would be naturally accounted for under the assumption that the EPP and Tense features are *retained* by a C-related projection in Old Spanish, but are *donated* to T in Modern Spanish (thus aligning Spanish with Biberauer & Roberts's (2010) feature-inheritance account of modern Romance). This in turn implies, given standard accounts of the left-peripheral displacement of topics and foci, that one of the major changes undergone by Spanish during the Golden Age was a "syntacticization of discourse" (in the sense of Haegeman & Hill 2013). In other words, displacement to the low-left periphery came to be driven, not by a purely formal EPP feature as previously, but rather by syntactic features with specific information-structure value (e.g., [+focus]).

---

[1]Throughout the paper, I will use terms such as "C-related", "the low left periphery", "the C-domain", "V-to-C movement", etc. as ways of referring to Salvi's P2 position in the low left periphery. I take no position on what more specific projection within an articulated CP might be relevant as I believe the choice does not materially affect the proposed analysis. See, for example, Walkden (2015) for some possibilities in Germanic. Strictly speaking, as discussed in §4.2, it is possible that Spanish does not even possess FocusP as a syntactic projection during the medieval period because, as I will suggest, the relevant syntactic features have yet to develop.

2 P2 and the low left periphery of Old Spanish

As noted by various authors (e.g., Sitaridou 2011; Poole 2013), Old Spanish possessed various constructions in which an element displaced to the low left periphery was interpreted as topical or focal. The phenomenon of interpolation is of particular relevance, as it appears that the element displaced to the low left periphery could indeed be either topical or focal (*contra* Poole's (2013) analysis). As such then, Salvi's Generalization with respect to the P2 position does seem to correctly describe Old Spanish.

2.1 New information focus

In her study of information structure in the *General Estoria* of Alfonso the Wise (13th century), Sitaridou (2011) notes that complements dislocated to a pre-verbal position can bear a number of information structure roles, including new information focus. (2) for example instantiates an operation she dubs "Focus Fronting" (174) (see also Cruschina 2008; Cruschina & Sitaridou 2009):

(2) (*General Estoria* 4, 13th c., Sitaridou 2011: (25))

    & los qui se   gozaron   con el to   derribamiento **penados**

    and the who REFL.3PL enjoy.FUT.3PL with the your fall   punished

    seran   por ello.

    be.FUT.3PL for this

    'And those who rejoice with your fall they will be punished for that.'

Unlike Modern Spanish, left-peripheral focus is not obligatorily contrastive. According to Sitaridou, the fronted participle in (2) simply encodes new information focus.

2.2 Topics

A clear demonstration that the P2 position could be occupied by topics is necessarily made more difficult by the fact that topics may also occupy Salvi's P1 position. However, cases containing a fronted object such as (3), which, as Sitaridou (2011: 170) notes, do appear to have a topic interpretation, would seem to be plausible candidates.

(3) (*General Estoria* 1, 13th c., Sitaridou 2011: (16))

    e   fue   / natural duna cibdat q<ue> dixieron fenis [...] Y   esta cibdat

    and was.3SG / native of.one city   which called.3PL Fenis   and this city

    poblo   fenis fijo dagenor...

    inhabited.3SG Fenis son of.Agenor

    'And he was from a city which was called Fenis... and this city was inhabited by Fenis, son of Agenor.'

Esta cibdat 'this city' in (3) resumes the previously mentioned city Fenis.

Cases described as "resumptive preposing" by Mackenzie (2010) are also plausibly instances of topics occupying Salvi's P2 position. Consider (4), originally discussed by Fontana (1993):[2]

(4)   (*General Estoria* 1, 13th c., Mackenzie 2010: (14))
      este logar mostro dios a abraam
      [this place God showed to Abraham]

As Mackenzie points out, the presence of *este* 'this' suggests that the preposed object is resuming something in the discourse, and his examination of the context reveals that *este* in fact resumes the phrase *una cabeça mas alta que todo el otro monte* 'a peak higher than the rest of the mountain' which is found in the preceding sentence. In that sense, (4) appears similar to (3) above.

Mackenzie observes that resumptively preposed elements are "topical within the discourse" (2010: 284), though, at the same time, claims that they are not "a topic in any syntactically relevant sense" (385). However, given a more articulated distinction between types of topics, phrases such as *este logar* in (4) would seem to plausibly constitute, for example, G-Topics in the sense of Bianchi & Frascarelli (2010). G-Topics are used to retrieve information already present within the conversational common ground content and are associated with topic continuity. These are also the structurally lowest topics within Bianci & Frascarelli's hierarchy. As such they would seem to naturally align with Salvi's P2 position. Additionally, as Mackenzie (2010: 392) notes, resumptively preposed elements are obligatorily adjacent to the verb, further suggesting that they do not occupy a high topic position along the lines of Salvi's P1 position.

2.3 Interpolation

The phenomenon of interpolation (e.g., Chenery 1905; Batllori et al. 1995; Poole 2013) is of particular interest in the context of the information structure of left-peripheral fronting in Old Spanish because it appears as though the interpolated element can be interpreted as either a topic or as a focus (partially *contra* Poole 2013).

In this construction, object and indirect object pronouns can appear separated from the finite verb by a short intervening constituent, for example an adverb, a short prepositional phrase, or a subject, as illustrated in (5):

(5)   (*Castigos e documentos de Sancho IV,* 13th c., Poole 2013: (4))
      ... &   vsa mal   del   buen entendimiento que **le**   **dios dio**.
      and uses badly of.the good understanding that him God gave.3SG

      '...and he makes poor use of the good understanding that God gave him.'

---

[2]Mackenzie's original examples, which lack morpheme-by-morpheme glosses, are reproduced verbatim in the text. For (4) the glosses would be:

(4)   este logar mostro   dios a abraam.
      this place showed.3s God to Abraham

      'God showed this place to Abraham.'

Poole (2013) argues that interpolation targets a low Topic position within the left periphery and that the interpolated element acts as a given or familiar topic. Consider the context in (6) preceding the instance of interpolation of *esto* 'that':[3]

(6) (*Crónica de 1344 I*, 14th c., Poole 2013: (19))
     Et estonçe les dixo el Rey que se salliesen de su tierra Et aquella gente a qujen esto dixo fueron se a la villa & tanto que **les esto dixo** luego se armaron muy bien & venjeron se al Rey onde yazia en su alcaçar & lidiaron conel & lo mataron.
     'And then the king said to them that they should leave his land. And those people to whom he said that went to the town and as soon as **he said that to them** they armed themselves well and went to the king where he rested in his fortress and fought with him and killed him.'

In (6), the interpolated element *esto* 'that', resumes the recently mentioned event *que se salliesen de su tierra* 'that they should leave his land', with said event also having been resumed by *esto* in the sentence immediately preceding the one in which *esto* is interpolated. As such, interpolation in (6) seems clearly to be an instance of topic continuity.

However, Poole (2013: 90) notes cases of interpolation such as (7), which are not straightforwardly associated with topicality.

(7) (*Calila e Dimna*, 13th c., Poole 2007: (13))
     manifiesta cosa es que lo feziste a tuerto et   sin   pecado que **te   él**
     manifest   thing is that it did.2SG unjustly and without sin   that you he
     fiziese.
     did.3SG
     'It's clear that you did it unjustly and without him having done you any wrong.'

From the context, the interpolated personal pronoun subject seems contrastive and even mildly emphatic. Other cases in which a personal pronoun are interpolated would seem to be even clearer.

(8) (*El Libro de Caballero Zifar* 14th c., Poole 2007: (2b))
     e   dixe   que **lo   yo auja** muerto.
     and said.1SG that him I   had killed
     'and I said that I had killed him.'

In (8), the interpolated subject pronoun is identical with the matrix clause subject, and in Modern Spanish would be obligatorily emphatic. Insofar as Old Spanish appears to be identical to Modern Spanish with respect to *pro*-drop, one would expect that the pronoun was interpreted as focal in Old Spanish as well. Thus it appears to be the case that the interpolated element may be interpreted as either a topic or as a focus.

---

[3]I omit for reasons of space the morpheme-by-morpheme gloss in (6) as the argument hinges on the larger discourse context, the relevant portions of which are explicated in the text.

Another interpolation-specific generalization which points to the correctness of Salvi's Medieval Romance characterization as it relates to Old Spanish concerns the elements which can precede the "interpolation cluster" – that is, the cluster of clitic pronoun, interpolated element and finite verb. In general, it is rare for anything to precede the interpolation cluster. It most commonly follows the Complementizer or other subordinating element. However, as Poole (2013) notes, in those cases in which an element does intervene between the complementizer and the interpolation cluster, the element is very plausibly topical. Consider (9), for example:

(9) (*General Estoria I*, 13th c., Poole 2013: (35))
& que *desta   manera* se   **non contrallan**   estas razones de Moysen &
and that of.that way   REFL NEG contradict.3PL those laws   of Moses   and
de Josepho.
of Joseph

'And in that way the laws of Moses and Joseph were not violated.'

Recall that Salvi claims that the P1 position in Medieval Romance, the position which precedes the P2 position, is a position which hosts thematic material. Given the presence of the demonstrative pronoun *esto* 'that', and the fact that it refers back to an element of the previous discourse, it seems plausible to assume that it occupies Salvi's P1 position.

2.4 XP co-occurrence restrictions in the low left periphery

The previous sections have illustrated various left-peripheral XP displacements in Old Spanish, arguing that Salvi's traditional generalization is correct insofar as it states that the P2 position in Old Spanish could be occupied by elements which were interpreted as topical or as focal. In addition however, recall that Salvi's generalization claims further that only one XP could occupy this left peripheral position. This predicts that there should be complementary distribution among the constructions discussed above, and this prediction appears to be correct.

First, these constructions all require that the pre-verbal element be immediately left-adjacent to the verb, from which complementarity of distribution then follows derivatively.[4] Sitaridou (2011: 174), for example, notes that the fronted element must be adjacent to the verb in order to be interpreted as new information focus.[5] Mackenzie (2010: 392) observes that verb-adjacency is also required for resumptive preposing, while Poole (2013), among others, notes that the same is true for interpolation.

Some further co-occurrence restrictions specific to interpolation also suggest that Salvi's generalization indeed applies to Old Spanish. As Poole (2013: 94–95) notes, interpolation is in complementary distribution with wh-operators, but not with relative clause operators. It can be found in all types of relative clauses, whether restrictive, non-

---

[4]See §3.1 below for more discussion regarding the significance of the verb-adjacency requirement.
[5]Obviously verb-adjacency is not a requirement for interpretation as a topic, given the availability of the P1 position for topics in addition to the P2 position.

restrictive or free, as in (10–12), but there appear to be no examples like the constructed (13).

(10) (*Siete Partidas*, 13th c.; Poole 2013: (51))
otra muger con *quien lo no pudiesse* fazer de derecho.
other woman with whom it not could.3SG do.INF of right
'...another woman with whom he had no right to [marry].'

(11) (*Gran Conquista de Ultramar*, 13th c., Poole 2013: (52))
ala   reyna halabra su madre de *quien os ya*   *diximos* en otros lugares
to.the queen H   his mother of whom you already said.1PL in other places
'...to Queen Halabra his mother, about whom we have already spoken elsewhere,...'

(12) (*El emperador Otas de Roma*, 14th c., Poole 2013: (53))
quien le   entonçe viese   griegos matar / & *espedaçar espedaçar bien*
who him then   saw.3SG Greeks kill   and butcher butcher well
ternja   *quele*   *deujan*   *doler*   *los braços*
would.have.3SG that.him should.3PL hurt.INF the arms
'Whoever saw him killing Greeks and butchering them would have had to have had aching arms....'

(13) (Poole 2013: (48))
  * ca   non sabedes quien *lo asi fiziese*
    because not know.2PL who   it thus did.3SG
'because you don't know who did it like that'

Under the assumption, following Poole (2013), that wh-operators occupy FocusP in Old Spanish in both main and embedded clauses, this suggests that Salvi's generalization is correct that only one element can occupy the P2 position. Wh-operators, which occupy P2, are incompatible with interpolation, which also occupies P2. Relative clause operators, which occupy a higher position (the specifier of ForceP), are not.

2.5 Extending Salvi's Generalization: elements which are neither topical nor focal

The previous sections motivated Salvi's (2012) generalization concerning elements which can precede the finite verb. However, evidence from quantifier fronting in Old Spanish (Mackenzie 2010) shows that the generalization can be extended in an important way: the single element which immediately precedes the finite verb can be not only *either* topical or focal, but also be *neither* topical *nor* focal.

Mackenzie (2010) notes examples such as (14) and (15), in which a fronted object quantifier appears in an immediately pre-verbal position.[6]

(14) (*General Estoria* IV, 13th c., Mackenzie 2010: (22))
      Si **ell omne algo deue**; faze gelo oluidar de guisa ques tiene que mas Rico es que otros omnes.

      [If a man owes something, it [wine] makes him forget it so that he holds himself to be richer than other men.]

(15) (*Estoria de España* II, 13th c., Mackenzie 2010: (23))
      Mas pero non fizo y quel **nada ualiesse** de lo que el querie.

      [But he didn't do there [anything] that was of any value to him in terms of what he wanted.]

As Poole (2016) observes, these fronted quantifiers are in complementary distribution with the other elements discussed above. Mackenzie himself (2010: 392) notes that they are in complementary distribution with other focus-fronted elements as well as with wh-elements and Poole (2016) notes that this complementarity extends to include interpolation. It therefore seems plausible to suggest that these are elements which occupy Salvi's P2 position.

The importance of the distributional observation stems from the information-structure of sentences in which this quantifier fronting has taken place. As Mackenzie (2010: 390) observes, "[h]owever hard one looks at examples like these..., it is impossible to see anything other than neutral assertions", ultimately concluding (*ibid.*) that constructions such as (14) and (15) instantiate wide or broad focus, and indeed labels the construction Wide Focus Fronting.

This intuition is confirmed by Poole (2016). As he notes, fronting such as that seen in (14) and (15) cannot instantiate any kind of information- or contrastive-focus. Neither can (14) and (15) instantiate verum/positive polarity focus, as the construction can be found in environments such as the complements of factive clauses, which, following Leonetti & Escandell-Vidal (2009), strongly disallow it:

---

[6] Again, for the relevant portions of Mackenzie's examples in (14) and (15), the morpheme-by-morpheme glosses are as follows:

(14) si ell omne algo   deue....
      If the man   something owes

      'If a man owes something....'

(15) ... quel   nada   ualiesse de lo que el quierie.
      that.him.DAT nothing values of it that he wanted

      '...[anything] that was of value to him in terms of what he wanted.'

(16)   (*Sermones*, early 16th c., Poole 2013: (4))

       y   así   atinaron a pedir   el bien y   desearlo con grandes ansias **viendo**
       and thus aimed.3PL to ask.INF the good and desire.it with grand   will   see.GER

       que nada   **podían**.
       that nothing could do.3PL

       'And thus they settled for praying for good and for desiring it with all their hearts, seeing that they could do nothing else.'

Neither can quantifiers of this sort serve as topics. Non-specific quantifiers such as *algo* 'something' in (14) simply cannot coherently be "what the sentence is about". Therefore, it appears to be the case that the fronted quantifier itself is not (and indeed cannot be) either a topic or a focus. If this is the case, then Salvi's P2 position can be occupied by not only topical or focal elements, but also elements which are *neither*.

3 Explaining Salvi's Generalization: EPP and tense features in the low left periphery

The extension of Salvi's Generalization to include elements which are neither foci nor topics is significant because it provides a clear direction to pursue with respect to the explanation: the displacement associated with Salvi's P2 position is triggered by a feature, hosted in the low left periphery, which does not itself possess any information-structure value (i.e., a feature such as Chomsky's (2000; 2001) EPP-feature, a "formal feature" in the sense of Frey (2006); Light (2012), or Biberauer et al.'s (2014) "movement triggering" feature). Such an approach would account for the fact that the position can be filled by one element only, and that the information-structure status of the element is irrelevant.

However, if Salvi's generalization regarding the P2 position ultimately derives from an extension of Biberauer & Roberts's (2010) feature-inheritance typology to Old Spanish (and therefore relates ultimately to Holmberg's (2015) V2 property), we should see evidence that the low left periphery not only retained an EPP-feature, but also that it retained a Tense feature. In other words, in addition to the evidence that XPs raise into the low left periphery in Old Spanish, we should also find evidence that the verb in Old Spanish raises to a position in the C-domain.

3.1 Verb-adjacency revisited

As mentioned above in §2.5, it has been noted by various authors in various contexts that the verb in Old Spanish must be linearly adjacent to elements which, by hypothesis, occupy a specifier position in the low left periphery. Sitaridou (2011: 175), following Cruschina (2008), notes for example that strict adjacency is required between the verb and focus fronted elements, as exemplified by (17):

(17) (*General Estoria* 1, 13th c. Sitaridou 2011: (23b))
      Fuerça *fizieron* los sabios e   los altos omnes en el   nombre d' esta cibdad.
      power made.3PL the savants and the high men   in the name   of this city

      'The savants and the men of high standing imposed power in the name of the city.'

Under the assumption that the focus-fronted object occupies a position in the low left periphery (such as FocusP), the strict linear adjacency would be accounted for under the assumption that the verb moves to a head position in the same area of the clause. As also noted above, verb-adjacency is also a requirement for resumptive preposing and interpolation: if these elements are correctly analyzed as occupying the low left periphery (see Sitaridou 2011: Section 3 and the references cited there), then a natural explanation for the observed linear adjacency with respect to the finite verb is that it too has raised to a C-related position.

3.2 Sitaridou (2012) on tests for V-raising to the C-domain

In addition, contra Sitaridou 2012, there do appear to be phenomena which suggest that there is V-raising to the C-domain in Old Spanish. In her survey of a number of medieval Romance varieties, Sitaridou (2012) enumerates a number of traditional syntactic tests which are claimed to provide evidence that the verb moves to a position higher than T°.[7] She concludes on the basis of these tests that the verb did obligatorily raise to the C-domain in Old French, among other varieties, but that this was not the case in Old Spanish. However, there do appear to be examples in Old Spanish which parallel the examples offered for Old French, once one moves beyond the one text that Sitaridou examines (the *General Estoria* of Alfonso X).

One traditional argument/test concerns the position of the verb relative to various adverbs which are very high on Cinque's (1999) adverb hierarchy. She notes, for example, that in Old French the verb can appear higher than adverbs such as *vraiment* 'really'.

(18) (Sitaridou 2012: (52b))
      Et *je* croy   vraiement.
      and I think.1SG really

      'And I really believe.'

Although high, speaker-oriented adverbs are generally not found in Old Spanish, one can find examples in which the finite verb precedes polarity focus *bien* 'well' (cf. Hernanz 2006; Batllori & Hernanz 2013).[8]

---

[7] Her proposal more specifically is that the verb moves to Fin°.
[8] All unattributed examples from Old Spanish are taken from the *Corpus del Español* (Davies 2002).

(19)   (*Cuento de Tristán de Leonís*, 14th c.)
     yo creo   **bien** que el era tristan ca   non es enel mundo caualler
     I   believe.1SG well that he was T   because NEG is in.the world man
     que tanto   pudiese fazer.
     that so.much could   do.INF

     'I really believe that he was Tristan because there is no [other] man in the world
     who could do so much.'

(20)   (*Estoria de España*, 13th c.)
     Et   todo omne que viesse la posada que el çid tenie   **dirie**
     And every man that saw.3SG the ship   that The Cid had.3SG would say.3SG
     bien   que era   vna grant hueste.
     indeed that was.3SG a   great host

     'And everyone who saw the ship that The Cid had would indeed say that it was a
     great military force.'

The use and interpretation of *bien* in examples such as (19) and (20) (particularly (19))
appears entirely parallel to the case of Old French *vraiment* above. More specifically,
whether polarity focus items occupy a ΣP/PolP phrase between TP and the C-domain or
some higher projection within the C-domain itself, examples such as (19) and (20) would
seem to show that the verb in Old Spanish did indeed undergo "V-to-C movement", on
analogy with the French cases.

    Another class of examples which Sitaridou argues provides evidence that the verb
raises to a high position in Old French are cases such as (21):

(21)   (Sitaridou 2012: (53a))
     pour la grant amour ai   *je* pourchacie ...
     for the great love   have.1SG I pursued

     'For the great love I have pursued'

Following Benincà 1994, Sitaridou argues (2012: 589–90) that this inversion pattern, in
which the subject pronoun appears between the auxiliary and the past participle, is evidence of obligatory V-to-C raising. Once again, moving beyond her very specific corpus,
it is not difficult to find examples parallel to the Old French example in (21).

(22)   (*General Estoria IV*, 13th c.)
     &   de Caripdis. de quien **auemos** **nos contado** enla tercera parte desta
     And of C   of who have.1PL we related in.the third   part of.that
     estoria
     history

     '...and about Caripdis, about whom we have spoken in the third part of that
     history...'

(23) (*Gran Conquista de Ultramar*, 13th c.)
      Todo aquesto **he**   **yo hablado** conel   duque Gudufre.
      All   these   have.1SG I   spoken with.the duke G

      'I have spoken about all of this with Duke Gudufre.'

Therefore, it appears as though there is some parallel evidence based on the traditional tests which Sitaridou (2012) discusses in Old French for thinking that the verb in Old Spanish does indeed raise to some C-related position, and therefore that the C-domain hosted a Tense feature.

3.3 The diachrony of P2 fronting and its relation to V-to-C raising

A further reason for thinking that both EPP and Tense features are located in the low left periphery in Old Spanish comes from the diachronic development of some of the constructions discussed above. An examination of the *Corpus del Español* reveals that those instances of low left-peripheral fronting unequivocally triggered by a discourse-neutral EPP feature decline in parallel with verb-initial declaratives with a post-verbal object. If the EPP-feature and the tense feature are somehow linked, as suggested by Biberauer & Roberts's (2010) typological analysis, this parallel decline would be expected.

   Consider first the diachrony of two particular instances of movement to Salvi's P2 position: interpolation and wide focus fronting. Recall from §2.3 above that the element which intervenes between the clitic pronoun and the finite verb in interpolation structures can be interpreted in some cases as topics and in other cases as foci. This suggests that the trigger for the fronting of that element is a feature which is independent of any particular information-structure interpretation. A logical conclusion therefore is that the trigger is a "pure" EPP or movement-triggering feature. A similar conclusion can be reached in the case of Mackenzie's (2010) Wide Focus Fronting (§2.5). Elements such as non-specific *algo* are attracted to the low left periphery, but insofar as these elements cannot be interpreted either as topics or foci, it must be a pure movement-triggering feature which attracts them.

   An examination of the *Corpus del Español* shows that interpolation of negation, while robustly attested during the 13th and 14th centuries, declines significantly in the 15th century and is essentially extinct by the 16th. Clausal negation, as in (24), is one of the most commonly interpolated elements and Poole (2013) claims that it too instantiates XP movement to the low left periphery.

(24) (*El Conde Lucanor*, 14th c.)
      Et   desque vio   que **lo non fazia**....
      and since   saw.3SG that it NEG would.do.3SG

      'And since he saw that he wouldn't do it....'

As Table 1 shows, relative instances of the subordinating Complementizer *que* 'that' or *si* 'if', followed by an object pronoun, followed by clausal negation, followed by a finite verb (indicative, conditional or subjunctive) remain unchanged during the 13th and 14th

centuries. However, they decline to less than a quarter of that value in the 15th century, and only a handful of cases are to be found by the beginning of the Golden Age period.[9]

Table 1: Corpus del Español : *que/si ObjPn no/non [vi*]/[vc*]/[vs*]*

Period	13th c.	14th c.	15th c.	16th c.
Instances	1745	718	479	4
Per Million Words	259.84	268.96	58.69	0.23

A similar diachronic trajectory is seen with respect to Mackenzie's (2010) Wide Focus Fronting. One relatively common example is the fronting of *esto* 'this' in examples such as (25).

(25) (*Gran Conquista de Ultramar*, 13th c.)
     Quando **el   emperador esto oyo**   ouo muy gran miedo.
     When   the emperor   this heard had very great fear

     'When the emperor heard this, he became very afraid.'

Like interpolation, Wide Focus Fronting declines significantly in the 15th century relative to the 13th and 14th, and is nearly extinct by the 16th.

Table 2: *Corpus del Español*: Det N *esto* V

Period	13th c.	14th c.	15th c.	16th c.
Instances	108	56	102	36
Per Million Words	16.08	20.98	12.50	2.11

Interestingly, in parallel with the decline of these XP-fronting constructions, there is some evidence to suggest that verb-raising to a high position also declines. As Fontana (1993: Section 3.4.2) notes, one traditional diagnostic for V-to-C raising in the literature on various Germanic varieties (e.g., Modern Yiddish and Icelandic) is the grammaticality of verb-initial declarative sentences, and sentences such as (26) are very common in Old Spanish, particularly in main clauses introduced by *and* (or variant).

---

[9]During the 13th and 14th centuries, non-interpolated clausal negation (i.e., the order no/non ObjPn V) is found approximately equally frequently. However, in the 15th century, non-interpolation appears approximately 5.5 times more frequently, and is over 3100 times more frequent in the 16th century. See Poole (2013: Section 1) for further discussion.

(26) (*Estoria de España*, 13th c.; Fontana 1993: (74a))

    & **fizo** el   papa penitencia & **dixo** Sant Antidio la   missa en su lugar &

    & did the pope penance   & said sant Antidio the mass in his place &

    consagro   la   crisma.

    consecrated the host

    'And the pope did penance & S. A. said the mass in his place and consecrated the Host.'

Fontana notes (1993: 249) that the percentage of verb-initial declaratives followed by a clitic pronoun (thereby even more clearly suggesting that the verb has raised to a relatively high position) declines from the 12th to the 16th centuries, and it appears to decline in a way reminiscent of the XP-fronting data seen above.

Table 3: V-Cl vs Cl-V order

Period	12th c.	13th c.	14th c.	15th c.	16th c.
V – Cl order observed vs. Cl – V order	84%	85%	87%	68%	14%

Data from a representative search of the *Corpus del Español* paints a similar picture. Though the *Corpus del Español* does not contain any texts from the 12th century, a search for a coordinating conjunction followed by an indicative verb form with an enclitic plural indirect-object pronoun shows a significant decline from the 14th to the 15th centuries to near extinction in the 16th century.

Table 4: *Corpus del Español:* [cc*] *les.[vi*] minus all 2sg verb forms

Period	13th c.	14th c.	15th c.	16th c.
Frequency	46	84	82	47
Per Million Words	6.85	31.47	10.04	2.76

To summarize then, the data in the tables above suggests that XP-fronting triggered by a "pure" EPP or movement-triggering feature undergoes a diachronic decline which bears some resemblance to the decline seen in V-to-C raising.

4 Convergence: EPP/tense feature inheritance and some implications

4.1 Biberauer & Roberts's (2010) feature-inheritance approach to syntactic typology

As mentioned at various points above, a central claim of this paper is that the synchronic and diachronic descriptive facts discussed in Sections 2 and 3 can be naturally accounted for using Biberauer & Roberts's (2010) feature inheritance typological approach: EPP- and T-features are *retained* in the C-domain in Old Spanish, but *donated* to T in Modern Spanish.

Following Ouali's (2008) classification, uninterpretable features present on the phase head C may either be "kept", "shared" or "donated". They are retained by the phase-head in the first case, but either copied or given over entirely to a phase-internal non-phase head in the latter two cases respectively. Biberauer & Roberts suggest that Ouali's feature-inheritance classification system can be usefully extended into language typology. By way of illustration, Biberauer & Roberts argue that phi- and T-features are donated to T in Romance and English (leading to V-to-T movement in Romance because of the presence of rich tense) but are kept in Continental Germanic, leading to V-to-C raising, one part of the well-known verb-second effect. These options also apply in the case of XP movement-triggering features such as the EPP-feature. In Mainland Scandinavian, for example, the EPP-feature present in C is shared with T. As a result, both a traditional verb-second and English-style EPP effect is seen. (See Biberauer & Roberts 2010: Section 3 for further discussion and examples.)

For Old Spanish then, the claim would be that both the EPP and Tense features were retained in the C-domain. This accounts first for the distribution of elements seen in the low left periphery as part of Salvi's (Extended) Generalization regarding the P2 position. There can be only one element, and because it is attracted by a pure EPP/movement-triggering feature, it can be either topical, focal, or neither. The fact that the T-feature is also kept results in the verb being attracted to this position within the low left periphery, which places it adjacent to the element in Salvi's P2 position.

The diachronic data seen in §3.3 finds a natural account under the assumption that at some point during the Spanish Golden Age period, the EPP and Tense features ceased being retained in the C domain, and were instead donated to T. This explains why certain cases of low-left-peripheral fronting appear to decline to extinction in parallel with cases of verb-initial declaratives with an enclitic object pronoun.

Such an approach to the diachronic data aligns with Biberauer & Roberts's (2010) typological account of Modern Romance. As mentioned above, on Biberauer & Roberts's analysis of Modern Romance, the EPP feature is donated to T, but the requirement is met by a deleted pronoun in the case of null subject languages such as Italian and Spanish. The T-feature is also donated from C to T, which, because of rich tense, results in V-to-T movement. We therefore have a straightforward characterization of (part of) the diachronic change that took place between Old Spanish and Modern Spanish.

4.2 Some synchronic and diachronic implications of the proposed approach: (re)visiting V2 and a "syntacticization of discourse"

Synchroncially, the proposed account takes a clear position in the debate concerning whether or not Old Spanish was a verb-second language.[10] On Holmberg's (2015) characterization, there are two components to the V2 property, which may be independently realized.

(27)   a. A functional head in the left periphery attracts the finite verb.

b. This functional head requires that a constituent move to its specifier position.

The characteristics in (27) appear to describe exactly the situation in Old Spanish, as discussed in the above sections. Indeed, as Holmberg notes (2015: 276) the property in (27b) "may be formalized as a "generalised EPP-feature", along the lines of Roberts (2004)".

Salvi's Generalization regarding the P1 position, the position which immediately precedes P2, then becomes the logical explanation for the well-attested instances of V3 (and other) orders in Old Spanish. The P1 position hosts topics, and I have suggested that it finds a natural correspondent in the high topic position within an articulated CP. Given that topics in this position can be iterated (Salvi 2012: 103), the existence of these orders does not undermine the claim that Old Spanish was a verb-second language.[11,12]

Diachronically, the proposed change in the behaviour of the features associated with C suggests that Spanish underwent a "syntacticization of discourse".[13] Consider first the relation between syntax and information structure in Old Spanish implied by the analysis outlined above. Movement to the low left periphery is triggered by a pure movement-triggering feature. Elements which are attracted by this feature can, however, ultimately receive an information-structure interpretation. Recall example (2) above:

(2)   (*General Estoria* 4, 13th c., Sitaridou 2011: (25))

& los qui se gozaron con el to derribamiento **penados**
and the who REFL.3PL enjoy.FUT.3PL with the your fall punished
seran por ello.
be.FUT.3PL for this

'And those who rejoice with your fall they will be punished for that.'

---

[10]The former position is represented by work such as Fontana (1993), while e.g. Sitaridou (2012) argues for the latter position.

[11]Ott (2014: Fn 34) suggests that his ellipsis approach to Contrastive Left-Dislocation could be extended to account for Romance Clitic Left Dislocation phenomena. Should such an extension prove to be successful, Old Spanish might more closely resemble a "traditional" verb-second language such as Modern German.

[12]V1 declarative orders do exist in Old Spanish, but as Poole (2016) argues, they exhibit a specific information structure interpretation: wide or broad focus. With respect to the satisfaction of the EPP-feature, there are a number of logical possibilities, including a base-generated "default" operator associated with sentence-level focus or declarative force, or perhaps even attraction of the entire TP, which would plausibly entail a wide focus interpretation. However, I leave this question for future research.

[13]The term is originally due to Haegeman & Hill (2013). See Sitaridou (2011: 160) for some initial speculation regarding Old Spanish and Poole (2016) for much further discussion.

Following Sitaridou (2011), I assume that the fronted participle is interpreted as focalized, but this is not because the movement is triggered or driven by a syntactic information-structure-specific feature such as [+focus]. In other words, elements are not attracted to Salvi's P2 position in the low left periphery for discourse or information-structure reasons per se. It follows therefore that, in Old Spanish, information structure interpretation is in some way post-syntactic.[14]

The analysis of interpolation in particular becomes potentially important in this context. As discussed above, it appears as though interpolated elements may be interpreted as either topical (6) or focal (8).

(6) (*Crónica de 1344 I*, 14th c., Poole 2013: (19))
Et estonçe les dixo el Rey que se salliesen de su tierra Et aquella gente a qujen esto dixo fueron se a la villa & tanto que **les esto dixo** luego se armaron muy bien & venjeron se al Rey onde yazia en su alcaçar & lidiaron conel & lo mataron.

'And then the king said to them that they should leave his land. And those people to whom he said that went to the town and as soon as **he said that to them** they armed themselves well and went to the king where he rested in his fortress and fought with him and killed him.'

(8) (*El Libro de Caballero Zifar* 14th c., Poole 2007: (2b))
e   dixe   que **lo   yo auja** muerto.
and said.1SG that him I   had killed

'and I said that I had killed him.'

Under the assumption that cases such as these are instances of "the same" syntactic phenomenon – that is to say, truly two representations of the same syntactic process – then information-structure interpretation in Old Spanish must have been post-syntactic.

However, if access to the low left periphery in Old Spanish is mediated by an information-structurally neutral EPP feature which is retained in the C-domain, and, as discussed above, the diachronic change in Spanish involves the donation of this feature to T, then some method must have been developed by which access to the low left periphery was regained, given that Modern Spanish unquestionably has such access.

Poole (2016) suggests that one of the major syntactic changes to take place during the Spanish Golden Age period is that information-structure-specific syntactic features, such as [+focus], are developed.[15] This predicts, for example, the loss of left-peripheral wide focus fronting, as seen in §3 above. Interestingly, as Poole (2016) notes, two word orders which signal wide/broad focus in Old Spanish, Mackenzie's (2010) fronted quantifiers and the verb-initial declarative constructions referred to in the previous section,

---

[14]See, e.g., Cinque (1993), Reinhart (2006) and Sheehan (2010) for the suggestion that focus might be accounted for in prosodic terms.

[15]Note that if in fact the innovated feature which is responsible for focus is [+contrast] rather than [+focus], following Lopez 2009, that would account for the fact that left-peripheral focus is obligatorily contrastive in Modern Spanish but not in Old Spanish.

come in later varieties to signal verum/positive polarity focus. Poole suggests that this is an indication that displacement is driven in these later varieties by an information-structurally specified syntactic feature. In essence, low left-peripheral wide/focus is precluded because access to low left periphery now requires prior identification as a topicalized or focalized element, and therefore an element in the low left periphery which cannot be a topic must be focalizing *something*. Poole's suggestion is that these elements have in fact first been attracted to the specifier of ΣP/PolP, the projection which encodes sentence polarity, and represent focalization of that category, accounting for the verum focus interpretation.[16]

Acknowledgements

Thanks to Maria Maza, the audience at the 2014 Meeting of the Linguistics Association of Great Britain and two anonymous reviewers for many helpful comments and suggestions.

References

Batllori, Montserrat & Maria-Lluïsa Hernanz. 2013. Emphatic polarity particles in Spanish and Catalan. *Lingua* 128. 9–30.

Batllori, Montserrat, Carlos Sánchez & Avel·lina Suñer. 1995. The incidence of interpolation on the word order of Romance languages. *Catalan Working Papers in Linguistics* 4(2). 185–209. http://ddd.uab.cat/record/21183. [4 December 2015].

Benincà, Paola. 1994. Osservazioni sulla sintassi dei testi di Lio Mazor. In Paola Benincà (ed.), *La variazione sintattica: Studi di dialettologia romanza*, 163–176. Bologna: Il Mulino.

Bianchi, Valentina & Mara Frascarelli. 2010. Is 'topic' a root phenomenon? *Iberia: An International Journal of Theoretical Linguistics* 2(1). 43–88.

Biberauer, Theresa, Anders Holmberg & Ian Roberts. 2014. A syntactic universal and its consequences. *Linguistic Inquiry* 45. 169–225.

Biberauer, Theresa & Ian Roberts. 2010. Subjects, tense and verb-movement. In Theresa Biberauer, Anders Holmberg, Ian Roberts & Michelle Sheehan (eds.), *Parametric variation: Null subjects in minimalist theory*, 263–303. Cambridge: Cambridge University Press.

Chenery, Winthrop Holt. 1905. Object pronouns in dependent clauses: A study in Old Spanish word-order. *Publications of the Modern Language Association of America* 20. 1–151.

Chomsky, Noam. 2000. Minimalist inquiries: The framework. In Roger Martin, David Michaels & Juan Uriagereka (eds.), *Step by step: Essays on minimalist syntax in honor of Howard Lasnik*, 89–155. Cambridge: MIT Press.

---

[16] See Poole 2016 for much further discussion and Poole 2011 for another potentially relevant diachronic development relating to n-words.

Chomsky, Noam. 2001. Derivation by phase. In Michael Kenstowicz (ed.), *Ken Hale: A life in language*, 1–52. Cambridge: MIT Press.

Cinque, Guglielmo. 1993. A null theory of phrase and compound stress. *Linguistic Inquiry* 24. 239–97.

Cinque, Guglielmo. 1999. *Adverbs and functional heads: A cross-linguistic perspective.* Oxford: Oxford University Press.

Cruschina, Silvio. 2008. *Discourse-related features and the syntax of peripheral positions: A comparative study of Sicilian and other Romance languages.* University of Cambridge dissertation.

Cruschina, Silvio & Ioanna Sitaridou. 2009. From modern to old Romance: The interaction of information structure and word order. Paper given at the XI Diachronic Generative Syntax (DiGS), Universidade de Campinas, 20-22/08/2009.

Davies, Mark. 2002. *Corpus del Español (100 million words, 1200s–1900s).* http://www.corpusdelespanol.org/.

Fontana, Josep M. 1993. *Phrase structure and the syntax of clitics in the history of Spanish.* University of Pennsylvania dissertation.

Frey, Werner. 2006. Contrast and movement to the German prefield. In Valéria Molnar & Susanne Winkler (eds.), *The architecture of focus*, 235–264. Berlin: Mouton de Gruyter.

Haegeman, Liliane & Virginia Hill. 2013. The syntactization of discourse. In Raffaela Folli, Christina Sevdalli & Robert Truswell (eds.), *Syntax and its limits* (Oxford Studies in Theoretical Linguistics), 370–390. Oxford: Oxford University Press.

Hernanz, Maria-Lluïsa. 2006. Emphatic polarity and C in Spanish. In Laura Brugè (ed.), *Studies in Spanish syntax*, 105–150. Venezia: Libreria Editrice Cafoscarina.

Holmberg, Anders. 2015. Verb second. In Tibor Kiss & Artemis Alexiadou (eds.), *Syntax – Theory and analysis: An international handbook*, 2nd edn., 342–382. Berlin: de Gruyter.

Leonetti, Manuel & Victoria Escandell-Vidal. 2009. Fronting and Verum Focus in Spanish. In Andreas Dufter & Daniel Jacob (eds.), *Focus and background in Romance languages*, 155–204. Amsterdam: John Benjamins.

Light, Caitlin. 2012. *The syntax and semantics of fronting in Germanic.* University of Pennsylvania dissertation.

Lopez, Luis. 2009. *A derivational syntax for information structure.* Oxford: Oxford University Press.

Mackenzie, Ian. 2010. Refining the V2 hypothesis for Old Spanish. *Bulletin of Hispanic Studies* 87(4). 379–396.

Ott, Dennis. 2014. An ellipsis approach to contrastive left-dislocation. *Linguistic Inquiry* 45(2). 269–303.

Ouali, Hamid. 2008. On C-to-T φ-feature transfer: The nature of agreement and anti-agreement in Berber. In Roberta D'Alessandro, Susan Fischer & Gunnar Hrafn Hrafnbjargarson (eds.), *Agreement restrictions*, 159–80. Berlin: Walter de Gruyter.

Poole, Geoffrey. 2007. Interpolation and the left periphery in Old Spanish. *Newcastle Working Papers in Linguistics* 13. 188–216.

Poole, Geoffrey. 2011. Focus and the development of N-words in Spanish. In Janine Burns, Haike Jacobs & Tobias Scheer (eds.), *Romance Languages and Linguistic Theory 2009: Selected Papers from "Going Romance", Nice 2009*, 291–303. Amsterdam: John Benjamins.

Poole, Geoffrey. 2013. Interpolation, verb-second, and the low left periphery in Old Spanish. *Iberia: An International Journal of Theoretical Linguistics* 5(1). 69–98.

Poole, Geoffrey. 2016. Focus and the syntacticization of discourse in Spanish. In Ernestina Carrilho, Alexandra Fiéis, Maria Lobo & Sandra Pereira (eds.), *Romance languages and linguistic theory 10: Selected papers from "Going Romance" 28, Lisbon*, 191–210. Amsterdam: John Benjamins.

Reinhart, Tanya. 2006. *Interface strategies: Optimal and costly computations*. Cambridge, MA: MIT Press.

Rizzi, Luigi. 1997. The fine structure of the left periphery. In Liliane Haegeman (ed.), *Elements of grammar: A handbook of generative syntax*, 281–337. Dordrecht: Kluwer.

Salvi, Giampaolo. 2012. On the nature of the V2 system of Medieval Romance. In Laura Brugé, Anna Cardinaletti, Giuliana Giusti, Nicola Munaro & Cecilia Poletto (eds.), *Functional heads: The cartography of syntactic structures*, vol. 7, 103–111. Oxford: Oxford University Press.

Sheehan, Michelle. 2010. 'Free' inversion in Romance and the Null Subject Parameter. In Theresa Biberauer, Anders Holmberg, Ian Roberts & Michelle Sheehan (eds.), *Parametric Variation: Null Subjects in Minimalist Theory*, 231–262. Cambridge: Cambridge University Press.

Sitaridou, Ioanna. 2011. Word order and information structure in Old Spanish. *Catalan Journal of Linguistics* 10. 159–184.

Sitaridou, Ioanna. 2012. A comparative study of word order in Old Romance. *Folia Linguistica* 46(2). 553–604.

Walkden, George. 2015. Verb-third in early West Germanic: A comparative perspective. In Theresa Biberauer & George Walkden (eds.), *Syntax over time: Lexical, morphological, and information-structural interactions* (Oxford Studies in Diachronic and Historical Linguistics 15), 236–248. Oxford: Oxford University Press.

Chapter 4

Finite sentences in Finnish: Word order, morphology, and information structure

Urpo Nikanne
Åbo Akademi University, Finland

According to Holmberg et al. (1993) the finite sentence of Finnish is a structure with 2–6 functional heads. In this article, the theory is developed further and the functional heads are reanalyzed. The functional categories are divided into two categories: (i) lexical categories Neg, Aux, V, and C; (ii) morphological categories: AgrS, T, and Ptc. These categories are in separate tiers, and the tiers are linked to each other. Both lexical and morphological categories are hierarchically organized, and the linking between the tiers follows these hierarchies. The result of the reanalysis is a system that does not involve movement nor a complicated constituent structure of functional categories even though the desired properties of the previous analysis remain.

1 Introduction

Anders Holmberg and his colleagues came up with an analysis of the Finnish finite sentence in the early 1990s (Holmberg et al. 1993). The analysis was based on the so-called incorporation theory in which finite verb morphology assumed to be a result of a head-to-head movement of the verb: the verb was raised from one functional head (e.g. tense, mood, subject agreement, etc.) to another, and the functional heads were attached to the verb. The finite verb morphology was therefore a mirror image of the syntactic structure (Pollock 1989; Baker 1988; Chomsky 1995), etc.). In the Minimalist Theory (Chomsky 1995), the basic idea has remained the same, but, instead of picking up affixes along its head-to-head movement upwards in the syntactic structure, the verb checks that the morphological features it is carrying are compatible with the features in the syntactic tree.

Traditionally, the word order of Finnish has been characterized as free. According to Vilkuna (1989), the word order in Finnish finite sentences is constraint by information structure. There are designated word order positions for the topic of the sentence and a phrase that carries a contrastive focus. Holmberg & Nikanne (1994; 2002; 2008) have

Urpo Nikanne. 2017. Finite sentences in Finnish: Word order, morphology, and information structure. In Laura R. Bailey & Michelle Sheehan (eds.), *Order and structure in syntax I: Word order and syntactic structure*, 69–97. Berlin: Language Science Press. DOI:10.5281/zenodo.1117710

shown that the word (verb or negation word) carrying the subject agreement suffixes has its own designated position in the finite sentence word order.

The theory presented by Anders Holmberg and his colleagues (Holmberg et al. 1993; Holmberg & Nikanne 2002, etc.) is so far the most advanced model of the finite sentence of Finnish. It is able to combine the Finnish finite sentence morphology and syntax in an elegant way. As linguists, however, it is our duty always to seek for new ways to see language and try to come up with theories that can replace the old ones. That is the purpose of this article.

At first, I explain how the theory by Holmberg and his colleagues works. Then, I discuss how it can be improved. After that, I suggest improvements that are based on a "micro-modular" theory of language. The micro-modular theory, Tiernet, is a version of Conceptual Semantics (Jackendoff 1983; 1990; 2002, etc.) explained and motivated in detail in Nikanne (forthcoming).

2 Finnish finite sentence: the basic facts

The Finnish finite verb has the morphological structure given in Table 1.

Table 1: Morphological structure of the Finnish verb

verb stem	(+ passive)	+ tense/mood	+ subject agreement	
istu ['sit']		+ *i*	+ *mme* [1PL SUBJ. AGR]	'we sat down'
istu ['sit']		+ *isi*	+ *mme* [1PL SUBJ. AGR]	'we would sit down'
istu ['sit']	+ *tt* [PASSIVE]	+ *i* [PAST]	+ *in* [PASS SUBJ. AGR.]	'it was sat down'
istu ['sit']	+ *tta* [PASSIVE]	+ *isi* [CONDITIONAL]	+ *in* [PASS SUBJ. AGR.]	'it would have been sat down'

There are two things in the Finnish finite morphology that might be confusing: (i) the tense and mood markers are in complementary distribution; and (ii) in addition to the passive marker *ttA* the passive form has an AgrS suffix *-Vn* when the negation word or the auxiliary are not present.

In addition to the predicate verb, there are two more words that may carry finite affixes. The auxiliary *ole-* 'be' in the perfect and pluperfect tenses and the negation word *e(i)-* 'not' in negated sentences. In the perfect and pluperfect tenses, the predicate verb is in the perfect participle form. Here is an example of the paradigm (the finite morphemes are separated with a dash):

(1)   a. Present active (3rd person plural)
        Tytöt istu-vat tuolilla.
        girls sit-3PL chair.ADE
        'The girls sit on the chair.'

      b. Present passive
        Istu-ta-an   tuolilla.
        sit-PASS-PASS chair.ADE
        'It is sat on the chair.'
        'One sits on the chair.'

(2)   a. Simple past active (3rd person plural)
        Tytöt istu-i-vat   tuolilla.
        girls sit-PAST-3PL chair.ADE
        'The girls sat on the chair.'

      b. Simple past passive
        Istu-tt-i-in   tuolilla.
        sit-PASS-PAST-PASS chair.ADE
        'It was sat on the chair.'
        'One sat on the chair.'

(3)   a. Conditional present active (3rd person plural)
        Tytöt istu-isi-vat   tuolilla.
        girls sit-COND-3PL chair.ADE
        'The girls would sit on the chair.'

      b. Conditional present passive
        Istu-tta-isi-in   tuolilla.
        sit-PASS-COND-PASS chair.ADE
        'One would sit on the chair.'

(4)   a. Perfect tense active (3rd person plural)
        Tytöt o-vat istu-nee-t tuolilla.
        girls be-3PL sit-PTC-3PL chair.ADE
        'The girls have sat on the chair.'

      b. Perfect tense passive
        On   istu-tt-u   tuolilla.
        be-3SG sit-PASS-PTC chair.ADE
        'It has been sat on the chair.'
        'One has sat on the chair.'

(5)   a. Pluperfect tense active (3rd person plural)
        Tytöt ol-i-vat   istu-nee-t tuolilla.
        girls be-PAST-3PL sit-PTC-3PL chair-ADE
        'The girls had sat on the chair.'

    b. Pluperfect tense passive

        Ol-i   istu-tt-u   tuolilla.

        be-PAST.3SG sit-PASS-PTC chair.ADE

        'It was sat on the chair.'

        'One had sat on the chair.'

(6) a. Negative past active (3rd person plural)

        Tytöt ei-vät   istu-nee-t tuolilla.

        girls not-3PL sit-PTC-PL chair.ADE

        'The girls did not sit on the chair.'

    b. Negative past passive

        Ei   istu-tt-u   tuolilla.

        not.3SG sit-PASS-PTC chair.ADE

        'It was not sat on the chair.'

(7) a. Negative perfect tense active (3rd person plural)

        Tytöt ei-vät   ole istu-neet tuolilla.

        girls not-3PL be sit-PTC.PL chair.ADE

        'The girls have not sat on the chair.'

    b. Negative perfect tense passive

        Ei   ole istu-tt-u   tuolilla.

        not-3SG be sit-PASS-PTC chair.ADE

        'It has not been sat on the chair.'

(8) a. Negative pluperfect tense:

        Tytöt ei-vät   ol-leet   istu-neet tuolilla.

        girls not-3PL be-PTC-PL sit-PTC-PL chair.ADE

        'The girls had not sat on the chair.'

    b. Negative pluperfect tense passive

        Ei   ol-lut istu-tt-u   tuolilla.

        not.3SG be-PTC sit-PASS-PTC chair.ADE

        'It had not been sat on the chair.'

3 Anders Holmberg's et al. theory of Finnish finite sentence

According to Holmberg & Nikanne (2002) (based on the analysis of Holmberg et al. 1993), the Finnish finite sentence in its fullest possible form is as in (9). The category F (= finite) in Holmberg & Nikanne's (2002) analysis is marked in (9) as AgrS in order to show the relation between the morphology and syntactic structure. (This is not a radical difference; see the discussion of the node F instead of AgrS in Holmberg & Nikanne 2002.)

(9)   The maximal structure of the Finnish finite sentence

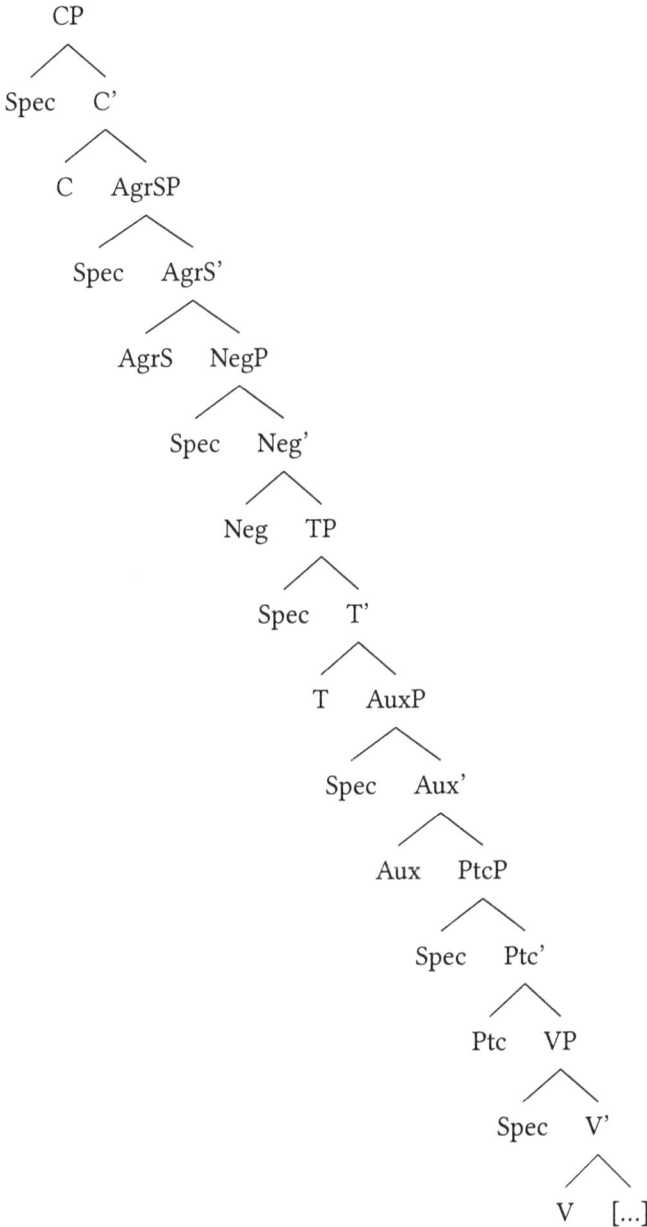

```
CP
├── Spec
└── C'
    ├── C
    └── AgrSP
        ├── Spec
        └── AgrS'
            ├── AgrS
            └── NegP
                ├── Spec
                └── Neg'
                    ├── Neg
                    └── TP
                        ├── Spec
                        └── T'
                            ├── T
                            └── AuxP
                                ├── Spec
                                └── Aux'
                                    ├── Aux
                                    └── PtcP
                                        ├── Spec
                                        └── Ptc'
                                            ├── Ptc
                                            └── VP
                                                ├── Spec
                                                └── V'
                                                    ├── V
                                                    └── [...]
```

"C" stands for Complementizer, "AgrS" for subject agreement (i.e. person 1SG, 2SG, 3SG, 1PL, 2PL, 3PL, and the passive agreement ending), "Neg" for negation, "T" for tempus (i.e. present, past) and in Finnish also modus (i.e. conditional, potential, imperative), "Aux" for auxiliary verb (olla 'be'), "Ptc" for participial (past, present), and "Spec" for specifier.

NB: "Constituency" is marked according to the convention introduced by Petrova (2011): the "ball" at the end of the line indicates the end in which the dominated element (the daughter) is. The benefit of this convention is that it does not require that the mother phrase is above the daughter.

The passive marker *ttA* is base generated in the Spec(VP), the assumed original position for the subject. In standard Finnish, the passive voice is in a complementary distribution with an overt subject.

Only AgrS and T are obligatory. Those are the morphemes that are in an affirmative present or simple past tense forms (see examples 1–8 above).

The D-structure of the sentence *Istu-i-mme tuolilla* [sit-PAST-1PL chair.ADE] 'We sat on the chair' is given in (10). The information on the finite sentence morphology is in the functional positions, and the subject NP is in the Spec(VP) position; note that then both arguments of the verb *istu-* 'sit' are in the maximal projection whose head the verb is.

The derivation from D-structure to S-structure is illustrated in (10): The verb undergoes a head movement from the head of the VP position (V) via the head of the Tense/Mood phrase (T) to the head of the AgrSP position (AgrS). The morphological structure is a mirror image of the head-to-head movement chain. The subject NP is assumed to be base generated in the Spec(VP) position. As the subject NP is in the nominative case and the AgrS feature (1PL) is compatible with the person and number of the subject NP, the sentence is grammatical. The verb and the subject NP leave behind traces in the positions in which they land on the way to their S-structure positions.

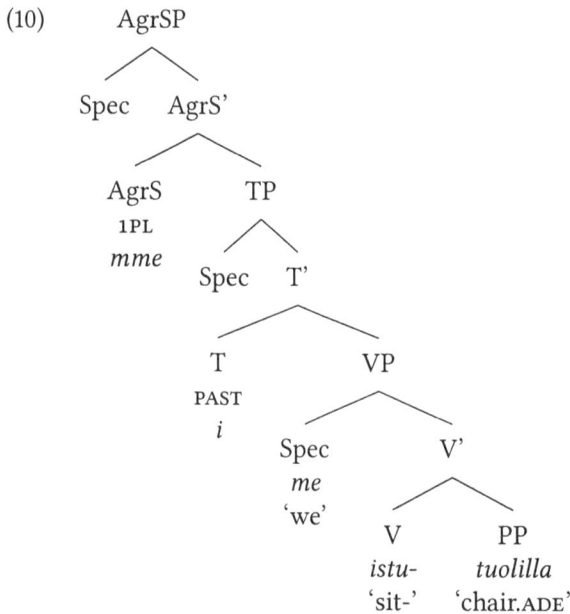

(10)   AgrSP

    Spec   AgrS'

        AgrS   TP
        1PL
        mme
                Spec   T'

                    T   VP
                    PAST
                    i
                        Spec   V'
                        me
                        'we'
                                V   PP
                                istu-   *tuolilla*
                                'sit-'   'chair.ADE'

The S-structure is given in (11), with the solid arrows indicating the movements. The finite morphology, as it appears in the surface structure, is given in the grey box, and the dashed arrow points to syntactic position of the inflected element. (In 12–14, in order to avoid too many arrows, only the movements of V and Aux are shown.)

(11)

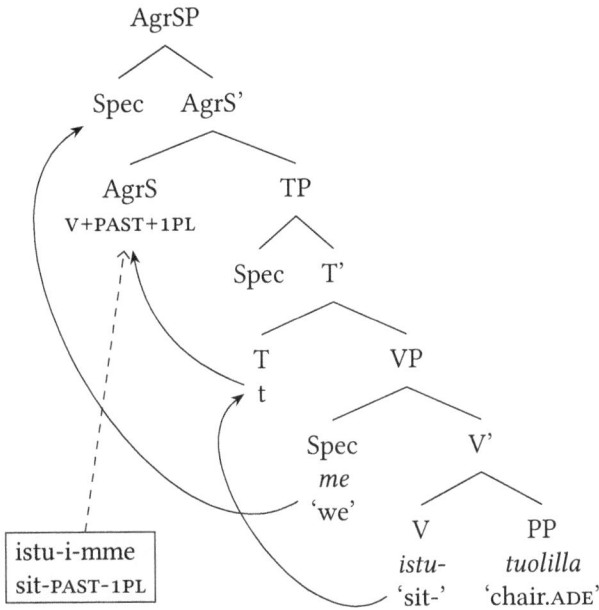

The passive marker is base generated in the specifier position of the VP. This is the position in which the subject argument is supposed to be base generated. The surface structure is derived as follows:

(12)

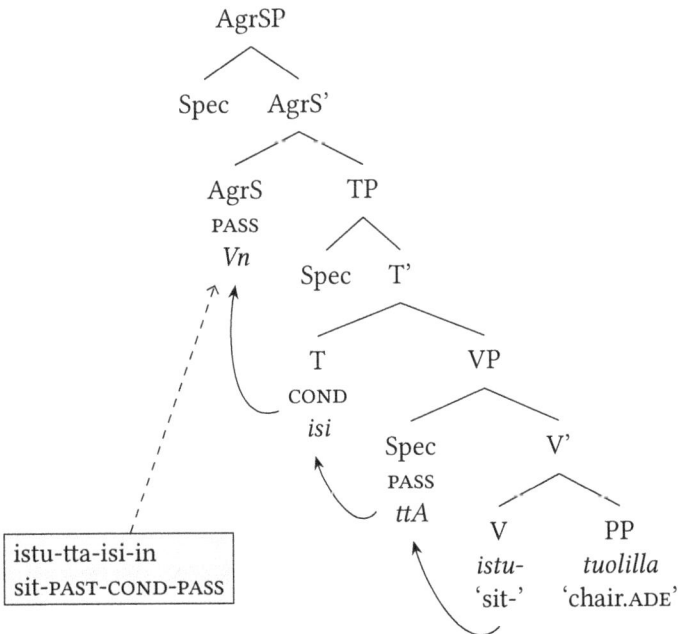

If the auxiliary *olla* 'be' is present, i.e. in the perfect or pluperfect tense, the Aux undergoes a head movement from the head of the auxiliary phrase position (Aux) to AgrS. Then, the verb moves from V to the head of the participial phrase position (Ptc).

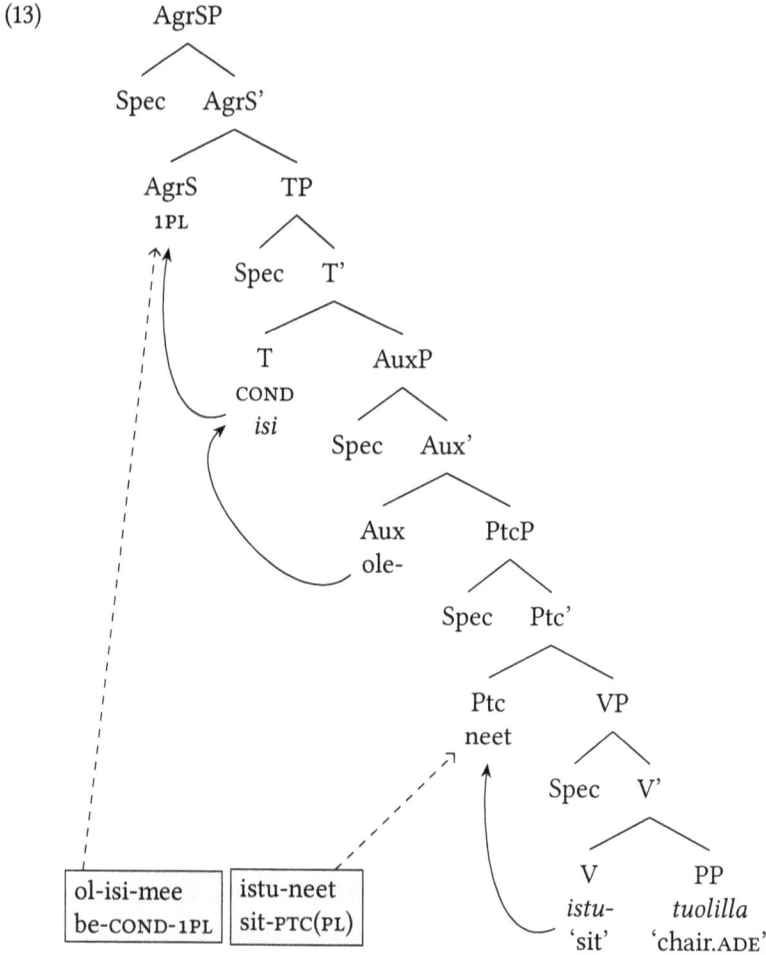

(13)

```
                AgrSP
               /    \
            Spec    AgrS'
                   /    \
               AgrS      TP
               1PL      /  \
                     Spec   T'
                           /  \
                          T    AuxP
                        COND  /    \
                         isi Spec   Aux'
                                   /    \
                                 Aux    PtcP
                                 ole-  /    \
                                    Spec    Ptc'
                                           /    \
                                         Ptc    VP
                                        neet   /  \
                                            Spec   V'
                                                  /   \
                                                 V     PP
                                               istu-  tuolilla
                                               'sit'  'chair.ADE'
```

ol-isi-mee	istu-neet
be-COND-1PL	sit-PTC(PL)

If the negation is present, the negation word *ei* undergoes a movement from the head of the negation phrase (Neg) to AgrS. Then, the auxiliary moves from Aux to T and the predicate verb from V to Ptc.

(14)

```
AgrSP
├── Spec
└── AgrS'
    ├── AgrS
    │   1PL
    │   mme
    └── NegP
        ├── Spec
        └── Neg'
            ├── Neg
            │   e-
            └── TP
                ├── Spec
                └── T'
                    ├── T
                    │   COND
                    │   isi
                    └── AuxP
                        ├── Spec
                        └── Aux'
                            ├── Aux
                            │   ole-
                            └── PtcP
                                ├── Spec
                                └── Ptc'
                                    ├── Ptc
                                    │   neet
                                    └── VP
                                        ├── Spec
                                        └── V'
                                            ├── V
                                            │   istu-
                                            │   'sit'
                                            └── PP
                                                tuolilla
                                                'chair.ADE'
```

e-mme	ol-isi	istu-neet
neg-1PL	be-COND	sit-PTC(PL)

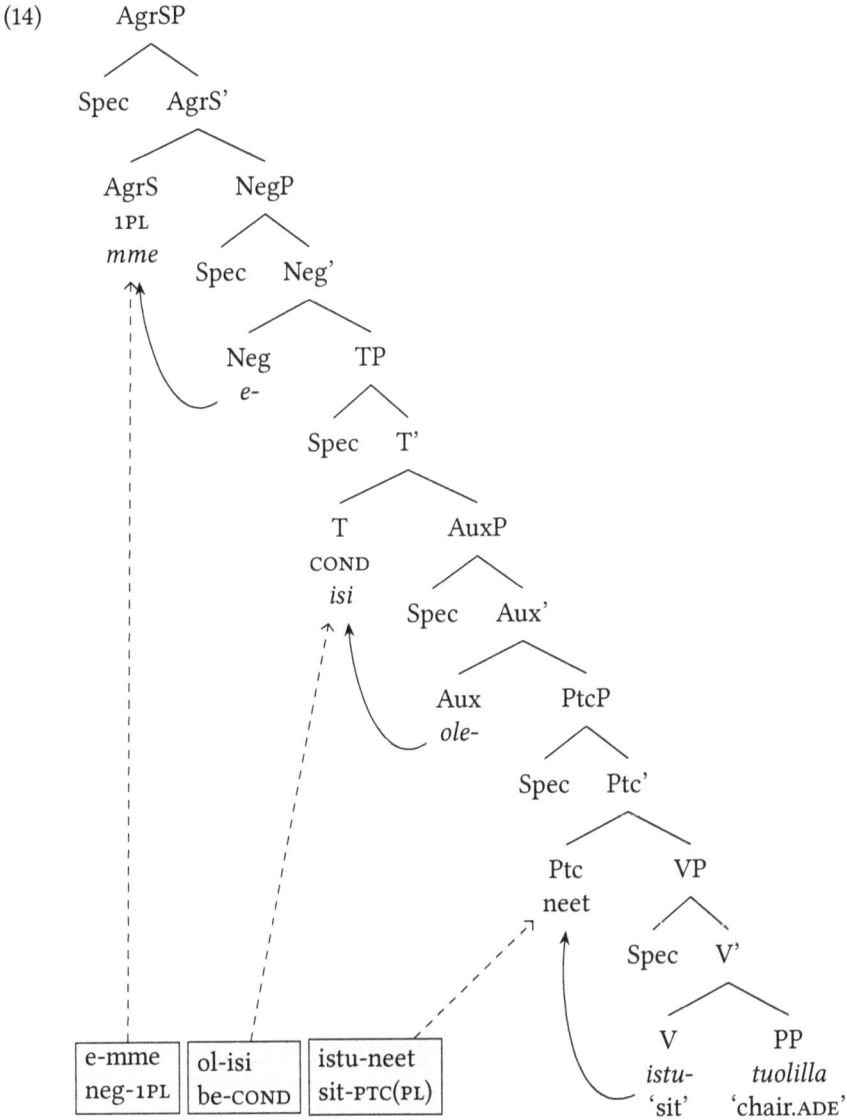

The Complementizer phrase (CP) is understood traditionally as a projection of a Complementizer word, such as a subordinating conjunction (15a), wh-word (15b), or contrastively focused element (15c,d). According to Maria Vilkuna (1989 etc.), the two initial positions of the Finnish finite sentence are reserved for a contrastively focused element (the first position) and the topic of the sentence (the second position). The topic of the sentence can be the first element if there is no contrastively focused element present. According to Holmberg & Nikanne (1994), the contrast position is Spec(CP) position and the topic position is Spec(AgrSP).

(15)

```
                    CP
              ┌──────┴──────┐
            Spec           C'
             ┊         ┌────┴────┐
             ┊         C       AgrSP
             ┊         ┊    ┌─────┴─────┐
             ┊         ┊  Spec        AgrS'
             ┊         ┊   ┊      ┌─────┴─────┐
             ┊         ┊   ┊    AgrS        TP
             ┊         ┊   ┊     ┊     ┌─────┴─────┐
             ┊         ┊   ┊     ┊   Spec        T'
             ┊         ┊   ┊     ┊    ┊     ┌─────┴─────┐
             ┊         ┊   ┊     ┊    ┊     T         PtcP
             ┊         ┊   ┊     ┊    ┊     ┊     ┌─────┴─────┐
             ┊         ┊   ┊     ┊    ┊     ┊   Spec        Ptc'
             ┊         ┊   ┊     ┊    ┊     ┊    ┊     ┌─────┴─────┐
             ┊         ┊   ┊     ┊    ┊     ┊    ┊    Ptc       [...]
             ┊         ┊   ┊     ┊    ┊     ┊    ┊     ┊
           millä_i   tytöt    eivät  olisi  istuneet
```

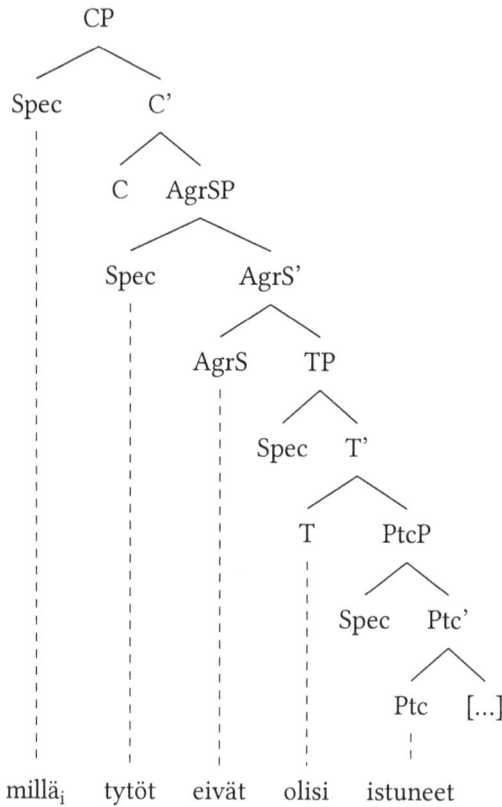

a. millä_i   tytöt   eivät olisi   istuneet t_i?'
   what.ADE girl.PL(NOM) not.3PL be.COND sit.PTC.PL

   'What would the girls not have sat on?'
   (WH-WORD AS ADVERBIAL; TOPIC 'girls')

b. Spec(CP)   Spec(AgrSP) AgrS   T   Ptc
   ketkä_i   t_i   eivät olisi   istuneet tuolilla?
   who.PL(NOM) *t*   not.3PL be.COND sit.PTC.PL chair.ADE

   'Who(PL) would not have sat on the chair?'
   (WH-WORD AS SUBJECT; TOPIC 'who')

c. Spec(CP)   Spec(AgrSP) AgrS   T   Ptc
   tuolilla_i tytöt   eivät olisi   istuneet t_i.
   chair.ADE girl.PL(NOM) not.3PL be.COND sit.PTC.PL *t*

   'It is the chair that the girls would not have sat on.'
   (CONTRASTIVE FOCUS ON 'on the chair'; TOPIC: 'girls')

d. Spec(CP) Spec(AgrSP) AgrS T   Ptc
   eivät_i   tytöt   t_i olisi   istuneet tuolilla.
   not.3PL   girl.PL(NOM) *t* be.COND sit.PTC.PL chair.ADE

   'It is not the case that the girls would have sat on the chair.'
   (FOCUS ON NEGATION; TOPIC: 'girls')

Similar models based on functional categories have been suggested for many other languages besides Finnish, e.g. French (starting Pollock 1989), Swedish (Holmberg & Platzack 1995, Italian (e.g. Cinque 1999), etc. The suggested sentence structures are very similar to that proposed for Finnish. The differences suggested for different languages have to do with the exact set and the mutual order of the categories.

4 What can be done better?

The model of finite sentence based on functional categories works well, and it has without any doubt been the most advanced model of the Finnish finite sentence so far. However, there is always room for progress. In the sections that follow, I will show that the benefits of the theory by Holmberg et al. can be developed into a simpler theory that even better shows the relationship between finite sentence syntax and morphology.

The two areas that need further development are the theory of constituents and keeping morphological and lexical categories apart from each other:

Constituents: Traditionally, a constituent is defined as a unit that moves as a whole, is deleted as a whole, etc. In addition, in the X'-theory, a constituent is a projection of its head. This definition fits well with the good old-fashioned constituents like NP, PP, AP, and AdvP. The constituents headed by functional categories are much more abstract and they have been introduced to the theory mostly for theory internal reasons. The functional categories C and I and their respective projections CP and IP in Chomsky (1986) enabled the X'-theory cover the sentence structure in its entirety. Before that, the sentence (S) was the only constituent that did not have head and an X'-structure. These new "functional" constituents differ from the old-fashioned constituents, which are based on lexical categories. As the door was open for abstract functional constituents, they have been assumed to play a role even in non-finite categories, such as NPs (or DPs). The development has led to a more and more abstract syntax, and at the same time, the idea of constituency has shifted further and further away from its original definition, particularly when it comes to the sentence level constituents headed by functional categories C, I, and the categories suggested to be parts of I (see the analysis of Finnish in §3 above). The theory of syntax should make a difference between the old fashioned constituents and functional categories as they are two different things, at least in the finite sentence.

Separating lexical and morphological categories: In Finnish, for instance, the categories Neg, Aux, and V must always be raised from their original positions, and they never appear without morphological suffices AgrS, T or Ptc. The categories AgrS, T or Ptc on the other hand cannot appear alone. The "mirror image" effect is explained but it is difficult to justify a complicated model of constituent structure in which the head nodes of the lexical categories must always be moved out of their projections (constituents which they are head words of) and at the same time there are constituents headed by heads that never appear alone without a lexical category.

The expansion of the number of functional categories may be a consequence of aiming at a universal description of grammar. A universal (or cross-linguistically relevant) description of the grammar requires that the overall systems of world's languages are described in a comparable manner, not that for instance each part of the grammar, e.g. finite sentences, must be assumed to have the same underlying structure in all languages. Thus, even if we can argue for a category, feature or element in one language, we do not need to generalize the same analysis to all languages. In mainstream generative grammar, syntactic constituent structure has been the most important part of grammar, and many phenomena have been analyzed as syntactic. That leads to, as it seems to me, unnecessarily, complicated syntactic constituent analyses of constituent structure. (For arguments against unnecessarily abstract syntax in mainstream generative grammar, see also Culicover & Jackendoff 2005.)

One motivation in generative grammar for analysing finite sentence as a constituent tree has been that the grammatical functions subject and object as well as assigning grammatical cases can be defined as positions in the constituent tree. Two most important morpho-syntactic feature of the grammatical subject is that the finite predicate verb agrees with the nominative subject in person and number. In Finnish, the word order may vary because the information structure is marked in the word order (see Vilkuna 1989), and still the predicate verb of a finite sentence agrees with the (nominative) subject, no matter where the subject is located. For instance in (16), the verb *istua* 'sit' agrees with the subject *tytöt* [girl.PL.NOM] despite the word order (S = subject, V = predicate verb, X = object or adverbial):

(16) SVX: Tytöt   istuivat   tuolilla.
            girl.PL.NOM sit.PAST.3PL chair.ADE

            'The girls sat on the chair.'

    XVS: Tuolilla   istuivat   tytöt.
            chair.ADE sit.PAST.3PL girl.PL.NOM

    SXV: Tytöt   tuolilla   istuivat.
            girl.PL.NOM chair.ADE sit.PAST.3PL

    XSV: Tuolilla   tytöt   istuivat.
            chair.ADE girl.PL.NOM sit.PAST.3PL

There is, thus, no obvious reason to assume that the subject of the sentence must have a particular syntactic position or that the grammatical cases for the subject (NOM) and the object (PAR or ACC) are assigned to particular positions in the constituent tree.

5 A new look at the finite sentence of Finnish

In this section, I will suggest an alternative way to analyse the morpho-syntactic structure of the Finnish finite sentence.

5.1 From constituents to tiers

The analysis is based on Tiernet Theory (Nikanne 1990; 2002; 2008; forthcoming; Pörn 2004; Paulsen 2011; Petrova 2011), which is a generative theory of grammar and based on Jackendoff's Conceptual Semantics (1972; 1983; 1987; 2002). The characteristic property of Tiernet is that the grammar is based on several very simple micro-modules and links between the micro-representations generated by these micro-modules. (See Nikanne forthcoming, for a detailed introduction to the theory.)

The binary constituent structure in (9) (based on Holmberg et al. 1993) can be presented in a horizontal position so that the maximal and middle nodes are at one level, and heads and specifiers on another level, as shown in Figure 1. The head and specifier nodes are linked to other domains of the language system: information structure, (inflectional) morphology, and lexical categories. The sentence initial positions Spec(CP) and Spec(AgrSP) are reserved for information structure. The functional head positions AgrS, Neg, T, Aux, Ptc, and V are linked to morphological and lexical categories. It is worth pointing out that every second functional head, AgrS, T, and Ptc, are linked to morphological categories and every second functional head, Neg, Aux, and V, are linked to lexical categories. The category C is typically understood to be linked to conjunctions, but there are theories in which C is associated with abstract features of various kinds (having to do with questions, emphasis, etc.).

In the analyses that follow, we abandon constituent structure as the universal architecture of syntax and functional nodes as syntactic categories. Information structure, morphology, and word order are treated as separate tiers. In this way, we are able to reach the goals set above: (i) to avoid unnecessarily abstract syntactic constituents, and (ii) to keep the lexical and morphological categories apart when it comes to finite sentence. In order to do this, we need to use a slightly different set of tools than before:

(i) Hierarchies and linking are applied instead of movements.

(ii) Lexical categories, morphological categories, and finite features are kept in separate tiers instead of putting them all in the same syntactic constituent structure.

5.2 Morphology

The **finite sentence morphological categories** (**fsm-categories**) of Finnish are AgrS, T, Ptc, and Pass. Instead of assuming a head movement, we analyse them as hierarchically organized. The hierarchy is the same as the linear order in Holmberg et al.'s (1993) constituent structure:

(17) *Hierarchy of Fsm-Categories*
      AgrS > T > Ptc > Pass

The finite sentence morphological categories select the finite sentence lexical categories in a strict hierarchical order. The status of a morphological category in the hierarchy of fsm-categories determines its place in the picking order. The highest morpholog-

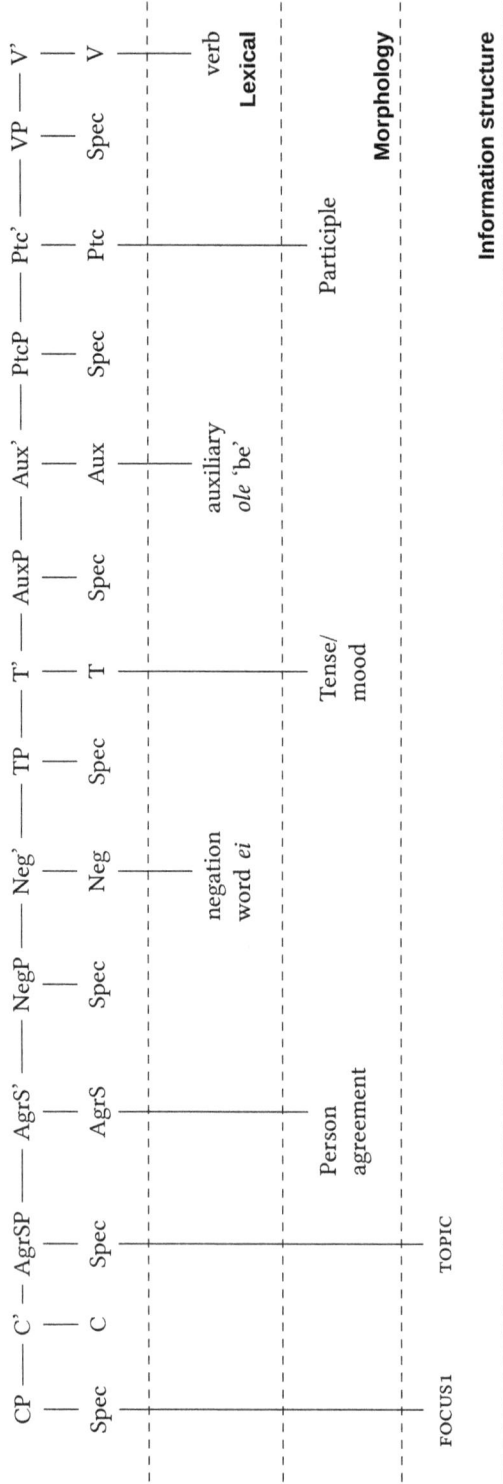

Figure 1: Information structure, morphology, and lexical categories in the Finnish finite sentence.

ical category has the right to select the most desired lexical categories. The desirability of lexical categories is determined in another hierarchy.

In the hierarchy of fsm-categories, there is one difference compared to Holmberg et al. (1993), namely that passive is part of the hierarchy but it is not is not a functional head in the theory of Holmberg et al. As we have abandoned the functional constituent heads, we can – or should – treat passive in the same way as the rest of the finite sentence morphology. As already pointed out above, the Finnish passive has two parts: the passive marker (*ttA*)[1] next to the verb stem and the passive personal ending (*Vn*)[2] in the position of AgrS-endings:

(18)   *istu-ta-an* [sit-PASS-PASS] 'it is sat'
       istu-tt-i-in [sit-PASS-PAST-PASS] 'it was sat'
       istu-tta-isi-in [sit-PASS-COND-PASS] 'it would be sat'
       istu-tta-ne-en [sit-PASS-POT-PASS] 'it probably will be sat'

In the perfect and pluperfect tense, the passive marker is in the participial:

(19)   *on istu-tt-u* [be.3SG sit-PASS-PASTPTC] 'it has been sat'
       oli istu-tt-u [be.PAST.3SG sit-PASS-PASTPTC] 'it had been sat'

The person of the auxiliary *olla* 'be' is traditionally analyzed as 3SG as 3SG is the neutral or default person in the Finnish grammar. In colloquial Finnish, the perfect and pluperfect tenses are not always following the pattern given above: it is common to double the passive morphology in the auxiliary: *ol-la-an istu-tt-u* [be-PASS-PASS sit-PASS-PASTPTC] 'it has been done' instead of *on istu-tt-u* [be.3SG sit-PASS-PASTPTC] 'it has been sat.'

As mentioned above, the lexical categories of the finite sentence form a hierarchy. I use the term **finite sentence lexical categories (fsl-categories)** for the lexical categories that are characteristic for the finite sentence, i.e. Neg, Aux, and V. The hierarchy of these categories is as follows:

(20)   *Hierarchy of Finite Sentence Lexical Categories*
       Neg > Aux > V

The higher the lexical category is in the hierarchy the more valuable it is from the point of view of morphological categories. Just as was the case with morphological categories, the hierarchy of lexical categories corresponds to their order in the syntactic tree in the constituent analysis by Holmberg et al. (1993).

The morphological form follows from general principles.

(21)   *Linking between Finite Sentence Morphological and Lexical Categories*
       A.   Each fsl-category must always be selected by at least one fsm-category.

---

[1]The suffix *ttA* (in which A indicates *a* or *ä* depending on the vowel harmony) is sensitive to its morphophonological context and may appear as *tta, ttä, ta, tä, tt, t, la, lä, ra,* or *rä*. This alternation is, however, beyond the scope of this article.

[2]The V in the suffix *Vn* indicates vowel lengthening: V appears as the lengthening of the preceding vowel.

B. Fsm-categories select a maximal number of fs-morphological categories from left to right following the lexical and morphological hierarchies, with exceptions (i) and (ii).

(i) Neg can only be selected by AgrS.

(ii) Ptc can only select V.

The principles of selection based on these hierarchies correspond to the head movement in Holmberg et al. (1993).

The morphological categories must have values. These values are called φ-features in generative grammar. I will call them **finite features**. Traditionally, the finite sentence morphology has been divided into such categories as voice, tense, mood, person and number. Thus, the morphological category T may carry such finite features as present tense, past tense, conditional mood, imperative mood, or potential mood. AgrS may carry person and number features, or the passive feature.

The finite features are organized in a constituent structure as in Figure 2 (PASS = passive, PRES = present tense, COND = conditional mood, IMP = imperative mood, POT = potential mood). Arrow indicates selection, i.e. dependency relation).

All the finite features of a finite sentence are "collected" by constituency to the same m-root. The m-root represents the whole set of features, and it selects (arrow indicates selection) a finite sentence morphological category. The organization of the finite features is very much the same as in traditional grammars. The new idea is the linking between finite features and finite sentence morphology. The feature system above is based on the grammar of Finnish, but most parts of it are similar to other languages. The finite sentence morphemes (fsm-categories) and the linking between the morphological categories and the features is more language specific.

The fsm-categories can carry different finite features, i.e. they can carry a part of the constituent tree in Figure 2. The restrictions – and possibilities – for categories of AgrS, T, and Ptc to carry finite features are given in (22). The circles show the range of finite features each fsm-category may carry in Finnish.

(22) The possible finite features of the fsm-categories AgrS, T, Ptc, and Pass in Finnish.

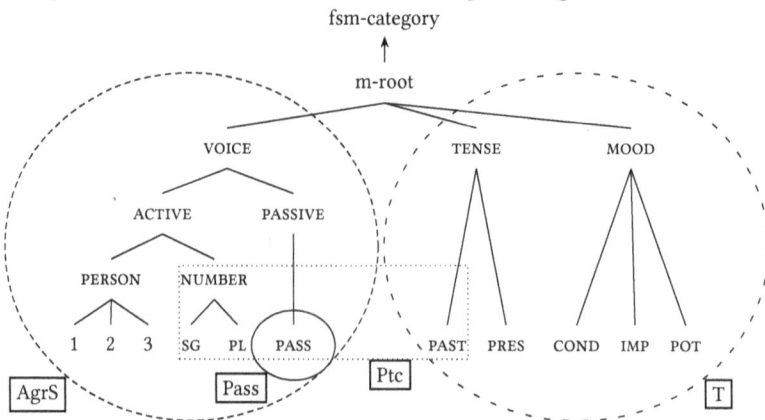

fsl-category (Neg > Aux > V)

Finite sentence lexical categories

fsm-category (AgrS > T > Ptc > Pass)

Finite sentence morphological categories

Finite features

m-root

VOICE   TENSE   MOOD

ACTIVE   PASSIVE

PERSON   NUMBER

1   2   3   SG   PL   PASS   PAST   PRES   COND   IMP   POT

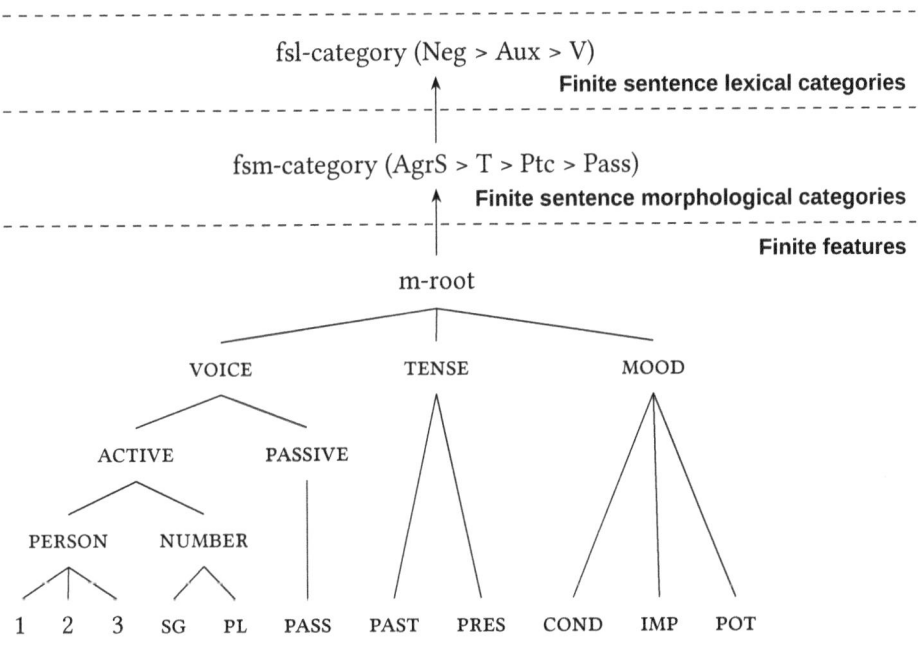

Figure 2: The hierarchy of finite features and linking between finite features, fsm-categories and fsl-categories.

The categories AgrS and T do not share any values but Ptc can carry a part of the values of AgrS, namely number and passive, as well as a part of the values of T, namely past or present. The person values can only be carried by AgrS and the mood values only by T. The main principle is that the branches in the fs-morphological constituent structure must be interpreted as "pick only one," with the excpetion that VOICE can co-occur wth TENSE and MOOD and PERSON can co-occur with NUMBER. We can formulate this into a principle of Finnish grammar:

(23) *Co-occurrence of finite features in Finnish*
The sisters of the finite feature constituent structure cannot co-occur in the same finite sentence, except (i) and (ii).
(i)   VOICE, TENSE, and MOOD can co-occur with each other.
(ii) PERSON can co-occur with NUMBER.

We should keep in mind that the finite sentence is a whole, and one finite sentence can only express one set of finite features (as represented in figure 3). There is only one set of fsm-categories per finite sentence, and therefore we can say that the finiteness of the finite sentence is based on the morphology. The only exception of this is TENSE, which we will discuss shortly. As a reminder of this, I mark the set of fsm-categories that belong to the same finite sentence with brackets and subscript index **fs** ("finite sentence").

The principle of the unity of the finite sentence can be formulated as follows:

(24) *Finite sentence as a unit (in Finnish)*
In a finite sentence, there cannot be more than one instance of each finite feature. The only exception is TENSE of which there can be two instances.

The perfect and pluperfect tense can be described as having two instances of tense: one in auxiliary and another one in the participle. This is an exception to the main principle that each finite feature cannot be expressed more than once.

In theory by Holmberg & al. the functional heads AgrS and T were supposed to always be present in a finite sentence of Finnish. We must add this principle in the present system. In addition, the lexical category V is always present in a finite sentence. The principle is as follows:

(25) *Obligatory categories in Finnish finite sentence*
The fsm-categories AgrS and T as well as the fsl-category V are obligatory in a finite sentence.

Here is an example of the system. The example in (26) *istuisimme* [eat.COND.1PL] 'we would eat' can be analyzed as follows and *istumme* [eat.1PL] 'we sit':

(26) a. istuisimme
eat-COND-1PL

'we would eat'

```
COND      1              PL
  |       |              |
       PERSON    NUMBER
             \    /
            ACTIVE
              |
MOOD        VOICE
  |           |
root        root
  ↓           ↓
[fs T      AgrS]
      \    /
        V
```

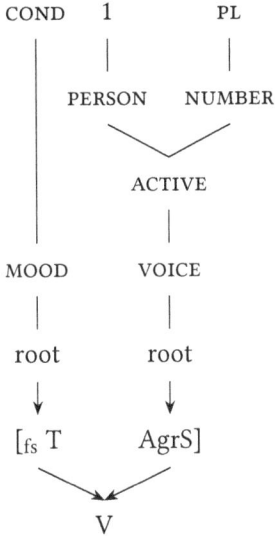

b. istumme
sit-1PL

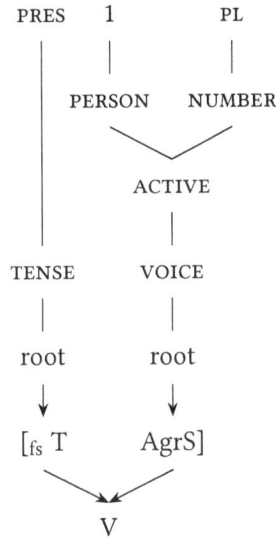

```
PRES      1              PL
  |       |              |
       PERSON    NUMBER
               \    /
              ACTIVE
                |
TENSE         VOICE
  |             |
root          root
  ↓             ↓
[fs T        AgrS]
        \    /
          V
```

The perfect and pluperfect tenses can be analyzed as follows:

(27) a. olemme istuneet
be-1PL   sit-PASTPTC-PL

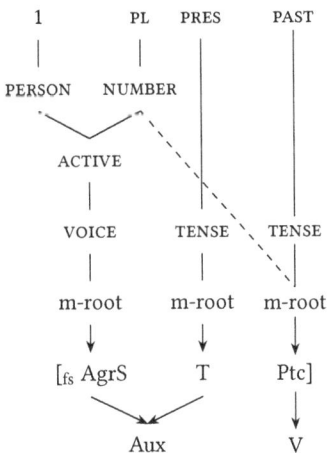

```
  1         PL    PRES    PAST
  |         |      |       |
PERSON   NUMBER    |       |
      \    /       |       |
     ACTIVE        |       |
       |           |       |
     VOICE       TENSE   TENSE
       |           |       |
     m-root     m-root   m-root
       ↓           ↓       ↓
   [fs AgrS       T      Ptc]
        \    /            |
          Aux             V
```

b. olimme   istuneet
be-PAST-1PL sit-PASTPTC-PL

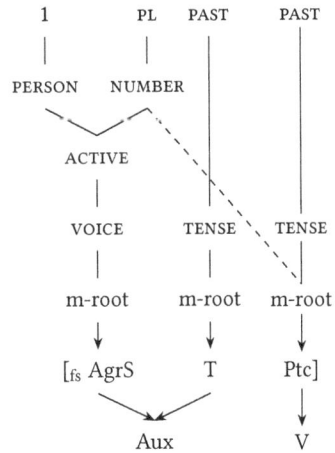

```
  1         PL    PAST    PAST
  |         |      |       |
PERSON   NUMBER    |       |
      \    /       |       |
     ACTIVE        |       |
       |           |       |
     VOICE       TENSE   TENSE
       |           |       |
     m-root     m-root   m-root
       ↓           ↓       ↓
   [fs AgrS       T      Ptc]
        \    /            |
          Aux             V
```

The participles used in the finite sentence are in the same number (SG or PL) as the whole finite sentence morphology. This agreement can be described as feature spreading. The feature spreading is marked by dashed constituent lines. The spreading lines are linked directly to the m-root: the participial forms are just agreeing with the number of the finite sentence. The primary expression of number is in the morphological form of the negation word.

As discussed earlier, the Finnish morpho-syntax is peculiar in the way that the finite features tense and mood cannot co-occur in the same finite verb: the fsm-category T expresses either mood or tense but not both. There is however, a solution: participle. If tense and mood co-occur, the mood is expressed by fsm-category T that selects Aux and tense by fsm-category Ptc that selects V, for instance in (28).

(28) olisimme   istuneet
      be-COND-1PL sit-PASTPTC-PL

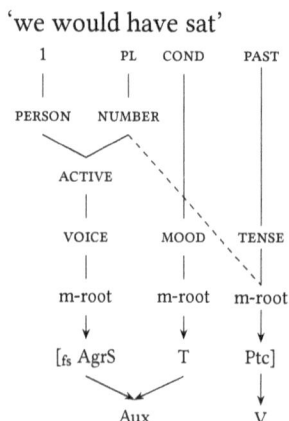

'we would have sat'

```
   1          PL    COND      PAST
   |          |      |         |
PERSON    NUMBER
     \      /                 |
      ACTIVE    ------        |
        |             \       |
      VOICE         MOOD  \  TENSE
        |             |     \  |
     m-root        m-root   m-root
        ↓             ↓        ↓
     [fs AgrS        T        Ptc]
        \        /             |
          Aux                  V
```

In this way, both tense and mood can be expressed in the same finite sentence even though they do not have room in the same verb form.

Another morphological peculiarity in Finnish is that passive is expressed by two endings: the passive marker and the passive personal suffix. For instance:

(29) istu-tt-i-in
      sit-PASS-PAST-PASS

'it was sat'

I suggest the following solution:

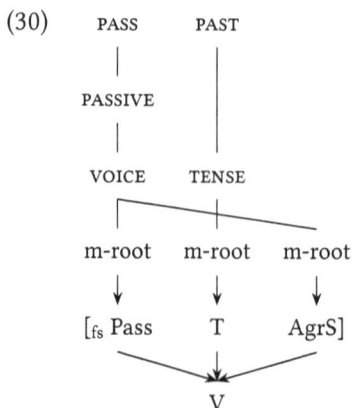

(30)   PASS   PAST
         | |
      PASSIVE |
         | |
       VOICE   TENSE
         ┌─────────┼─────────┐
       m-root   m-root   m-root
         ↓   ↓   ↓
      [fs Pass   T   AgrS]
          \ | /
                   ↓
                   V

88

The solution in (31) is rather obvious in a "nonlinear" morphology as the present approach. The node VOICE is shared by the m-roots of the fsm-categories Pass and AgrS. Hakulinen & Karlsson (1979) suggest that passive is "the fourth person." The motivation is that the passive form has a person suffix, i.e. AgrS. In the present approach, it is not necessary to assume a fourth person. The passive is just linked to the fsm-category AgrS, in addition to the fsm-category Pass, and the passive voice is expressed in two fsm-categories.

The negation word *e(i)* 'not' is selected by the fsm-category AgrS. The mood or the tense are then expressed by the verb:

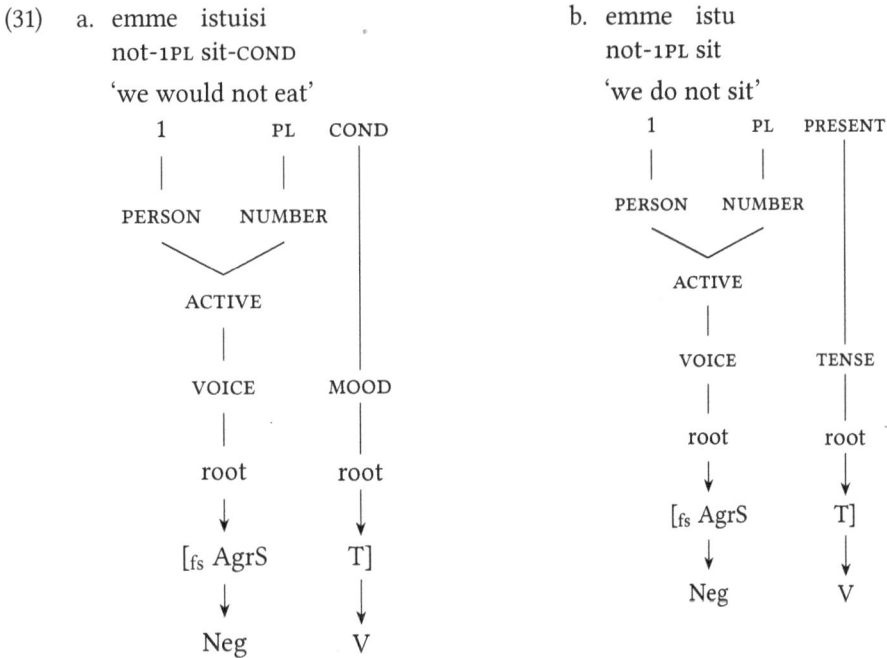

(31) a. emme istuisi
           not-1PL sit-COND

           'we would not eat'

    b. emme istu
           not-1PL sit

           'we do not sit'

We need to stipulate an exception to the system. But this stipulation is something that any system – known so far – must do. There is a third peculiarity in Finnish: if the finite sentence has a negation word, the verb or the auxiliary appears in the participial form in the past tense. The auxiliary is in the participial form in the pluperfect as the pluperfect (normally) consists of an auxiliary in the past tense plus the verb in a past participial form:

(32) a. Tyttö   ei   istunut   tuolissa.
         girl.NOM not.3SG sit.PASTPTC chair.INE

         'The girl did not sit on the chair.'

         (Negation and past tense: V in a participial form.)

    b. Tytöt   eivät istuneet   tuolissa.
         girl.PL.NOM not.3PL sit.PASTPTC chair.INE

         'The girls did not sit on the chair.'

         (Negation and perfect tense: Aux appears in a participial form.)

c. Tytöt   eivät   ole istuneet   tuolissa.
   girl.PL.NOM not.3PL be sit.PASTPTC chair.INE

'The girl did have not sat on the chair.'

(Negation and pluperfect tense: Aux appears in a participial form.)

This exception can tentatively be formalized as follows (i.e. the past tense morphology of Aux or V is replaced by the participial form in the presence of Neg).

(33)   *Past tense in the negative sentence in Finnish*
       If the fs-morphological category AgrS selects Neg, then the value PAST of the fs-morphological category T appears as past participle.

Thus, the fsm-category that selects verb in (32a) and the auxiliary in (32b, 32c) is functionally T but it appears as a participial. The participial form is able to express tense, and the Finnish grammar takes an advantage of this property in the perfect and the pluperfect tenses. Why the (simple) past tense is expressed using a participial form in negative sentence, seems to be just a strange detail of the Finnish grammar. What we know, however, that this is made possible by the facts (i) that a particcple *can* be selected by tense and that (ii) the person and number select the negation word when it is possible.

For instance the finite forms in (32) can be described as in (34):

(34)   a. ei   istunut   b. eivät   istuneet
          not-3SG sit-PASTPTC   not-3PL sit-PASTPTC-PL

       '(she/he/it) did not sit'   '(they) did not sit'

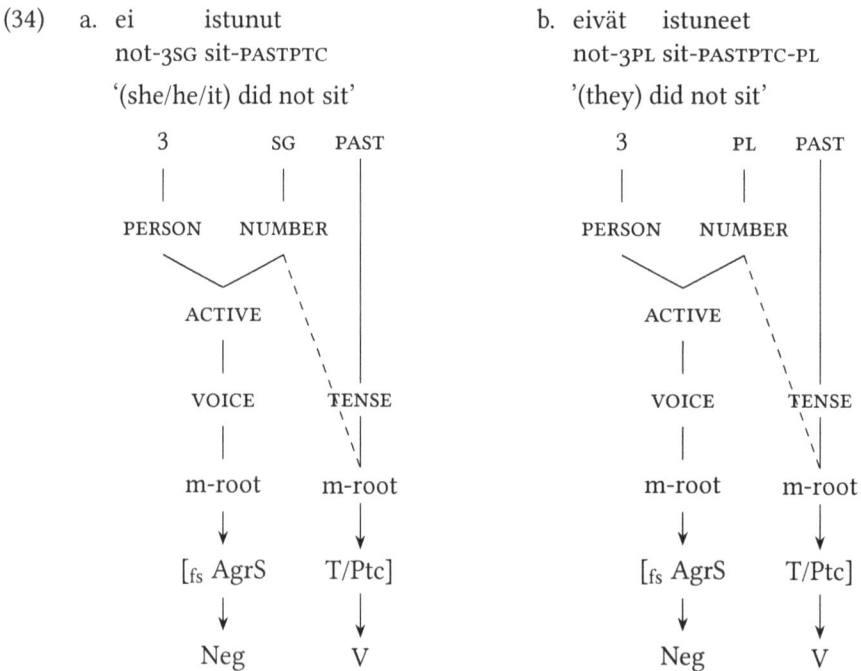

c. eivät   ole istuneet
   not-PL be sit-PASTPTC-PL

   '(they) have not sat'

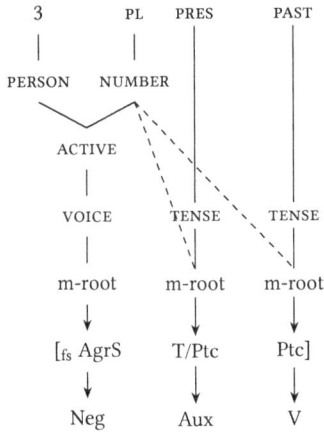

```
    3        PL   PRES     PAST
    |        |
 PERSON   NUMBER
     \      /  \
     ACTIVE
       |
     VOICE    TENSE      TENSE
       |
     m-root   m-root    m-root
       ↓        ↓         ↓
   [fs AgrS    T/Ptc     Ptc]
       ↓        ↓         ↓
     Neg       Aux        V
```

d. eivät   olleet   istuneet
   not-PL3 be-PASTPTC-PL sit-PASTPTC-PL

   '(they) had not sat'

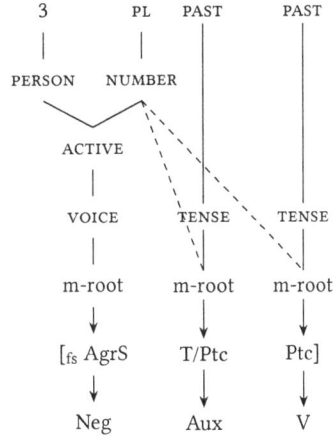

```
    3        PL   PAST     PAST
    |        |
 PERSON   NUMBER
     \      /  \
     ACTIVE
       |
     VOICE    TENSE      TENSE
       |
     m-root   m-root    m-root
       ↓        ↓         ↓
   [fs AgrS    T/Ptc     Ptc]
       ↓        ↓         ↓
     Neg       Aux        V
```

The fact that tense is expressed by a participle in negative sentences is marked as T/Ptc, which should be understood like T that is replaced by Ptc.

When it comes to the ability of the participle form to express tense, the Finnish grammar uses it also when the T is selected by MOOD. Here for instance is the past tense (or perfect tense, if you like) of the conditional mood (the example (28) is repeated here as (35)):

(35) olisimme   istuneet
      be-COND-3PL sit-PASTPTC-3PL

      'we would have sat'

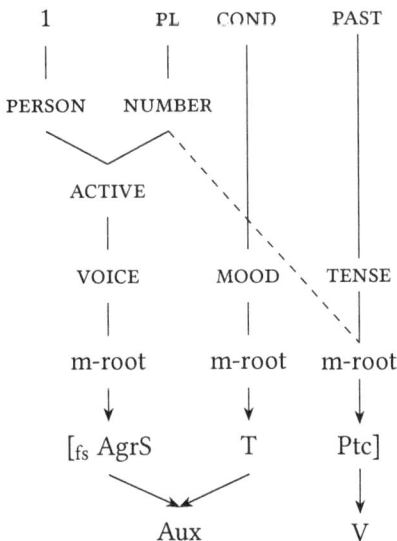

```
    1        PL   COND     PAST
    |        |
 PERSON   NUMBER
     \      /  \
     ACTIVE
       |
     VOICE    MOOD       TENSE
       |        |
     m-root   m-root    m-root
       ↓        ↓         ↓
   [fs AgrS     T        Ptc]
       \       /          ↓
         Aux              V
```

The pluperfect of negative sentences in Standard Finnish has passive marker only in the participial form of the V (40a). In colloquial Finnish, it is, however, very common to have the passive marker both in the participial form of the auxiliary and the participial form of the verb. (School teachers tend to have a hard time trying to make children use the Standard Finnish form, and even educated adult writers often use the colloquial form.)

(36)   a. ei ollut   istuttu
           not be-PASTPTC sit-PASS-PASTPTC

       'it had not been sat'

```
   PASS              PAST          PAST
    |                 |             |
 PASSIVE           TENSE         TENSE

  VOICE

  m-root           m-root        m-root
    ↓                ↓             ↓
 [fs AgrS          T/Ptc          Ptc]
    ↓                ↓             ↓
  Neg              Aux            V
```

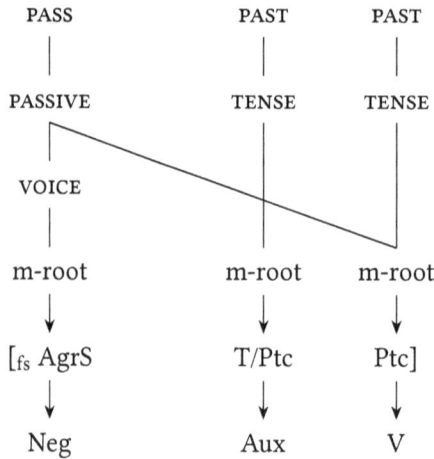

       b. ei oltu   istuttu   (colloquial)
           not be-PASS-PASTPTC sit-PASS-PTC

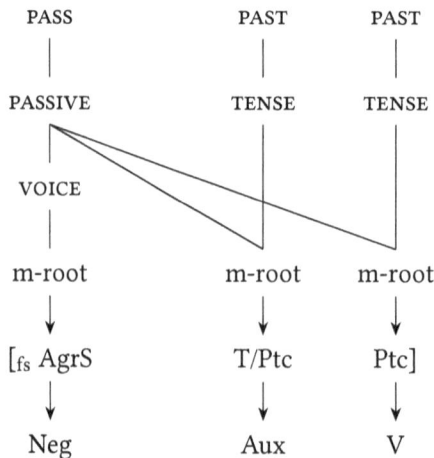

           'it had not been sat'

```
   PASS              PAST          PAST
    |                 |             |
 PASSIVE           TENSE         TENSE

  VOICE

  m-root           m-root        m-root
    ↓                ↓             ↓
 [fs AgrS          T/Ptc          Ptc]
    ↓                ↓             ↓
  Neg              Aux            V
```

In the light of the present nonlinear micro-modular approach, it is easy to understand why the colloquial form (36b) is so appealing: the passive is spread across the whole finite sentence, just like in the present the simple past tense. The Standard Finnish form must be learned separately as skipping the category T/Ptc is somewhat unnatural.

5.3 Word order and information structure in tiers

The system suggested above covers the finite features, as well as the finite sentence morphology. One thing that is not covered is word order. Word order is a linear system, and I suggest that the system, the word order tier, is simply a linear order of word order positions, and the lexical, morphological, syntactic, and other elements are linked to these positions. Here is a suggestion for the word order tier:

(37) **Word order tier**

    0 $\dashrightarrow$ 1 $\dashrightarrow$ 2 $\dashrightarrow$ 3 $\dashrightarrow$ 4 $\dashrightarrow$ 5 $\dashrightarrow$ …

The notation X $\dashrightarrow$ Y indicates 'X immediately precedes Y in linear order.' Linear order is an asymmetric relation: if A precedes B, then B does not precede A. It has a direction: if A precedes B and B precedes C, then A precedes C. The notation indicates this asymmetry and direction.

The importance of the linear order in a modular model of grammar has lately been emphasized by Sadock (2012: 111–113). The technical difference between the word-order tier suggested above and Sadock's model is that Sadock suggests that linear order is a uniformly either left- or right-branching tree structure, which leads to an unambiguous linear order of the terminal nodes. The word-order tier above is an assumption that is one step simpler, as the relation "precede" simply states the linear order. We will see how far we can get with the null-hypothesis.

The information structure categories TOPIC and FOCUS1 (a.k.a. "contrastive focus") have their designated positions Spec(CP) and Spec(AgrSP). According to Vilkuna (1989), the word order of Finnish is based on categories such as CONTRAST (our FOCUS1) and TOPIC, so in Finnish, the information structure must be linked to the word order tier. The word inflected in the AgrS-morphology sits in the AgrS-position. Compared to the functional constituent tree of Holmberg et al. (1993), the word order position 0 corresponds to Spec(CP), 1 corresponds to C, 2 to Spec(AgrSP), and 3 to AgrS.

The designated positions of the information structure categories and the AgrS can be found in the word order tier:

(38) *Fixed links between information structure and word-order in Finnish*
    FOCUS1 always selects word order position 0 and TOPIC always selects position 2.

The position of the word inflected in the AgrS-morphology can be formulated as follows:

(39) *Fixed link between fsm-category AgrS and word-order in Finnish*
    AgrS always selects word order position 3.

The question words such as *mikä* 'what', *kuka* 'who', *miten* 'how', *millloin* 'when', etc. are linked to position 0. One interpretation is, naturally, that a question word has a contrastive focus as it represents the missing piece of information that is in the focus of the question sentence.

Position 1 is needed for an expletive in certain structures, when the information structure must be made visible (Nikanne forthcoming).

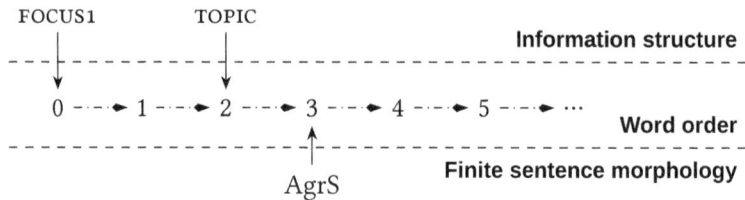

Figure 3: The fixed links between the word order tier, information structure, and finite sentence morphology in Finnish.

The morphological category AgrS is fixed to position 3. The morphological categories have right to pick the higher position according to the morphological hierarchy. If Neg and Aux are not present, T and Agr appear as inflectional categories of V, and they are located in position 3 as in (40). Ptc has the right for position 4 if Neg is not present and T is in position 3 together with AgrS, as illustrated in (40). If all the fs-lexical categories (Neg, Aux and V) are present, T (here: conditional mood) is in position 4 and Ptc (here past participial plural) in position 5. The active voice sentences given in (1–8) are repeated below as (40). The word-order position is marked above each sentence, and the categories of other tiers fixed to that position (FOCUS1, TOPIC, and AgrS) are marked above the word order position:

(40)   a. FOCUS1   TOPIC   AgrS
            0   2   3   4   5
            millä$_i$ tytöt   eivät olisi   istuneet
            what.ADE girl.PL(NOM) not.3PL be.COND sit.PTC.PL

'What would the girls not have sat on?'
(WH-WORD AS ADVERBIAL; TOPIC 'girls')

  b. FOCUS1   TOPIC AgrS
            0   2   3   4   5
            ketkä$_i$ t$_i$ eivät olisi   istuneet
            who.PL(NOM) *t*   not.3PL be.COND sit.PTC.PL

'Who(PL) would not have sat on the chair?'
(WH-WORD AS SUBJECT; TOPIC 'who')

c. FOCUS1   TOPIC   AgrS
    0   2   3   4   5

tuolilla$_i$	tytöt	eivät	olisi	istuneet
chair.ADE	girl.PL(NOM)	not.3PL	be.COND	sit.PTC.PL

'It is the chair that the girls would not have sat on.'
(FOCUS ON 'on the chair', TOPIC: 'girls')

d. FOCUS1 TOPIC   AgrS
    0   2   3   4   5

eivät$_i$	tytöt	t$_i$	olisi	istuneet	tuolilla.
not.3PL	girl.PL(NOM)	t	be.COND	sit.PTC.PL	chair.ADE

'It is not the case that the girls would have sat on the chair.'
(FOCUS ON NEGATION; TOPIC: 'girls')

6 Conclusion

In this article, the finite sentence of Finnish is analyzed as a unit that consists of three tiers: finite sentence features, finite sentence morphology, and finite sentence lexical categories. In addition, I have suggested that word order is based on a simple one dimensional tier that takes care of the linear order of different tiers. The suggested system allows us to give up abstract syntax when it comes to constituent structure with functional categories and head movement. The Tiernet-model of finite sentence resembles traditional grammars:

(i) Morphological and lexical categories are kept apart.

(ii) Finite features are very close to those assumed traditionally.

Grammars of languages may differ at least in the following ways:

(i) The inventory of the finite features, lexical categories, and morphological categories may be different in different languages.

(ii) The links between the features and the morphological and lexical features may differ in different languages.

Abbreviations

Abbreviations used in this article follow the Leipzig Glossing Rules' instructions for word-by-word transcription, available at: https://www.eva.mpg.de/lingua/pdf/Glossing-Rules.pdf. Additionally used:

ADE the adessive case 'on' / 'at'   PTC participle

Acknowledgements

I would like to thank the editors Laura Bailey and Michelle Sheehan as well as the two anonymous reviewers for their valuable help with the article. The remaining mistakes are my own. The theory presented in this article would not have been possible without my good friend Anders Holmberg, with whom I have had the pleasure to work on the structure of the finite sentence of Finnish.

References

Baker, Mark. 1988. *Incorporation.* Cambridge: MIT Press.

Chomsky, Noam. 1986. *Barriers.* Cambridge, MA: MIT Press.

Chomsky, Noam. 1995. *The minimalist program.* Cambridge: MIT Press.

Cinque, Guglielmo. 1999. *Adverbs and functional heads: A cross-linguistic perspective.* Oxford: Oxford University Press.

Culicover, Peter W. & Ray Jackendoff. 2005. *Simpler syntax.* Oxford/New York: Oxford University Press.

Hakulinen, Auli & Fred Karlsson. 1979. *Nykysuomen lauseoppia.* Helsinki: Finnish Literature Society.

Holmberg, Anders & Urpo Nikanne. 1994. Expletives and subject positions in Finnish. In Mercè Gonzàlez (ed.), *NELS 24: Proceedings of the North East Linguistics Society,* 173–187. Amherst: University of Massachusetts.

Holmberg, Anders & Urpo Nikanne. 2002. Expletives, subjects, and topics in Finnish. In Peter Svenonius (ed.), *Subjects, expletives, and the EPP,* 71–105. Oxford: Oxford University Press.

Holmberg, Anders & Urpo Nikanne. 2008. Subject doubling in Finnish: The role of deficient pronouns. In Marika Lekakou Sjef Barbiers Olaf Koeneman & Margreet van der Ham (eds.), *Microvariation in syntactic doubling,* 325–349. Bingley: Emerald.

Holmberg, Anders, Urpo Nikanne, Hannu Reime, Irmeli Oraviita & Trond Trosterud. 1993. The structure of INFL and the finite clause in Finnish. In Anders Holmberg & Urpo Nikanne (eds.), *Case and other functional categories in Finnish syntax* (Studies in Generative Grammar 39), 176–206. Berlin: Mouton de Gruyter.

Holmberg, Anders & Christer Platzack. 1995. *The role of inflection in Scandinavian syntax.* Oxford: Oxford University Press.

Jackendoff, Ray S. 1972. *Semantic interpretation in generative grammar.* Cambridge, MA: The MIT Press.

Jackendoff, Ray S. 1983. *Semantics and cognition.* Cambridge: MIT Press.

Jackendoff, Ray S. 1987. The status of thematic relations in linguistic theory. *Linguistic Inquiry* 18. 369–411.

Jackendoff, Ray S. 1990. *Semantic structures.* Cambridge: MIT Press.

Jackendoff, Ray S. 2002. *Foundations of language: Brain, meaning, grammar, evolution.* Oxford: Oxford University Press.

Nikanne, Urpo. Forthcoming. *Tiernet: A micro-modular approach to conceptual semantics.* Amsterdam: John Benjamins.

Nikanne, Urpo. 1990. *Zones and tiers: A study of argument structure.* Helsinki: Finnish Literature Society.

Nikanne, Urpo. 2002. Kerrokset ja kytkennät. http://web.abo.fi/fak/hf/fin/kurssit/KONSEM/yleista.htm.

Nikanne, Urpo. 2008. Conceptual semantics. In Jan-Ola Östman & Jef Verschueren (eds.), *Handbook of pragmatics*, 1–21. Amsterdam: John Benjamins.

Paulsen, Geda. 2011. *Causation and dominance: A study of Finnish causative verbs expressing social dominance.* Åbo: Åbo Akademi University Press.

Petrova, Oksana. 2011. *'Of pearls and pigs': A conceptual-semantic tiernet approach to formal representation of structure and variation of phraseological units.* Åbo: Åbo Akademi University Press.

Pollock, Jean-Yves. 1989. Verb movement, universal grammar, and the structure of IP. *Linguistic Inquiry* 20(3). 365–424.

Pörn, Michaela. 2004. *Suomen tunnekausatiiviverbit ja niiden lausemaiset täydennykset.* Helsinki: Finnish Literature Society.

Sadock, Jerrold M. 2012. *The modular architecture of grammar.* Cambridge: Cambridge University Press.

Vilkuna, Maria. 1989. *Free word order in Finnish: Its syntax and discourse functions.* Helsinki: Finnish Literature Society.

Chapter 5

Scandinavian object shift is phonology

Nomi Erteschik-Shir
Ben Gurion University

Gunlög Josefsson
Lund University

The problem addressed in this paper is a case of word order microvariation in Mainland Scandinavian: optional vs. obligatory Object Shift (OS). Following standard assumptions (see Selkirk 1996), weak object pronouns are assumed to be affixal clitics at PF which do not themselves have the status of prosodic words. Since adverbs (including negation), are unsuitable as hosts, weak object pronouns may undergo OS, in other words precede adverbs, ending up encliticized onto the preceding verb or subject. In standard Danish, OS is obligatory; the order adverb+weak pronoun is blocked. However, in Swedish, OS is optional, as is the case for some Danish dialects, spoken in the southeastern island area. In our paper we explain the distribution of optional vs. obligatory OS by the phonological properties of the two varieties. What "optional OS" in Swedish and varieties of Danish have in common is the occurrence of a tonal accent, which creates a larger phonological unit than the minimal prosodic word, a Tonal Unit. We propose that the mechanism that allows a weak pronoun to remain in the canonical position in Swedish and the southeastern island dialects in Danish, is the availability of tonal accent. The tonal accent enables the inclusion of the pronoun in such a unit. Standard Danish, on the other hand, lacks tonal accent altogether which is why OS is obligatory in this dialect.

1 Introduction

Since Holmberg 1986, pronominal object shift, OS, in the Mainland Scandinavian languages, henceforth MSc, has become a widely studied and carefully described phenomenon. It refers to the placement of a weak object pronoun to the left of a sentence adverb, such as the negation, (1a), instead of in the canonical position for objects, which is to the right of a sentence adverb, (1b).

Nomi Erteschik-Shir & Gunlög Josefsson. 2017. Scandinavian object shift is phonology. In Laura R. Bailey & Michelle Sheehan (eds.), *Order and structure in syntax I: Word order and syntactic structure*, 99–115. Berlin: Language Science Press. DOI:10.5281/zenodo.1117700

(1) Swedish

    a. Jag mötte honom inte.
       I   met   him   not

      'I didn't meet him.'

    b. Jag mötte inte honom.
       I   met not him

      'I didn't meet him.'

Following standard assumptions (see Selkirk 1996), we assume that weak object pronouns are affixal clitics at PF which do not themselves have the status of prosodic words, and that this holds generally for OS in MSc. Whether or not OS is obligatory, however, varies among the MSc languages and varieties. In this article we will concentrate on Danish and Swedish. However, we are convinced that the ideas proposed here can be applied more generally in MSc. Somewhat simplified, OS is obligatory in most Danish dialects, except for certain areas in southern Denmark (for example the dialect spoken on the island of Ærø), where OS is optional. In Swedish OS is optional, except for Fenno-Swedish and Oevdalian Swedish.[1]

In this paper we demonstrate that optionality of OS in MSc is conditioned by language- and variety-specific phonological properties, and thus PF is responsible for at least some microvariation in word order. Our argument however goes further: We claim, following Erteschik-Shir 2005a and Josefsson 2010; 2012, that OS in the Mainland Scandinavian languages is in fact driven by phonology. The basis of our claim is the well-known requirement of weak pronouns to incorporate, and thus to form a prosodic unit with a legitimate host. In the shifted word order, the host is the preceding verbal or nominal element. This is shown in the Danish examples below.[2]

(2) Danish

    a. Jeg mødte ham ikke.
       I   met=him   not

      'I didn't meet him.'

    b. Hvorfor mødte Peter ham ikke.
       why   met   Peter=him not

      'Why didn't Peter meet him.'

At first glance it could be tempting to explain the variation by assuming a word order parameter that would determine whether adverbs may be hosts or not.[3] However, such a solution would be a simple reformulation of the empirical observation, thus circular and

---

[1]It should be pointed out that our study is restricted to pronominal shift in the Mainland Scandinavian languages. Naturally, it would be interesting to explore to what extent our findings could be applied to full DP shift, as in Icelandic, but that question will not be explored in this article.

[2]Similar examples could be drawn from the other MSc dialects, except for Fenno-Swedish, discussed in §5.

[3]Negation behaves like other adverbs in Scandinavian and is therefore classified as an adverb here.

devoid of explanatory force. Therefore, we will hold on to the generalization that adverbs in general are not legitimate hosts for prosodic incorporation or cliticization, thus that weak pronouns cannot cliticize onto adverbs in any of the MSc varieties.[4] Instead, we argue that the varieties that allow optional OS – varieties where the weak object pronoun may follow an adverb as in (1b) – offer another possibility of prosodic incorporation, namely a prosodic unit created by (the presence of) tonal accent. (This will be elaborated in §4.)

The idea that prosodic factors determine OS is important more generally, since it shows that PF can be responsible for microvariation in word order. If this is the case, the claim that word order is entirely determined by syntax is put into question.

2 Previous proposals on OS, phonology, and information structure

The idea that OS has phonological properties has been suggested in the literature. More specifically it has been proposed that weak object pronouns are clitics or clitic-like elements (see Holmberg 1991: 167; Josefsson 1992; 1993; 1994; 2010; 2012; Déprez 1994: 122; Hellan 1994; 2005; Bobaljik & Jonas 1996: 207; Diesing 1996: 77; Diesing 1997: 41; Erteschik-Shir 2005a,b; Hosono 2010; 2013).

The fact that stressed pronouns cannot undergo OS inspired Holmberg (1999: 25–28) to propose that OS is driven by a formal feature related to information structure. Holmberg suggests that objects that undergo OS are marked [-Focus], and that they need to be c-commanded by a category marked [+Focus]. The reason shift never takes place across verbs, verb particles, or prepositions (for Holmberg's Generalization, see Holmberg 1986; 1999) would be that such categories are inherently marked [-Focus], which means that there would be no trigger for movement of the object to a higher position. Adverbs, on the other hand, are not marked [-Focus] in this framework, which would explain why they do not block OS. The requirement that a [-Focus] element has to be licensed by a [+Focus] element would, in fact, be what forces movement. A suggestion along the same lines was suggested in Platzack (1996), where a feature Repel F was introduced. The role of this feature is to force a [-Focus] element, for example, to move out of a focus domain.

3 Phonological background

Since our account is phonological in nature, a short introduction to the phonological theory which we base our analysis on is called for.

---

[4]Languages vary as to which elements can host prosodic incorporation or cliticization. In Scandinavian languages, for example, but not in English, nominals can host these processes. We do not expect to find adjoined modifiers, such as adverbs as hosts crosslinguistically. In the cases we discuss here, the formation of the prosodic unit between the adverb and the weak pronoun is due to the tonal accent, not to the capability of the adverb to be a host for incorporation.

3.1 Stress and (minimal) prosodic words in MSc

Basing their claims on Swedish, Myrberg & Riad (2013), see also Riad (2013), define a minimal prosodic word in terms of culminativity; a minimal prosodic word is a constituent with exactly one stress. Consequently, most simplex words and derivations are minimal prosodic words. A compound, such as *hus-båt* (house-boat) 'house boat' and certain derivations, for example *tvätt-bar* (wash-BAR) 'washable', have two stresses, primary stress on the first constituent, and secondary stress on the second constituent, which means that they consist of two minimal prosodic words [ˈhʉːsˌboːt] and [ˈtvetˌbaːr]. Compounds and other prosodic words with two stresses are classified as maximal prosodic words. These are discussed in §3.2.

Following Selkirk 1996, there is no one-to-one correspondence between prosodic and morphosyntactic words. For instance, the PP *med bil* 'with car', as in *Vi åkte med bil* 'We went by car', is pronounced as a minimal prosodic word: [məˈbiːl], and the unit has the same prosodic contour as e.g. the morphosyntactic word *banan* 'banana': [baˈnɑːn]. In a similar way, weak object pronouns may incorporate into prosodic words. Riad (2013: 131) exemplifies this with the verb *gav* 'gave' [ˈgɑːv], followed by the object pronoun *henne* 'her' (pronounced [ˈhənə] in isolation), which may form a minimal prosodic word, [ˈgɑːvənə] 'gave her'. The loss of /h/ in this position indicates that the first syllable of *henne* is neither stressed, nor initial in a prosodic word. (/h/ only occurs initially in minimal prosodic words in Swedish.) Furthermore, the syllabification is *ga.ve.ne* (rather than *gav.e.ne*), which indicates a single syllabification domain, i.e. a single minimal prosodic word.

As we have seen, Riad discusses examples of verb + weak object pronouns. However, if we include weak subject pronouns in the discussion, we conclude that the formation of prosodic words does not depend on syntactic constituency. The sequence *jag såg* 'I saw' [jaˈsoː] in *jag såg hönor* 'I saw chickens' forms one prosodic word, distinct from the object *hönor* 'chickens' [ˈhøːnər], which is a prosodic word by itself: [jaˈsoːˈhøːnər] – it is possible to make a break before *hönor*. Furthermore, it would be incorrect to leave the [h] sound out in this example, *[ˈøːnər], which is a strong indication that the object *hönor* 'chickens' is a (minimal) prosodic word of its own in this case. Further support that *hönor* 'chickens' in the example in question is a minimal prosodic word on its own is supported by the fact that it has Accent 2, as opposed to *jag såg* 'I saw', which has Accent 1. Assuming that verb + object form a syntactic constituent, the subject + verb example shows that a prosodic word can consist of units that are not syntactic.

What will be important in the following is the assumption that weak object pronouns are pronouns that have to incorporate into a prosodic word.

3.2 Tonal accent and tonal units in Mainland Scandinavian

In addition to stress, most Swedish and Norwegian dialects, as well as some Southern Danish dialects, distinguish two tonal accents: Accent 1 and Accent 2. These accents may differentiate word pairs with two or more syllables in these languages. The actual tone contour differs between dialects, but a typical Stockholm variant is shown below:

(3) Stockholm Swedish (from Riad 2013: 184)

					word accent	focus accent
anden	'the duck'	[$^{1\prime}$andən]	→	Accent 1	HL*	L*H
anden	'the ghost'	[$^{2\prime}$andən]	→	Accent 2	H*L	H*LH

In Standard Swedish, compounds and words derived by suffixes generally have Accent 2:

(4) a. *hus-båt* (house-boat) 'houseboat' [$^{2\prime}$hʉːsˌboːt]

b. *tvätt-bar* (wash-BAR) 'washable' [$^{2\prime}$tvɛtˌbɑːr]

In those varieties of Scandinavian that have tone, tone creates a domain that is larger than that of the minimal prosodic word. Domains larger than the (minimal) prosodic word domain, but smaller than the phonological phrase have been recognized and discussed in the literature, cf. Vigário's "Prosodic Word Group", PWG, (Vigário 2010). According to Vigário, PWGs are formed by different mechanisms in different languages, and tonal accent is one of these. The type of PWG that interests us here is the one based on tonal accent, which corresponds roughly to Kristoffersen's "Accent Phrase" (Kristoffersen 2000) and Riad's "maximal prosodic word" (Riad 2013).[5] In what follows we will use the term "Tonal Unit", TU, when referring to the type of PWG that is defined by Tone. Thus, *husbåt* and *tvättbar* in (4) are both TUs.

TUs may be formed by a verb + a weak object pronoun; in such cases the tone of the verb determines the tone of the whole TU. From a prosodic point of view, the weak pronoun has the same properties as inflection. Consider the Swedish examples in (5):

(5) a. *gav* 'gave' + *henne* 'her':   [$^{1\prime}$gɑːv]$_\omega$ + [$^{2\prime}$hənə]$_\omega$ →   [$^{1\prime}$gɑːvənə]$_{TU}$

b. *gillar* 'likes' + *henne* 'her':   [$^{2\prime}$jɪlar]$_\omega$ + [$^{2\prime}$hənə]$_\omega$ →   [$^{2\prime}$jɪlarənə]$_{TU}$

c. *gav* 'gave' + *det* 'it':   [$^{1\prime}$gɑːv]$_\omega$ + [$^{1\prime}$də]$_\omega$ →   [$^{1\prime}$gɑːvdə]$_{TU}$

d. *gillar* 'likes'+ *det* 'it':   [$^{2\prime}$jɪlar]$_\omega$ + [$^{1\prime}$də]$_\omega$ →   [$^{2\prime}$jɪladə]$_{TU}$

As (5) shows, an Accent 1 verb + a weak object pronoun gives rise to an Accent 1 TU, and an Accent 2 verb + a weak object pronoun gives rise to an Accent 2 TU, regardless of the tone of the pronoun in isolation.

4 Tonal units and object shift in MSc

As should be evident by now, we assume that weak object pronouns are affixal clitics at PF which do not themselves have the status of prosodic words (see also Selkirk 1996). All instances of OS in MSc are thus instances of incorporation. The purpose of our study, however, is to explain the fact that OS is obligatory in some varieties of MSc, optional in some, and unavailable in others. As will be evident as we go along, this will be explained

---

[5]For the term maximal prosodic word, see also Myrberg & Riad (2013). Other, related terms are "Tonal Foot" (Fretheim & Nilsen 1989) and "Prosodic Word" (Bruce 1998; Hansson 2003).

by an additional means of incorporation, available in some varieties, but not in others. We will concentrate our study on Swedish and Danish.

Somewhat simplified, the general picture in the generative literature is that OS is obligatory in Danish, but optional in Swedish (Josefsson 2003; 2010). One way of explaining this difference would be to assume that adverbs are potential hosts for weak pronouns in Swedish, but not in Danish. However, allowing the adverb to provide a host in those languages or dialects in which OS is optional would be a stipulation. Therefore, there must be a different mechanism which licenses the prosodic incorporation of a pronoun into an element which does not provide a legitimate host, such as an adverb.

If we take a closer look at the data, the empirical facts become a bit more complex. For instance, Pedersen (1993) points out that there are Danish dialects where OS is optional – similar to the situation in Swedish.

Interestingly enough, the dialects where OS is optional coincide to a large extent with the presence of a tone accent distinction, as described above.[6] There is a basic overlap between the optional OS area and the tone accent area. We propose that this is not a coincidence; the presence vs. absence of tonal accent has implications for syntax. Tonal accent may, in fact, drive syntax.

Recall the idea that unstressed pronouns are clitics or clitic-like elements that have to incorporate prosodically. Consider (5), repeated here:

(5) a. *gav* 'gave' + *henne* 'her': $[^{1'}\text{gaːv}]_\omega + [^{2'}\text{hənə}]_\omega \rightarrow [^{1'}\text{gaːvənə}]_{TU}$
   b. *gillar* 'likes' + *henne* 'her': $[^{2'}\text{jɪlar}]_\omega + [^{2'}\text{hənə}]_\omega \rightarrow [^{2'}\text{jɪlarənə}]_{TU}$
   c. *gav* 'gave' + *det* 'it': $[^{1'}\text{gaːv}]_\omega + [^{1'}\text{də}]_\omega \rightarrow [^{1'}\text{gaːvdə}]_{TU}$
   d. *gillar* 'likes'+ *det* 'it': $[^{2'}\text{jɪlar}]_\omega + [^{1'}\text{də}]_\omega \rightarrow [^{2'}\text{jɪladə}]_{TU}$

The native speakers' judgement that sequences such as those in (5) form TUs are confirmed by the Praat diagrams in Figure 1 and 2, which show the sequences *köper dom* (buy.PRS them) 'buys them', where the verb has Accent 1, and *hämtar dem* (fetch.PRS them) 'fetches them'), where the verb has Accent 2.

We suggest that weak pronouns may incorporate in the unit created by the TU, also when the preceding element is an adverb. For example, in (1b) *Jag mötte inte honom* (I met him not) 'I didn't meet him', the weak pronoun *honom* 'him' is incorporated in the same TU as the preceding adverb *inte* 'not'. Crucially, this does not mean that the adverb is the host for the pronoun; it is the tonal accent which allows the formation of this prosodic unit. The possibility of incorporating weak object pronouns into a TU is possible only in those varieties of MSc that have TUs, that is those varieties that have tonal accent.

If our proposal is correct, we predict that the sequence adverb + a weak object pronoun displays a tone contour, specified as Accent 1 or Accent 2. More specifically, we predict that an Accent 1 adverb + weak object pronoun will have an Accent 1 contour, and an Accent 2 adverb + weak object pronoun an Accent 2 contour. To a native speaker's ear, this seems indeed to be the case in Swedish. For example *inte honom* (see 1b) has Accent

---

[6]For a map showing the Danish dialects with a tonal accent distinction, see http://dialekt.ku.dk/dialektkort/ kort 3 'map 3'.

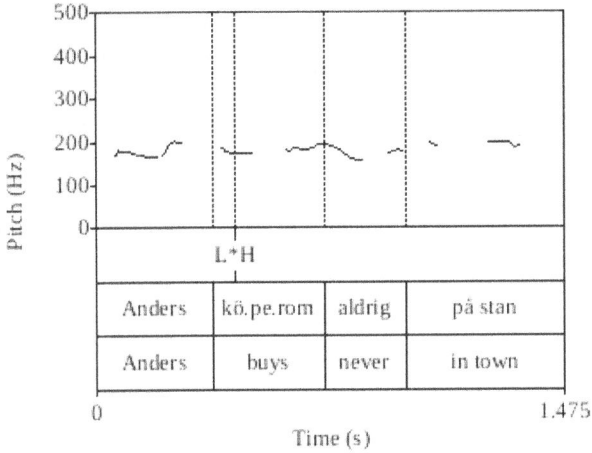

Figure 1: Swedish TU formation, Accent 1 verb *köper* (buy.PRS) + *dom* (them) 'buys them'.

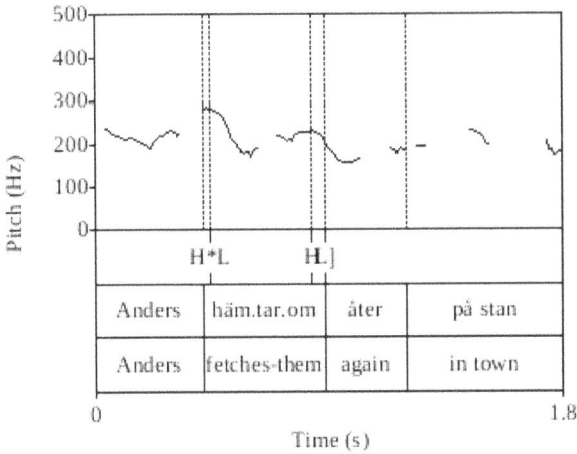

Figure 2: Swedish TU formation, Accent 2 verb *hämtar* (fetch.PRS) + *dem* 'fetches them'

2, whereas *faktiskt honom* Accent 1. (The adverb *faktiskt* 'in fact' has Accent 1, and the adverb *inte* Accent 2.)

The Praat diagrams show adverb + weak pronoun sequences. Recall that the prosodic structure of Accent 1 in Swedish is L*H (L%) (see (3) above). This is also what we find for the sequence *åter dom* 'again them' in Figure 3.

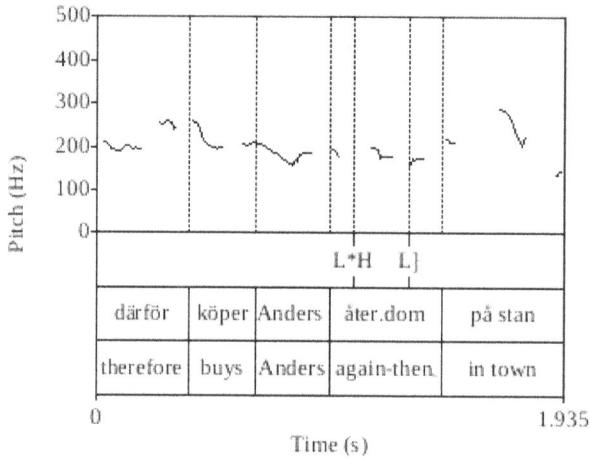

Figure 3: Swedish TU formation, Accent 1 adverb + pronoun → Accent 1

The prosodic structure of Accent 2 in Swedish is H*LH (L%) (see (3b) above). This is also what we find for the sequence *aldrig dom* 'never them' in Figure 4.

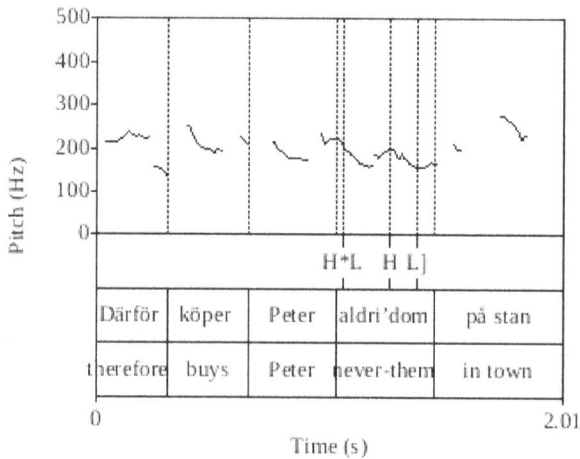

Figure 4: Swedish TU formation, Accent 2 adverb + pronoun → Accent 2

As we can see, the sequences *åter dem* and *aldrig dem* make up one TU. The tone, Accent 1 or Accent 2, is determined by the tone of the adverb. This supports our claim that weak object pronouns may form TUs with adverbs.

Ærø Danish instantiates another dialect with both tonal distinctions and optional OS and therefore provides a strong case in favor of the current proposal. As pointed out above, tonal distinctions are limited to certain south Danish dialects which vary greatly in the way the tones are instantiated. The prediction concerning the particular tone to be found on the sequence of adverb(s) + pronoun(s) is again that the tone of the unit depends on the tone of the first element.

In the Ærø dialect Accent 1 rises until the stressed syllable and then descends, whereas Accent 2 has an initial descending tone followed by a rise at the end of the word. The descending tone is more pronounced in Accent 1 and the rising tone is more pronounced in Accent 2.[7] This is shown in Figures 5 and 6.

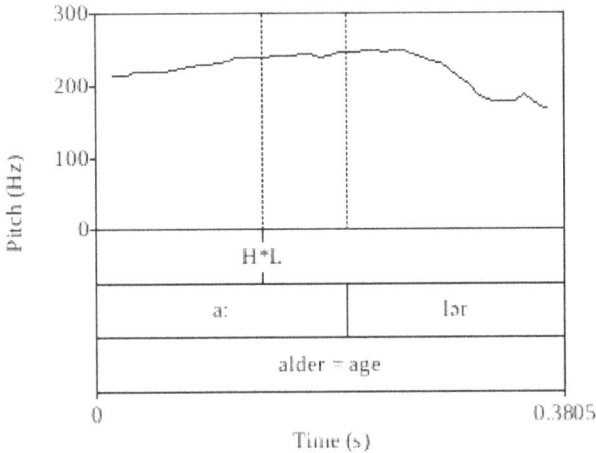

Figure 5: The Ærø dialect, Accent 1 *alder* 'age', pronounced [1]aller.

Figure 7 shows the sequence *så henne* 'saw her', which has the same prosodic contour as the Accent 1 *alder* 'age' in Figure 5.

Figure 8 shows the sequence *henter dem*, with the Accent 2 verb *henter* (fetch.PRS) 'fetches' + the pronoun *dem* 'them'. The sequence *henter dem* 'fetches them' has the same prosodic contour as the Accent 2 *aldrig* 'never' in Figure 5.

Let us now consider the sequence adverb + pronoun, in other words cases of non-shift in the Ærø dialect. The prediction is that the result will be the same as in the corresponding sentences in Swedish, namely that adverb + weak pronoun will form a TU. Consider first the sequence *lige* 'just' + *dem* 'them'. The adverb *lige* 'just' is an Accent 1 adverb (see Figure 9).

---

[7]See Kroman 1947 for an extensive description of tonal accents in this dialect.

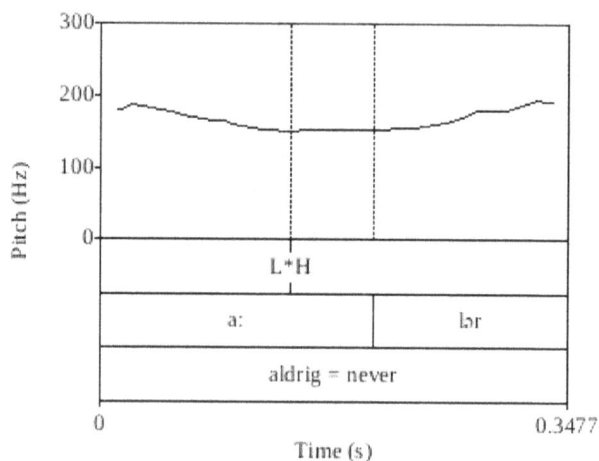

Figure 6: The Ærø dialect, Accent 2 *aldrig* 'never', pronounced [2]aller.

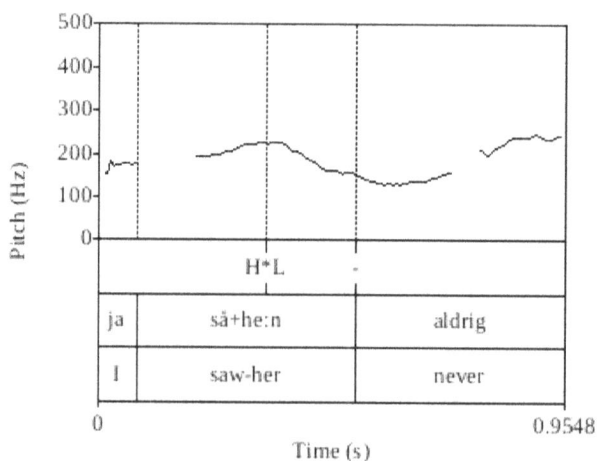

Figure 7: The Ærø dialect, Accent 1 verb + pronoun → Accent 1 TU

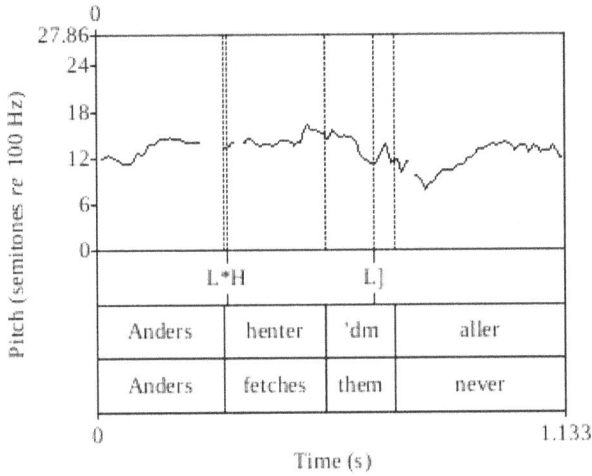

Figure 8: The Ærø dialect, Accent 2 verb + pronoun → Accent 2 TU

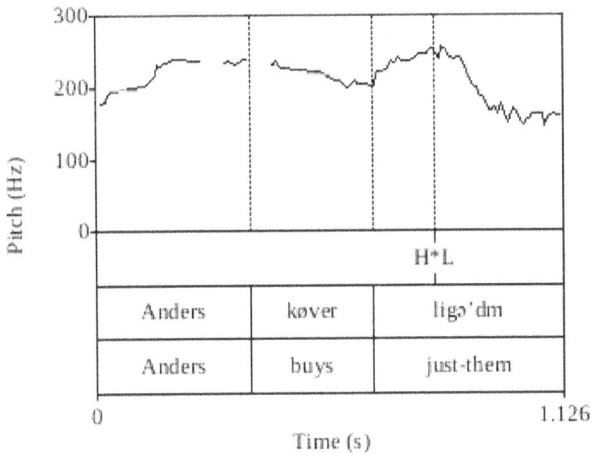

Figure 9: The Ærø dialect, Accent 1 adverb + pronoun → Accent 1 TU

We also predict that an Accent 2 adverb + pronoun will give rise to an Accent 2 TU (see Figure 10).

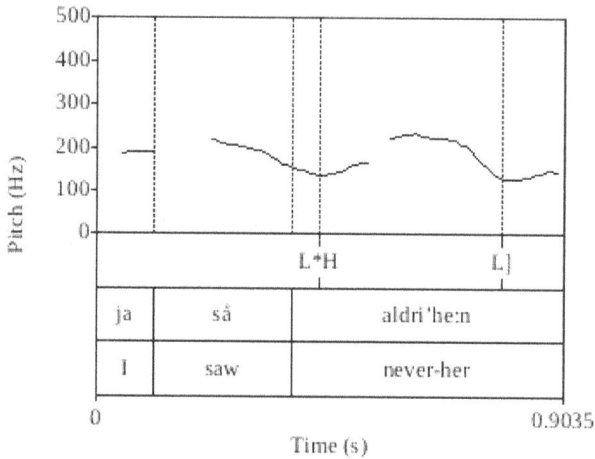

Figure 10: The Ærø dialect, Accent 2 adverb *aldrig* 'never' + pronoun → Accent 2 TU

As we have seen, the prediction is supported: the sequence adverb + weak pronoun forms a TU, in the same way as in Swedish.

As an experiment, three Ærø informants were asked to repeat sentences where the object pronoun had undergone OS. All three informants reversed most of the test sentences with OS and rendered them with the object following the adverb. This was consistently the case with the adverb 'not' (*ikke* in standard Danish, *it* in the Ærø dialect) but not with the longer adverbs, e.g. *aldrig* 'never'. As will be shown below for Falster-Danish, monosyllabic adverbs, or cases in which adverbs become monosyllabic due to apocope, must cliticize in certain dialects rendering the order V-Adverb-pronoun. This is preferred in Ærø-Danish, but not required.

5 Potential counterexamples: Norwegian Vesttrødersk, Danish Lolland-Falster and Fenno-Swedish

The Lolland-Falster dialect has been claimed to have optional Object Shift, i.e., to allow the order adverb + weak pronoun even though tonal distinctions are absent from these dialects. Fenno-Swedish poses another problem: OS has been claimed to be absent in this dialect – even though there is no tonal accent distinction.

Our prosodic analysis of object-shifted and non-object-shifted sentences in Swedish and Ærøese shows that the weak pronouns in both orders are tonally incorporated into their hosts. We argue that the formation of a TU consisting of adverb + pronoun requires a tonal accent but that the existence of tonal accent does not necessarily force optional OS. This is attested in Norwegian. In Vesttrødersk (=Nordmørsk), for example, Object Shift is strongly preferred. In the dialect of Trødersk spoken in most parts of Trønde-lag (e.g., Trondheim), however, negation undergoes apocope (*ikkje* → *itj*) resulting in a monosyllabic clitic. In this dialect and with this adverb, pronouncing the pronoun in situ is strongly preferred. If we assume that the word order *såg itj'n* (saw=not=it) 'didn't see it' is due to the clitic nature of the negative adverb, we have an explanation of the difference between these two dialects and the limitation of the phenomenon to the clitic adverb. We recorded both these dialects and verified these facts.

This phenomenon in Norwegian gave us the inspiration for an explanation of the seem-ing exceptional properties of Lolland-Falster Danish. As it turns out one of the properties of the Lolland-Falster dialect is that it has apocope and that negation is monosyllabic. In order to verify that this is what is going on, recordings were made of two speakers of the Falster dialect in April 2015. (It should be noted that speakers of the dialect are no longer easy to find and can be found only among the older generation). It turned out that our hypothesis was correct: both speakers had obligatory Object Shift, as in standard Danish, for all adverbs except for the clitic adverbs *ik* 'not' and *jo* 'as presumed'. The recordings clearly show clitic clusters for these adverbs as illustrated in Figure 11. Note that the weak element is an adverb, *her* 'here'. However, the weak adverbs *der* 'there' and *her* 'here' undergo OS in Danish.

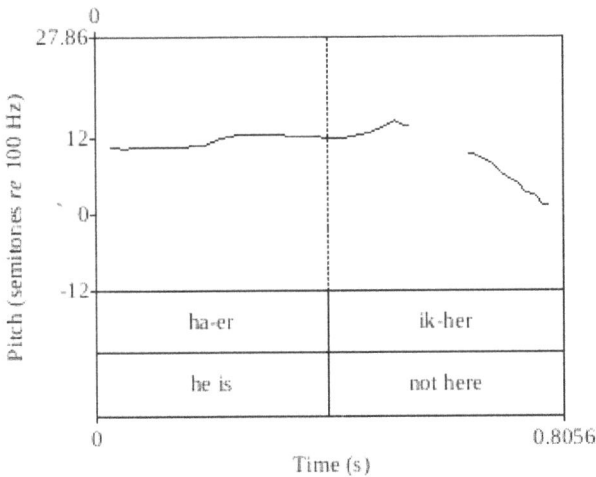

Figure 11: The Lolland-Falster dialect, the negation *ik* + *her* 'here'

Interestingly the following example was produced spontaneously:

(6) Jeg kender+jo+ik+(h)am.
     I   know=JO=NEG=him
     'I don't know him.'

We were happy to conclude that this Danish dialect does not, in fact, provide a problem for our thesis. Falster Danish has obligatory Object Shift, as we predict for a dialect without tonal distinctions. The cases of in-situ weak pronouns are limited to clitic adverbs, which cliticize into the verbs, themselves forming a clitic-cluster with the following weak adverbs. We were surprised to discover that Pedersen's (1993) claim that OS is optional in the Lolland-Falster dialect was in fact limited to the negative adverb.

Fenno-Swedish presents a different problem since OS is not available (Bergroth 1917: 72). Fenno-Swedish differs significantly from Standard Swedish in not having tonal distinctions, contra our prediction. Kiparsky (2008: 17) includes pronouns in his list of function words with short stressed syllables in Helsinki Swedish. This indicates that pronouns in this dialect are not prosodically weak. If this is indeed the case, our prediction does not apply to Fenno-Swedish since this dialect would not require incorporation of weak pronouns into the adverb, and it is only such incorporation which requires the formation of a TU. The lack of tonal distinctions in Fenno-Swedish would then no longer be a problem. In May 2015, three speakers of Fenno-Swedish from Helsinki were recorded and the findings were that the given pronouns were not reduced and definitely not incorporated in the preceding adverbs.

More investigation is needed, of course, but initial data indicates that neither Falster Danish nor Fenno-Swedish contradict our accent-based analysis of the optionality of OS.

6 Architectural implications

In previous work we have each independently examined the phonological properties of OS. Here we focus on the optionality of Object Shift and show that leaving the weak pronoun in situ is licensed by tonal accent, further strengthening our argument for the claim that OS is determined by PF. Leaving OS in MSc to phonology allows for at least some cases of word order to be determined in the phonology. Since the full range of properties of OS has not to-date been given a satisfactory syntactic account, this is a good result and falls nicely within the proposal in Berwick & Chomsky (2011), that displacement is constrained by the syntactic computational system, and the PF externalization system is responsible for at least microvariation. One implementation of this approach would have OS operate in the computational system and have PF act as a filter on its output. The only "advantage" of this approach is to exclude movement from PF in the case of OS. Another would be to have the position of the object fully determined by phonological processes and constraints. This implementation raises questions concerning what reordering in phonology would look like, and what other word order phenomena belong at PF.

7 Summary

We have come a long way in verifying our initial hypothesis concerning the connection between word order and prosody. In particular, we have found that the order adverb + weak pronoun forms a Tonal Unit licensed by a single unifying accent which is not limited to syntactic constituents.

The three seeming exceptions to this generalization, Vesttrødersk Norwegian, Lolland-Falster Danish, and Fenno-Swedish have been shown to receive explanations following from the particular prosodic properties of each of these dialects: apocope in the former two, and the lack of reduction of weak pronouns in the latter.

In addition to explaining the variation in Object Shift in the various dialects we also provide a deeper understanding of the prosodic properties of the dialects in question as well as furthering the understanding of the prosody/word-order interface in general.

Acknowledgements

First and foremost we want to thank Anders Holmberg for having inspired us to write this paper, and also for being inspirational over the years – in many different areas of linguistics. Anders' greatness stems from a mind open to new ideas, curiosity and an eye for small details as well as broad generalizations. Thank you, Anders!

The research for this work was funded by the Israel Science Foundation Grant No. 302/13. We are indebted to Björn Koenlein for valuable assistance in the interpretation of the prosodic data. We would also like to thank an anonymous reviewer for valuable comments. Earlier versions of this paper have been presented at Hebrew University, Jerusalem; Tel Aviv University; the 25th Scandinavian Conference of Linguistics, Reykjavik, May 2013; and at the Grammar seminar, Centre of Languages and Literature, Lund University, March 2014. We would like to thank the participants at those occasions for valuable input. All remaining errors and inadequacies are our own.

References

Bergroth, Hugo. 1917. *Finlandssvenska: Handledning till Undvikande av Provinsialismer i Tal och Skrift.* Helsingfors: Holger Schildts Förlag.

Berwick, Robert & Noam Chomsky. 2011. The biolinguistic program: The current state of its evolution and development. In Anna Maria Di Sciullo & Cedric Boeckx (eds.), *The biolinguistic enterprise: New perspectives on the evolution and nature of the human language faculty,* 19–41. Oxford: Oxford University Press.

Bobaljik, Jonathan David & Dianne Jonas. 1996. Subject positions and the roles of TP. *Linguistic Inquiry* 27. 195–236.

Bruce, Gösta. 1998. *Allmän och svensk prosodi* (Praktisk Lingvistik 16). Lund: Lund University.

Déprez, Viviane. 1994. Parameters of object movement. In Norbert Corver & Henk van Riemsdijk (eds.), *Studies on scrambling: Movement and non-movement approaches to free word-order phenomena,* 101–152. Berlin: Mouton de Gruyter.

Diesing, Molly. 1996. Semantic variables and object shift. In Höskuldur Thráinsson, Samuel David Epstein & Steve Peter (eds.), *Studies in comparative Germanic syntax,* vol. II, 66–84. Dordrecht: Kluwer.

Diesing, Molly. 1997. Yiddish VP order and the typology of object movement in Germanic. *Natural Language & Linguistic Theory* 15. 369–427.

Erteschik-Shir, Nomi. 2005a. Sound patterns of syntax: Object shift. *Theoretical Linguistics* 31. 47–93.

Erteschik-Shir, Nomi. 2005b. What is syntax? *Theoretical Linguistics* 31. 263–274.

Fretheim, Thorstein & Randi Alice Nilsen. 1989. Terminal rise and rise-fall tunes in East Norwegian intonation. *Nordic Journal of Linguistics* 12. 155–182.

Hansson, Petra. 2003. *Prosodic phrasing in spontaneous Swedish* (Travaux de l'Institute de Linguistique de Lund 43). Lund: Gleerup.

Hellan, Lars. 1994. A note on clitics in Norwegian. In Henk van Riemsdijk & Lars Hellan (eds.), *Clitics: Their origin status and position.* Tilburg: ESF-EUROTYP.

Hellan, Lars. 2005. Comments on Erteschik-Shir's article. *Theoretical Linguistics* 31. 137–145.

Holmberg, Anders. 1986. *Word order and syntactic features in the Scandinavian languages and English.* Stockholm: Stockholm University dissertation.

Holmberg, Anders. 1991. The distribution of Scandinavian weak pronouns. In Henk van Riemsdijk & Luigi Rizzi (eds.), *Clitics and their hosts,* 155–173. Tilburg: Tilburg University.

Holmberg, Anders. 1999. Remarks on Holmberg's Generalization. *Studia Linguistica* 53(1). 1–39.

Hosono, Mayumi. 2010. Scandinavian object shift as the cause of downstep. *Working Papers in Scandinavian Syntax* 85. 1–36.

Hosono, Mayumi. 2013. *Object shift in the Scandinavian languages: Syntax, information structure, and intonation.* Netherlands Graduate School of Linguistics dissertation.

Josefsson, Gunlög. 1992. Object shift and weak pronominals in Swedish. *Working Papers in Scandinavian Syntax* 49. 59–94.

Josefsson, Gunlög. 1993. Scandinavian pronouns and object shift. *Working Papers in Scandinavian Syntax* 52. 1–28.

Josefsson, Gunlög. 1994. Scandinavian pronouns and object shift. In Henk C. van Riemsdijk & Lars Hellan (eds.), *Clitics: Their origin, status and position,* 91–122. Tilburg: ESF-EUROTYP.

Josefsson, Gunlög. 2003. Four myths about object shift in Swedish – and the truth. In Lars-Olof Delsing, Cecilia Falk, Gunlög Josefsson & Halldór Á. Sigurðsson (eds.), *Grammar in focus vol. II. Festschrift for Christer Platzack, 18 Nov. 2003,* 199–208. Lund: Department of Scandinavian Languages, Lund University.

Josefsson, Gunlög. 2010. Object shift and optionality: An intricate interplay between syntax, prosody and information structure. *Working Papers in Scandinavian Syntax* 86. 1–24.

Josefsson, Gunlög. 2012. *Deconstructing object shift.* Ms., Scandinavian languages, Centre for Languages and Literature. Lund University.

Kiparsky, Paul. 2008. Fenno-Swedish quantity: Contrast in Stratal OT. In Andrew Nevins & Bert Vaux (eds.), *Rules, constraints, and phonological phenomena,* 185–219. Oxford: Oxford University Press.

Kristoffersen, Gjert. 2000. *The phonology of Norwegian*. Oxford: Oxford University Press.

Kroman, Erik. 1947. *Musikalsk akcent i dansk*. Copenhagen: Einar Munksgård.

Myrberg, Sara & Tomas Riad. 2013. The prosodic word in Swedish. In Eva Liina Asu & Partel Lippus (eds.), *Nordic prosody. Proceedings of the XIth conference, Tartu, 2012*, 255–264. Frankfurt am Main: Peter Lang.

Pedersen, Karen Margrethe. 1993. Lethedreglen og lighedsreglen, novation, ekspansion og resistens. In Karen Margrethe Pedersen & Inge Lise Pedersen (eds.), *Jyske studier, institut for dansk dialektforsknings publikationer*, 199–218. København: C. A. Reitzels Forlag.

Platzack, Christer. 1996. Germanic verb second languages – Attract vs. Repel: On optionality, A-bar movement and the symmetrical/asymmetrical Verb Second hypothesis. In Ewald Lang & Gisela Zifonun (eds.), *Deutsch — typologisch*, 92–120. Berlin: Walter de Gruyter.

Riad, Tomas. 2013. *The phonology of Swedish*. Oxford: Oxford University Press.

Selkirk, Elisabeth. 1996. The prosodic structure of function words. In James L. Morgan & Katherine Demuth (eds.), *Signal to syntax: Bootstrapping from speech to grammar in early acquisition*, 187–213. Mahwah, NJ: Lawrence Erlbaum Associates.

Vigário, Marina. 2010. Prosodic structure between the prosodic word and the phonological phrase: Recursive nodes or an independent domain? *The Linguistic Review* 27.

Chapter 6

Mainland Scandinavian object shift and the puzzling ergative pattern in Aleut

Ellen Woolford

University of Massachussetts

Eskimo-Aleut languages turn out to have the same two types of object shift that Holmberg (1986) describes for Scandinavian. Specific objects move out of the VP in Inuit (Bittner & Hale 1996) and I argue that object shift also occurs in Aleut, but it is limited to pronouns as in Mainland Scandinavian. Aleut differs from Mainland Scandinavian in that, for independent reasons, only third pronouns successfully undergo object shift. Shifting first and second person pronouns is blocked by PCC-like constraints on the portmanteau agreement that occurs in object shift constructions. Shifting reflexives is also blocked, because it would incur a violation of the Anaphor Agreement Effect. The surface pattern in Aleut has been described as one where ergative case marks the subject only when another argument in the clause is null. I argue that there is no direct cause and effect relationship between these. The key is the fact that pronouns that agree are not spelled out. Agreement correlates with ergative case because, as in Inuit, ergative case marks the subject in Aleut only when the object moves out of the VP, and in this situation, again as in Inuit, there is portmanteau agreement with the ergative subject and nominative object in object shift constructions. Like Inuit, Aleut has possessor raising/stranding so that the possessor of an object can undergo object shift, trigger agreement, and thus pro drop. From the English translations of Aleut sentences, it initially appears that null objects of prepositions also correlate with ergative subjects, but Aleut, like Inuit, has possessed relational nouns which function like prepositions if they take locative case. These also allow possessor raising and object shift, with the same consequences described above.

1 Introduction

Holmberg (1986) establishes that Scandinavian languages divide into two types with respect to the kind of objects that undergo object shift (movement of an object out of the VP to a position below the subject): In Mainland Scandinavian languages such as Swedish, only pronouns undergo object shift, as in (1), while Icelandic allows all specific objects to undergo object shift, as in (2)[1]:

---

[1]The verb moves out of the VP to 'second position'. Objects that precede the negative have undergone object shift.

Ellen Woolford. 2017. Mainland Scandinavian object shift and the puzzling ergative pattern in Aleut. In Laura R. Bailey & Michelle Sheehan (eds.), *Order and structure in syntax I: Word order and syntactic structure*, 117–133. Berlin: Language Science Press. DOI:10.5281/zenodo.1117744

(1) Swedish (Holmberg 1986: 242)
Johan köpte   den inte.
John bought it   not

'John did not buy it.'

(2) Swedish (Holmberg 1986: 242)
*Johan köpte boken   inte.
John   bought book.the not

'John did not buy the book.'

(3) Icelandic (Holmberg 1986: 2)
Jón keypti bókina ekki.
John bought book.the not

'John did not buy the book.'

The goal of this paper is to show that the Eskimo-Aleut languages divide into the same two types. Inuit parallels Icelandic in that specific objects undergo object shift (Bittner & Hale 1996).[2] In this paper I argue that, despite its obfuscating surface complexity, Aleut is like the Mainland Scandinavian languages in that only pronouns undergo object shift.

There are some additional consequences of object shift in the Eskimo-Aleut languages which are not present in the Scandinavian languages. In clauses with object shift in the Eskimo-Aleut languages, the case pattern is ergative-nominative, and the agreement is portmanteau, reflecting features of both the ergative subject and the nominative object.[3] The two types of object shift produce two slightly different surface case and agreement patterns in Inuit versus Aleut. In Inuit, the subject is ergative and the agreement is portmanteau when the object is specific, because specific objects undergo object shift in Inuit. In contrast, in Aleut, the subject is ergative and the agreement is portmanteau only if the object is a pronoun, because only pronouns undergo object shift in Aleut.

Additional complications in Aleut (to be discussed below) produce a surface ergative pattern which initially seems entirely unlike that of other ergative languages, even that of the related language Inuit. The Aleut pattern has been described as marking the subject with ergative case if and only if there is a null argument elsewhere in the clause

---

(i) a. Structure without object shift: [subject V$_i$ neg [$_{VP}$ t$_i$ object]]

b. Structure with object shift: [subject V$_i$ object$_j$ neg [$_{VP}$ t$_i$ t$_j$]]

[2] Although object shift is typically associated with Scandinavian languages, it is known to occur in other languages, such as Turkish (Diesing 1996) and Hindi (Bhatt & Anagnostopoulou 1996). See Thráinsson (2001) for an overview of object shift. Bittner & Hale (1996) show that specific objects move out of the VP in Inuit/West Greenlandic; although they do not label this movement as object shift, it nevertheless fits the definition of object shift as movement of an object out of the VP to a position below the subject.

[3] Exactly why object shift alters the case pattern in Eskimo-Aleut languages is controversial. Bittner & Hale (1996), working within dependency case theory, claim that shifting the object brings it close enough to the subject to allow it to serve as a case competitor. Woolford (2015) suggests that object shift creates a defective intervention effect that can be avoided by a 'last resort' use of ergative case on the subject.

(Bergsland 1997; Boyle 2000; Sadock 2000; 2009). This surprising correlation between ergative case and null arguments has been referred to as the Aleut Effect:

(4) *Description of The Aleut Ergative Pattern (the Aleut Effect)*:
    In Aleut, the subject gets ergative case if and only if there is a null NP elsewhere in the clause.

This description of the Aleut pattern contrasts sharply with the ergative pattern in Inuit, following Bittner & Hale (1996):

(5) *The Inuit Ergative Pattern*:
    In Inuit Greenlandic, the subject is marked with ergative case if and only if the object moves out of the VP, and only specific objects move out of the VP.

Despite this apparent dissimilarity, Hale (1997) nevertheless suggests that the analysis of Inuit in Bittner & Hale (1996) can be extended to Aleut.[4] Hale sketches an analysis wherein only null pronouns move out of the VP in Aleut.[5] Sadock (2000) and Boyle (2000) point out that Hale's account of Aleut suffers from various technical problems, and does not account for all of the Aleut data. While Hale's proposal to extend Bittner and Hale's account of Inuit to Aleut is incomplete, and handicapped by some now outmoded assumptions of the framework of Chomsky (1995), I argue that his basic idea is correct: object shift is the key to understanding the case patterns of both Inuit and Aleut. I show that the differences between these two languages stem from the difference in what type of objects undergo object shift; specific objects object shift in Inuit but only pronouns undergo object shift in Aleut, a difference that parallels the two types of object shift that Holmberg (1986) shows occurs in Scandinavian languages.

With the benefit of improvements in syntactic theory since Hale's 1997 paper, particularly in the area of case and agreement, and with the benefit of excellent subsequent work on other Native American languages, I am able to present an account of the complex Aleut pattern which preserves Hale's basic idea: subjects get ergative case only when the object moves out of the VP in both Inuit and Aleut, however the two languages differ in what kind of objects move out of the VP. Nevertheless, I argue that Hale's proposal has one important factor backwards: Hale postulates that pronouns undergo object shift only if they are null in Aleut.[6] In contrast, I argue that cause and effect goes in the other

---

[4]Fortescue (1985: 6) also recognizes the parallel between Aleut and other Eskimo languages with respect to constructions with and without an ergative subject and agreement with both the subject and the object.

[5]Hale (1997) proposes that only null objects move out of the VP in Aleut, and assuming that case drives movement, following Chomsky (1995), he postulates that null pronouns in Aleut lack case and must therefore move to get case. Boyle (2000) shares this assumption that only null pronouns that move out of the VP, although his motivation for the movement is different: a need for null pronouns to be licensed by moving to Spec TP. Merchant (2011) suggests the movement of null pronouns in Aleut is like clitic movement in other languages.

[6]To limit object shift to null pronouns, Hale (1997) claims that overt pronouns get case in situ, but null pronouns have to move to get case. Aside from the problem of why this would be so, case no longer drives movement in more recent versions of theory (e.g. Chomsky 1995; 2000). Moreover, under the assumption that the decision as to which pronouns will and will not be pronounced (spelled out) is not made until PF, there is no distinction between overt and null pronouns in syntax.

direction: pronouns are null only if they undergo object shift, because only shifted pronouns are in a position to trigger agreement, and only agreeing pronouns can be pro dropped (not spelled out/pronounced at PF), in both Aleut and Inuit.

A complication in Aleut is that object shifting some kinds of pronouns is blocked because it would cause the derivation to crash. Object shifting first and second person pronouns out of the VP is blocked by PCC-like effects on the resulting portmanteau agreement (with the ergative subject and nominative object), similar to what we see in dative-nominative constructions in Icelandic with first and second person objects (Sigurðsson 1996).[7] Thus first and second person object do not undergo object shift in Aleut, and thus they do not agree. Because they do not agree, they cannot be pro dropped (null). Thus first and second person object pronouns are overt and in situ in Aleut. Object shift of reflexives is also blocked, due to the Anaphor Agreement Effect (Rizzi 1990; Woolford 1999).[8]

The proposed analysis of Aleut does not posit anything new. The complex Aleut pattern results from the interaction of nine known syntactic and morphological properties, each of which is independently motivated in other languages. Almost all of these properties have been documented in Inuit and/or other Native American languages such as Nez Perce and Navajo:[9]

(6) *Nine Independently Motivated Properties of Aleut*:
1. Mainland Scandinavian type object shift (pronouns only)
2. Possessor raising, as in Inuit (Bittner 1994: 71) and Nez Perce (Deal 2010).
3. Possessed positional nouns/nominal stems in Aleut which have the function of postpositions (Fortescue 1985; Bergsland 1997)
4. Ergative subject only in object shift constructions (as in Inuit and Nez Perce)[10]
5. Portmanteau agreement with subject and object in object shift constructions (as in Inuit)
6. Object shift of reflexives is blocked in Aleut, as in Inuit (Bittner 1994: 82) and Nez Perce (Deal 2010), which is an instances of the Anaphor Agreement Effect (Rizzi 1990; Woolford 1999)
7. Object shift of first and second person objects is blocked because the resulting portmanteau agreement from probing both the ergative subject and the nominative object would incur a PCC-type violation (cf. Icelandic dative subject constructions (Sigurðsson 1996))

---

[7]PCC stands for Person Case Constraint. Bonet (1994) formulated this constraint to account for person restrictions on sequences of a dative and accusative clitic in Romance. This term has been extended to apply to person restrictions on agreement in clauses with a dative subject and a nominative object in Icelandic and other languages. See Anagnostopoulou (2005) for discussion and additional references.

[8]Reflexives are prohibited in positions construed with agreement (Rizzi 1990).

[9]This contrasts with the view expressed in Boyle 2000 that Aleut syntax is unlike that of any other language.

[10]Since Bittner & Hale (1996) established that there is a type of ergative language where ergative case is used on the subject only when the object moves out of the VP, additional languages of this type have emerged, e.g. Nez Perce and Niuean. See Woolford (2015) for a survey and discussion of this type of ergative language.

8. Pro-drop of pronouns that agree (as in Inuit (Bok-Bennema 1983; 1991))
9. Fronted topical objects, with a resumptive pronoun in situ (as in Navajo Speas 1990; Willie 1991) and as argued for Aleut by Boyle (2000))

The conclusion of this paper is that the Aleut Effect, that is, the observed surface correlation between ergative case on the subject and a null argument elsewhere in the clause in Aleut is a true correlation, but there is no direct causal relation. Both ergative subjects and null objects are independent, indirect consequences of Mainland Type Object Shift of pronouns:

- Pronouns that undergo object shift agree, and agreeing pronouns are dropped (null) in Eskimo Aleut languages, as in many languages.

- Object shift places the object in a local relation with the subject, which requires ergative case on the subject in the Eskimo-Aleut languages, as in Niuean and Nez Perce.[11]

This paper is organized as follows. The data and the proposed analysis of basic transitive clauses in Aleut, with a comparison to Inuit, is presented in §2. This section includes a discussion of clauses with a fronted topical object, clauses with a first or second person object, and clauses with a reflexive object. §3 focuses on possessor raising constructions in Aleut, where the raised possessor behaves like any object, just as in Inuit and Nez Perce. §4 turns to possessed relational/positional nouns in Aleut, which also allow possessor raising. §5 discusses some remaining questions and §6 is the conclusion.

2 Transitive clauses in Inuit and Aleut

2.1 Object shift

Object shift occurs in both Inuit and Aleut, but the two languages differ as to what kind of object undergoes object shift, paralleling the Scandinavian languages. Inuit is like Icelandic wherein specific objects undergo object shift, while non-specific objects do not. Bittner (1994) gives the following minimal pair. In the example in (7), the object is specific: there is one specific book which Juuna has not got:

(7) Inuit (Bittner 1994: 2)
Junna-p atuagaq ataasiq tigu-sima-nngi-laa.
Junaa-ERG book one get-PERF-NEG-IND.3SG.SG
'There is one book which Juuna hasn't got (yet).'

Bittner argues that the specific object has moved out of the VP, based on evidence involving the scope of negation.

(8) [Junna-ERG one book_i [_VP t_i got.neg]]

---

[11]See Woolford (2015) for a survey and discussion of this type of ergative language.

The case pattern in object shift constructions in Inuit is ergative-nominative, with portmanteau agreement resulting from the multiple agree relation created when T probes to and through the ergative subject down to the nominative object.

In contrast, in the example in (9), the object is non-specific. This object "can only take narrow scope, indicating that it remains below negation, inside the VP" (Bittner 1994: 35).

(9) Inuit (Bittner 1994: 35)
Juuna ataukka-mik ataasi-mik tigu-si-sima-nngi-la-q.
Junna book-INSTR   one-INSTR get-AP-PERF-NEG-IND-3SG

'Juuna has not got one book.'

(10)   [Junna-ERG [$_{VP}$ one book got]]

Here the subject has nominative case and the agreement is only with the subject.

Although we don't see a word order change in the above pair of examples, more ergative languages of this type have emerged in the linguistics literature, and for some there is clear word order evidence. One of these is Niuean. Massam (2010) gives the following pair of examples from Niuean where word order changes indicate whether or not object shift has occurred before the VP fronting that characterizes this verb initial language. In the example in (11), there is a specific object and object shift occurred before VP fronting. The resulting word order is VSO and the case pattern is ergative nominative:

(11)   Niuean (Massam 2010: 98)
[VSO specific object][12]
Ne inu   e   Sione e   kofe.
past drink ERG Sione NOM coffee

'Sione drank the coffee.'

(12)   a. Base order: S [$_{VP}$ V O]
        b. Order after object shift: S O$_i$ [$_{VP}$ V t$_i$]
        c. Order after VP fronting [$_{VP}$ V t] S O

In contrast, the example in (13) has a non-specific object and no object shift has occurred. The object thus fronts with the verb inside the fronted VP, so that the resulting word order is VOS:

(13)   Niuean (Massam 2010: 98)
[VOS non-specific object]
Ne inu   kofe   a   Sione.
PAST drink coffee NOM Sione

Sione drank coffee.

---

[12] In Niuean the ergative case morpheme for proper nouns, *e*, happens to look just like the nominative case morpheme for common nouns, *e*.

(14) a. Base order: S [$_{VP}$ V O]

b. Order after VP fronting: [$_{VP}$ V O] S

I argue that Aleut manifests a pattern similar to the related Inuit language, the difference being that only pronouns undergo object shift in Aleut, paralleling Mainland Scandinavian. Transitive clauses with non-pronominal arguments have an ordinary nominative-accusative case pattern in Aleut (although neither case is marked) and agreement is only with the subject:

(15) Aleut (Boyle 2000: 2 (1a) from Bergsland & Dirks 1981: 32)
Piitra-x̂   Ivaana-x̂ kidu-ku-x̂.
Peter-3SG John-3SG help-PRES-3SG
'Peter is helping John.'

Non-pronominal objects remain in situ in the VP in Aleut:

(16) [Peter(NOM) [$_{VP}$ John(ACC) V-3SG]]

In contrast, I argue that (third person) pronoun objects undergo object shift in Aleut, as in Mainland Scandinavian.[13] The case pattern in object shift constructions in Aleut is ergative-nominative, as in Inuit (Bittner 1994; Bittner & Hale 1996). The agreement is portmanteau, expressing features from both the ergative subject and the nominative object:[14]

(17) Aleut (Boyle 2000: 3 (1b) from Bergsland & Dirks 1981: 32)
Piitra-m   kidu-ku-u.
Peter-ERG help-PRES-3SG/3SG
'Peter is helping him.'

(18) [Peter-ERG pro.NOM$_i$ [$_{VP}$ t$_i$ V-3SG/3SG]]

The object pronoun is not pronounced (not spelled out at PF) because it agrees and agreeing pronouns drop in Aleut, as in Inuit. We see both subject and object pronoun drop in the following Aleut example:

---

[13] We will see below that the object shift construction is blocked with first and second person objects, as well as with reflexive objects in Aleut.

[14] The ergative case is labeled 'relative' in descriptive work on Aleut. The portmanteau agreement series is referred to as the anaphoric series, reflecting the fact that this series identifies the feature of a null object. Work on Aleut generally uses the traditional typological label 'absolutive' for the object of a clause with an ergative subject, however the term 'absolutive' was meant to be the neutral label of a typological pattern (Dixon 1994) rather than the label of an actual case. As Bittner (1994) argues for the related language Inuit/West Greenlandic, the identity of this case is nominative in Aleut. There are ergative languages that have accusative objects, e.g. Warlpiri (Legate 2006), but accusative objects do not participate in portmanteau agreement with the subject.

(19)   Aleut (Boyle 2000: 3 (5) from Bergsland & Dirks 1981: 10)
       Kidu-ku-ngis.
       help-PRES-3/3PL
       'They are helping him/her/them.'

Bok-Bennema (1983) gives the following examples with subject and object pronoun drop from Yupi'k:

(20)   Yup'ik (Bok-Bennema 1983: 1)
       Yurar-tug.
       dance-IND.3SG
       'She/he is dancing.'

(21)   Yup'ik (Bok-Bennema 1983: 2)
       Tangrr-aa.
       see-IND.3/3
       'He/she sees him/her/it.

2.2 Topical objects

Aleut allows a topical object to precede the clause, with a resumptive pronoun in situ, as in example (23):

(22)   Aleut (Boyle 2000: 3 (6a) from Bergsland 1969: 27)
       Tayaĝu-x̂ qa-x̂   qa-ku-x̂.
       man-SG   fish-SG eat-PRES-3SG.
       'The man is eating the fish.'

(23)   Aleut (Boyle 2000: 4 (6b) from Bergsland 1969: 27)
       qa-x̂   tayaĝu-m qa-ku-u.
       fish-SGᵢ man-ERG eat-PRES-3/3SG
       'The fish, the man is eating it.'

This is not movement leaving a trace, but rather a base generated topic linked to a resumptive pronoun in situ (Boyle 2000), paralleling what Willie (1991) and Speas (1990) argue for in Navajo. As with any pronoun object, this resumptive pronoun undergoes object shift, triggers agreement on the verb, and is thus not spelled out at PF (pro-dropped):

(24)   fishᵢ [man-ERG pro.NOMᵢ [VP tᵢ V-3/3]]

2.3 First and second person objects

Something different happens with first and second person objects; these do not undergo object shift, do not agree, and must thus be spelled out at PF. The case pattern is nominative-accusative, as in any transitive clause without object shift in Aleut:

(25) Aleut (Bergsland 1997: 344)
      Tayag^u-x̂   ting   kidu-ku-x^^.
      man-3SG(NOM) me(ACC) help-PRES-3SG

      'The man is helping me.'

I argue that the object shift construction is blocked/crashes with first and second person objects because the portmanteau agreement that would result violates PCC-type
constraints, similar to what has been observed in Icelandic dative subject constructions
with first and second person nominative objects, as in Sigurðsson 1996; 2004:[15]

(26) Icelandic (Sigurðsson 2004: 148)
      Honum mundu   alltaf   líka þeir.
      him.DAT would.3PL always like they.NOM

      'He would always like them.'

(27) Icelandic (Sigurðsson 2004: 148)
      *Honum munduð   alltaf   líka þið.
      him.DAT would.2PL always like you.NOM

      'He would always like you.'

Thus the only grammatical version of this construction in Aleut is the one without
object shift, as in (25), because it has a nominative-accusative case pattern and agreement
only with the subject.[16]

2.4 The pattern with reflexive objects

In both Inuit and Aleut, object shift is blocked (or the object shift construction crashes)
when the object is a reflexive. We see this for Inuit in the following pair of examples from
Bittner 1994. The Inuit example in (28) has a specific object, which undergoes object shift,
with the resulting ergative-nominative case pattern. In contrast, in the example in (29)
with a reflexive object, object shift has not occurred and the case pattern is nominative-
dative:

(28) Inuit (Bittner 1994: 82)
      Suulu(t)-p Kaali aallaa-vaa.
      Suulu-ERG Kaali shoot-IND.3SG/3SG

      'Suulut shot Kaali.'

---

[15]See Anagnostopoulou (2005) for discussion and additional references on PCC effects.

[16]In contrast to Aleut, the related language Inuit allows first and second person objects to undergo object
shift. We know that PCC-type effects are not universal, and that languages that do manifest PCC effects
vary widely in exactly which feature combinations are prohibited; however, we may be able to identify
a more specific reason why first and second person objects are allowed to undergo object shift in Inuit,
in contrast to Aleut. In addition to portmanteau agreement, Inuit has pronominal clitics which suffix to
the portmanteau agreement. When a first or second person object moves out of the VP, Inuit may avoid
some PCC-type violations by encoding only the number of the object in the portmanteau agreement, and
encoding the first or second person feature of the object in a separate pronominal clitic. See Fortescue
(1985) and Woolford (2016).

(29) Inuit (Bittner 1994: 82)
      Sullut immi-nut aallaa-vuq.
      Sullut self-DAT shoot-IND.3SG
      'Suulut shot himself.'

The object shift version of the reflexive object example is ungrammatical:

(30) Inuit (Bittner 1994: 82)
      *Suulu(t)-p immi aallaa-vaa.
      Sullut-ERG self   shoot-IND.3SG/3SG
      'Suulut shot himself.'

This is an example of the Anaphor Agreement effect (Rizzi 1990; Woolford 1999): anaphors cannot occur in positions normally associated with agreement.[17]

We see the same pattern with reflexive objects in Aleut. The following example in (31) has a pronoun subject (which is not spelled out because it agrees), and an overt reflexive object. The agreement, which is only with the subject, tells us that object shift has not occurred. Although the subject pronoun is not spelled out, because it agrees, the reflexive pronoun has to be spelled out because it does not agree:

(31) Aleut (Bergsland 1969: 139)
      Txin   achixa-ku-x̂.
      3.REFL.SG teach-PRES-3SG
      'He taught himself.'

This contrasts with the example in (32) with a pronoun object that is disjoint in reference with the subject. Here we see by the portmanteau agreement on the verb that object shift has occurred. The shifted object is dropped (not spelled out at PF) because it agrees.

(32) Aleut (Bergsland 1969: 139)
      Kidu-ku-u.
      help-PRES-3/3SG
      'He is helping him.'

3 Possessed objects

3.1 Possessor raising

Pronominal possessors of objects behave like pronominal objects in Aleut. I argue that this is due to possessor raising, paralleling Nez Perce (Deal 2013).[18] Nez Perce is like Aleut in that it has object shift resulting in an ergative subject and portmanteau agreement, and

---

[17]The Anaphor Agreement Effect appears to be universal (Woolford 1999), but why it holds is still a mystery.
[18]Bittner (1994: 71–72) shows that Inuit allows possessor raising, but only with some verbs.

it also has clearly transitive clauses without object shift where the subject is nominative and agreement is only with the subject.

(33) Nez Perce (Rude 1988: 552)
Háama   hi-'wí-ye   wewúkiye.
man(NOM) 3-shoot-ASP elk(ACC)

'The man shot an elk.'

(34) Nez Perce (Rude 1988: 552)
Háama-nm pée-'wi-ye   wewúkiye-ne.
man-ERG   3/3-shoot-ASP elk-OBJ

'The man shot an elk.'

In terms of what kind of object undergoes object shift, Nez Perce is more like Inuit and Icelandic in that non-pronominal arguments can undergo object shift. According to Rude (1982; 1986), it is the more topical objects that undergo object shift in Nez Perce, and less topical objects do not.

Nez Perce allows possessor raising, as Deal (2013) shows, and raised possessors undergo object shift; as in other object shift constructions in Nez Perce, the subject is ergative and the agreement is portmanteau and the object takes the case glossed as objective:[19]

(35) Nez Perce (Deal 2013: 398 (14) from Rude 1986: 119)
Hi-nees-hex-ne'ny-e ma-may'as-na pist.
3rd-PL.OBJ-see-μ-PAST PL-child-OBJ   father

'He saw the children's father.'

In contrast, we see an unraised possessor in the following example in (36). The first object has undergone object shift, and we see the genitive possessor in the second object:

(36) Nez Perce (Deal 2013: 400 (20a))
'Ew-'nii-se   Tatlo-na Angel-nim taaqmaał.
3OBJ-give-IMPERF Tatlo-OBJ Angel-GEN hat

'I'm giving Tatlo Angel's hat.'

In contrast to Nez Perce, Aleut only allows pronominal possessors to undergo possessor raising and object shift.[20] The pair of examples below shows the contrast between an NP possessor in (37), and a pronominal possessor in (38). In (37), there is no object shift, which is what we expect with non-pronominal objects in Aleut; thus the subject case is nominative and the agreement on the verb is only with the nominative subject:

---

[19]See Deal (2013) for a discussion of the morpheme she glosses as μ.

[20]Deal (2013) argues that object shift is directly from the possessor position, without a separate step of possessor raising in Nez Perce. This could be true of Aleut as well.

(37)   Aleut (Boyle 2000: 3 (4a) from Bergsland 1997: 144)
       Piitra-x̂   [hal-s   ada-a]   kidu-ku-x̂.
       Peter-3SG [boy-PL father-3/3] help-PRES-3SG
       'Peter is helping the boys' father.'

In contrast in (38) below the possessor of the object is a pronoun. This pronoun undergoes object shift, and we see all the usual consequences of object shift in Aleut. The subject is ergative and the shifted plural pronoun is cross-referenced in the portmanteau agreement on the verb. Because it agrees, the object shifted pronoun is not pronounced (i.e. it is pro-dropped):

(38)   Aleut (Bergsland 1997: 144)
       Piitra-m   ada-ngis   kidu-ku-ngis.
       Peter-ERG father-3/3PL help-TNS-3/3PL
       'Peter is helping their father.'

(39)   [Peter-ERG their.NOM$_i$ [[t $_i$ father] help-3/3PL]]

3.2 No object shift of coreferent possessors

Aleut parallels Nez Perce as well in constructions where the pronominal possessor of the object is coreferent with the subject. Here object shift is blocked in both languages, and Deal's account of why extends to Aleut. Deal (2013: 413) points out that Binding Condition B rules out a pronominal object being coreferent with the subject, as in the Nez Perce example in (40) where the pronominal possessor has undergone object shift (as evidenced by the ergative subject and portmanteau agreement on the verb):

(40)   Nez Perce (Deal 2013: 413 (54a))
       Pit'iin'-im paa-'yax̂-na'ny-a   'ip-ne   picpic.
       girl-ERG   3/3-find-μ-REM.PAST his/her-OBJ cat
       'The girl$_i$ found his/her$_j$ cat.' (no coreference)

If there is coreference, only the version without object shift (and without ergative case and portmanteau agreement) in (41) is grammatical:

(41)   Nez Perce (Deal 2013: 413 (54b))
       Pit'iin'   hi-'yaax̂-n-a   ['ip-nimi picpic].
       girl(NOM) 3-find-ASP-REM.PAST [her-GEN cat]
       'The girl$_i$ found her$_i$ cat.' (coreference)

If the object shifted pronoun were to be interpreted as a reflexive rather than an ordinary pronoun, coreference in (41) would also be ruled out, but for a different reason: the reflexive pronount would agree and that would be an instance of the Anaphor Agreement Effect: anaphors are barred from positions that agree. Thus the only solution is to block object shift when there is co-reference between the subject and the possessor of an object.

The same pattern is found in Aleut. When a pronoun possessor undergoes object shift, it cannot be interpreted as coreferent with the subject:

(42) Aleut (Bergsland 1997: 54)
      Hla-m   [ada-a   ] kidu-ku-u.
      boy-ERG$_i$ pro$_j$ [t$_j$ father-3/3] help-PRES-3/3
      'The boy$_i$ is helping his $_j$ father.' (no coreference)

As Deal (2013) concludes for Nez Perce, this is due to Binding Condition B which prohibits coreference between a pronoun object and a c-commanding subject in the same clause.

Coreference is only possible if the pronoun possessor does *not* undergo object shift, as in (43). We can tell that object shift has not occurred in (43) because the subject is not ergative and the verbal agreement is only with the subject.

(43) Aleut (Bergsland 1997: 54)
      Hla-x̂   [ada-an   ] kidu-ku-x̂.
      boy-SG(NOM)$_i$ [pro$_i$ father-3.REFL] help-TNS-SG
      'Peter is helping his (own) father.'

Note that the pronoun possessor is null (not spelled out) even in its base position inside the object NP in (43) because it agrees with the head noun, and agreeing pronouns are dropped (not spelled out).

4 Possessed relational nouns in Aleut

From the English translations of the following examples, one could easily get the impression that the subject is ergative in Aleut when the object of a PP is null, and as far as we know, object shift does not occur out of PPs. However, these constructions do not actually involve PPs, but rather possessed directional nouns with an oblique case suffix (Fortescue 1985, Bergsland 1997: 47). These constructions work like the possessed object constructions discussed above in §3. The version of the sentence in (44) has a non-pronominal NP possessor, which remains in situ, since only pronouns undergo object shift in Aleut. In contrast, the version of the sentence in (45) has a pronominal possessor, which does undergo object shift.

(44) Aleut (Bergsland 1997: 126)
      Piitra-x̂   tayagu-m had-a-   huya-ku-x̂.
      Peter-3SG man-GEN direction-3/3-LOC go-PRES-3SG
      'Peter is going toward the man (in the man's direction).'

(45)   Aleut (Bergsland 1997: 127)
       Piitra-m   had-a-n   huya-ku-u.
       Peter-ERG direction-3/3-LOC go-PRES-3/3SG

       'Peter is going toward him/her (in his/her direction).'

We observe the same differences in the case and agreement patterns in these examples as we do in examples (37) and (38) in §3.

5 Remaining questions

There are remaining issues concerning Aleut grammar that have not been discussed in this paper. One is the question that Sadock (2000) asks: what determines which features are expressed by the agreement morphology in different constructions in Aleut? This paper addresses only part of this question, predicting when verbal agreement in clauses can and cannot be portmanteau; verbal agreement cannot be portmanteau unless object shift has occurred. However, the question of which agreement features will be spelled out at PF is a separate issue. Sadock suggests that in some instances, the choice of what agreement features to realize at PF, especially in agreement in DPs (which have not been discussed in this paper), can depend on functional/communicative factors.

Another remaining question concerns Aleut examples where (under the analysis proposed in this paper) object shift appears to occur out of some kind of embedded/adjunct clause. Berge (2010) cites the following pair of examples from Bergsland (1997: 248). In the first example in (46), the verb 'go.to.sleep' agrees only with its subject. In contrast, in the second example in (47), the agreement is portmanteau, also encoding the 3PL features of what looks like the null subject of the adjunct/embedded clause, "When (they) stopped talking":

(46)   Aleut, Atkan dialect (Berge 2010: 10)
       Hla-s   tunum-kada-ku-z-iin   ting saĝani-na-q.
       boy-PL talk-CESS-IND-PL-ENCL 1SG go.to.sleep-part-1SG

       'When the boys stopped talking, I went to sleep.'

(47)   Aleut, Atkan dialect (Berge 2010: 10)
       Tunum-kada-ku-z-iin   ting saĝani-qa-ning.
       talk-CESS-IND-PL-ENCL 1SG go.to.sleep-part.an-1SG/3PL.an

       'When they stopped talking, I went to sleep.'

One possible clue to understanding these particular examples is that the morpheme -*iin* which Berge glosses simply as 'enclitic' is actually the 2nd/3rd plural possessive ending on nouns −*iin*, as in *adam-aziin* 'to our fathers' (Bergsland 1997: 149). This suggests the possibility that what is translated as 'when they stopped talking' might be more accurately translated as '(at) their stopping-talking'. If so, this could be another instance of possessor raising.

Merchant (personal communication) suggests the possibility of a similar analysis of Aleut examples which, from their English translations, would appear to involve movement out of a relative clause. As Merchant notes in his 2011 paper "Some Aleut relative clauses have something like the form of a possessed clause." (Merchant 2011: 397)

6 Summary and conclusions

The goal of this paper has been to show that the Eskimo-Aleut languages parallel the Scandinavian languages in manifesting two types of object shift, one where only pronouns undergo object shift, and one where all specific objects undergo object shift. Aleut is like the Mainland Scandinavian languages in allowing only pronouns to undergo object shift, while Inuit is like Icelandic in allowing all specific objects to shift.

We have seen that the consequences of object shift are much more complex in the Eskimo Aleut languages than they are in Scandinavian languages. In the Eskimo-Aleut languages, clauses with object shift have an ergative subject and portmanteau agreement, in contrast to clauses without object shift which have a nominative subject and agreement only with the subject. These consequences of object shift have also been observed in other ergative languages such as Nez Perce and Niuean. Additional factors interacting with object shift in Aleut include possessed relational nouns instead of PPs and possessor raising.

A second goal of this paper has been to show that, although the surface pattern of Aleut shows a perfect correlation between ergative case on the subject and a null object (The Aleut Effect), this correlation does not reflect causation. Instead, object shift (interacting with other factors) causes both ergative subjects and null objects in Aleut. While the surface complexity of the Aleut pattern might initially seem to warrant adding significant generative machinery to the grammar, I have shown in this paper that the Aleut Effect follows automatically from a combination of nine grammatical constructions/factors, each of which is independently motivated in other languages.

Acknowledgements

It is a privilege to have been invited to contribute to this volume dedicated to Anders Holmberg in honor of his important contributions to linguistic theory. In my case, without his contributions in the area of object shift typology, I would never have been able to solve the mystery of the puzzle known as the Aleut Effect. I would like to thank Jason Merchant and Margaret Speas and two anonymous reviewers for reading this manuscript and providing many helpful comments.

References

Anagnostopoulou, Elena. 2005. Strong and weak person restrictions: A feature checking analysis. In Lorie Heggie & Francisco Ordóñez (eds.), *Clitic and affix combinations: Theoretical perspectives*, 199–235. Amsterdam: John Benjamins.

Berge, Anna. 2010. Unexpected non-anaphoric marking in Aleut. In Jan Wohlgemuth & Michael Cysouw (eds.), *Rara and rarissima: Documenting the fringes of linguistic diversity*, 1–22. Berlin: Walter de Gruyter.

Bergsland, Knut. 1969. A problem of transformation in Aleut. *Word* 25(1–3). 24–38.

Bergsland, Knut. 1997. *Aleut grammar: Unagam tunuganaan achixaasix*. Fairbanks, Alaska: Alaska Native Language Center.

Bergsland, Knut & Moses Dirks. 1981. *Atkan Aleut school grammar*. Anchorage: National Bilingual Materials Development Center, Rural Education, University of Alaska.

Bhatt, Rajesh & Elena Anagnostopoulou. 1996. Object shift and specificity: Evidence from ko-phrases in Hindi. In Lise Dobrin, Kora Singer & Lisa McNair (eds.), *CLS 32: Papers from the main session*, 11–22. Chicago: Chicago Linguistics Society.

Bittner, Maria. 1994. *Case, scope, and binding*. Dordrecht: Kluwer.

Bittner, Maria & Ken Hale. 1996. Ergativity: Toward a theory of a heterogeneous class. *Linguistic Inquiry* 27. 531–604.

Bok-Bennema, Reineke. 1983. On pro-drop pronominal anaphors in Eskimo. *Tilburg papers in language and literature* 37. 1–22.

Bok-Bennema, Reineke. 1991. *Case and agreement in Inuit*. New York: Foris.

Bonet, Eulalia. 1994. The person-case constraint: A morphological approach. *MIT working papers in linguistics* 22. 33–52.

Boyle, John. 2000. The Aleut effect: Competition at TP. In *Proceedings of CLS*, vol. 37, 221–38. Chicago.

Chomsky, Noam. 1995. *The minimalist program*. Cambridge, Massachusetts: MIT Press.

Chomsky, Noam. 2000. Minimalist inquiries: The framework. In Roger Martin, David Michaels & Juan Uriagereka (eds.), *Step by step: Essays on minimalist syntax in honor of Howard Lasnik*, 89–155. Cambridge: MIT Press.

Deal, Amy Rose. 2010. Ergative case and the transitive subject: A view from Nez Perce. *Natural Language & Linguistic Theory* 28. 73–120.

Deal, Amy Rose. 2013. Possessor raising. *Linguistic Inquiry* 44. 391–432.

Diesing, Molly. 1996. Semantic variables and object shift. In Samuel Epstein & Höskuldur Thráinsson (eds.), *Studies in comparative Germanic syntax*, vol. 2, 66–84. Dordrecht: Kluwer.

Dixon, Robert MW. 1994. *Ergativity*. Cambridge: Cambridge University Press.

Fortescue, Michael. 1985. Anaphoric agreement in Aleut. In Alide Machtelt Bolkestein, Casper de Groot & J. Lachlan Mackenzie (eds.), *Predicates and terms in functional grammar*, 105–126. Dordrecht: Foris.

Hale, Kenneth L. 1997. The Misumalpan causative construction. In Joan Bybee, John Haiman & Sandra Thompson (eds.), *Essays on language function and language type*, 199–216. Amsterdam: John Benjamins.

Holmberg, Anders. 1986. *Word order and syntactic features in the Scandinavian languages and English*. Stockholm: Dept. of General Linguistics, University of Stockholm dissertation.

Legate, Julie Anne. 2006. Split absolutive. In Alana Johns, Diane Massam & Juvenal Ndayiragije (eds.), *Ergativity*, 143–171. Dordrecht: Springer.

Massam, Diane. 2010. V1 or V2?: On the left in Niuean. *Lingua* 120(2). 284–302.

Merchant, Jason. 2011. Aleut case matters. In Etsuyo Yuasa Yuasa, Tista Bagchi & Katherine Beals (eds.), *Pragmatics and autolexical grammar: In honor of Jerry Sadock*, vol. 176, 193. Amsterdam: John Benjamins.

Rizzi, Luigi. 1990. On the anaphor-agreement effect. *Rivista di linguistica* 2(1). 27–42.

Rude, Noel. 1982. Promotion and topicality of Nez Perce objects. In Monica Macaulay & Orin Gensler (eds.), *Proceedings of the Eighth Annual Meeting of the Berkeley Linguistics Society*, 463–483. Berkeley: University of California.

Rude, Noel. 1986. Topicality, transitivity, and the direct object in Nez Perce. *IJAL* 52. 124–153.

Rude, Noel. 1988. Ergative, passive, and antipassive in Nez Perce. In Masayoshi Shibatani (ed.), *Passive and voice*, 547–560. Amsterdam: John Benjamins.

Sadock, Jerrold M. 2000. Aleut number agreement. In *Annual meeting of the Berkeley linguistics society*, vol. 26, 121–138. Berkeley, California.

Sadock, Jerrold M. 2009. The efficacy of anaphoricity in Aleut. In Marc-Antoine Mahieu & Nicole Tersis (eds.), *Variations on polysynthesis: The Eskaleut languages* (Typological Studies in Language 86), 97–113. Amsterdam: John Benjamins.

Sigurðsson, Halldór Ármann. 1996. Icelandic finite verb agreement. *Working Papers in Scandinavian Syntax* 57. 1–46.

Sigurðsson, Halldór Ármann. 2004. Icelandic non-nominative subjects: Facts and implications. In Peri Bhaskararao & Karumuri Venkata Subbarao (eds.), *Non-nominative subjects*, vol. 2 (Typological Studies in Language 61), 137–160. Amsterdam: John Benjamins.

Speas, Margaret. 1990. *Phrase structure in natural language* (Studies in natural language and linguistic theory 21). Dordrecht: Kluwer.

Thráinsson, Höskuldur. 2001. Object shift and scrambling. In Mark Baltin & Chris Collins (eds.), *The handbook of contemporary syntactic theory*, 148–202. Oxford: Blackwell.

Willie, MaryAnn. 1991. *Navajo pronouns and obviation*. Tucson: University of Arizona dissertation.

Woolford, Ellen. 1999. More on the anaphor agreement effect. *Linguistic Inquiry* 30(2). 257–287.

Woolford, Ellen. 2015. Ergativity and transitivity. *Linguistic Inquiry* 46(3). 489–531.

Woolford, Ellen. 2016. Two types of portmanteau agreement: Syntactic and morphological. In Geraldine Legendre, Michael T. Putnam, Henrietta de Swart & Erin Zaroukian (eds.), *Optimality theoretic syntax, semantics, and pragmatics: From uni-to bidirectional optimization*, 111–135. Oxford: Oxford University Press.

Chapter 7

Repairing Final-Over-Final Condition violations: Evidence from Basque verb clusters

Ricardo Etxepare

IKER UMR 5478-CNRS

Bill Haddican

CUNY, Queens College/Graduate Center

This article discusses implications of Basque modal constructions for representational models of Final-Over-Final Condition (FOFC) effects. We argue that FOFC-violating structures at an intermediate derivational level can be repaired by subsequent movement steps. The analysis entails that FOFC-violating structures are buildable by the syntax, contra narrow syntactic approaches to FOFC, and that FOFC evaluation instead applies in the phonology after copy deletion. Such a view of FOFC helps explain several recalcitrant word order restrictions on Basque modal constructions as well as variation in the effect of focus and negation on modal placement across Basque dialects.

1 Introduction

This article discusses some implications of Basque modal constructions for recent approaches to Final-Over-Final Condition (FOFC) effects. FOFC is a generalization originally by Holmberg (2000) about the interaction between dominance relations and {head, complement} ordering cross-linguistically. In particular, following much previous typological literature, Holmberg noted that "harmonic" sequences of head-initial and head-final phrases, as in (1a,1b) are common cross-linguistically, as are "disharmonic" sequences where a head-initial phrase dominates a head-final phrase, as in (1c) (Hawkins 1983; 1995). Holmberg noted that what is much rarer – possibly unattested in relevant domains – are instances of a head-final phrase dominating a head-initial phrase, as in (1d).

Ricardo Etxepare & Bill Haddican. 2017. Repairing Final-Over-Final Condition violations: Evidence from Basque verb clusters. In Laura R. Bailey & Michelle Sheehan (eds.), *Order and structure in syntax I: Word order and syntactic structure*, 135–157. Berlin: Language Science Press. DOI:10.5281/zenodo.1117702

(1) a. Harmonic, right-branching b. Harmonic, left-branching c. Disharmonic, attested d. Disharmonic, unattested (in relevant domains)

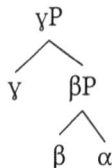

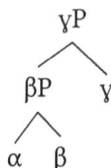

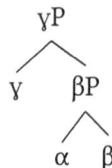

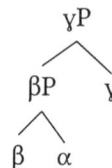

```
a.        γP              b.       γP            c.       γP          d.
        /    \                   /    \                /    \                        γP
       γ     βP                βP     γ              γ     βP                      /    \
            /  \              /  \                        /  \                   βP      γ
           β    α            α    β                      α    β                 /  \
                                                                               β    α
```

For the moment, let us summarize Holmberg's observation about the above interaction as in (2) (taken from Biberauer et al. (2014)).

(2) *The Final-over-Final condition (preliminary version)*
If β is a head-initial phrase and γ is a phrase immediately dominating β, then γ must be head-initial. If β is a head-final phrase, and γ is a phrase immediately dominating β, then γ can be head-initial or head-final.
(adapted from Biberauer et al. 2014)

Following Holmberg (2000), a now-considerable body of literature has described FOFC-effects cross-linguistically (Holmberg 2000; Biberauer et al. 2008; 2014; Sheehan 2013a,b) and diachronically (Biberauer et al. 2009; 2010). Formal approaches to FOFC effects have generally been of two types.[1] One approach, by Biberauer et al. (2014), takes FOFC effects to be a narrow syntactic phenomenon. Assuming the Linear Correspondence Axiom (LCA) (Kayne 1994), Biberauer et al. (2014) take effects such as (1) to reflect restrictions on roll-up movement, which follow, in turn, from minimality effects on the spreading of features which drive such movement. A second approach by Sheehan (2013a; 2013b; 2017) takes FOFC effects to be phonological in nature. On this approach, structures such as (1d) are bad because they cannot be linearized by the LCA (in Sheehan's modified form) at PF.

The two approaches crucially make different predictions about the possibility of derivational repair. The PF approach, but not the narrow syntax approach, predicts the possibility of a derivation where a FOFC-violating structure is built by the syntax, but repaired in some way before linearization – for instance by copy deletion of FOFC-violating structure. In contrast, the narrow syntax approach holds that FOFC-violating structures are never buildable by the syntax, and therefore predicts that the syntax should never have occasion to repair a FOFC-violating structure. The goal of this chapter is to describe a set of modal constructions in Basque where copy deletion appears to bleed FOFC. Assuming that copy deletion applies in the phonology, our evidence that FOFC evaluation follows copy deletion is therefore in keeping with a PF approach to FOFC effects in these

---

[1]We do not consider consider here Hawkins' (to appear) processing based approach to FOFC. See Sheehan (2017) for discussion.

dialects and not with a narrow syntactic approach. We do not take a position on how FOFC effects might be derived at PF.

The discussion is organized as follows. In §2, we introduce FOFC and describe PF vs. narrow syntactic approaches to this phenomenon. §3 reviews a set of facts described by Etxepare & Uribe-Etxebarria (2009) about the interaction between word order and structural complexity of modal complements in Basque modal constructions. In §4, we spell out the nature of the FOFC violation and FOFC repair involved in such constructions.

2 The Final-Over-Final Condition

2.1 Word order (dis)-harmony in mixed-head languages

We begin by illustrating FOFC effects with some examples from the literature. Holmberg's (2000) original characterization of FOFC was in the context of {Aux, O and VP} order patterns in Finnish as in (3). Finnish is typically VO, but in certain contexts allows both the object to precede the V and the V to precede the auxiliary, as illustrated in (3a–3c). What is not permitted, however, is a V-O-Aux order as shown in (3a), that is, where a head-final auxiliary selects a head-initial V, in violation of (2).

(3) a. *Milloin Jussi olisi   kirjoittanut romaanin?*
         when Jussi would-have written   INDEF-novel

         'When would Jussi have written a novel?'   [Aux-V-O]

     b. *Milloin Jussi olisi   romaanin   kirjoittanut?*
         when Jussi would-have INDEF-novel written

         'When would Jussi have written a novel?'   [Aux-O-V]

     c. *Milloin Jussi romaanin   kirjoittanut olisi?*
         When Jussi INDEF-novel written   would-have

         'When would Jussi have written a novel?'   [O-V-Aux]

     d. * *Milloin Jussi kirjoittanut romaanin   olisi?*
         when Jussi written   INDEF-novel would-have

         'When would Jussi have written a novel?'   **[*V-O-Aux]**
         (Holmberg 2000)

Similar facts come from the relative order of modals, infinitival verbs and their objects in Basque. Basque is canonically OV, but many speakers allow objects – especially heavy objects – to occur postverbally (Rijk 1969; Ortiz de Urbina 1989; Elordieta 2001). In addition, infinitival complements of modals may appear either to the right or the left of the selecting modal + auxiliary. When the infinitival complement appears to the right of its selecting modal as in (4a, 4b) both OV and VO orders are possible. When the infinitival appears to the left of its selecting modal, only the OV order is possible, a pattern again in keeping with (2).

(4) a. *Nahi zuen [hobetu bere ingelesa.]*
      want AUX improve REFL English

      'He/She wanted to improve his/her English.'   [Modal-Infin-Obj]

    b. *Nahi zuen [bere ingelesa hobetu.]*
      want AUX REFL English improve

      'He/She wanted to improve his/her English.'   [Modal-Obj-Infin]

    c. *[Bere ingelesa hobetu] nahi zuen.*
      REFL English improve want AUX

      'He/She wanted to improve his/her English.'   [Obj-Infin-Modal]

    d. *[*Hobetu bere ingelesa] nahi zuen.*
      improve REFL English want AUX

      'He/She wanted to improve his/her English.'   **[*Infin-Obj-Modal]**

Biberauer et al. (2014) note that without further qualification, (2) incorrectly rules out commonplace, well-formed structures in German of the kind shown in (5).

(5) a. *Johann hat [$_{VP}$ [$_{DP}$ einen Mann] gesehen.]*
      John has   a   man   seen

      'John has seen a man.'

    b. *Johann ist [$_{VP}$ [$_{PP}$ nach Berlin] gefahren.]*
      John is   to   Berlin gone

      'John has gone to Berlin.'
      (Biberauer et al. 2014)

(5a) involves a head-final VP containing a head-initial DP, and in (5b), the head-final VP contains a head initial PP, both in violation of (2). Biberauer et al. note that such exceptions to (2) can be explained in terms of the categorial status of α and β. That is, Biberauer et al. note that the cases in (5) differ from the Basque and Finnish cases just discussed in that the relevant α and β heads in (5), are categorially distinct – V is clearly of a different categorial status from both D (5a) and P (5b). By contrast, the Finnish examples in (3) all crucially involve a sequence of heads in the extended projection of the verb. Biberauer et al. capture this class of exceptions to (2) by restricting FOFC evaluation to an extended projection, and by defining the extended projection as in (6), where SPINE is defined as in (7).

(6) The Extended Projection of a lexical head L (EP(L)) is the sequence of categories
      EP = $\{\alpha_1 \ldots \alpha_i \ldots \alpha_n\}$ such that:

    i. α_i is in the spine defined by L; for each pair of heads <H_i, H_{i+1}> in EP;

    ii. H_i c-selects H_{i+1};

    iii. H_i is categorially non-distinct from H_{i+1}.

(7)   SPINE: A sequence of nodes $\Sigma = \{\alpha_1 \ldots \alpha_i \ldots \alpha_n\}$ forms a spine iff:

    i. α_n is a lexical head H^{min};

    ii. α_i is H^{-min}, a projection of α_n;

    iii.   for all $\alpha_{m > i}$ α is a head H' which c-selects either H or some $\alpha_j \in \Sigma$, or α is a projection of some $\alpha_j \in \Sigma$.

Biberauer et al.'s (6) and (7) are intended to formalize the intuition that the extended projection of a lexical head consists of all of the functional material in the c-selecting sequence above that lexical head up to the first categorially distinct element. Biberauer et al. assume that a sequence C-T-v-V is all part of the extended projection of V and will count as categorially non-distinct. In this way, Biberauer et al. intend FOFC to encompass disharmonies of the above type involving heads in a canonical clausal spine as well as those in a canonical nominal spine, but will not extend to sequences of heads with distinct categorial features, such as in cases where a CP is selected by n.

A second class of exceptions that Biberauer et al. focus on concerns Ā-movement. Biberauer et al. note that, across languages, topic- and focus-movements appear able to violate FOFC as described so far. In (8), for example, the head-initial, non-satellite VP raises to the left-periphery and spells-out to the left of its dominating head in violation of (2).

(8)   We expected John to eat the pies, and [eat the pies] he did ~~eat the pies~~.
    (Biberauer et al. 2014)

Biberauer et al. therefore also exclude Ā-movement from the scope of FOFC. Let us therefore adopt as our working characterization of FOFC the following from Biberauer et al. (2014).

(9)   *The Final-over-Final condition (amended version)*
    If β is a head-initial phrase and γ is a phrase immediately dominating β, then γ must be head-initial. If β is a head-final phrase, and γ is a phrase immediately dominating β, then γ can be head-initial or head-final, where:

    i.   β and γ are in the same Extended Projection;

    ii.   βP has not been Ā-moved to Spec, γP.

    (adapted from Biberauer et al. (2014))

We consider two main formal approaches to this generalization in the following sections.

2.2 Biberauer et al.'s narrow syntactic approach to FOFC

Biberauer et al. propose that FOFC effects, as described above, are a property of the syntactic component, reflecting a condition on movement. In particular, Biberauer et al. follow Kayne (1994) in assuming a universal spec-head-complement merged order, and that complement-head orders are a consequence of "roll up" – iterative complement-to-specifier movement in a given sequence. FOFC effects, from this perspective, are explained if the following two conditions apply to roll up: (i) it must start at the base of a given extended projection; and (ii) it proceeds monotonically, that is, it cannot start and stop and start again.

Biberauer et al. model these conditions in terms of constraints on spreading of a general movement-driving feature which they represent with the caret symbol, "^". This feature drives different kinds of movement depending on the formal features that it associates with: when "^" associates with edge features of a phase head, it will trigger Ā-movement; when associated with phi-features it will drive A-movement; and crucially for FOFC effects, when it associates with c-selectional features, it triggers movement of a complement to the spec of its selecting head.

Biberauer et al. assume further that this feature can "spread" up the tree. This spreading is crucially constrained in a way typically assumed for head movement, namely that it can skip no intervening heads. Biberauer et al. state this condition as in (10).

(10)   If a head α_i in the Extended Projection E of a lexical head L has ^ associated with its selection feature for a lower head α_{i+1}, then so does α_{i+1}.

The assumption of monotonic spreading therefore excludes the unattested start-stop-start pattern that will produce FOFC violations:

(11)   *Non-monotonic spreading of* ^
       *[X^ [Y [Z^]]]

Importantly, on Biberauer et al.'s approach, FOFC effects are a narrow syntactic phenomenon. FOFC-violating structures are not filtered out by interface conditions; rather they are simply not derivable on the approaches to merge and locality proposed by Biberauer et al. In the next section, we briefly contrast this approach with Sheehan's PF approach.

2.3 Sheehan's PF approach

Sheehan (2013a; 2013b; 2017) proposes that FOFC effects are a consequence of the way the phonology linearizes syntactic structures on a modified version of the LCA (Kayne 1994). Following Chomsky (1995) and Nunes (2004), Sheehan (2013a; 2013b) takes the LCA to be a linearization algorithm that orders syntactic objects in the phonological component. Sheehan's version of the LCA, however, differs from Kayne's in that it assumes that linearization maps not just according to c-command relations, but also *c-selection* relations. Indeed, in Sheehan's algorithm, precedence relations are first mapped by c-selection; c-command is an elsewhere condition. In addition, it adopts from head-parameter approaches the assumption that linearization of two categories in a c-selection relation is parametrized to the selecting head. We summarize this proposal in (12) from Sheehan (2013a,b).

(12) *Sheehan's (2013b) revised LCA*

    i. If a category A c-selects a category B, then A precedes/follows B at PF.

    ii. If no order is specified between A and B even transitively by (i), then A precedes B at PF if A asymmetrically c-commands B.

Let us consider now how these assumptions help derive the FOFC effects described in §2.1, returning to the structures in §1, repeated here.

(1) a. Harmonic, right-branching   b. Harmonic, left-branching   c. Disharmonic, attested   d. Disharmonic, unattested (in relevant domains)

In the harmonic (a) and (b) structures in (1), precedence relations are established unproblematically by parameter setting attaching to the c-selection relations between β and α and α and γ, pursuant to (12i). In (a), the precedence relations β > α and γ > β are established and by transitivity γ > α. In (b), α > β, β > γ are established by c-selection, and by transitivity α > γ. In the case of the disharmonic orders in (c) and (d), the condition in (12ii) becomes relevant. In the attested disharmonic order, (c), c-selectional relations will determine the orders γ > β and α > β. C-selectional relations, however, leave underdetermined the relative order of γ and α, that is, the choice between outputs γ > α > β and α > γ > β. The fall back c-command criterion in (12ii), however, determines γ > α. In the disharmonic structure in (d), c-selectional relations will likewise determine β > γ and β > α, leaving underdetermined the relative order of γ and α. Crucially, the c-command condition in (12ii) will then determine γ > α, yielding the output β > γ > α, and *not* the FOFC-violating order, β > α > γ. On this approach, the unavailability of FOFC-violating structures in the general case falls out of Sheehan's modified LCA, since the (d) structure in (1) is not linearizable on this approach.[2]

Sheehan's PF approach and Biberauer et al.'s narrow syntactic approach therefore make different predictions about the reparability of FOFC-violating structures in the syntax. Again, on the PF approach, but not the narrow syntactic approach a FOFC-violating structure should in principle be derivable in the syntax; it just will not be linearizable.

One possible case of FOFC repair noted in previous literature involves *Head-Final Filter* violations (Greenberg 1963; Williams 1982; Sheehan 2017). A well-known restriction on adjectival modification cross-linguistically is a ban on complements of prenominal

---

[2]Sheehan (2013b) does not take up the issue of how to express the exceptionality of Ā-movement and c-selectional relations between different extended projections as raised by Biberauer et al. (2014).

adjectives where the adjectival complement appears between the adjective and noun. (Williams 1982 called this the *Head-Final Filter.*) Sheehan (2017), in particular, argues that strings like (13c) should be analyzed as a FOFC effect and proposes a PF approach akin to the one described in §2.3.

(13) a. the proud man
      b. John is proud of his children.
      c. * the [γP [βP proud [αP of his children]] man]
      (adapted from Williams 1982)

As Sheehan notes, different languages employ different "compliance strategies" for contexts where a Head-Final Filter would otherwise arise. One such case involves extra-position of CP/PP complements of the prenominal adjective as in (14) and (15) in English and Slovenian respectively.

(14) a. a difficult book [for anyone to read]
      b. * a difficult [for anyone to read] book
      (adapted from Sheehan 2017)

(15) zavesten otrok, da je   vojna
      aware.M child.M that is.3SG war.F

      'a child aware that there is a war'
      (adapted from Sheehan 2017)

Sheehan (2017) follows Kayne (1994) in taking prenominal adjectives to be reduced relative clauses where the adjective raises from a postnominal position.

(16) [DP [CP [AP Adj [NP Noun ~~AP~~]]]]

Sheehan (2017) proposes that these repair effects might be reconciled with the PF approach to FOFC effects introduced above where FOFC-violating structures are not lin-earizable by the LCA. In particular, Sheehan suggests that the FOFC-violating structures might be repaired at copy deletion by "scattered deletion", whereby "extraposition" of the FOFC-offending CP/PP in cases like (14) and (15) are achieved by deleting the higher rather than the lower copy of these constituents in order for them to be linearizable by the modified LCA.

In the following discussion, we describe a similar set of facts from Basque verb clusters which suggest that chain reduction may bleed FOFC-violations in a similar way in the absence of scattered deletion.

3 Word order and the functional richness of modal complements in Basque

The core set of facts that we focus on come from observations by Etxepare, Uribe-Etxe-barria and colleagues concerning word order and the functional richness of infinitival complements of the modals *behar* 'need' and *nahi* 'want' (Etxepare & Uribe-Etxebarria 2009; 2012; Balza 2010). As illustrated in (17) the constituent headed by *ikusi*, 'see', can appear either to the left or the right of the selecting modal, *nahi*, 'want'.

(17)   a.   [Horrelakoak maiz-ago   ikusi] nahi nituzke.
            like.that.PL   often-more see   want AUX

       b.   Nahi nituzke [horrelakoak maiz-ago   ikusi.]
            want AUX   like.that.PL   often-more see

            'I'd like to see things like that more often.'

Etxepare & Uribe-Etxebarria (2009; 2012) and Balza (2010) note that the word order difference illustrated in (17) correlates with three other properties suggesting that the modal-infinitival order in (17b) can involve a functionally richer infinitival complement than (17a). We describe these in turn below.

3.1 Temporal modification

A first way in which infinitival>modal and modal>infinitival orders differ is in terms of the temporal independence of the non-finite constituent. In infinitival>modal orders, the infinitival phrase cannot contain a temporal modifier forcing a temporal interpretation of the event in the infinitival phrase that is different from that of the modal+auxiliary. In (18a), the infinitival phrase contains *gaur* 'today' with a temporal interpretation different from the past interpretation of the modal+auxiliary, and the result is poor. On the other hand, Etxepare and Uribe-Etxebarria report that this temporal difference is fine in modal>infinitival contexts such as (18b).

(18)   a.   * Jon-ek   atzo   [gaur etxe-a-n   ego-n] behar zuen.
            Jon-ERG yesterday today house-DEF-in be-INF need   AUX

       b.   Jon-ek   atzo   behar zuen ⌊gaur etxe-a-n   ego-n.⌋
            Jon-ERG yesterday need   AUX   today house-DEF-in be-INF

            'Yesterday Jon needed to be home today.'

Etxepare & Uribe-Etxebarria (2009; 2012) take these facts to indicate that, in modal>infinitival orders, the non-finite constituent may contain a T head with a tense value different from that of the matrix clause. In infinitive-modal orders, on the other hand, the non-finite constituent cannot contain a separate T head.

3.2 Agreement

A second difference between the word orders concerns agreement. Open class finite verbs in Basque are formed periphrastically, with a verb root (bearing any aspectual morphology) separate from the auxiliary that agrees in person and number with ergative, absolutive and dative arguments of the main verb. We illustrate this agreement in (19).[3] In the examples in (19), ergative, absolutive and dative arguments are all overt; however, we note that Basque allows pro-drop with all three of these argument types.

(19) a. Ni   joa-n na-iz.
     1SG.ABS go.PRF 1SG.ABS-ROOT

     'I have gone.'   [unaccusative]

    b. Katu-ek   ni   ikus-i na-u-te.
       cat-3PL.ERG 1SG.ABS see-PRF 1SG.ABS-ROOT-3PL.ERG

       'The cats have seen me.'   [monotransitive]

    c. Ni-k   liburu-ak   Jon-i   ema-n
      1SG-ERG books-PL.ABS Jon-DAT give-PRF
      d-i-zki-o-t.
      3SG.ABS-ROOT-ABS.PL-3SG.DAT-1SG.ERG

      'I have given Jon the book.'   [ditransitive]

    d. Ni   Jon-i   mintza-tzen na-tzai-o.
      1SG.ABS Jon-DAT speak-IPFV 1SG.ABS-ROOT-3SG.DAT

      'I speak to Jon.'   [applicative unaccusative]

In addition, modal verbs that take infinitival complements are transparent to plural absolutive and dative agreement marking in transitive constructions. In sentences with the modal *behar* 'must', agreement marking on the auxiliary is exhaustively determined by the argument structure of the lower verb as shown in (20), below.

(20) a. % Joan behar na-iz.
      go   must 1SG.ABS-ROOT

      'I must go.'[4]   [unaccusative]

    b. Katu-ek   ni   ikusi behar na-u-te.
       cat-3PL.ERG 1SG.ABS see   need 1SG.ABS-ROOT-3PL.ERG

       'The cats must see me.'   [monotransitive]

    c. Jon-i   liburu-ak   eman behar d-i-zki-o-t.
      Jon-DAT books-PL.ABS give   need 3.ABS-ROOT-PL.ABS-3SG.DAT-1SG.ERG

      'I must give Jon the books.'   [ditransitive]

As Etxepare & Uribe-Etxebarria (2009) note, both absolutive plural agreement and dative agreement patterns are constrained by the position of the infinitival. As shown in (21), in the modal>infinitival order, absolutive plural agreement is optional.

---

[3]On a closed class of synthetic verbs, tense and agreement marking appear affixed to the verb root in some aspectual contexts. Addressee agreement works similarly for these forms but we set these forms aside for expositional convenience.

[4]In some dialects, the modal *behar* determines the transitive auxiliary *edun in unaccusative contexts.

(21) a. Nahi n-it-u-z-ke   [horr-ela-ko-a-k   maiz-ago
          want 1SG.ERG-**PL.ABS**-ROOT-**PL.ABS**-IRR that-like-GEN-DEF-PL frequent-more
          ikus-i].
          see-INF

      b. Nahi n-u-ke   [horr-ela-ko-a-k   maiz-ago   ikus-i].
          want 1SG.ERG-ROOT-IRR that-like-GEN-DEF-PL frequent-more see-INF

          'I'd like to see things like that more often.'
          (Etxepare & Uribe-Etxebarria 2009)

In the infinitival>modal order, on the other hand, plural absolutive agreement on the auxiliary is obligatory.

(22) a. [Horr-ela-ko-a-k   maiz-ago   ikus-i] nahi
          that-like-GEN-DEF-PL frequent-more see-INF want
          n-it-u-z-ke.
          1SG.ERG-**PL.ABS**-ROOT-**PL.ABS**-IRR

      b. * [*Horr-ela-ko-a-k   maiz-ago   ikus-i*] *nahi nuke.*
          that-like-GEN-DEF-PL frequent-more see-INF want 1SG.ERG-ROOT-IRR

          'I'd like to see things like that more often.'
          (Etxepare & Uribe-Etxebarria 2009)

Agreement with dative arguments is similarly constrained. (23) shows that that dative agreement is optional in the modal>infinitival order.

(23) a. *Behar zen-i-e-ke*   [*zure guraso-ei   obeditu*].
          must 2ABS-ROOT-DAT.PL-IRR your parent-DAT.PL obey

      b. *Behar zen-u-ke*   [*zure guraso-ei   obeditu*].
          must 2ABS-ROOT-IRR your parent-DAT.PL obey

          'You should obey your parents.'
          (Etxepare & Uribe-Etxebarria 2009)

As shown in (24), this agreement is obligatory when the order is infinitival>modal:

(24) a. [Zure guraso-ei   obeditu] behar zen-i-e-ke.
          your parent-DAT.PL obey   must 2SG.ABS-ROOT-DAT.PL-IRR

      b. * [Zure guraso-ei   obeditu] behar zen-u-ke.
          your parent-DAT.PL obey   must 2SG.ABS-ROOT-IRR

          'You should obey your parents.'
          (Etxepare & Uribe-Etxebarria 2009)

These agreement restrictions stand to reason on the assumption that the loci for dative and absolutive case in transitive contexts is not T but rather some set of vP-internal heads – v and Appl for instance – and that the agreement morphemes on the auxiliary reflect head movement from v/Appl to T (Arregi & Molina-Azaola 2004; Rezac 2008). On this approach, the unavailability of dative and plural absolutive agreement on the finite auxiliary plausibly reflects the presence of a lower T blocking movement to the higher T.

3.3 Negation

The above sets of facts plausibly indicate that, in modal>infinitival but not infinitival>modal orders, the non-finite constituent may contain a T head. A final set of facts, however, suggests that in modal-infinitive orders the non-finite constituent can be somewhat larger than TP – containing minimally a TP-external negation projection. Balza (2010) and Etxepare & Uribe-Etxebarria (2009) observe that non-finite constituents to the left of the modal can never contain the sentential negation morpheme *ez*, which appears to the left of the auxiliary in Basque (Laka 1990). In contrast, when the infinitive appears to the right of the modal, *ez* can indeed appear. This contrast is illustrated in (25).

(25)   a. * [Ez eros-i] nahi/behar n-u-ke.
           NEG buy-INF want/need 1SG.ERG-ROOT-IRR

       b. Nahi/behar n-u-ke   [ez eros-i].
           want/need 1SG.ERG-ROOT-IRR NEG buy-INF

           'I want/need not to buy it.'
           (Etxepare & Uribe-Etxebarria 2009)

As Etxepare & Uribe-Etxebarria (2009) note, the negation in (25b) is not plausibly an instance of constituent negation since constituent negation does not license a higher, clausemate negative polarity item (NPI). Example (26a), illustrating constituent negation in a non-modal context, shows that the higher NPI *inork* 'anybody' is not licensed, unlike a true sentential negation context such as (26b).

(26)   a. * Inork   (ere) du ez eros-i.
           Anybody (at-all) AUX NEG buy-INF

           'Nobody at all bought it.'

       b. Inork   (ere) ez du eros-i.
           Anybody (at-all) NEG AUX buy-INF

           'Nobody at all bought it.'

(27) shows that *ez* in modal>infinitival contexts behaves like sentential negation in licensing the higher NPI, *deus*, 'anything'. Balza (2010) and Etxepare & Uribe-Etxebarria (2009) take these facts to indicate that the non-finite constituents in these environments can contain a negative head.

(27)   Nahi nuke deus   (ere) ez eros-i.
       want AUX anything at.all NEG buy-INF

       'I'd like to not buy anything (at all).'

To summarize, we have described four sets of facts drawn mainly from Etxepare & Uribe-Etxebarria (2009; 2012) and Balza (2010) suggesting that the two word orders discussed above correspond to different internal structures of the non-finite constituent. The infinitival phrase in infinitival>modal orders is smaller than TP – a vP, we'll assume – while the infinitival in modal>aux>infinitival orders can be a TP and may contain a TP-external negation position as well. We illustrate this proposal with the sequences of functional heads in (28), (repeated here) which abstract away from surface linear order.

(28)   a. Infinitival>modal orders: [T [Modal [v [V …

      b. Modal>infinitival orders: [T [Modal ([Neg) ([T) [v [V …

As noted earlier, Balza (2010) and Etxepare & Uribe-Etxebarria (2009) do not provide an account of the contrast in (28). In the following discussion, we argue that this contrast is explainable as a garden variety FOFC effect from the perspective of antisymmetric approaches to Basque.

4 FOFC and word order in Basque verb clusters

4.1 Antisymmetry and polarity-sensitive word order alternations

Basque is a *mixed-head* language: heads in the clausal spine below T appear to the right of their complements, while heads above T, including preverbal speech act and evidential particles appear to the left of their complements (Rijk 1969; Ortiz de Urbina 1989; 1994; Laka 1990; Elordieta 2001; Irurtzun 2007; Elordieta 2008). Most generative approaches to Basque have modeled these facts in terms of a head-directionality parameter: T and clausal heads below it take their complements to the left, while those heads above T take their complements to the right. The head-final nature of TP-internal projections, on this approach, usefully accounts the fact that in neutral declarative sentences like (29), the finite verb – presumably in T – appears sentence finally.

(29)   *Affirmative main clauses*
      Miren-ek Jon   ikus-i du.
      Miren-ERG Jon-ABS see-PRF AUX.3SG.ERG

      'Miren has seen Jon.'

In negative sentences, the negative morpheme *ez* appears left-adjacent to the auxiliary and the VP appears to the right of the auxiliary as in (30).

(30)   *Negative main clauses*
      Miren-ek ez   du   Jon   ikus-i.
      Miren-ERG NEG AUX.3SG.ERG Jon-ABS see-PRF

      'Miren hasn't seen Jon.'

Laka (1990) and Elordieta (2001; 2008) propose that these polarity effects reflect the fact that negation – which is head-initial on this approach – is first-merged outside TP in Basque, and that the inflected verb must head adjoin to negation as a way of providing lexical support for the clitic-like auxiliary. The Neg>Aux word order requires that this be right head adjunction as shown in (31). In affirmative sentences, Neg is not merged, and the auxiliary stays in its first-merged position in TP.

(31) *The head movement approach (Laka 1990)*

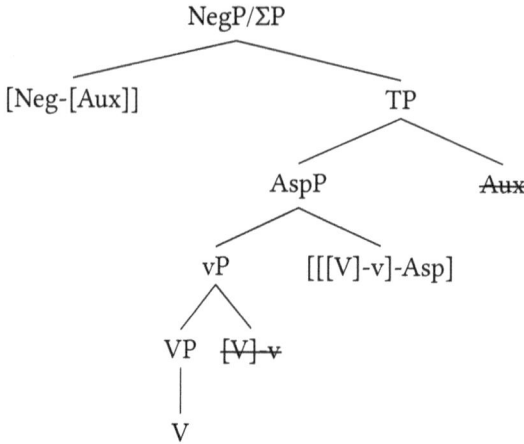

```
                      NegP/ΣP
              _____|_____
             |                 |
       [Neg-[Aux]]            TP
                          _____|_____
                         |           |
                       AspP         Aux
                     ___|___
                    |       |
                   vP   [[[V]-v]-Asp]
                  _|_
                 |   |
                VP  [V]-v
                 |
                 V
```

On an approach that eschews head-directionality parametrization, a different account is required for the polarity-sensitive word order alternations illustrated in (29) and (30). In particular, following Haddican (2004; 2008), we propose that (i) the left-branching structure of the extended VP is derived via roll up (Kayne 1994), and (ii) the relative order of the auxiliary and extended verbal projection reflects the presence or absence of fronting of the extended verbal projection, a constituent that we will label PolP, for reasons to be made clear shortly. We adopt Laka's (1990) seminal proposal that Basque has a left peripheral polarity head, Σ. We propose that this head probes for polarity-specified elements. Two such elements will be the the negative and the emphatic affirmative morphemes *ez* and *bai*, which we take to be polarity adverbs merged in the Spec of PolP. These forms, where present, will raise to Spec,ΣP, as illustrated in the negative example in (32).

(32) Ez-raising, negative contexts

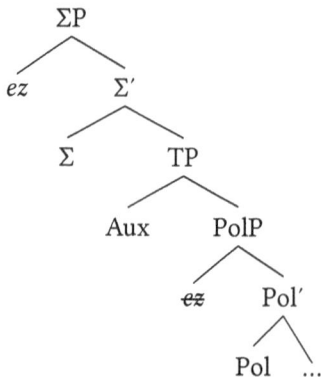

```
              ΣP
          ____|____
         |         |
        ez         Σ'
               ____|____
              |         |
              Σ         TP
                    ____|____
                   |         |
                  Aux       PolP
                        _____|_____
                       |           |
                       ez         Pol'
                               ____|____
                              |         |
                             Pol       ...
```

In affirmative root contexts, the position to the left of the auxiliary is not occupied by the negative morpheme *ez*, but rather by the extended projection of the verb. We propose that, in these contexts, in the absence of *ez*, the extended verbal phrase raises to Σ to satisfy the latter's polarity feature. Specifically, in the spirit of predicate fronting approaches to VSO and VOS word orders (Massam 2000; 2001; 2010; Coon 2010; 2012), let us assume that what raises is a PolP whose head contains an affirmative polarity [Aff] feature. In the verb-initial orders they analyze, Massam and Coon take the landing site of this movement to be TP/IP, and relate this movement to the featural needs of T/C. In Basque, we take this movement to be related to featural needs of a polarity-related morpheme, namely Σ. We illustrate this in (33).[5]

(33) *Affirmative orders*

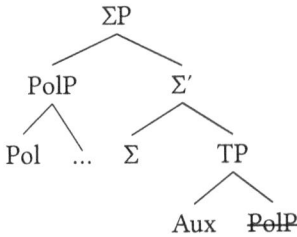

$$
\begin{array}{c}
\Sigma P \\
\diagup\diagdown \\
\mathrm{PolP} \qquad \Sigma' \\
\diagup\diagdown \qquad \diagup\diagdown \\
\mathrm{Pol}\ \ \dots\ \ \Sigma \qquad \mathrm{TP} \\
\diagup\diagdown \\
\mathrm{Aux}\ \ \sout{\mathrm{PolP}}
\end{array}
$$

Evidence in favor of predicate fronting in affirmative clauses comes from TP ellipsis sentences like (34) and (35). In both cases, the auxiliary in the second sentence is left unpronounced, plausibly as a banal case of TP ellipsis (Laka 1990). Interestingly, the elements which escape TP-ellipsis are different in affirmative and negative sentences: whereas in negative sentences (and in those involving contrastive affirmation) the verbal predicate is elided together with the finite auxiliary (35), in simple affirmative sentences the verbal predicate escapes TP-ellipsis, by virtue of obligatory predicate raising (34). On the head directionality approach, additional movement operations are required to derive such sentences.

(34) Jon-ek kafe-a erosi du, eta Ane-k, [$_{\Sigma P}$ [$_{PolP}$ [liburu-a leitu] Σ [$_{TP}$ ~~du~~].
    Jon-ERG coffee bought AUX and Ane-ERG   book-the read
    'Jon has bought coffee, and Ane has read the book.'

(35) Jon-ek kafe-a erosi du, baina Ane-k, [$_{\Sigma P}$ ez Σ ~~TP du kafe-a erosi~~].
    Jon-ERG coffee bought AUX but Ane-ERG   NEG
    'Jon has bought coffee, but Ane hasn't.'

Evidence that the extended VP indeed contains a polarity feature in affirmative contexts comes from polarity focus sentences like (36). Here, the extended VP raises to a left peripheral focus position and co-occurs with an affirmative denial interpretation, suggesting the raised verbal constituent is the locus of the affirmative feature.

---

[5]See Haddican (2004; 2008) and Etxepare & Uribe-Etxebarria (2009) for similar approaches.

(36) [*FocP* [*PolP* *Etorri*] [*TP* *da* *Iker.*]]
             come   AUX Iker

    'Iker HAS (indeed) come.'

What is important about this approach for the FOFC-effects focused on here is that TP is a left-headed projection that does not participate in roll-up movement; that is, the complement of T does not move to its spec. From this perspective, and assuming that non-fintite T is like finite T in not participating in roll-up movement, Etxepare and Uribe-Etxebarria's observed correlation between word order and size of the modal complement is explicable as a vanilla FOFC effect. That is, what makes the functionally richer constituents impossible in the infinitive>modal order is the presence of a head-complement structure in the spec of the modal phrase, in violation of (9). Specifically, the complement of the infinitival T is not spelled out in the spec of the non-finite T, but rather as the sister of T. The infinitival T itself then moves to the spec of the modal projection and runs afoul of (2). In contrast, vP-sized infinitives will not run afoul of FOFC, as stated in (2) and (9), since v *does* participate in roll-up; that is, it attracts its complement to its spec. We illustrate this proposal in (37) and (38).

(37) *FOFC-violating TP-raising*

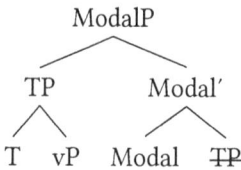

            ModalP
          ⌒
     TP   Modal′
     ⌒   ⌒
   T vP   Modal ~~TP~~

(38) *FOFC-compliant vP-raising*

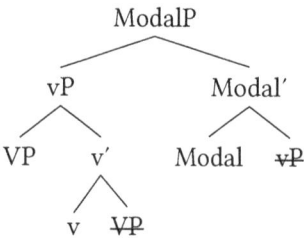

            ModalP
          ⌒
     vP   Modal′
     ⌒   ⌒
  VP   v′   Modal ~~vP~~
      ⌒
     v ~~VP~~

From the perspective of the antisymmetric approach to polarity-sensitive word order alternations described above, the structure-sensitivity of the word order alternations described by Etxepare & Uribe-Etxebarria (2009) is therefore predicted as a FOFC effect. From a mixed head perspective, where T takes its complement on the left, some other account of Etxepare and Uribe-Etxebarria's observation is required.[6]

---

[6]For the same reason, Sheehan's (2013a; 2013b; 2017) approach will fail to express the structure-sensitivity of these word order alternations as a FOFC phenomenon if T is parameterized to take its complement to its left. Sheehan's theory, though, entails no commitment to such a derivation versus an XP movement approach of the kind just proposed.

4.2 Repairing the violation

The account so far explains why vP-, but not TP-sized modal complements can raise to the specifier of the modal. Unaddressed so far is why TP-sized modal complements are licit when they appear to the right of the modal as in (17b). A further fact about the alternation in (17) that we take to be central to this issue is the fact that the modal-aux-infinitive order is most readily available in contexts in which the non-finite constituent to the right is focalized or contains a focus-bearing constituent. The modal+auxiliary sequence to the left is preferably defocused. From this perspective, sentences like (17b) are reminiscent of cases of right peripheral focus constructions as in (39) and (40).

(39) *Ardoa ekarri   diot (#) ANDONI-RI.*
      wine brought AUX   Andoni-DAT
      'I brought the wine to ANDONI.'
      (Elordieta 2001)

(40) *Monjak egin zigun [barruan utz-i.]*
      nuns   do AUX inside   leave-INF
      'The nuns LEFT US INSIDE.'
      (Haddican 2007)

Ortiz de Urbina (2002) and Uribe-Etxebarria (2003) propose that sentences such as (39) and (40) are derived by movement of the focused constituents to a left-peripheral focus position, followed by remnant movement of the non-focused portion of the sentence to a higher topic phrase. We illustrate this proposal in (41). As Ortiz de Urbina (2002) notes, this approach is supported by the fact that the remnant-moved material shares intonational properties with other pre-focus topic constituents.

(41) [TopP [*Ardoa ~~Andoni-ri~~ ekarri   diot*] *Top* [FocP [*Andoni-ri*   ]...]
              wine   brought AUX   Andoni-DAT
      'I brought the wine to ANDONI.'

Some support for remnant movement comes from the relative scope of focus and negation. When following the lexical verb, the favored scope of the focal constituent is maximal with regard to negation, as diagnosed by the continuation *and not DP*. In this regard, it behaves like left-peripheral foci as in (42b) (Ortiz de Urbina 2002).

(42) a. *Ez diot liburua   oparitu ANDONI-RI, eta ez   Miren-i.*
         NEG AUX book-the offered Andoni-DAT, and NEG Miren-DAT
         'The one I did not offer the book to is Andoni, and not Miren.'

      b. *ANDONI-RI ez   diot liburua   oparitu, eta ez   Miren-i.*
         Andoni-DAT NEG AUX book-the offered and NEG Miren-DAT
         'It is Andoni that I didn't offer the book to, and not Miren.'

Also, note that wide-scope foci in non-initial position must occupy the right edge of the clause as suggested by the fact that they cannot be followed linearly by clausal material:

(43) a. *Jon-ek   ez   du   liburu-rik irakurri BULEGOAN, eta ez   trenean.*
      Jon-ERG NEG AUX book-INF read   office-in   and NEG train-in

      'The place Jon did not read any book is the office, not the train.'

   b. *Jon-ek   ez   du   irakurri (liburu-rik) BULEGOAN (*liburu-rik), eta ez*
      Jon-ERG NEG has read   book-PART office-in   book-PART   and NEG

      trenean.
      train-in

      'The place Jon did not read any book is the office, not the train.'

The crux of our proposal about FOFC repair is as follows. In modal>infinitival orders such as (17b), affirmative PolP moves to ΣP, as usual. The FOFC-offending infinitival TP then subextracts to a Focus phrase, as in (44). The position of the modal to the left of the infinitival is derived via remnant topicalization, not shown here. Crucially, because the TP targets an A-bar position, this movement step is FOFC-exempt. (See Biberauer et al. (2014) for discussion.)

(44) *PolP movement to ΣP and sub-extraction of infinitival TP*

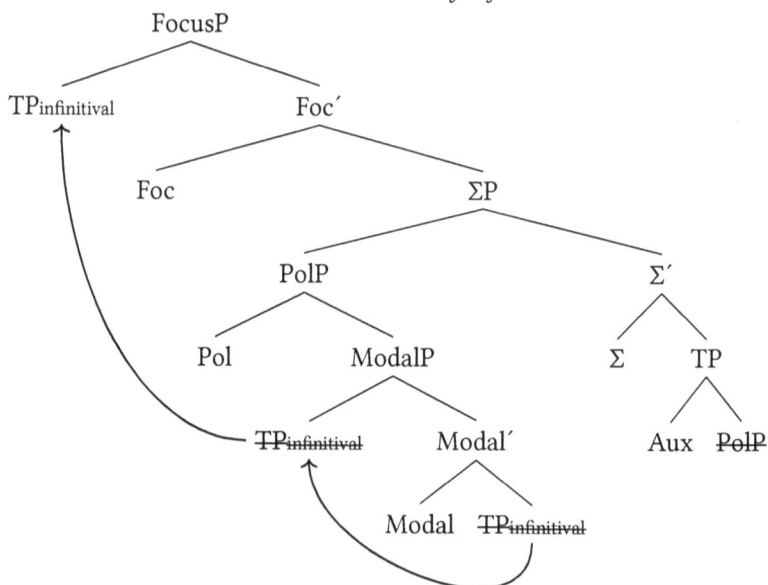

The derivation in (44) requires that freezing effects do not apply in this context (Collins 2005a,b). We do not consider in detail what conditions the availability of subextraction here, but note that independent evidence of the ability of focused constituents to extract from moved XPs come from examples like (45) and discussed by Elordieta (2008). Here, the *wh*-phrase, *norekin* 'with who', cyclically moves from within a moved CP.

(45) *Nor-ekin pentsa-tu duzu [CP ~~nor-ekin~~ ezkondu behar naiz-ela] agindu*
      who-with think-PRF AUX   who-with marry   must AUX-C   order
      didate-la ~~CP~~?
      AUX-C
      'Who did you think they told me I had to get married with?'

Subextraction of TP to the Focus Phrase is followed by remnant topicalization of ΣP, as in (41). Evidence that the modal in the relevant cases sits in a derived position comes from complex functional sequences preceding the non-finite constituent that cannot be generated in-situ (Etxepare & Uribe-Etxebarria 2009). Consider (46):

(46) *Nahi izan du   beranduago etorri.*
      want PRF AUX later   come
      'She/he has wanted to come later.'

In (46), the perfect head follows the modal, which it selects, and precedes the auxiliary, which in turn precedes the non-finite verb. The hierarchical relations among the different components of the matrix-clause functional sequence can be represented in terms of either a head-final structure or roll-up movement, but the relative ordering of that sequence and the non-finite verb cannot: the modal verb selects the non-finite TP, but the two elements appear on opposite sides of the sequence, and separated by other clausal heads. Remnant movement provides a simple rationale for this ordering, and is well attested in other Basque focal constructions. (47) lays out the derivational steps necessary to arrive to a configuration such as (46), starting from the merger of the Modal head with the TP-infinitival (47a):

(47) a. Merge modal *nahi* with infinitival TP:
         [ModalP *nahi* [TP *etorri*]]
      b. Infinitival TP rolls up with ModalP:
         [ModalP [TP *etorri*] *nahi* ~~TP~~]
      c. Merge Aspect (participle *izan*):
         [AspP *izan* [ModalP [TP *etorri*] *nahi*]]
      d. ModalP rolls up with AspP:
         [AspP [ModalP [TP *etorri*] *nahi*] *izan* ~~ModalP~~]
      e. Merge Pol and finite auxiliary in T:
         [TP *du* [PolP Pol [AspP [ModalP [TP *etorri*] *nahi*] *izan*]]]
      f. Merge Σ:
         [ΣP Σ [TP *du* [PolP Pol [AspP [ModalP [TP *etorri*] *nahi*] *izan*]]]]
      g. Predicate fronting – PolP raising to ΣP:
         [ΣP [PolP Pol [AspP [ModalP [TP *etorri*] *nahi*] *izan*]] Σ [TP *du* ~~PolP~~]]

    h. Merge focus head and move infinitival TP to spec, Foc:
[FocP [TP *etorri*] Foc [ΣP [PolP Pol [AspP [ModalP ~~etorri~~ *nahi*] *izan*]] Σ [TP *du*]]]

    i. Merge Topic head and remnant move ΣP to spec, Topic:
[TopP [ΣP [PolP Pol [AspP [ModalP *nahi*] *izan*]] Σ [TP *du*]] Top [FocP [TP *etorri*] Foc ~~ΣP~~]

To summarize, the importance of the foregoing facts for the debate between narrow syntactic and PF-based approaches to FOFC is that they suggest a derivation whereby a FOFC-violating structure is assembled, but then repaired by a subsequent movement step. The analysis, if correct, entails that Biberauer et al.'s narrow-syntax approach to FOFC, where FOFC-violating structures are simply not buildable in the syntax, cannot be correct. Rather, they suggest that copy-deletion can bleed FOFC. This, in turn, means that FOFC-evaluation is derivationally subsequent to copy-deletion, in the phonological component of the grammar on standard approaches (Nunes 2004).

5 Conclusion

This paper has presented an analysis of word-order restrictions in Basque modal constructions described in recent work by Etxepare & Uribe-Etxebarria (2009; 2012). We have shown that the relevant restrictions are explained as an utterly banal FOFC effect on antisymmetric approaches to Basque, but not on a traditional mixed head approach. The analysis of Basque verb clusters presented, if correct, entails that Biberauer et al.'s narrow syntactic approach to FOFC effects is not correct and instead recommends a PF-based approach. How this might be achieved, whether by Sheehan's promising analysis (2013a; 2013b) or another approach, might usefully be investigated in future work.

Acknowledgements

This chapter is dedicated to Anders Holmberg for his inspirational leadership in theoretical linguistics for a generation. We are grateful to him for his ideas, his mentorship and friendship. Thanks to Laura Bailey, Michelle Sheehan and an anonymous reviewer for helpful comments on this paper. Many thanks also to Beñat Oyharçabal, members of the Basque Dialect Grammar team and an audience at GLOW. This research is supported by a grant from the Spanish Ministerio de Ciencia e Innovación FFI2008-00240/FILO, FFI2008-05135/FILO and from the Basque Government GIC07/144-IT-210-07. All errors are our own.

References

Arregi, Karlos & Gainko Molina-Azaola. 2004. Restructuring in Basque and the theory of agreement. In *Proceedings of the 23rd West Coast Conference on Formal Linguistics*, 43–56.

Balza, Irene. 2010. Clausal architecture and morpho-syntactic structure from the point of view of modal verbs. Ms, University of the Basque Country (UPV/EHU).

Biberauer, Theresa, Anders Holmberg & Ian Roberts. 2008. Structure and linearization in disharmonic word orders. In Charles B. Chang & Hannah J. Haynie (eds.), *Proceedings of the 26th West Coast Conference on Formal Linguistics*, 96–104. Somerville, MA: Cascadilla Proceedings Project.

Biberauer, Theresa, Anders Holmberg & Ian Roberts. 2014. A syntactic universal and its consequences. *Linguistic Inquiry* 45. 169–225.

Biberauer, Theresa, Glenda Newton & Michelle Sheehan. 2009. Limiting synchronic and diachronic variation and change: The Final-Over-Final Constraint. *Language and Linguistics* 10(4). 699–741.

Biberauer, Theresa, Michelle Sheehan & Glenda Newton. 2010. Impossible changes and impossible borrowings. In Anne Breitbarth, Christopher Lucas, Sheila Watts & David Willis (eds.), *Continuity and change in grammar*, 35–60. Amsterdam: John Benjamins.

Chomsky, Noam. 1995. *The minimalist program*. Cambridge: MIT Press.

Collins, Chris. 2005a. A smuggling approach to raising in English. *Linguistic Inquiry* 36(2). 289–298.

Collins, Chris. 2005b. A smuggling approach to the passive in English. *Syntax* 8(2). 81–120.

Coon, Jessica. 2010. VOS as predicate fronting in Chol. *Lingua* 120(2). 354–378.

Coon, Jessica. 2012. Predication, predicate fronting, and what it takes to be a verb. Paper presented at NELS 43.

Elordieta, Arantzazu. 2001. *Verb movement and constituent permutation in Basque*. Utrecht: LOT.

Elordieta, Arantzazu. 2008. OA hizkuntzak: Oinarrizko hurrenkeraz eta hurrenkera eratorriez. In Iñigo Arteatx, Xabier Artiagoitia & Arantzazu Elordieta (eds.), *Antisimetriaren hipotesia vs. Buru parametroa: Euskararen oinarrizko hurrenkera ezbaian*, 93–126. Bilbao: EHUko Argitalpen Zerbitzua.

Etxepare, Ricardo & Myriam Uribe-Etxebarria. 2009. Hitz hurrenkera eta birregituraketa euskaraz. *Anuario del Seminario de Filología Vasca Julio de Urquijo* 43(1-2). 335–355.

Etxepare, Ricardo & Myriam Uribe-Etxebarria. 2012. Denominal necessity modals in Basque. In Urtzi Etxeberria, Ricardo Etxepare & Myriam Uribe-Etxebarria (eds.), *Denominal necessity modals in Basque*, vol. 187, 283–332. Amsterdam: John Benjamins.

Greenberg, Joseph H. 1963. Some universals of grammar with particular reference to the order of meaningful elements. *Universals of Language* 2. 73–113.

Haddican, Bill. 2004. Sentence polarity and word order in Basque. *Linguistic Review* 21. 87–124.

Haddican, Bill. 2007. On *egin: Do*-support and VP focus in Central and Western Basque. *Natural Language & Linguistic Theory* 25(4). 735–764.

Haddican, Bill. 2008. Euskal perpausaren oinarrizko espez-buru-osagarri hurrenkeraren aldeko argudio batzuk. In Iñigo Arteatx, Xabier Artiagoitia & Arantzazu Elordieta (eds.), *Antisimetriaren hipotesia vs. Buru parametroa: Euskararen oinarrizko hurrenkera ezbaian*, 69–96. Bilbao: EHUko Argitalpen Zerbitzua.

Hawkins, John A. 1983. *Word order universals*. New York: Academic Press.

Hawkins, John A. 1995. *A performance theory of order and constituency*. Vol. 73. New York: Cambridge University Press.

Holmberg, Anders. 2000. Deriving OV order in Finnish. In Peter Svenonius (ed.), *The derivation of VO and OV*, 123–152. Amsterdam: John Benjamins.

Irurtzun, Aritz. 2007. *The grammar of focus at the interfaces*. Vitoria-Gasteiz: University of the Basque Country (UPV/EHU) dissertation.

Kayne, Richard S. 1994. *The antisymmetry of syntax*. Cambridge: The MIT Press.

Laka, Itziar. 1990. *Negation in syntax, on the nature of functional categories and projections*. Massachusetts Institute of Technology, Dept. of Linguistics & Philosophy dissertation.

Massam, Diane. 2000. VSO and VOS: Aspects of Niuean word order. In Andrew Carnie & Eithne Guilfoyle (eds.), *The syntax of verb initial languages*, 97–116. Oxford: Oxford University Press.

Massam, Diane. 2001. Pseudo noun incorporation in niuean. *Natural Language & Linguistic Theory* 19(1). 153–197.

Massam, Diane. 2010. V1 or V2?: On the left in Niuean. *Lingua* 120(2). 284–302.

Nunes, Jairo. 2004. *Linearization of chains and sideward movement*. Cambridge, MA: MIT Press.

Ortiz de Urbina, Jon. 1989. *Some parameters in the grammar of Basque*. Dordrecht: Foris Publications.

Ortiz de Urbina, Jon. 1994. Verb-initial patterns in Basque and Breton. *Lingua* 94(2). 125–153.

Ortiz de Urbina, Jon. 2002. Focus of correction and remnant movement in Basque. In Xabier Artiagoitia (ed.), *Erramu Boneta. Festschrift for Rudolf PG de Rijk*, 511–524. Bilbao, Basque Country: University of the Basque Country.

Rezac, Milan. 2008. The syntax of eccentric agreement: The Person Case Constraint and absolutive displacement in Basque. *Natural Language & Linguistic Theory* 26(1). 61–106.

Rijk, Rudolf PG de. 1969. Is Basque an SOV language? *Fontes linguae vasconum: Studia et documenta* 1(3). 319–352.

Sheehan, Michelle. 2013a. Explaining the Final-over-Final Constraint: Formal and functional approaches. In Theresa Biberauer & Michelle Sheehan (eds.), *Theoretical approaches to disharmonic word orders*, 407–468. Oxford: Oxford University Press.

Sheehan, Michelle. 2013b. Some implications of a copy theory of labeling. *Syntax* 16(4). 362–396.

Sheehan, Michelle. 2017. The Final-over-Final Condition and the Head-Final Filter. In Michelle Sheehan, Theresa Biberauer, Ian Roberts & Anders Holmberg (eds.), *The Final-over-Final Condition*, 121–150. Cambridge, Mass.: MIT Press.

Uribe-Etxebarria, Myriam. 2003. Euskararen eta hizkuntza erromanikoen foko egituren arteko zenbait paralelotasunez. In *Euskal gramatikari eta literaturari buruzko jardunaldiak XXI. Mendearen atarian (i-ii)*, 437–457.

Williams, Edwin. 1982. Another argument that passive is transformational. *Linguistic Inquiry* 13(1). 160–163.

Chapter 8

Head-initial postpositional phrases in North Sámi

Marit Julien
Lund University

Most adpositions in North Sámi are postpositions – they follow their complements in the surface order. Nouns, on the other hand, invariably precede their complements. Strikingly, when the nominal complement of a postposition has its own complement, the complement of the noun follows after the postposition, so that the nominal phrase ends up being discontinuous, split by the postposition. This is an indication that North Sámi postpositions are prepositions underlyingly, and that the surface order is the result of the complement of P moving to the Spec of a higher functional head. The complement of the noun is however spelled out in the lower position. Neither the complement stranding approach of Sheehan (2009) nor the FOFC of Holmberg (2000) and Biberauer et al. (2008; 2014) can fully explain this pattern. Instead, in North Sámi a more specific requirement appears to be at work, which dictates that a postposition must follow immediately after the nominal head of its complement. A similar effect is seen with possessors, which precede the possessees but also leave their complements behind in postnominal position.

1 Introduction

There are in principle two possible explanations for the ordering contrast between prepositional and postpositional phrases. One is that a (possibly local) head parameter gives prepositions when set to <HEAD FIRST> but postpositions when set to <HEAD LAST>. The other is that the underlying order is the same in both cases, so that the two surface orders result from one or more movement operations.

In this paper I will present data from North Sámi which indicate that postpositional phrases in this language result from movement of the complement of the adposition from a position following the adposition to a position preceding it. In other words, North Sámi postpositions are prepositions underlyingly.

A striking feature of North Sámi postpositional phrases is that if the nominal complement of the postposition has its own complement, then this complement will follow the postposition, arguably in the position where it originates. At first glance, the observed pattern appears to be similar to the complement stranding phenomenon described in

Marit Julien. 2017. Head-initial postpositional phrases in North Sámi. In Laura R. Bailey & Michelle Sheehan (eds.), *Order and structure in syntax I: Word order and syntactic structure*, 159–176. Berlin: Language Science Press. DOI:10.5281/zenodo.1117706

Sheehan (2009), while the resulting order appears to be consistent with the Final-Over-Final-Condition proposed by Holmberg (2000) and Biberauer et al. (2008; 2014). If the constructions in question are investigated in more detail, however, it turns out that they are not entirely in accordance with either approach. Instead, the surface order seen in North Sámi seems to reflect a specific requirement that a postposition must immediately follow the lexical head of its complement.

2 The ordering of nouns and adpositions in North Sámi

In North Sámi, most adpositions follow their complement in the surface order, as in (1). That is, they are postpositions.[1] We can also note that complements of adpositions have genitive case.[2] Here and in following examples I boldface the relevant syntactic head (adposition or noun) and underline its complement.

(1) <u>mánáidgárddiid</u>   **várás**
     kindergarten.PL.GEN for

     'for (the) kindergartens'

Nouns, on the other hand, precede their complements, while adnominal adjectives precede nouns. This is shown in (2), where the adjective *ođđa* 'new' and the head noun *láhka* 'law' precede the complement PP *mánáidgárddiid várás* 'for kindergartens':

(2) ođđa **láhka**   <u>mánáidgárddiid</u>   várás
     new law.NOM kindergarten.PL.GEN for

     'a/the new law for kindergartens'

Now if a structure like (2) is to be embedded under a P, the result is as shown in (3):

(3) <u>ođđa lága</u>   **birra** <u>mánáidgárddiid</u>   várás
     new   law.GEN about kindergarten.PL.GEN for

     'about a/the new law for kindergartens'

We see here that the complement of the higher P ends up being discontinuous. While the noun and the adjective precede the higher P *birra* 'about', the PP complement of the noun follows the higher P.

The same pattern is seen in all cases where the nominal complement of a postposition has a postnominal modifier: the postposition invariably appears between the noun and

---

[1]North Sámi also has a few prepositions. An example is *miehtá* 'all over', which is shown in (i).

(i) Sii galget   galledit joatkkaskuvllaid   **miehtá** riikka.
     they shall.PRES.3PL visit.INF secondary.school.PL.ACC all.over country.GEN

     'They are going to visit secondary schools all over the country.'

[2]The examples in this paper are taken from the North Sámi corpus developed by Giellatekno, Centre for Saami language technology at the University of Tromsø. See http://gtweb.uit.no/korp/.

the postnominal modifier of the noun. The postnominal modifier of the noun can be a case-marked noun, as in (4), where the noun *olbmuid* 'people' is modified by the noun *govas*, which carries locative case and means 'in the picture'. As we see, the postposition *birra* 'about' intervenes between *olbmuid* and *govas*.

(4) Eará olbmuid   **birra** <u>govas</u>   sus   eai   lean   gal
     other person.PL.GEN about picture.LOC s/he.LOC NEG.3PL be.PAST.CONNEG PRT
     dieđut.
     information.PL.NOM

     'S/he had no information about other people in the picture.'

One can also note here that the modifying noun *govas* 'in the picture' is only loosely connected to the head noun *olbmuid* 'people' semantically. In some approaches modifiers of this type would be referred to as "adjuncts". It is clear, though, that all postnominal modifiers of nouns show the same behaviour when their containing noun phrase is the complement of a postposition. Thus, in (5) the postpositional phrase *mielli alde* 'on the river bank', which modifies the head noun *johtalus(a)* 'traffic' and which might be taken to be an adjunct in the nominal phrase, is separated from that head noun by the postposition *dáfus* 'concerning' in the same way as the modifying PP is separated from the head noun in (3):

(5) Johtalusa **dáfus**   <u>mielli   alde</u>, ferte   atnit   čielggasin
     traffic.GEN concerning river.bank.GEN on   must.PRES.3SG consider.INF clear.ESS
     ahte ...
     that ...

     'Concerning traffic on the river bank, one must consider it clear that ...'

Hence, the semantic relation between the head noun and the modifier does not make any difference. To keep things simple I will refer to all postnominal modifiers as complements.

The complement of the noun can also be an infinitival clause, as in (6), or a finite clause, as in (7). In either case, the clause follows the postposition – *birra* 'about' in (6), *vuostá* 'against' in (7) – while the noun and prenominal modifiers precede it.[3]

(6) Departemeanta sáhttá   addit   láhkaásahusaid   <u>gildosa</u>
     department.NOM can.PRES.3SG give.INF statutory.law.PL.ACC prohibition.GEN
     birra <u>guolástit ja   bivdit   dihto   guovlluin.</u>
     about fish.INF   and hunt.INF certain area.PL.LOC

     'The department can issue statutory laws about the prohibition of fishing and hunting in certain areas.'

---

[3]Nouns that are complements of numerals in the nominative singular appear in the genitive singular in North Sámi, as seen in (7).

(7) Eanetlohku jienastii Sáme-dikki evttohusa **vuostá** ahte
majority.NOM vote.PAST.3SG Sámi-parliament.GEN proposal.GEN against that

dat njeallje ođđa áirasa galget mannat dan
DEM.NOM four.NOM new representative.GEN shall.3PL go.INF DEM

sohkabeallái mii lea unnitlogus.
gender.ILL which.NOM is minority.LOC

'The majority voted against the proposal from the Sámi Parliament that the four
new representatives should go to that gender which is in minority.'

In all likelihood, the noun *lága* in (3) underlyingly forms a constituent with the PP
mánáidgárddiid várás, just like it does in (2). Similarly, the noun *olbmuid* forms a constituent with the noun *govas* in (4), and the same holds of the noun and the PP in (5) as
well as of the noun and the clause in (6) and (7). There are two possible ways in which
the surface order seen in these examples can be derived. Either the postpositions take
their complements to the left, and the final PP in (3), the locative noun in (4), the PP in
(5) and the clauses in (6) and (7) have been moved to the right of the postposition, or
else the postpositions take their complements to the right, but parts of the complements
move to the left of the postposition. In the next section, I will take a closer look at these
two possibilities.

3 Leftward or rightward movement?

Let us start by considering the underlying structure that must be postulated for (3) if
North Sámi postpositions take their complement to the left to begin with. I sketch this
structure schematically in (8). The nominal complement of the postposition P_2 precedes
P_2, and it consists of the head noun N, the prenominal adjective A and the postnominal
complement PP_1. In order not to jump to any conclusions concerning the category of
the nominal complement, I use the label XP here.

(8) a. $[_{PP2} [_{XP}$ A N $PP_1] P_2]$

b. * $[_{PP2} [_{XP}$ ođđa lága $[_{PP1}$ mánáidgárddiid várás]] birra]
new law.GEN kindergarten.PL.GEN for about

'about a/the new law for kindergartens'

From the structure in (8), the order seen in (3) above can be derived by movement of
PP_1 to the right of P_2, as shown in (9):

(9) a. $[[_{PP2} [_{XP}$ A N ~~PP₁~~$] P_2] PP_1]$

b. $[[_{PP2} [_{XP}$ ođđa lága ~~PP₁~~$]$ birra $] [_{PP1}$ mánáidgárddiid várás]]
new law.GEN about kindergarten.PL.GEN for

'about a/the new law for kindergartens'

We see that on the assumption that North Sámi postpositional phrases are head-final, the operation that is needed to get the right order is descriptively quite simple: all that is required is movement of the complement of the noun embedded under the higher P. As indicated in (9), one would probably have to say that the moved constituent right-adjoins to the higher PP. The problem with this proposal is that there is no obvious motivation for the movement operation.

As an alternative, one might want to propose that the landing site of the moved complement is the specifier position of a higher head Y, which has PP$_2$ as its complement to the left and takes its specifier to the right. The resulting structure would be as shown in (10).

(10)   [$_{YP}$ [$_{PP2}$ [$_{XP}$ A N ~~PP$_1$~~] P$_2$] Y PP$_1$]

There are however also certain problems with this proposal. Firstly, few or no cases of specifiers located to the right are attested in natural languages (see e.g. Kayne 1994). Secondly, the trigger for the movement remains mysterious – what property of Y could cause attraction of constituents as different as nouns, PPs and finite and non-finite clauses, across other elements in the nominal phrase?

The assumption that North Sámi PPs are underlyingly head-final does not lead to any satisfactory explanation for the orders that arise when the nominal complement of P has its own complement. So let us look instead at the consequences of taking North Sámi PPs to be underlyingly head-initial. Phrases like the one in (3) would then have the structure shown in (11) after the higher P has been merged over the nominal phrase:

(11)   a.   [$_{PP2}$ P$_2$ [$_{XP}$ A N PP$_1$]]

    b.   * [$_{PP2}$ **birra** [$_{XP}$ odda lága   [$_{PP1}$ mánáidgárddiid   várás]]]
            about   new law.GEN   kindergarten.PL.GEN for

      'about a/the new law for kindergartens'

Then a movement operation applies to (11) which gives as net result the structure sketched in (12):

(12)   a.   [[$_{ZP}$ A N] ... P$_2$ [$_{XP}$ ~~A N~~ PP$_1$]]

    b.   [[$_{ZP}$ odda lága   ] birra [$_{XP}$ ~~ZP~~ mánáidgárddiid   várás]]
            new law.GEN   about   kindergarten.PL.GEN for

      'about a/the new law for kindergartens'

Here some constituent ZP, which contains the adjective and the noun, has moved to the left of the higher adposition, while the complement of N is left behind. However, there cannot be any constituent that contains the adjective and the noun but excludes the complement of N. This means that there is more involved in the derivation of (3) than what is indicated in (12).

One possible derivation is shown in (13). Here PP$_1$ has moved to the Spec of a head Y which is located above PP$_2$. Assuming that adpositions are associated with functional domains, one could take Y to be a head in the functional domain of P_2. Then the whole nominal phrase, from which PP_1 has been extracted, moves to the Spec of an even higher head Z, while P_2 itself moves to Z, presumably via Y (a step not shown here).

(13) $[_{ZP} [_{XP} \text{A N } \overline{PP_1}] \text{ P2-Z } [_{YP} PP_1 \text{ Y } [_{PP2} \overline{P_2 [_{XP} \text{A N } PP_1]}]]]$

This derivation might be possible, but it is complicated, and it involves a number of movement operations that would have to be motivated.

I will propose instead a much simpler derivation, which I sketch in (14). Here the nominal complement of P moves as a whole to the Spec of a functional head p above P. The noun, and the elements that precede it inside the nominal phrase, are spelled out in the higher position, while any phrase YP that is the complement of the noun is spelled out in the lower position. Thus, the surface order is partly a matter of spellout.

(14) a. $[_{pP} [_{XP} \text{A N } \overline{YP}] \text{ p } [_{PP} \text{P } [_{XP} \overline{\text{A N}} \text{ YP }]]]$

   b. $[_{pP} [_{XP} \text{ oð\eth a lága } \overline{PP}] \text{ p } [_{PP} \text{ birra } [_{XP} \overline{\text{oð\eth a lága}} [_{PP} \text{ mánáidgárddiid}$
      new law.GEN   about   kindergarten.PL.GEN
      várás]]]]
      for

   'about a/the new law for kindergartens'

This analysis has a number of advantages. The problems related to extraction of complements of different types disappear, since there is no extraction of complements. The landing site is unproblematic, since it is a higher specifier position to the left, and the trigger is likely to be a feature of the attracting head.

As an alternative to the movement sketched in (14), one might want to propose that the nominal complement of P raises to the specifier of P. However, it has been proposed for adpositional phrases in many other languages that they contain functional elements – see e.g. Koopman (2000) and the articles in Cinque & Rizzi (2010). It is likely, then, that North Sámi postpositional phrases also contain more elements that just P. We also have indications that at least some postpositions in North Sámi are structurally complex.

In particular, many postpositions with local meaning come in several variants that are differentiated by suffixes. Some examples are given in (15):

(15)

	LOCATION	GOAL	PATH	
a.	bálddas	báldii	báldal	'beside'
b.	duohken	duohkái	duogi	'behind'
c.	gaskkas	gaskii	gaskal	'between'
d.	geahčen	geahčai	geaže	'at/to/past the end of'
e.	maŋis	maŋŋái	maŋil	'after'
f.	vuolde	vuollái	vuole	'under'

These postpositions consist of an invariant, root-like part plus endings that encode either location, goal of movement or path of movement. In order to show how this works in context, I give in (16) one example with each of the three postpositions that correspond to English *under*:

(16) a. Gávdnen   iežan   niibbi   <u>duorggaid</u> **vuolde.**
         find.PAST.1SG own.1SG knife.ACC twig.PL.GEN at.under

         'I found my knife under the (heap of) twigs.'

      b. Doppe čakŋala   <u>liegga gokčasa</u>   **vuollái.**
         there creep.PRES.3S warm blanket.GEN to.under

         'There s/he creeps under a/the warm blanket.'

      c. Geaidnu manai   <u>bávtte</u> **vuole.**
         road.NOM go.PAST.3SG cliff.GEN past.under

         'The road passed under a cliff.'

Pantcheva (2011) argues that spatial expressions involve a universal hierarchy of elements which can be given as follows: Route > Source > Goal > Place. The North Sámi
data are compatible with this claim, although the hierarchical ordering is not directly
visible in this language, since there are no containment relations between the relevant
markers. We can nevertheless take the postpositions in (15) to reflect the postpositional
base, which corresponds to the Axial Part in Pantcheva (2011) and also in Svenonius
(2006), in combination with an element that spells out one of the heads Route, Goal or
Place.[4] This means that the North Sámi postpositions are structurally complex, so that
there are landing sites in Spec positions above P for constituents that move out of the
complement of P.

This suffices to motivate the analysis that I propose of the constructions exemplified
in (3–7) above. I will continue to refer to the functional head above P as p, and I will
not discuss its identity any further here. The p head has an EPP feature which forces the
nominal complement of P to move to Spec-pP. This means that the real postposition is p.
But note that the morphology of the complex postpositions shown in (15) suggests that P
head-moves to p, since the elements that I take to be realisations of p are suffixed to the
postpositional bases, which I take to be realisations of P. In any case, if the nominal complement of P contains a complement of N, then this complement of N will obligatorily
be spelled out in the lower position.

4 Sheehan (2009) on complement stranding

Sheehan (2009) discusses data from English which bear a striking resemblance to the
North Sámi examples shown above. In English, PP complements of nouns and adjectives
can in some cases be left behind when the nominal or adjectival phrase moves to a higher
position. Two of Sheehan's examples are given in (17):

(17) a. A new book has come out about String Theory.

      b. How certain are you that the Mets will win?

---

[4]There is no specialised marking of Source in North Sámi. Instead, the forms that encode Place can also be
interpreted as Source. However, Svenonius (2009) argues that the source reading is always imposed from
outside of the phrase that carries the marking – for example by a motion verb or by some other element
expressing transition. Hence, there appears to be no reflex of the Source head in this language.

As we see, the PP complement of the noun *book* in (17a) and the CP complement of the adjective *certain* in (17b) have apparently been left behind after movement of their containing constituent. Sheehan analyses this phenomenon, which she calls *complement stranding*, as a consequence of the linearization procedure. I will summarise her analysis very briefly here.

In the structure in (18), the phrase β has been moved from the complement position of θ to the specifier position of α. Assuming that asymmetric c-command maps to linear precedence, in accordance with the Linear Correspondence Axiom (LCA) proposed by Kayne (1994), Sheehan notes that β's complement λ does not asymmetrically c-command anything in either of its positions. Moreover, in its higher position λ_2 it cannot be ordered with respect to α and θ, since it neither asymmetrically c-commands nor is asymmetrically c-commanded by either of them, on her definition of c-command. Consequently, only the base-generated copy of λ is a legitimate target for PF.

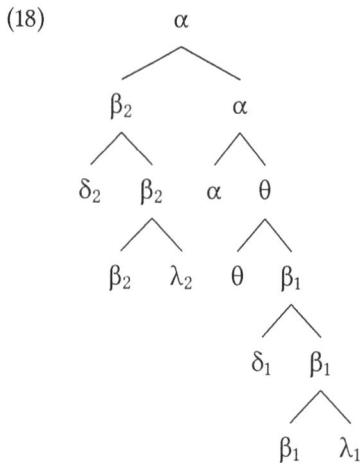

(18)

$$
\begin{array}{c}
\alpha \\
\diagup \diagdown \\
\beta_2 \qquad \alpha \\
\diagup\diagdown \quad \diagup\diagdown \\
\delta_2 \quad \beta_2 \quad \alpha \quad \theta \\
\diagup\diagdown \quad \diagup\diagdown \\
\beta_2 \ \lambda_2 \quad \theta \ \beta_1 \\
\diagup\diagdown \\
\delta_1 \ \beta_1 \\
\diagup\diagdown \\
\beta_1 \ \lambda_1
\end{array}
$$

However, as Sheehan also points out, this analysis predicts that in a phrase that moves from a complement position to a specifier position, the complement of the highest head inside that phrase will be stranded. For example, if the highest head in the nominal phrase *many books about morphology* is a Num head, with *many* located in the NumP projection, we might expect the complement of Num to be stranded, as in (19a), instead of the complement of N, as in (19b), the grammatical version.

(19) a. * Many have been borrowed books about morphology.

  b. Many books have been borrowed about morphology.

To get around this potential problem, Sheehan suggests that the Num head attracts its complement to its specifier position, and that this is the operation where the decision to spell out the complement of N in the low position is made. After movement of the complement of Num, the N will be sitting in a Spec position, so that linearization problems do not arise if the nominal phrase moves further.

Importantly, complement stranding in English is subject to certain restrictions. It is not allowed in specific DPs or in complements of verbs which force a concrete reading on their complement. Thus, complement stranding is not possible in (20), where the moved nominal phrase is definite, nor in (21), where the moved nominal phrase gets a concrete reading since it is underlyingly the object of *destroy*:

(20) a. This book about String Theory has finally come out.

  b. * This book has finally come out about String Theory.

(21) a. A book about String Theory has been destroyed.

  b. * A book has been destroyed about String Theory.

Sheehan (2009) argues that complement stranding is not possible in nominals that are strong islands. Thus, the possibility of stranding goes hand in hand with the possibility of extraction. Inspired by Uriagereka (1999) Sheehan takes islandhood to mean that the phrase in question goes to Spell-Out as soon as it is formed, and she suggests that a D head triggers Spell-Out – presumably because D is a phase head. It follows that when a DP is formed, it will go to Spell-Out as a unit, and there can be no subsequent extraction and no split phonological realisation. But if the nominal phrase is not a DP, it will go to Spell-Out together with its containing phase, and as a consequence, complement stranding will be triggered.

Following this line of reasoning, Sheehan further suggests that in cases where complement stranding appears to be optional in English, we are actually dealing with two different structures: nominals that strand their complements are NPs, while nominals that do not are DPs.

5 The Final-Over-Final Condition

The Final-Over-Final Condition is a constraint on syntactic ordering originally proposed in Holmberg (2000) and formulated as follows in Biberauer et al. (2014: 171):

(22) The Final-Over-Final Condition (FOFC)
  A head-final phrase αP cannot dominate a head-initial phrase βP, where α and β are heads in the same extended projection.

In the paper just mentioned, and also in Biberauer et al. (2008), a wealth of data from many languages is presented as evidence that the generalisation holds.

Concerning the nominal domain, Biberauer, Holmberg & Roberts take adpositions to belong to the same extended projection as their nominal complements. The pattern seen in the Finnish examples in (23) (from Biberauer et al. 2014: 187) can then be explained with reference to the FOFC. The Finnish adposition *yli* 'via over, across' can be a preposition or a postposition. When it is a preposition, it can take a nominal complement which contains a PP following the noun, as in (23a). But when it is a postposition, as in (23b), it cannot.

(23) a. **yli** [rajan [maitten välillä]]
     across border countries between

     'across the border between the countries'

 b. * [rajan [maitten välillä]] **yli**
     border countries between across

Biberauer, Holmberg & Robert then observe that Finnish has an alternative way to express the contents of the nominal phrase in (23ab), with an adjectival expression instead of a complement PP. The adjectival expression is prenominal, and consequently, a nominal phrase containing this expression can be embedded under a preposition, as in (24a), or under a postposition, as in (24b).

(24) a. **yli** [[maitten väli-se-n   ] rajan]
     across   countries between-ADJ-GEN border

     'across the border between the countries'

 b. [[maitten väli-se-n   ] rajan] **yli**
    countries between-ADJ-GEN border across

     'across the border between the countries'

The authors do not comment on the internal structure of the nominal phrases seen in these examples – they just state that the nominal phrase is head-initial in (23) but head-final in (24). Thus, they take the noun to be the head of the nominal phrase, which means that the adjectival phrase in (24) must be contained in the projection of the noun.

The FOFC is a descriptive generalisation and does not in itself say anything about the underlying mechanism. Sheehan (2009) points out that if one assumes, with Kayne (1994), that the LCA holds, and also that head-final orders result from roll-up movement, then only one additional restriction is needed to make sure that all resulting orders comply with the Final-Over-Final Condition – namely, that roll-up movement must begin at the bottom of the tree. It follows that the orders Aux – Verb – Object and Object – Verb – Auxiliary can be derived, for example, but not the order Verb – Object – Auxiliary. On this point Sheehan (2009) is fully in agreement with Biberauer et al. (2014). The potential advantage of Sheehan's approach is that it also offers an account of stranded complements. On her analysis, if a head-initial phrase like [Verb Object] is moved to the Spec of an auxiliary, then the lower copy of the object will be spelled out, so that the result is Verb – Aux – Object instead of Verb – Object – Auxiliary. In other words, on this approach derivations that violate the FOFC are not ungrammatical – they just do not lead to head-initial phrases being spelled out in front of their selecting heads.

6 North Sámi again

The account of complement stranding and of the FOFC presented in Sheehan (2009) appear at first glance to be relevant also for the ordering pattern seen in North Sámi postpositional phrases, where, if a nominal phrase containing a complement of the noun moves to the left of a selecting adposition, then the complement will be spelled out in the lower position. However, the complement stranding that can be observed in North Sámi postpositional phrases differs in several respects from the cases of stranding discussed by Sheehan. Firstly, in the North Sámi case there is no optionality. A noun that moves from the complement position of P to a position immediately preceding P in the linear order – to Spec,pP on my analysis – obligatorily leaves its complement behind. This holds also for nominal phrases that get a specific or definite reading, as seen in examples (25) and (26).

(25) Modealla lea hukse-juvvon <u>dan ipmárdusa</u> **nala** <u>ahte lea</u>
model.NOM is build-PASS.PTCP DEM.GEN understanding.GEN upon that is
<u>dásseárvu guovtti álbmoga gaskka.</u>
equality.NOM two.GEN people.GEN between
'The model is built upon the understanding that there is equality between two peoples.'

(26) Filbma lea <u>sin agálaš rahčama</u> **birra** <u>doalahit guohtun-eatnamiid.</u>
film.NOM is their eternal struggle.GEN about keep.INF grazing-land.PL.ACC
'The film is about their ever-lasting struggle to keep their grazing lands.'

North Sámi does not have obligatory articles,[5] and the categorical status of nominal phrases in this language is not entirely clear. It *is* clear, though, that the demonstrative *dan* in (25) and the possessor *sin* in (26) give their containing nominal phrases a definite reading. In addition, if we assume that adnominal adjectives are located in designated Spec positions above nP/NP, as proposed by Cinque (1994; 2010), and that other adnominal modifiers are also related to functional heads, it follows that both nominal phrases have functional structure above the nP/NP level. The presence of a demonstrative in (25) and of a possessor in (26) might be taken to indicate that both phrases are actually DPs. In any case, both phrases are of the type that would not allow complement stranding in English.

Secondly, while complement stranding is obligatory in postpositional phrases, in other cases a phrase that moves from a complement position to a specifier position can take its complement along. An example is seen in the passive construction in (27), where the nominal phrase headed by *gažaldagat* 'questions' has moved from object position to the surface subject position. Notably, the complex postpositional phrase which is the complement of *gažaldagat* is carried along – without this causing any linearization problems. Also note that there are no modifiers in front of the highest nominal here, and the phrase as a whole gets an indefinite reading, so that it appears to be of the type that would strand its complement in English.

---

[5]Nowadays, due to influence from Scandinavian, demonstratives are often used as definite articles while the numeral *okta* 'one' or the indefinite pronoun *muhtun* 'some' appear as indefinite articles.

(27) **Gažaldagat**   doarjagiid   hárrái
question.PL.NOM support.scheme.PL.GEN concerning
boazodoallo-šiehtadusa   olis   fertejit čielggad-uvvot dábálaš
reindeer.husbandry-agreement.GEN based.on must.3PL clarify-PASS.INF regular
šiehtadallamiid   bokte.
negotiation.PL.GEN by.means.of

'Questions concerning the reindeer husbandry agreement funding scheme must be settled by means of regular negotiations.'

In (28), a similar nominal phrase, headed by a noun without prenominal modifiers and allowing an indefinite reading, has left its PP complement behind when moving to a higher position. The phrase is the sole argument of an unaccusative verb, and it might be taken to originate in complement position.

(28) Dađistaga leat **dutkan-gáldut**   lassán-an   sápmelaččaid birra.
gradually are research-source.PL.NOM expand-PTCP Sámi.PL.GEN   about

'Gradually, research sources about the Sámi have expanded.'

Now consider (29), which is another passive construction. This time the passive subject has a demonstrative in initial position, which could be taken to mean that it is a DP, or at least that it has functional structure above nP/NP. Again, it carries its PP complement along to the surface subject position.

(29) Dát iešguđetge **doaimmat**   sáme-giela   várás leat hábme-juvvon
these separate   activity.PL.NOM sámi-language.GEN for   are form-PASS.PTCP
iešguđetge sektor-surggiin.
separate   sector-branch.PL.LOC

'These different activities for the Sámi language are designed in the different sector branches.'

It seems clear that complement stranding is not restricted in the same way in North Sámi as in English. Moreover, in cases where a nominal phrase moves to the front of a postposition, and the complement of the noun is a PP, there is in fact roll-up movement in the lower part of the structure. This was seen in example (3), which I repeat here as (30a). The structure is shown schematically in (30b).

(30) a. <u>ođđa lága</u>   **birra** <u>mánáidgárddiid</u>   várás
new law.GEN about kindergarten.PL.GEN for

'about a/the new law for kindergartens'

b. [$_{pP2}$ [$_{XP}$ A N ~~pP₁~~] p₂ [$_{PP2}$ P₂ [$_{XP}$ ~~A N~~ [$_{pP1}$ XP p₁ [$_{PP1}$ P₁ ~~XP~~]]]]]

Since the complement of the lower P has moved to the lower Spec,pP, there should be no linearization problems when the XP containing the lower PP moves to the Spec of the higher p – everything inside XP will precede the lower P, and consequently, all these elements should also precede the higher P after movement. In spite of this, the complement of the noun is left behind when the nominal phrase moves in front of the higher P. Hence, linearization does not appear to be the issue here.

If we go on to consider North Sámi postpositional phrases in light of the FOFC, the first point to be noted is that North Sámi nominal phrases are in fact head-initial. This is seen in the subject nominal phrase in (31), where the order is demonstrative – numeral – adjective – noun. In other words, elements that are located higher up in the syntactic structure consistently precede elements that are located lower down.

(31) Dat   guokte maŋemus iskosa čájehedje   ahte das eai
      DEM.NOM two.NOM latest   test.GEN show.PAST.3PL that it.LOC NEG.3PL
      lean   bakteriijat.
      be.PAST.CONNEG bacterium.PL.NOM

      'Those two latest tests showed that there were no bacteria in it.'

Consistently head-final nominal phrases have the opposite order, noun – adjective – numeral – demonstrative, as in the West Greenlandic nominal phrase in (32) (from Fortescue 1984: 118):

(32) qimmit qaqurtut marluk taakku
      dog.PL white.PL two   those

      'those two white dogs'

This means that PPs like those in (25) and (26) clearly violate the FOFC – if the p-P complex belongs to the nominal extended projection. In (25), the order is Dem – N – P, while in (26), it is Poss – A – N – P. In both cases, a head-initial phrase precedes the P.

Confronted with these constructions, the FOFC can be saved only if we assume that the postposition and the noun define separate extended projections. And in fact, this assumption is not entirely unreasonable, at least not for North Sámi. Many North Sámi postpositions have developed from nouns, and in many cases the nominal source is still easily recognised. For example, the string *joavkkuid gaskkas* can be parsed either as a possessor followed by a possessee in the locative case, as in (33a), or as a postposition preceded by its complement, as in (33b).

(33) a. joavkkuid   gaskka-s
         group.PL.GEN gap-LOC

         'in the groups' gap'

      b. joavkkuid   gaskkas
         group.PL.GEN between

         'between the groups'

In (33a) the nominal possessor, while contained in the functional domain of the possessee, necessarily also has its own functional domain. The example in (33b) could be taken to have a similar structure, the main difference being that the head of the larger functional domain here is of the category P.

If the line of reasoning that I have presented here is correct, neither the complement stranding approach presented in Sheehan (2009) nor the FOFC of Holmberg (2000) and Biberauer et al. (2008; 2014) can explain the ordering seen in North Sámi postpositional phrases. In North Sámi, there appears to be a restriction that applies specifically to postpositions, dictating that when the constituent immediately preceding the postposition is a nominal phrase, it must have the head noun as its final element. The restriction is mainly phonological in nature, since it forces the complement of the noun, if there is one, to be spelled out in the lower position.

An observation can now be added which concerns pronominal phrases. If the complement of a postposition is a pronominal phrase, then the pronoun need not be in final position within that phrase. An example is given in (34):

(34) Mun jurddašan   nu din_____ (buohkaid) **birra**.
      I   think.PRES.1SG so you.PL.GEN all.PL.GEN about

      'I think so much about you (all).'

If D is where person features are located, as Longobardi (2008) proposes, then *din* 'you' is in D, while the quantifier *buohkaid* 'all' is a position below D. Crucially, there is no requirement that *din* should appear immediately in front of the postposition, so that the quantifier can freely be added.[6]

7 A note on relative clauses

A pattern similar to the complement stranding seen with North Sámi postpositions is also obligatory in cases where a noun combines with a relative clause. Relative clauses in North Sámi follow their correlates, as illustrated in (35), where the relative clause *maid áigguiga rasttildit* 'which the two of them wanted to cross' follows the noun *jogaš* 'small river':

(35) **jogaš**   maid_____ áigguiga_____ rasttildit
      river.DIM.NOM which.ACC want.PAST.3DU cross.INF

      'a small river which the two of them wanted to cross'

If the nominal phrase in (35) is to be the complement of a postposition, the result is as shown in (36) – the nominal correlate of the relative clause precedes the postposition while the relative clause follows it:

(36) De   olliiga   jogaža   **lusa** maid_____ áigguiga_____ rasttildit.
      then arrive.PAST.3DU river.DIM.GEN to   which.ACC want.PAST.3DU cross.INF

      'Then the two of them reached a small river which they wanted to cross.'

---

[6]The pronominal part *din* is also optional, from a formal point of view, but *buohkaid* 'all' would get a third person interpretation if *din* is left out.

The construction in (36), with the relative clause separated from its correlate by an intervening postposition, is reminiscent of the cases of relative clause stranding discussed in Kayne (1994). Kayne assumes a raising analysis of relative clauses, which means that the correlate originates inside the relative clause and moves to the highest Spec of that clause. It is then to be expected that the correlate should in principle be able to move even higher, leaving the relative clause behind.

The raising analysis of relative clauses has attracted much attention. It has however also been challenged, among others by Platzack (2000) and Schmitt (2000), who both argued that relative clauses are CP complements of N. A well-known objection against the raising analysis has to do with morphological case, which presents a problem that can also be seen in the North Sámi example in (37):

(37) Mun in   diehtán   maidege   dan   dili   **birra**
     I   NEG.1SG know.PAST.CONNEG anything.ACC DEM.GEN situation.GEN about

     mas   son   elii.
     which.LOC s/he.NOM live.PAST.3SG

     'I did not know anything about the situation that s/he lived in.'

Here the correlate *dili* 'situation' has genitive case, as a consequence of being the complement of the postposition, while the relative pronoun *mas*, which introduces the relative clause, has locative case, in accordance with the syntactic function of the relativised element. This situation poses a problem for the raising analysis of relative clauses, which takes the relative pronoun and the correlate to originate as one constituent. It is possible to get around the problem – see e.g. Bianchi (2000) – but I would like instead to consider here the consequences of assuming that the relative clause is the complement of the correlate.

On a complement analysis of relative clauses, examples like (38) indicate that in North Sámi, complement stranding applies to relative clauses in the same way as it applies to other complements of nouns that move to pre-postpositional position, since on this analysis there is no constituent that contains the noun and the prenominal modifiers – a demonstrative and an adjective – but excludes the relative clause.

(38) Mun illudin   dan   čáppa skeaŋkka **ovddas** maid
     I   be.happy.PAST.1SG that.GEN beautiful gift.GEN for   which.ACC
     Vilges   ledjen   ožžon.
     Vilge.LOC be.PAST.1SG get.PTCP

     'I was happy for the beautiful present that I had got from Vilge.'

Once relative clauses are included in the discussion, it is also possible to draw a parallel between postpositional phrases on the one hand and possessor constructions on the other. As we saw already in (33a), possessors in North Sámi precede the possessee, and they are marked with genitive case. But if the possessor contains a relative clause, the relative clause follows the possessee. This is shown in (39), where the possessor phrase is headed by a pronoun, and in (40), where the possessor phrase is headed by a noun.

(39) Čájeha maid <u>sin</u> **nummáriid** geat leat geahččalan
show.PRES.3SG also 3PL.GEN number.PL.ACC who.PL.NOM be.PRES.3PL try.PTCP
dutnje riŋget.
you.ILL call.INF
'It also shows the numbers of those who have tried to call you.'

(40) Mun galggan olbmástalla-goahtit <u>dan</u> <u>máná</u> **váhnemiin**
I shall.PRES.1SG make.friends-begin.INF DEM.GEN child.GEN parent.COM
gii munno máná lea givssidan.
who.NOM 1.DU.GEN child.ACC is bully.PTCP
'I will begin to make friends with the parent of the child who has bullied our child.'

In other words, the possessee intervenes between the nominal head of the possessor phrase and the complement of that head in the same way as postpositions intervene between the head of its complement and the complement of that head. Two conclusions can be drawn from this fact. First, possessors in North Sámi originate in a position which is lower than the surface position of the possessed noun. Second, the same mechanism and the same restriction might be at work in possessed nominal phrases as well as in postpositional phrases. In both cases, the nominal head of a complement nominal phrase must immediately precede the complement-taking head.

8 Conclusion

We have seen that North Sámi postpositions are not strictly postpositional after all. If the nominal complement of a postposition has its own complement, then the complement of the noun will follow the postposition in the linear order, although the noun itself and all elements that precede it within the nominal phrase precede the postposition. In other words, in these cases the complement of the postposition gets a discontinuous realisation.

The observed pattern is not explained by the Final-Over-Final Condition (Holmberg 2000), since the preposed complement of the postposition is head initial. If the postposition is not a part of the extended projection of the noun, then the Final-Over-Final Condition does not apply at all. The Complement Stranding approach of Sheehan (2009) appears to be more relevant, but it turns out that the restrictions that regulate Complement Stranding in English do not carry over to North Sámi.

My conclusion concerning the North Sámi pattern is as follows. North Sámi postpositions take their complement to the right underlyingly. The complement of P is attracted to the Spec of p, a functional head above P, but if the nominal head of that complement has its own complement, the latter will be spelled out in the lower position. However, this does not happen as a consequence of the linearization problems that Sheehan (2009) discusses. It is instead due to a more specific requirement that the postposition must follow immediately after the nominal head of its complement. A similar effect is seen with possessors, which are spelled out in prenominal position but leave their complement behind in postnominal position. As it stands, however, the requirement that I propose here only refers to the surface order. The deeper nature of the requirement will have to be investigated further.

Acknowledgements

The research for this paper was financially supported by Bank of Sweden Tercentenary Foundation, grant no. P12-0188:1.

References

Bianchi, Valentina. 2000. The raising analysis of relative clauses: A reply to Borsley. *Linguistic Inquiry* 31. 123–140.

Biberauer, Theresa, Anders Holmberg & Ian Roberts. 2008. Structure and linearization in disharmonic word orders. In Charles B. Chang & Hannah J. Haynie (eds.), *Proceedings of the 26th West Coast Conference on Formal Linguistics*, 96–104. Somerville, MA: Cascadilla Proceedings Project.

Biberauer, Theresa, Anders Holmberg & Ian Roberts. 2014. A syntactic universal and its consequences. *Linguistic Inquiry* 45. 169–225.

Cinque, Guglielmo. 1994. On the evidence for partial N-movement in the Romance DP. In Guglielmo Cinque, Jan Koster, Jean-Yves Pollock, Luigi Rizzi & Raffaella Zanuttini (eds.), *Paths towards universal grammar*, 85–110. Washington, D.C: Georgetown University Press.

Cinque, Guglielmo. 2010. *The syntax of adjectives. A comparative study*. Cambridge, MA: MIT Press.

Cinque, Guglielmo & Luigi Rizzi (eds.). 2010. *Mapping spatial PPs*. Vol. 6 (The Cartography of Syntactic Structures). New York: Oxford University Press.

Fortescue, Michael. 1984. *West Greenlandic*. London: Croom Helm.

Holmberg, Anders. 2000. Deriving OV order in Finnish. In Peter Svenonius (ed.), *The derivation of VO and OV*, 123–152. Amsterdam: John Benjamins.

Kayne, Richard S. 1994. *The antisymmetry of syntax*. Cambridge: The MIT Press.

Koopman, Hilda J. 2000. Prepositions, postpositions, circumpositions, and particles: The structure of Dutch PPs. In Hilda J. Koopman (ed.), *The syntax of specifiers and heads: Collected essays of Hilda J. Koopman*, 204–260. London: Routledge.

Longobardi, Giuseppe. 2008. Reference to individuals, person, and the variety of mapping parameters. In Henrik Høeg Müller & Alex Klinge (eds.), *Essays on nominal determination: From morphology to discourse management*, 189–211. Amsterdam: John Benjamins.

Pantcheva, Marina Blagoeva. 2011. *Decomposing path. The nanosyntax of directional expressions*. CASTL, University of Tromsø dissertation.

Platzack, Christer. 2000. A Complement-of-N° account of restrictive and non-restrictive relatives: The case of Swedish. In Artemis Alexiadou, Paul Law, André Meinunger & Chris Wilder (eds.), *The syntax of relative clauses*, 265–308. Amsterdam: John Benjamins.

Schmitt, Cristina. 2000. Some consequences of the complement analysis for relative clauses, demonstratives, and the wrong adjectives. In Artemis Alexiadou, Paul Law, André Meinunger & Chris Wilder (eds.), *The syntax of relative clauses*, 309–348. Amsterdam: John Benjamins.

Sheehan, Michelle. 2009. The Final-over-Final constraint as a result of complement stranding. *Newcastle Working Papers in Linguistics* 15. 104–125.

Svenonius, Peter. 2006. The emergence of axial parts. *Tromsø Working Papers in Language and Linguistics (Nordlyd)* 33(1). 49–77.

Svenonius, Peter. 2009. *Location and source in North Sámi*. Ms., CASTL, University of Tromsø.

Uriagereka, Juan. 1999. Multiple spell-out. In Norbert Hornstein & Samuel David Epstein (eds.), *Working minimalism*, 251–282. Cambridge, MA: MIT Press.

Chapter 9

Probing the nature of the Final-over-Final Condition: The perspective from adpositions

Theresa Biberauer
University of Cambridge and Stellenbosch University

This paper considers the behaviour of adpositional structures in relation to the Final-over-Final Condition (FOFC) as originally formulated in Holmberg (2000). More specifically, it focuses on superficially FOFC-violating PP-structures of two main kinds – (i) circumpositional structures in which a head-initial locative preposition appears to be dominated by a head-final directional postposition, and (ii) head-initial PPs surfacing in preverbal position, i.e. structures in which head-initial PPs appear to be dominated by head-final VPs. The distribution and internal make-up of these structures, it is argued, points to a characterization of FOFC that crucially references extended projections, in the sense of Grimshaw.

1 Introduction

This paper considers the behaviour of adpositional structures in relation to the Final-over-Final Condition (FOFC). FOFC's initial formulation, due to Anders Holmberg, is given in (1) (the significance of the *unrestricted* characterization will become clear below):

(1) **The Final-over-Final Condition (FOFC) – unrestricted version**
If a phrase α is head-initial, then the phrase β immediately dominating α is head-initial. If α is head-final, β can be head-final or head-initial. (Holmberg 2000: 124)

Adposition-containing structures pose two distinct challenges to (1). Firstly, we observe that there are languages, notably including all members of the West Germanic family and also languages in what Stilo (2005) designates the Iranian "buffer zone" between Turkic and Semitic, that permit circumpositional structures in which a head-initial locative

Theresa Biberauer. 2017. Probing the nature of the Final-over-Final Condition: The perspective from adpositions. In Laura R. Bailey & Michelle Sheehan (eds.), *Order and structure in syntax I: Word order and syntactic structure*, 177–216. Berlin: Language Science Press.
DOI:10.5281/zenodo.1117694

preposition appears to be dominated by a head-final directional postposition. Consider Afrikaans (2) in this connection:[1]

(2) Hy loop **by** die deur **uit**.
     he walk by the door out
     'He walks out of the door.'

Secondly, as first noted by Sheehan (2008), we observe that OV-languages with initial PPs frequently seem to extrapose these PPs. (3) illustrates:

(3) (Kairiru, Papua New Guinea)
     Ei porritamiok a-pik   [**gege-i**   nat nai].
     3SG axe   3SG-take from-3SG child that
     '(S)he took the axe from that child.' (Wivell 1981: 151, via Hawkins 2008: 170)

This pattern superficially resembles the head-initial CP-extraposition pattern (near-)universally observed in OV-languages (see Dryer 2009).[2] Consider (4) by way of illustration:

(4) (Bengali)
     Chele-Ta Sune-che   [**je** or baba aS   -be].
     boy-CF   hear-PAST.3SG C his father come -FUT.3SG
     'The boy heard that his father will come.' (Bayer 2001: 14)

Significantly, CP-extraposition produces a FOFC-compliant structure in languages which otherwise have the ingredients to produce FOFC-violating structures: as schematised in (5), a head-final VP dominating a head-initial CP, as in (5a), would violate (1); extraposition of head-initial CP circumvents this, producing a FOFC-compliant structure (5b):[3]

(5) a. [$_{VP}$ [$_{CP}$ C TP] V] – FOFC-violating structure

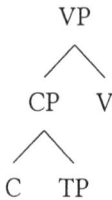

              VP
             ╱ ╲
           CP   V
          ╱ ╲
         C   TP

---

[1] Unless otherwise indicated, all Afrikaans examples were constructed by the author, a native-speaker. The data in question is entirely uncontroversial.

[2] Dryer (2009) highlights two exceptions to the extraposition pattern, Harar Oromo and Akkadian; see Biberauer (2017) for discussion suggesting that even these do not constitute FOFC violations.

[3] See Holmberg (2000: 135) for discussion of another striking case in which languages with the potential to violate FOFC – in this case, by being VO-languages with a head-final WANT-element – do not in fact do so.

b. [$_{VP}$ V [$_{CP}$ C TP]] – FOFC-compliant structure[4]

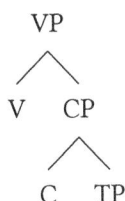

```
        VP
       /  \
      V    CP
          /  \
         C    TP
```

To the extent that OV-languages with head-initial PPs extrapose those PPs, they superficially appear to be employing another FOFC-compliance strategy (cf. Sheehan 2013). Importantly, however, the PP-extraposition pattern differs from the CP-extraposition one in not consistently being obligatory or, in some cases, even possible.

This paper's objective is to show how closer investigation of adpositional patterns like those in (3–4) reinforces the correctness of the view that FOFC is a narrower condition than originally envisaged in Holmberg (2000). More specifically, I will show that the notion of 'Extended Projection' (Grimshaw 1991 *et seq.*) is central to its formulation in the manner stated in (6) (*pace* i.a. Sheehan 2013; Hawkins 2013, Etxepare & Haddican 2017):

(6) **The Final-over-Final Condition (FOFC) – restricted version**
A head-final phrase αP cannot dominate a head-initial phrase βP where α and β are heads in the same Extended Projection.
(Biberauer, Holmberg, et al. 2014: 171)

Against this background, it emerges firstly, that the distribution of head-initial PPs in OV-languages does not constitute a challenge to the proposal that FOFC is a hierarchical universal in the sense of Whitman (2008), and, secondly, that attested circumpositional structures and, similarly, structures where head-final Ps dominate head-initial nominals also do not appear to instantiate FOFC-violating structures.

The paper is structured as follows: §2 briefly introduces the on-going debate regarding the nature of FOFC, which, I argue, PPs give us important insight into; §3 then considers the external distribution of head-initial PPs in OV-languages (these are expected to require obligatory extraposition on a (1)-type definition of FOFC, whereas a (6)-type definition does not rule out preverbal placement); §4 focuses on the PP-internal distribution of head-final Ps in languages with head-initial nominals and/or head-initial Ps (both (1)- and (6)-type FOFC predict head-final and head-initial Ps not to be able to co-occur in circumpositional structures, except where the latter dominate the former, giving initial-over-final structures; and (1)- but not (6)-type FOFC predicts that the combination of head-initial nominals and head-final PPs should not be attested); §5 concludes.

---

[4](5b) is a simplified structure, which does not correspond to any of the extraposition structures that have been proposed in the literature; the intention is simply to show that a postverbal head-initial CP will not violate FOFC. The question of the right analysis for extraposed CPs is a very interesting one in relation to which numerous questions remain open (see Biberauer & Sheehan 2012 for some FOFC-oriented discussion and references; see also note 10).

2 FOFC: What kind of condition is it?

FOFC has been argued to hold over a wide range of domains, ruling out structures including the following (see Biberauer, Holmberg, et al. 2014; Sheehan et al. 2017 for overview discussion and references, also of cases that superficially appear to instantiate the structures below):

(7) a. $^*[_{VP}$ VO] Aux
     b. $^*[_{VP}$ VO]... C
     c. $^*[_{PolP}$ Pol TP] C
     d. $^*[_{Asp}$ Asp VP] T
     e. $^*[_{D(em)P}\ [_{NumP}$ Num NP] D(em)]

It has also been shown to regulate diachronic change, including that taking place in contact scenarios (see Biberauer et al. 2009; 2010). Word-order changes necessarily proceed along FOFC-compliant pathways of the kind schematized in (8) and not along FOFC-violating routes like those in (9) [FOFC-violation **bold underlined** in each case]:

(8) a. [[[O V] I] C] > [C [[O V] I]] > [C [I [O V]]] > [C [I [V O]]]
     b. [C [I [V O]]] > [C [I [O V]]] > [C [[O V] I]] > [[[O V] I] C]

(9) a. *[[[O V] I] C] > [[**I [O V]**] C] > [C [I [O V]]] > [C [I [V O]]]
     b. *[[[O V] I] C] > [[**V O] I] C**] > [[**I [V O]] C**] > [C [I [V O]]]
     c. *[C [I [V O]]] > [C [[**V O] I**]] > [C [[O V] I]] > [[[O V] I] C]
     d. *[C [I [V O]]] > [[**I [V O]] C**] > [[**V O] I] C**] > [[[O V] I] C]

Given evidence such as the above, the question that arises is what kind of condition FOFC in fact **is**. Proposals to date include that it is a:

(10) a. (tendential) processing/parsing effect (Cecchetto 2013; Hawkins 2013,[5] Philip 2013; Mobbs 2015)
     b. (tendential) product of diachronic forces (Whitman 2013)
     c. superficial/"late" PF condition (Sheehan 2013; N. Richards 2016, Etxepare & Haddican 2017)
     d. deep syntactic condition (Biberauer et al. 2009 *et seq.*, Cecchetto 2013)

---

[5]It is worth noting that Hawkins (2013) disputes the validity of FOFC as a distinct condition on word-order variation, pointing out that it appears to be simultaneously too strong (in ruling out attested structures, including those that are the focus of this paper), and too weak (in failing to rule out unattested structures that don't meet the characterisation in (1) (see following note), but seem intuitively similar, e.g. extraposed head-final CPs of the kind we will discuss in §3.2; see (i) below; and, if one adopts (6) – which Hawkins rejects – the absence of head-initial relative clauses in languages with head-final nominals; see (ii) below).

(i) * $[_{VP}$ V $[_{CP}$ TP C]] – unattested (Hawkins 1990; though see §3.2 and note 29)

(ii) * $[_{NP}\ [_{CP}$ C TP] N] – unattested (Lehmann 1984)

His analysis therefore attempts to account for FOFC-type disharmony in processing-efficiency terms that also apply to initial-over-final (i.e. inverse-FOFC) disharmony.

With the exception of Cecchetto (2013), which we discuss under (10d) below, (10a,b)-type approaches allow for less commonly attested, but nevertheless genuine exceptions to (1)/(6):[6] FOFC on this view is a statistical universal, no different to the more robust of the cross-categorial word-order generalizations initially proposed by Greenberg (1963). Distinguishing between three sub-types of Greenbergian generalization – cross-categorial, hierarchical and derivational generalizations (Whitman 2008: 234; see also §5 below) – Whitman (*op. cit.*) argues that cross-categorial word-order generalizations are necessarily statistical, with Whitman (2013) specifically arguing that this is also the case for FOFC, interpreted as in (6). (10a,b), then, do not specifically rule out any of the structures we are concerned with in this paper, although processing and/or historical considerations may limit their attestation. They will be relevant to the present discussion in that we will consider the extent to which the types of external (processing and/or diachronic) forces proposed by the relevant authors correctly predict the (un)availability of the adpositional structures that are the main focus of this paper.

(10c) allows for syntax-internal final-over-initial structures, as long as these are not realized as such at PF, i.e. spellout considerations of different kinds preclude the realization of FOFC violations, with the result that apparent violations, such as those under discussion in this paper, must be shown to instantiate structures that do not pose the same spellout obstacle as unattested final-over-initial structures. For Sheehan (2013) and Etxepare & Haddican (2017 [this volume]), who build on Sheehan's analysis, FOFC-effects arise as a result of a linearization difficulty that emerges in the presence of complex specifiers (cf. also Uriagereka 1999, who first observes that LCA-based linearization of such specifiers requires an "induction step" over and above the "basic" asymmetric c-command statement standardly associated with the LCA of Kayne 1994).[7] As this difficulty arguably does not arise where a complex specifier has already been spelled out, a situation which has been argued to produce islands (see Sheehan 2013 for discussion and references), such structures are expected to be permitted. In the FOFC domain, this produces the prediction that apparently FOFC-violating structures will involve a head-initial *island* dominated by a head-final structure, regardless of the categorial specifications of the initial and final phrases: as the linearization difficulty outlined above applies equally to all complex specifiers, regardless of whether they are categorially the same or different to the projection with which they are merging, Sheehan is necessarily committed to the

---

[6]Cecchetto and Hawkins both assume unrestricted FOFC as in (1), while Whitman operates with restricted (6). The class of FOFC-violating structures that their approaches predict to be disfavoured, but nevertheless possible are therefore different, with the former authors interpreting a larger range of actually attested structures as being FOFC-violating – not only those in which a head-final XP dominates a head-initial one within its own Extended Projection, but also those in which this configuration involves a head-final XP dominating a head-initial one belonging to a **different** Extended Projection (e.g. a head-final VP dominating a head-initial PP, one of the cases of interest in this chapter).

[7]Worth noting here is that Sheehan and Etxepare & Haddican, like Biberauer, Holmberg, et al. (2014), assume head-final orders to be derived via some kind of movement. In these terms, a head-initial XP located in a (derived) specifier position constitutes a potential FOFC-violation; whether it is a *real* violation or not depends on the different assumptions these authors make about the nature of FOFC (see main text).

unrestricted FOFC in (1).[8] Consider (11), which depicts the linearization options for complex specifiers in Sheehan's (2013) system; YP represents a complex specifier and Z the head whose specifier it has, in accordance with standard minimalist assumptions about how structure is generated, merged (11a) or moved (11b,c) to create:

(11)   a. $[_{ZP} [_{YP} Y XP] Z ...]$

     b. $[_{ZP} [_{YP} Y XP] Z ... \cancel{[_{YP} Y XP]}]$

     c. $[_{ZP} [_{YP} Y \cancel{XP}] Z ... [_{YP} \cancel{Y} XP]]$

(11a) represents the case of a complex specifier spelled out in its first-merge position; the prediction is that these will necessarily be islands, with YP having been spelled out prior to merger with Z. (11b) involves a moved complex specifier, which has again been spelled out prior to movement, with the result that it can be spelled out in its derived position, again as an island. (11a)- and (11b)-type structures will be superficially FOFC-violating as Z will give the appearance of being final in relation to head-initial YP. (11c), on the other hand, involves a complex specifier which has *not* been spelled out prior to merger with Z; in Sheehan's system, head-initial YP cannot be spelled out in its derived position, requiring a "scattered deletion"-type operation which produces an extraposition structure, Y-Z-XP (see Sheehan 2013 for details). For this proposal, then, superficially FOFC-violating head-initial *island-containing* structures are predicted to be possible, and we also expect to see extraposition structures of a particular kind in contexts where a non-island apparently FOFC-violating structure might be expected. The examples in (12) illustrate – in simplified form – how this proposal would apply in the case of potentially FOFC-violating VOAux structures (a broadly Kaynian analysis is assumed, and ~~strikethrough~~ indicates lower copies):

(12)   a.   *... þæt [_{TP} ænig mon [_{VP} atellan [_{DP} ealne þone demm]] mæge]
         that   any man   relate   all   the   misery can
         [pseudo-Old English, based on attested (12b)]

     b.   [_{TP} þæt ænig mon [_{VP} atellan ~~ealne þone demm~~] mæge [~~atellan~~ ealne þone
            that any man   relate all the misery   can relate all   the
            demm]] > þæt ænig mon atellan mæge ealne þone demm
            misery

       '... that any man can relate all the misery ... '
       [Old English, Pintzuk 2005: 13 (coorosiu, Or_2:8.52.6.998), cited in Sheehan
       2013: 429]

Here the idea is that VP movement into the Aux-domain would result in the creation of a complex specifier containing the moved VO-VP. If VP were an island, it could be spelled out in the pre-auxiliary position, giving VOAux order of the kind illustrated in (12a). This is a scenario which potentially arises for VP-fronting structures in null-subject

---

[8]This means that not only the, in crosslinguistic terms, less common structures that are of central interest in this paper, but also undeniably more widely attested structures like head-initial nominals in OV languages must be interpreted as involving head-initial islands wherever they surface preverbally (see Sheehan (2013) for initial discussion).

languages.[9] Since "regular" (i.e. non-focused or topicalized) VPs presumably do not constitute islands, however, (12a) is unattested, not only in Old English, but also more generally. What we do see, however, are structures like that illustrated in (12b), where V is spelled out in pre-Aux position with O following; this is Sheehan's "scattered deleted" structure (11c) above, i.e. $[_{TP} [_{VP} V \Theta] T [_{VP} \cancel{V} O]]$.[10]

---

[9] The Sardinian example below illustrates:

(i) Sardinian
$[_{CP} [_{VP}$ **Tunkatu su barkone** $] C [_{TP}$ asa-T$]]$.
       shut   the window   have.2SG
'It's shut the window you have!' (Jones 1988: 339)

Here we have surface VOAux, but the structure, crucially, involves A-bar movement. VP can therefore plausibly be viewed as an island, with the result that it does not violate FOFC on Sheehan's account. It likewise does not violate FOFC on the Extended Projection (EP)-oriented analysis advocated in BHR and also in this paper as FOFC only applies to structures in which the specifier is occupied by the categorially identical head-initial XP that constitutes the complement of its head, i.e. where the EP-sister of a head X has "rolled up" into its specifier (see Biberauer 2017 for more detailed discussion).

The German examples in (ii) underline the striking difference between VOAux involving basic/neutral structures – which exhibit the ill-formedness expected in terms of FOFC (iib) – and VOAux structures involving non-neutral/A-bar movement-containing structures – which are well-formed (iia) (here, as elsewhere, we offer simplified structural representations):

(ii) a. Colloquial German
    $[_{CP} [_{VP}$ **Gesprochen mit ihr**$]$ hat-C $[_{TP}$ er t$_{that}$ nicht mehr t$_{VP}$$]]$
        spoken   with her has   he   not   more
    'As for speaking with her, he no longer did that.'

    b. * ... dass er nicht mehr gesprochen mit ihr hat.
          that he not   more spoken   with her has

    c. ... dass er nicht mehr gesprochen hat mit ihr.
         that he not   more spoken   has with her
    '... that he didn't talk to her anymore.' (Haider 2013: 80)

Exactly the same pattern emerges in Afrikaans, which permits PP-stranding much more readily than German.

[10] Assuming CP-complements to be embedded within a (non-island-inducing and often not overtly realized) nominal shell, as suggested for different reasons by i.a. Kayne (2008); Arsenijević (2009); Moulton (2009; 2013; 2015); Biberauer & Sheehan (2012), and Franco (2012), the CP-extraposition pattern that is typical of "non-rigid" OV-languages with head-initial CPs instantiates this "scattered deletion" pattern. This is schematized in (i), with (ii) providing an example from Afrikaans:

(i) $[_{VP} [_{nP}$ n $[_{CP}$ C TP$]]$ V $[_{nP}$ n $[_{CP}$ C TP$]]]$

(ii) Hy het **dit** geweet $[_{CP}$ **dat** ons nie 'n kans   het nie.$]$
    he has it   known   that us not a chance have POL
    'He knew it that we didn't have a chance.'

Of course, if CPs are embedded within this type of nominal shell, preverbal head-initial CPs would not violate FOFC on (6)-type interpretations of this condition, raising the question why they are nevertheless always extraposed, a matter I will not go into here. Also worth noting is the fact that the grammatical PP-extraposition structure in (iic) in the immediately preceding footnote instantiates a further case of the "scattered deletion" structure predicted by Sheehan's proposals.

Richards' PF-oriented proposals, in turn, rule out FOFC-violating structures occurring *within* the same phasal domain, or, more accurately, within the same spellout domain, with these latter corresponding to the domains defined by the original Phase Impenetrability Condition proposed in Chomsky (2000) and schematized for (a simplified version of) the clausal domain in (13) (see N. Richards 2016: Chapter 5 for detailed discussion):

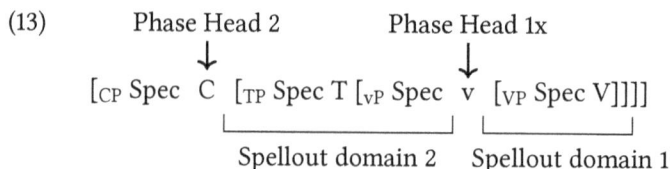

(13)   Phase Head 2   Phase Head 1x

$[_{CP}$ Spec   C $[_{TP}$ Spec T $[_{vP}$ Spec v $[_{VP}$ Spec V]]]]

Spellout domain 2   Spellout domain 1

For Richards, then, FOFC is an even more restricted condition than (6), holding only *within*, but not *across* phasal domains, and thus also not across an entire Extended Projection. VOAux is therefore ruled out wherever the VO-containing VP and Aux are spelled out together upon completion of a phase. One circumstance where this applies would be where V raises to v and the auxiliary is merged within the T-domain, as the v- and T-space will always be spelled out together at the point where C is merged; another is where V remains in situ, but the auxiliary is merged within the first phase, below the phase head (rather clearly, the proposal would make incorrect predictions in the absence of suitably articulated phasal domains, i.e. clausal structure entailing more than the bare V-v-T-C structure typically cited in the minimalist literature; see Biberauer & Roberts 2015 for discussion of one route via which to "join up" bare minimalist and more articulated approaches to clause structure).[11] Where Aux is T, VO-Aux is, in principle at least, available, which looks to be correct if we consider the attestation of VOT(ense) structures, featuring specifically Tense-marking auxiliaries: as already noted by Greenberg (1963), who consequently excluded non-inflecting auxiliaries from his V, O and Aux investigations, VOT is attested in systems where T does not inflect (see also Dryer 1992 and Biberauer 2017 for discussion, and see note 9 for another superficial VOAux structure that would be compatible with Richards' proposals). One complication here is the fact that there is no obvious explanation for why languages with **inflecting** T-auxiliaries do not permit VOAux structures, which seems to be the case (cf. Biberauer 2017 for further discussion).

---

[11]To the extent that they had not yet grammaticalised into T-elements, but instantiated spellouts of lower, non-phasal v-related heads, the Old and early Middle English auxiliaries would instantiate the types of auxiliary elements that Richards' proposals would predict to be incompatible with VOAux configurations, an accurate prediction (see Biberauer & Roberts 2010 for discussion of the plausibility of assuming non-T status for auxiliaries at the relevant stage). If, as is commonly assumed, the relevant pre-auxiliary constructions were biclausal, though, it is less clear that VOAux would be predicted to be ruled out. This looks like the incorrect prediction for earlier English, but it might fit with recent discoveries about the syntax of Latin, which permitted VO-Aux structures under certain clearly defined circumstances (cf. Danckaert to appear for discussion); these circumstances would, however, also be amenable to explanation on the basis of a (6)-type interpretation of FOFC. As the details remain to be worked out, we leave this matter aside here, noting only that Richards' proposals do entail different predictions for mono- and biclausal VOAux-containing structures.

The same question arises in relation to C-elements in VOC structures. For Richards, VOC is predicted to be possible where C belongs to the same clause as V, e.g. where it is a matrix C-particle of the type found in Sinitic and many other languages (cf. Biberauer 2017 for discussion); these particles are never spelled out at the same time as V, even if V undergoes raising into the higher phase. Structures of this type certainly exist, as predicted. More problematically, though, Richards' approach predicts that embedded clauses with VO-ordering should be compatible with final C-heads (e.g. complementizers). This is, however, strikingly at odds with typological findings about the distribution of **non-particle** subordinating complementizers (see again Dryer 2009, and also Biberauer 2017): VOC of this type simply does not seem to occur (see Biberauer 2017 for discussion of the two apparent counterexamples, neither of which ultimately constitute genuine VOC structures). Precisely why there should be such a striking difference between (subordinating) Complementizer elements of the kind that typologists have traditionally paid attention to and complementizer-particles is unclear on this approach.[12] More generally, the question for this approach, as should now be clear, is why the "inflecting" versus "non-inflecting" distinction should matter as it seems to: "inflecting" elements may not surface in FOFC-violating structures, regardless of how close or far a final inflecting element is from head-initial structure that is also part of its projection line (=Extended Projection), while "non-inflecting" elements may, again seemingly irrespective of the distance between them and the projecting initial element.

In the specific context of the structures we will be focusing our attention on here, Richards' approach does not rule out [$_{VP}$ [$_{PP}$ P DP] V]-type structures as PP defines its own spellout domain, meaning that PP and V could combine to produce structures of the type found in West Germanic and discussed further in §3.1. To the extent that final Ps can be shown to be located in a higher phase than the head-initial XPs they dominate (see §4 below), it also does not exclude [$_{PP}$ [$_{PP}$ P DP] P]- or [$_{PP}$ [$_{DP}$ D NP] P]-type structures. As we will see below, this approach is therefore as "strict" as the strictest version of (10d) when it comes to the adpositional structures that are the primary concern in this paper. These two approaches do, however, differ in respect of the predictions they make about the nature of the final elements dominating the head-initial XPs, a point we will return to in the following sections.

The final type of approach, (10d), outright bans the generation, at any stage of the syntactic derivation, of FOFC-violating structures; in other words, for these researchers, the ban on FOFC-violating structures is "deep", extending to the syntactic computation,

---

[12] By contrast, the (6)-type, Extended Projection-oriented interpretation of this condition does allow us to understand why particle and inflecting instantiations of "the same" category do not distribute identically as far as FOFC is concerned. The key here is that particles can, on independent grounds, be shown not to be part of the Extended Projection of the verb, while the complementizers that have been the traditional focus of typological research – which typically encode multiple clause-related properties (subordination, force, finiteness, mood, etc.) – rather clearly are, at least on the assumption that Extended Projection-defining elements share features, with the result that they can Agree with one another (see Biberauer 2017 for further discussion).

which may not at any point produce final-over-initial structures.[13] These approaches also crucially understand FOFC as in (6), i.e. as a condition which necessarily makes reference to Extended Projections. In terms of this type of approach, then, VOAux and VOC are always ruled out where Aux and C can be shown to contribute to the Extended Projection of the verb, i.e. where they reflect or are sensitive to formally encoded[14] verb-related properties like finiteness, mood, agreement, etc. (see Biberauer 2017 for detailed discussion). To the extent that elements that have been designated as 'particles' do not give evidence of a formal connection with the verb (see note 15), we expect them to be able to surface in apparently FOFC-violating structures, thus accounting for the structures mentioned above and also those more generally discussed in Biberauer (2017).

Strikingly, Cecchetto (2013) proposes a parsing-motivated rationale as the basis for the "deep" ban on FOFC assumed in (10d)-type approaches. Building on Hawkins' Performance-Grammar Correspondence model – i.e. the idea that grammars conventionalize syntactic structures in proportion to their degree of preference in performance – and the dependency-parsing ideas originally proposed to account for the Right Roof Constraint (Fodor 1978, Rochemont 1992) and elaborated in Ackema & Neeleman (2002), Cecchetto argues that structures in which a selecting head follows and is not immediately adjacent to the head it selects will never become conventionalized in Hawkins's sense; as a result, structures of this type are ruled out for "deep" reasons. Importantly, his approach distinguishes between heads that select another head within a single Extended Projection (e.g. v and V or C and T) and heads which select elements outside of their Extended Projection (e.g. V and P).[15] The former are heads which select for the specific featural content of the selected head, and thus, by hypothesis, have to precede it to satisfy parsing

---

[13] Haider (2013) also explicitly states that FOFC-violating structures are ruled out by his Basic Branching Condition (BBC) as this Condition requires functional heads always to be head-initial, regardless of the headedness of the lexical projection they dominate (cf. p.71 and section 5.2 for discussion). Crucially, however, this holds only of **derived** functional heads, i.e. those which are the target of head-movement or "feature attraction" (long-distance Agree, effectively). In his own words, "a functional projection is a *functional extension of a lexical projection* if and only if the lexical content for the *non-lexical functional head* position is derived. ... Note that according to this definition, a projection of a *lexical* functional head (e.g. a lexical Complementizer or a determiner) does not qualify as the *functional extension* of the complement of the functional head." (emphasis in the original; p.71). Final complementizers or question markers are thus equally ruled in, as his note 7 directly states, leaving us with no account of the VOC discrepancy that also poses a challenge for Richards' analysis (see main-text discussion), or, indeed, of any structures in which a "functional head is furnished with its own lexical content" (*ibid.*).

[14] The *formally encoded* qualification here is crucial: auxiliary and complementizer-elements which are sensitive to semantic properties that give no evidence of having been formally encoded via features that are visible Narrow Syntax-internally (cf. Chomsky 1995, Biberauer 2011 *et seq.*) in the relevant verbal system will, by hypothesis, not lead acquirers to postulate a formally instantiated connection between auxiliaries and complementizers; following on from Grimshaw's original definition of 'Extended Projection', we take the **formal** connection between verbs and higher verb-related elements like auxiliaries and complementizers to be crucial in establishing whether an element qualifies as part of an Extended Projection and, hence, whether it obeys (6)-type FOFC or not. Cf. also Wiltschko (2014 *et seq.*) on the difference between projecting versus modifying elements, which delivers the vital distinction in play here.

[15] CPs take on an interesting place in this context, clearly not being part of the same Extended Projection as the selecting V, but differing from nominal and adpositional selectees in sharing the [V]-related features associated with verbal Extended Projections. We leave this challenging case aside here, but see also note 11.

requirements; the latter involve heads which arguably select for phrasal complements (PPs) rather than individual heads, with the result that head-head adjacency is not specifically required. In one of the cases of interest to us in this paper, for example, V selects for a PP, rather than the P-head of the PP; as the featural relationship is between V and a phrase, that phrase can precede its selector, with the location of the head of the phrase being immaterial.[16]

Insofar as the specific focus of this paper is concerned, then, head-initial PPs in OV languages are not predicted by (10d)-analyses to be problematic, and neither are postpositions dominating head-initial nominals that can be shown not to be part of the Extended Projection of the nominal; similarly, postpositions dominating prepositions in circumpositional structures will only be problematic if they are part of the same Extended Projection. The difference between (10c) and (10d) is thus that the former predicts FOFC to hold across a more limited domain within an Extended Projection, with the latter also highlighting the relevance of the formal make-up of elements within an Extended Projection – broadly speaking, the difference between Extended Projection-defining heads versus non-projecting/modifying elements.

Having introduced the nature of the debate surrounding the nature of FOFC, let us now consider the adpositional structures that are our principal focus in this paper.

3 The external distribution of head-initial PPs in OV-languages

This section will be concerned with the external distribution of head-initial PPs in OV-languages. If FOFC is unrestricted, as in (1), we would expect systems of this kind either to extrapose their head-initial PPs in the manner observed for head-initial CPs (cf. (4) above), or, if Sheehan (2013) is correct, for preverbally occurring head-initial PPs to be islands, with "scattered deletion" structures arising where this is not the case (cf. 11b vs 11c above). If FOFC is restricted as in (6) or as in N. Richards's (2016) proposal, head-initial PPs are not expected to show any special behaviour. If external considerations such as processing are a factor, we expect the relevant processing considerations to determine the nature of possible versus impossible structures. What we will see is that the distribution of head-initial PPs in OV languages does not exhibit the patterns (10a,b) would lead us to expect; both (10c) and (10d) are compatible with the observed data, however.

We start with a consideration of OV Germanic (§3.1), before looking specifically at languages which, at first sight, appear to exhibit the obligatory PP extraposition pattern predicted by unrestricted (1-type) interpretations of FOFC, i.e. (10c)-type approaches (§3.2).

---

[16]Cf. also i.a. Baltin (1989), Payne (1993), Williams (2003), Sportiche (2005), Bruening (2009), Fowlie (2014), and Bruening et al. (2015) for argumentation focusing on completely different phenomena that also points to the fact that selection **across** Extended Projections is fundamentally different to selection within an Extended Projection. This is also necessarily the case in the context of theoretical approaches like Nanosyntax (cf. i.a. Starke 2009 and Pretorius in progress for discussion).

3.1 The distribution of head-initial PPs in OV West Germanic

In all OV West Germanic languages, it is unproblematic for head-initial PPs, like nominal complements, to surface preverbally. The illustrations in this section will mostly come from Afrikaans, the most extraposition-tolerating modern OV Germanic system. As (15) shows, mixed OV/VO Mòcheno,[17] which extraposes even more readily than Afrikaans, also permits preverbal PP-placement (the labelled bracketing is simplified for expository convenience):

(14) (Afrikaans)

    a. Ek het [$_{VP}$ [$_{PP}$ **in die bos**] **geloop**].
       I have   in the bush walked

       'I walked in the bush.'

    b. Ek sal [$_{VP}$ die presente [$_{PP}$ **vir/aan hulle**] **gee**].
       I shall   the presents   for/to   them give

       'I will give the presents to them.'

    c. Ek het [$_{VP}$ [$_{PP}$ **(vir) haar**] **gegroet**].
       I have   for her   greeted

       'I greeted her.'

(15) (Mòcheno)
    Gester   hot der Mario **en de Maria** a puach gem.
    yesterday has the Mario to the Mary a book given

    'Yesterday Mario gave Mary a book.' (Cognola 2012: 46)

(14a,b) illustrate the preverbal placement of adjunct and argument PPs respectively, while (14c) instantiates an innovated structure in modern Afrikaans, a form of differential object-marking involving the preposition *vir*, which also serves, as (14b) shows, as one of the options for marking indirect objects. As the comparison between (16a) and (16b) shows, *vir* is optional where an object has undergone leftward scrambling, but obligatory where it is in its unscrambled position:

(16) a. Ek het **(vir) haar** / **Sarie** gister   gegroet.
       I have for her / Sarah yesterday greeted

       'I greeted her/Sarah yesterday.'

    b. Ek het gister   *(vir) haar** / **Sarie** gegroet.
       I have yesterday for   her / Sarah greeted

       'I greeted her/Sarah yesterday.'

---

[17] Mòcheno, also known as Fersentalerisch, is an Upper German variety spoken in three villages in the Fersina valley in the Trentino province of northern Italy. Like neighbouring Cimbrian, it has been strongly influenced by contact with local varieties of Italian.

Assuming, in line with standard assumptions about West Germanic scrambling (cf. i.a. M. Richards 2004, Haider 2005, and Chocano 2007), that scrambled elements are located outside of VP, whereas their unscrambled counterparts are located VP-internally, the data in (16) mean that Afrikaans has innovated a context in which a head-initial PP is dominated by a head-final VP, namely (16b). This is *contra* what we might expect on the unrestricted interpretation of FOFC in (1), where it should never be possible for any head-initial XP to be dominated by a head-final XP.[18] Even more significantly in view of the (1)-induced expectation that OV-languages with initial PPs should permit these to be extraposed (cf. (3) above), it is completely impossible to extrapose a differentially object-marked nominal. As (17) shows, such objects are as unextraposable (17a) as their non-object-marked counterparts (17b) and nominal objects more generally (17c):

(17) a. * Ek het gister gegroet **vir haar** / **Sarie**.
     I have yesterday greeted for her / Sarah

  b. * Ek het gister gegroet **daardie meisie**.
     I have yesterday greeted that girl

  c. * Ek het gister gelees **daardie boek**.
     I have yesterday read that book

Further, as (18) shows, it is (colloquially) possible to extrapose from a differentially object-marked object (18b):

(18) a. Ek het net gister **vir Sarie wat by Sam-hulle bly** gegroet.
     I have just yesterday for Sarah what by Sam-them stay greeted

     'I greeted Sarah who lives with Sam and them just yesterday.'

  b. Ek het net gister **vir Sarie** gegroet **wat by Sam-hulle bly**.
     I have just yesterday for Sarah greated what by Sam-them stay

Strikingly, however, this extraposition does not resolve the superficial violation of (1) – [vp [pp P DP] V] – although it does decrease the number of elements that need to be parsed in order to identify the verb's PP-complement, which is in line with the Minimize Domains component of Hawkins' (1994 *et seq.*) processing proposals.[19] It also does not reflect the kind of extraposition pattern predicted by Sheehan's (2013) approach: a non-island PP-complement would, on this proposal, be expected to be linearized as in (19), which is, however, ungrammatical:

---

[18] It is usually thought (*pace* Haider 2013 and this author's previous work) that the verbal functional structure immediately above VP is also head-final in West Germanic systems, meaning that scrambling of a head-initial PP will still result in a configuration where a head-final PP is dominated by a head-final verbal XP; the point here, though, is that *vir*-structures of the kind illustrated in (16b) represent a **novel** final-over-initial structure, i.e. an innovation of the kind that FOFC should rule out (see Biberauer et al. 2009, Biberauer et al. 2010).

[19] Minimize Domains (MiD): The human processor prefers to minimize the connected sequences of linguistic forms and their conventionally associated syntactic and semantic properties in which relations of combination and/or dependency are processed. (Hawkins 2004: 32)

(19) a. ... [PP vir Sarie wat by Sam-hulle bly] gegroet [PP vir Sarie wat by Sam-hulle bly]

  b. * Ek het net gister   vir gegroet **Sarie wat by Sam-hulle bly.**
      I   have just yesterday for greeted Sarah what by Sam-them stay

As already hinted at above, there are other kinds of head-initial PPs in Afrikaans – and also to a lesser extent in Dutch and to an even lesser extent in German – that can extrapose, particularly in the spoken language. Consider the following examples (the judgments below reflect those of the author and, additionally, 11 native-speakers, who were asked to consider the acceptability of these structures in their own spoken Afrikaans[20]):

(20) a. Ek het geloop **in die bos.** (contrast 14a)
      I   have walked in the bush

      'I walked in the bush.'

  b. Ek sal   die present gee **vir** / **aan** [??] **hulle** / **iemand   wat dit sal**
      I   shall the present give for   to   them   someone what it shall
      waardeer.
      appreciate

      'I will give the present to them/someone who will appreciate it.'

  c. Ek het gereken **op hom.**
      I   have counted on him

      'I counted on him.'

(21) a. ... dat ek [AP [PP **met die antwoord**] tevrede] is.
          that I   with the answer   satisfied am

      '... that I am satisfied with the answer.'

  b. ... dat ek [AP tevrede [PP **met die antwoord**]] is.
          that I   satisfied   with the answer   am

  c. ... dat ek [AP tevrede] is [PP **met die antwoord**].
          that I   satisfied am   with the answer

Here we see that adjunct PPs readily extrapose (20a), while argument PPs can be more resistant to extraposition, although weight considerations of the sort that one might expect to play a role in an approach like that of Hawkins (1994 *et seq.*) can ameliorate argument-extraposition to the point of full acceptability (20b). Since argument PPs do not constitute islands – cf. the stranding examples in (22c) and (23c) – the requirement that precisely these head-initial PPs must be placed before their selector and cannot be extraposed constitutes a challenge to Sheehan's proposed analysis, in terms of which, recall, superficially FOFC-violating structures like [VP [PP P DP] V] and [AP [PP P DP] A] are predicted to involve head-initial **islands**:

---

[20]My informants were all native-speakers of Afrikaans, who either live in South Africa or use the language daily. They ranged in age from 17 to 65, and none are speakers of a markedly regional variety.

(22) a. (Afrikaans)
     Ek het   [VP [PP **op hom**] gereken].
     I   have   on him   counted

     'I counted on him.'

  b. (Standard Afrikaans)
     Op wie het jy   [VP [PP ~~op wie~~] gereken]?
     on who have you   counted

     'On whom were you counting?' (piedpiping)

  c. (Colloquial Afrikaans)
     Wie het jy   [VP [PP ~~wie~~[21] **op** ~~wie~~] gereken?]
     who have you   on   counted

     'Who were you counting on?' (stranding)

(23) a. Ek is   [AP [PP **met daardie student**] tevrede].
     I   am   with that   student satisfied

     'I am satisfied with the answer.'

  b. (Standard Afrikaans)
     Met wie is jy   [AP [PP met wie] tevrede]?
     with who are you   satisfied

     'With whom are you satisfied?' (piedpiping)

  c. (Colloquial Afrikaans)
     Wie is jy   [AP [PP ~~wie~~ **mee** ~~wie~~] tevrede]?
     who are you   with   satisfied

     'Who are you satisfied with?'

Importantly, PP-selecting verbs like *reken* in (20c) differ from ditransitives like *gee* in (20b) in that they do permit extraposition as an alternative to preverbal placement. Interestingly, the same is true for the PP-complements of adjectival predicates; thus (21c) is as readily accepted by the informants I consulted as (21a), while (21b) is more marked, but was nevertheless also accepted by all informants. Here, both Hawkins' and Sheehan's proposed analyses may facilitate insight into the observed extraposition patterns, though not into the optionality between (21a) and (21c); further, neither of these approaches would seem to have anything to say about the difference between (21b) and the corresponding verbal-complement pattern, VOAux, which is, of course, sharply ungrammatical – cf. (iib) in note 10, which is presented as (24a) here, with (24b) showing that the same pattern holds for Afrikaans:

---

[21]There is strong evidence that *wh*-extraction in Afrikaans, as in other (West Germanic) languages, involves extraction via the PP-edge (cf. Abels 2003; 2012 for detailed discussion). As (23c) shows, a subset of Afrikaans Ps undergo form-change when *wh*- and other pronominal elements pass through their specifiers; in this case, *met* ('with') becomes *mee*.

(24) a. (German)
　　　　*... dass er nicht mehr [AuxP [VP gesprochen [PP mit ihr]] hat]
　　　　　　that he not more　　　　　spoken　　　　with her has
　　　b. (Afrikaans)
　　　　*... dat hy nie meer [AuxP [VP gepraat [PP met haar]] het]
　　　　　　that he not more　　　　spoken　　with her　has

Importantly, PP-complements of copulas constitute an exception to the pattern that has emerged above: regardless of length, they cannot be fully extraposed (25b)[22]; where a complement-PP features independently extraposable material (e.g. the adjunct-PP in 25c), extraposition of this latter material is, however, possible, something which fits with the more general pattern in Afrikaans:

(25) a. ... dat ek **by die huis** met die eindelose tuine　is.
　　　　　　that I　by the house with the endless　gardens am

　　　　'... that I am at house with the endless gardens.'

　　　b. *... dat ek is **by die huis** (met die eindelose tuine).
　　　　　　that I　am by the house with the endless　gardens

　　　c. ... dat ek **by die huis** is met die eindelose tuine.
　　　　　　that I　by the house am with the endless　gardens

As was the case for (18b) above, the extraposition pattern in (25c) does not ameliorate the (1)-type FOFC-violation, although it does conform to MiD (see note 20).

Taken together, then, what the OV West Germanic data considered here seem to show is that:

- head-initial PPs are not banned from positions in which they superficially appear to violate (1), with some structures, like the copula-complements just considered (25), and the differentially marked objects discussed in (16–18), actually *requiring* superficially (1)-violating structures, and that

- it does not appear to be the case that all of the apparently (1)-violating structures constitute islands (cf. the data in 22–23).

Unexplained at this point, however, is why PP-extraposition should seem to be *necessary* in at least some OV-systems outside of West Germanic. This fact, first noted by Sheehan (2008), leaves open the possibility that West Germanic head-initial PPs may be crosslinguistically unusual and thus deserving of more detailed study in the FOFC context. The following section presents an empirical argument that this is not in fact the case, and that the conclusion reached here – namely that the external distribution of head-initial PPs in OV Germanic points to the inadequacy of (1)-type and also of at least some PF-oriented interpretations of FOFC – should stand.

---

[22]This mirrors the more generally observed pattern in Dutch, which, as Broekhuis (2013: 65) notes, consistently requires predicative complements to precede their selector, regardless of its nature.

3.2 The distribution of head-initial PPs in OV systems more generally

As Sheehan (2008; 2013) notes, head-initial PPs in OV systems are less common than head-final PPs in VO systems, i.e. the distribution of disharmony predicted by FOFC. Consultation of the *World Atlas of Language Structures* (*WALS* 2013) reveals that the current survey features just 14 OV and preposition systems, as opposed to 41 VO-languages with postpositions. Worth noting here, though, is that the West Germanic languages, like others exhibiting both pre- and postpositions, are not included in this total.[23] Nevertheless, what Sheehan (2008) showed for the 10 OV-plus-preposition systems registered in *WALS* 2008[24] is that 5 of these (Persian, Neo-Aramaic, Iraqw, Päri and Tobelo) necessarily require PPs to be extraposed, while Mangarrayi does not obviously have Ps, and all the other systems, barring Sorbian, permit both pre- and postverbal placement of PPs.[25] (25), deriving from Sheehan (2013: 435–436), illustrates structures from two of the obligatorily PP-postposing systems:

(26)   a. (Päri)

        Á-lw'ʌʌr' **kí**   **kwàc.**

        1SG-fear   PREP leopard

        'I am afraid of leopards.' (Anderson 1988: 303)

     b. (Iraqw)

        I-   na   ta'<a'>ín   **ay dí-r**   **konkomo.**

        3SG- PAST run<HAB>3SGM PREP place.F-CON cock

        'He ran to the place where the cock was.' (Mous 1993: 100)

Evidently, then, there are languages that avoid (1)-violating PP-V structures via an extraposition pattern that superficially resembles the CP-extraposition pattern in (4); furthermore, those that do not obligatorily do so all, with the exception of Afro-Asiatic Tigré (see below), belong to a single language family, Indo-European.

Closer consideration of the obligatory-extraposition systems – Persian, Neo-Aramaic, Iraqw, Päri and Tobelo – however highlights an important fact about the nature of the OV found in these systems: they are what Hawkins (2008) terms *OVX* systems, i.e. languages in which only nominal objects precede the verb, but elements of other kinds (e.g. PPs, CPs, etc.) follow it. For Hawkins, these languages are "basically VO" (see below and note 29 for further discussion)[26], a typological observation which is also readily understandable in (broadly Kaynian) generative terms. In these terms, these systems can be insightfully distinguished from more systematic (i.e. more consistently head-final) OV-languages in respect of the trigger underlying head-final orderings: in OVX languages,

---

[23]The OV-plus-preposition systems given in *WALS* 2013 are: Central Kurdish (Indo-European), Persian (Indo-European), Tajik (Indo-European), Sorbian (Indo-European), Iraqw (Afro-Asiatic), Neo-Aramaic (Afro-Asiatic), Tigré (Afro-Asiatic), Tigrinya (Afro-Asiatic), Päri (Nilo-Saharan), Tobelo (West Papuan), Tuvaluan (Austronesian), Mangarrayi (Australian), Kuku-Yalanji (Australian), and Tapiéte (Tupian).

[24]These 10 are those given in the previous footnote, except Kuku-Yalanji, Tapiéte, Tigrinya, and Tuvaluan.

[25]Sorbian is known to have had contact with German, which also exhibits fairly rigid, though, as noted in the previous section, not exceptionless PP-V behaviour.

[26]Interestingly, Persian and Neo-Aramaic are known to have derived from initially VO-systems.

this is a specifically **nominal**-oriented trigger (e.g. a phi-probe on v); in more generally OV-systems, v (and, possibly, a contiguous subset of the verbal heads dominating it) will have a less specialized trigger – possibly a "blind" diacritic of the kind assumed in Biberauer, Holmberg, et al. (2014) – resulting in more V-final patterns;[27] and in rigid OV-languages (e.g. Japanese and Malayalam), the "blind" diacritic is associated with all the heads making up the clausal spine, delivering consistently V-final structures. This gives the (simplified) OV-typology in (27) (cf. Biberauer & Sheehan 2013 for discussion and references):

(27) a. **rigid** OV: consistently V-final, e.g. Japanese, Malayalam, Sinhala, Korean, Kannada

   b. **intermediate OV**: DP/PP-V-CP/PP, e.g. West Germanic, Turkish, Hindi

   c. **OVX OV**: DP-V-X, e.g. Nupe, Mande (Niger-Congo), Päri, Iraqw, and Neo-Aramaic

Taking this into account, then, we can understand obligatory PP-extraposition as a reflex not of a FOFC-compliance strategy of the kind observed in the CP-domain (cf. again (4) above and also the discussion below), but, instead, of a particular type of OV-system.

That this seems to be the correct conclusion is strongly suggested by a very surprising and, to the best of our knowledge, to date unremarked-on fact about the nature of the PPs in OVX systems. As Hawkins (2008: 183) shows in a table demonstrating the headedness of PP in OVX systems (see Table 1 below), 14/21 languages that he considers (i.e. 67%) are *postpositional*, and, of the remaining 7 languages, some are designated as having "no dominant order". Table 1 reproduces Hawkins' table, while (28) illustrates OVX systems which extrapose *post*positional PPs:

Table 1: Headedness of PP in different types of OV and VO languages

Language type	Postpositions	Prepositions or No dominant order
XOV	97% (32)	3% (1)
OXV	94% (15)	6% (1)
OVX	67% (14)	33% (7)
VO	14% (22)	86% (134)

---

[27] As will be clear from the discussion in §3.1, structures in which PPs and CPs "leak" past V are possible in these systems. On the view that head-final structures are always derived, data of this kind can be accounted for by appealing to devices like a "scattered-deletion" mechanism of the kind proposed by Sheehan (2013; see main text) or remnant fronting which strands the extraposed XP. What is crucial is that the explanation should allow us to understand the difference between extraposable and non-extraposable XPs, which is, as things stand, an unresolved matter.

(28) a. (Supyire)

U sí sìɲciiyí   cya **mìì á**.
2SG FUT firewood.DEF seek 1SG POST

'She will fetch firewood for me.' (Carlson 1994: 274)

b. (Koyraboro Senni)

Ay ga   nooru wiri ay **baaba ga**.
1SG IMPF money seek 1SG father POST

'I will seek money from my father.' (Heath 1999: 139)

The OVX PP-facts, then, constitute a striking exception to the more general head-initial orientation of OVX systems: where we might have expected the postverbal PPs in OVX systems to be head-initial, making these systems more VO-like in the usual generative sense (i.e. more consistently head-initial), what we in fact find is that these PPs are head-final, i.e. that there are at least two lexical heads in these systems that are head-final.[28] In the present context, the fact that the extraposed PPs are head-final is particularly significant as it suggests that PP-extraposition in OVX systems is not correlated with PP-headedness in the way that CP-extraposition is. To see this, consider Bayer's (2001) discussion of CP-placement possibilities in languages like Bengali which have both initial and final C-elements. These can be schematized as follows:

(29) a. $V [_{CP} C [_{TP}...]]$

b. $[_{CP} [_{TP} ...T] C] V$

c. $* [_{CP} C[_{TP}...]] V$

d. $?? V [_{CP} [_{TP} ...\textbf{T}] \textbf{C}]$

Here we see that head-initial CPs must be extraposed (29a vs 29c) and that head-final CPs are perfect in preverbal position and only very marginally available (hence:

---

[28]It is worth noting that Hawkins' characterization of OVX languages as "basically VO" is not undermined by the fact that these languages so frequently have head-final PPs. This becomes clear from the way he leads into the table representing the adpositional headedness facts (Table 1 in the main text): "The OVX languages should be more head-initial and have head ordering correlations more like those of VO. ... For correlations involving postpositions vs. prepositions within a PP as XP, there is a clear tendency in this direction: one third of OVX languages have either prepositions or no dominant order within PP and are transitional between the overwhelmingly postpositional XOV and OXV and the predominantly preposi-tional VO" (p.183). In clausal placement terms, then, postverbal PPs fit the VO pattern, departing from the preverbal placement patterns – XOV and OXV – observed in OV languages. To the extent that OVX languages can be shown to have been "more OV" – i.e. more consistently head-final and thus less amenable to extraposition – at earlier points in their history, it may be that the 14 OV languages in Hawkins' sample afford insight into the way in which OV languages become more VO at the lowest levels of clausal structure: PP extraposition **precedes** a change in PP headedness. From a (1)-type FOFC perspective, this would be the expected sequence as VP dominates PP, and head-final to head-initial changes are expected to proceed top-down (cf. (8) above); on the (6)-type view being advocated here, the sequence of changes could as easily be the reverse, though, as V and P do not form part of the same extended projection line. As stable OV systems with head-initial PPs are clearly attested (see main text), there do not seem to be FOFC-based grounds for ruling out the reverse sequence of changes. Systems which have undergone these changes – like Persian and Neo-Aramaic (see note 27) – would nevertheless be interesting to investigate.

??) postverbally (29b vs 29d).[29] Extraposition of head-final CPs, then, appears to be, at best, very marginal, whereas head-final PP-extraposition is *required* in two-thirds of OVX systems (cf. Table 1).

OVX systems clearly merit much closer attention than has been the case to date – also because the obligatory extraposition of postpositional PPs would seem to entail a decrease in processing efficiency, a point that Hawkins (2008) does not address.[30] For our purposes, though, it seems that the following conclusions can be drawn about the FOFC-relevant insights afforded by the external distribution of PPs in OV-languages:

(i) uncontroversial unrestricted (i.e. (1)-type) FOFC-violating preverbal prepositional PP structures can be found in West Germanic and elsewhere (Persian, Sorbian, etc);

(ii) obligatory PP-extraposition in OV-languages is characteristic of OVX-type OV languages, which are "minimally OV", exhibiting many traits found in VO languages, i.e. there is an independent reason why we see PP-extraposition in the relevant languages, one which is not in force in more fundamentally OV languages; and

(iii) because PP-extraposition affects postpositional PPs twice as frequently as prepositional PPs, PP-extraposition cannot be viewed as a FOFC-compliance strategy parallel to CP-extraposition; it appears to apply independently of the need to create FOFC-compliant structures.

Taken together, these facts suggest, firstly, that a more restricted (6)-type interpretation of FOFC is required, and also that the distribution of PPs in OV-languages cannot always be viewed as being straightforwardly dictated by processing considerations (see again note 31).

---

[29] That head-final CP-extraposition is not crashingly bad in the way immediately preverbal placement of head-initial CPs is (29d vs 29c) is worth noting in the context of one of Hawkins' (2013) objections to FOFC as a condition that is too weak (see note 6). Hawkins' argument is that the two structures are equally bad, but this does not seem to be the case.

[30] That the postverbal placement of head-final PPs is not predicted to be optimal in processing efficiency terms is shown in the schematic representations in (i-ii) below:

(i) [$_{VP}$ [$_{PP}$ NP P] V]]

(ii) [$_{VP}$ V [$_{PP}$ NP P]]

As the structures show, immediately preverbal placement – XVO as in (i) – would be more efficient as selectee and selector are immediately adjacent in this case, in contrast to (ii), where the NP necessarily intervenes between V and the PP it selects (since PPs **always** extrapose in OVX languages, we can reason on the basis of selected – i.e. argument – PPs as these will necessarily be affected in the way described here; it is, of course, the case that PPs can also function as adjuncts). Interestingly, a preliminary investigation of the distribution of Hungarian PPs – which are most commonly postpositional – reveals that native-speakers are very happy to accept these in postverbal rather than the optimal preverbal position when the PPs in question are short (3 words, rather than 5 or 7 words; cf. Benson 2016 for discussion). Cursory investigation of some of the OVX languages listed on WALS suggests that length may more generally be a relevant consideration as the languages in question lack articles, and nominals appear to extrapose their complements, in the same way that Vs in these languages generally do. These patterns clearly deserve more detailed investigation.

In the following section, we will consider evidence from the internal make-up of PPs in languages featuring superficially (6)-type FOFC-violating structures in order to further support this conclusion.

4 The internal distribution of head-final Ps in languages with head-initial Ps (and nominals)

Our presentation in this section will again focus mostly on Afrikaans, a language that has been described as having all of the ingredients that are of principal interest to us here, namely prepositions, postpositions and circumpositions (and head-initial nominals).

4.1 A closer look at the Afrikaans adpositional system

(30) illustrates Afrikaans' head-initial nominals, prepositions, postpositions and circumpositions:

(30)   a. die boek **oor**   Chomsky
              the book about Chomsky

              'the book about Chomsky'

      b. Hulle loop die bos **in**/ skool **toe**.
             they walk the bush in school to

             'They walk into the bush/to school.'

      c. Hy loop **by** die huis   **uit**.
             he walk by the house out

             'He walks out of the house.'

If *in* and *toe* in (29b) combine with head-initial *die bos/skool* as part of the Extended Projection of N, as shown in (31), they will violate (6)-type FOFC (see i.a. Ledgeway 2012, and Sheehan & van der Wal 2015 for an argument in favour of the idea that Ps constitute part of the Extended Projection of fully extended nominals):

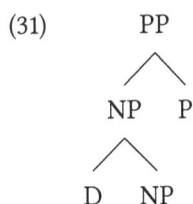

(31)   PP

         /‾‾\

        NP P

      /‾‾\

     D NP

Similarly, *by die huis uit* in (30c) will violate (6)-type FOFC if it can be shown that *uit* dominates *by*, as diagrammed in (32):

(32)
$$PP$$

```
        PP
       /  \
     PP     P
    /  \
   P    NP
```

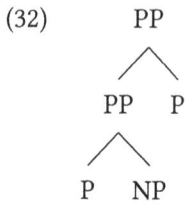

This does indeed seem to be the case as closer inspection of Afrikaans circumpositional structures reveals – and the same is true, more generally, for (non-English) West Germanic (cf. den Dikken 2010a and Koopman 2000; 2010 for two much-cited, comprehensive discussions of Dutch). More specifically, prepositions in these structures typically express location, while postpositions express direction,[31] and it is by now well established that P_{DIR} dominates P_{LOC} as shown in (33):[32]

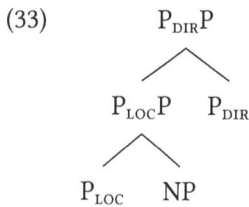

(33)
```
        P_DIR P
        /    \
    P_LOC P    P_DIR
    /   \
 P_LOC   NP
```

Various considerations, however, point to the need for care when it comes to simply assuming that Afrikaans' pre- and postpositions are equivalent types of element which can therefore be equally straightforwardly interpreted as elements belonging to the same Extended Projection. Consider, for example, the data in (34–37):

(34) a. Hulle het   [$_{PP}$ in die bos] geloop.
          they have   in the bush walked

          'They walked (around) in the bush.'

      b. Hulle het geloop [$_{PP}$ in die bos].
          They have walked   in the bush

          'They walked (around) in the bush.'

(35) a. Hulle het [$_{PP}$ die bos in] geloop.[33]
          they have   the bush in walked

          'They walked into the bush.'

---

[31] See Pretorius (2015; in preparation) for more detailed discussion, which also highlights some counterexamples to this generalization, however (see also J. Oosthuizen 2000, and H. Oosthuizen 2009).

[32] To the extent that P_{DIR} can be shown to be part of a different phasal domain to P_{LOC}, it will not violate the very restricted FOFC assumed by N. Richards (2016). In phasal terms, P_{DIR} could well be a plausible candidate for *p* (cf. Svenonius 2007; 2010), but we leave this matter aside here as it will emerge in the main text that there are good reasons not to worry about postpositional P_{DIR} as a violator of less restricted (6)-type FOFC; in other words, the restriction that Richards' proposed analysis would impose is not required as there are independent considerations.

b. *Hulle het   geloop [PP die bos   **in**].
   they   have walked   the bush in

Here we see a striking difference in extraposition possibilities, apparently depending on whether the PP is headed by a preposition or a postposition. Thus the PP headed by the prepositional (locative) *in* in (34) readily undergoes extraposition (cf. also the extraposition cases illustrated in (20–22) above), but it is not possible to extrapose postpositional PPs like (35). The data in (36–37), however, highlight the fact that this pre- versus postpositional distributional dichotomy is too simple:

(36) a. Hulle het   [PP **vir reën**] gebid.
        they have   for rain   prayed

        'They prayed for rain.'

     b. Hulle het   gebid [PP **vir reën**].
        they have prayed   for rain

        'They prayed for rain.'

(37) a. Hulle het   [PP **daarvoor**] gebid.
        they have   there.for   prayed

        'They prayed for it.'

     b. Hulle het   gebid [PP **daarvoor**].
        they have prayed   there.for

        'They prayed for it.'

(38) a. (Colloquial Afrikaans)
        Hulle het   [PP **vir dit**] gebid.
        they have   for it   prayed

        'They prayed for it.'

     b. Hulle het   gebid [PP **vir dit**].
        they have prayed   for it

        'They prayed for it.'

As (37b) shows, postpositions can extrapose when they are combined with so-called *R-pronouns*, i.e. pronouns in which a superficially locative R-containing form has replaced the expected pronominal form: here *daar* ('there') has replaced neuter *dit* ('it'), for example. Strikingly, though, it is not just the form of the pronoun that differs from what might be expected here; the P also takes on a different form as *vir* in (36) becomes *voor* in (37). The expected pronominal and prepositional forms are both possible in colloquial Afrikaans, but must co-occur as indicated in (38).[34]

---

[33] The adposition *in* offers a particularly clear illustration of the dominant preposition = location while post-position = direction pattern in Afrikaans. The same pattern holds in Dutch (see i.a. den Dikken 2010b: 27).

[34] *Vir daar* ('for there') and *voor dit* ('before it/that') are both possible in Afrikaans, but have different meanings, as the bracketed translations indicate.

Appealing to similarities with the behaviour of adpositions in Hungarian and other languages, Vos (2013) proposes that *voor* is in fact the *agreeing* counterpart of *vir*. That this is the correct intuition will become clear from our discussion of (47) below. For the moment, it suffices to note the important point that Afrikaans postpositions appear to be of at least two types: a non-alternating, non-extraposable type of the kind illustrated in (35), and an alternating, extraposable type of the kind illustrated in (37).

Focusing, then, on the extraposition discrepancy between preposition-containing (34) and postposition-containing (35): Pretorius (2015) suggests a potential reason for it, proposing that postpositions in Afrikaans, for the most part, instantiate the particle-component of particle verbs (I suggest that the alternating postpositions just introduced are the exception here, a matter to which we return below). Simplifying greatly, this has implications of the following kind for (35) (in the representations to follow, we leave aside considerations such as the fact that the object DP would probably have to originate to the left of the particle V in (4.1a'), where the moved object DP would be located, etc.):

(39)   a.   Hulle het   [$_{PP}$ die bos   in] geloop. (=35a) ✗
            they   have   the bush in   walked

            'They walked into the bush.'

       a.'   Hulle het [$_{VP}$ [$_{DP}$ die bos] [$_{particleV}$ **in** geloop^{35}]]. ✓

       b.   *Hulle het   geloop [$_{PP}$ die bos   in]. (=35b)
            they   have walked   the bush in

The idea here is that *in* is structurally represented in such a way that it is spelled out as part of V as in (4.1a'), rather than as part of the object as in (35/4.1a). This proposal rests on an intuition – fleshed out in more detail in Pretorius (2015; in preparation), but developed in a different way here – that also underlies the proposal made in den Dikken (2010b) for (standard spoken) Dutch, and part of what Aelbrecht & den Dikken (2013) propose in their analysis of identical doubling structures in certain Belgian varieties (e.g. Asse, illustrated in 40b), namely that postpositional elements are structurally deficient. To see how this is the case, consider, firstly, the data in (40):

(40)   a.   (Afrikaans)
            Hulle het   **in** die bos   **in** geloop.
            they   have in the bush in walked

            'They walked into the bush.'

       b.   (Asse Dutch)
            Hij is **op** den berg **op** geklommen.
            he   is on the hill   on climbed

            'He climbed onto the hill.'

---

[35]Importantly, *in geloop* ('walked in') here is distinct from *ingeloop* ('done in, cheated'). The distinction is readily captured by appealing to the distinction between separable (*in geloop*) versus non-separable particle verbs, though. Worth noting is that Afrikaans spelling conventions do not reflect the analysis proposed here; instead, they distinguish between "regular" particle verbs, which are written as a single word, and postposition-containing structures, in which the postposition – which, here, is simply another verbal particle – is written separately from the verb. I will continue to follow the Afrikaans spelling conventions in my presentation and discussion of the data.

Here we see sentences in which apparently identical pre- and postpositions create what seems to be a circumpositional structure, with the usual directional interpretation associated with these structures.[36] Importantly, both *in loop* ('walk in') and *op klim* ('climb up') exist as (directional) particle verbs in the respective varieties. Drawing on the further observation that both Dutch and Afrikaans have silent GO, which surfaces in structures like (41) (cf. Van Riemsdijk 2002 and Biberauer & Oosthuizen 2011), a (simplified) structure of the kind in (42) suggests itself to account for (40):

(41) a. (Afrikaans)
> Hy is dorp toe [GEGAAN].[37]
> he is town to gone

> 'He has gone to town.'

  b. (Gaan)
> Sy moet lughawe toe [GAAN].
> she must airport   to GO

> 'She must go to the airport.'

(42)

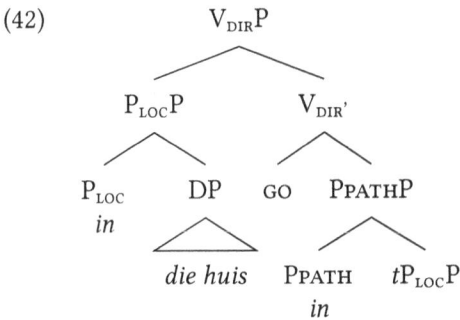

In (41), we see directionally interpreted structures that superficially lack a lexical verb. Van Riemsdijk (2002) provides convincing argumentation that this is only apparently the case, and that a silent motion verb, GO, is in fact present in the structure. If this silent verb is also present in directional circumpositional structures like (40) and in directional postpositional structures more generally, we can understand why the "postpositions" in both types of directional structures are not in fact postpositions at all. Consider (42) to

---

[36] As J. Oosthuizen (2000) and Aelbrecht & den Dikken (2013) both note, certain colloquial varieties appear to be in the process of *extending* this pattern to locative PPs; but it is clear in both cases that directional PPs were the starting point for this unusual pattern, an important consideration in view of the availability of silent GO (see main text).

[37] Since Afrikaans differs from Dutch in lacking HAVE VS BE auxiliary selection in compound tenses, it might at first sight seem implausible to assume the presence of van Riemsdijk's silent GO in structures like (41a), which contains a form of BE. Given the systematic discrepancies between null and overt elements of "the same" kind, however (cf. i.a. Nunes 2004; Kayne 2010; Biggs 2014; Douglas 2015 and Biberauer 2017), and also the minimal specification associated with BE in Afrikaans, as in Dutch, this become less troubling, however.

see why this is so. In this simplified structure, we follow den Dikken (2010a; 2010b) in assuming a PP-structure in which $P_{Loc}P$ is selected by $P_{PATH}P$ which is, in turn, potentially dominated by $P_{DIR}P$ (see also Koopman 2010 for a variant of this proposal). The presence of silent GO, however, raises the possibility of structures in which the directionality component is represented not by a fully-fledged $P_{DIR}P$, but instead, by a V that incorporates DIR, the silent V_{DIR} GO, i.e. a structure in which the PP-component is defective, with part of what PPs can contribute to directional meaning being contributed by the verbal entity with which they combine rather than by the PP itself.[38] Significantly in the current context, this structure does not violate (6)-type FOFC.

That directional postpositions appear to be defective compared to locative prepositions has already been demonstrated in (34–35) above, and the same discrepancy emerges when we consider the few directional prepositions in Afrikaans relative to their postpositional counterparts. Contrast (43) with (35), repeated here as (44), for example:

(43) a. Hy het **na die swembad**   gehardloop.
          he has to the swimming.pool run

          'He ran to the swimming pool.'

      b. Hy het gehardloop **na die swembad**.[39]
          he has run   to the swimming.pool

(44) a. Hulle het die bos **in** geloop.
          they have the bush in walked

          'They walked into the bush.'

      b. *Hulle het   geloop die bos   **in**.
          they   have walked the bush in

While prepositional *na*-PPs can extrapose, postpositional *in*-phrases like those in (35/44b) cannot. Aelbrecht & den Dikken (2013) propose that the $P_{DIR}P$-component of identical doubling structures lacks the full functional structure associated with the locative component of the circumposition: in lexicalization (and also "spanning"; see note 38) terms, we can think of this as doubling Ps being unspecified for DIR, with the result that they cannot themselves project PDIRP (*in* in (42) is the head of PPATHP). Here, we propose that this is also more generally true of directional postpositions in Afrikaans (and in West Germanic more generally).

This has two immediate consequences. The first of these is that P_{PATH} will incorporate with V_{DIR}, and, from there, into the lexical verb with which the V_{DIR}-structure is ultimately merged. Assuming the approach to incorporation in Roberts (2010), P_{PATH} constitutes a defective goal in relation to V_{DIR}, as it lacks the DIR-specification present

---

[38] In Pretorius (2015), these options are conceived of as the consequence of different 'spanning' choices (cf. Svenonius 2011; 2016).

[39] Significantly, the circumpositional variant of this structure, in which *na* is reinforced by *toe* – *Hulle het gehardloop na die swembad toe* – is also readily acceptable, in sharp contrast to the pattern to be discussed below and illustrated in (43). We return to this matter below.

on the latter head;[40] the incorporated P_{PATH}-V_{DIR}-structure, in turn, is plausibly a defective goal in relation to the lexical verb, which will bear verbal specifications typical of fully-fledged overt lexical items (cf. again the references cited above on the idea that null elements lack properties associated with their overt "counterparts", and i.a. Pesetsky 1995 and Bošković & Lasnik 2003). Taken together, these incorporations predict that postpositional Ps in Afrikaans (and Dutch) will always precede the lexical verb. This, in turn, allows us to understand why extraposition structures such as those in (35/44b) are barred: postpositional *in* must incorporate with a higher verbal head in order to be licensed, and, as such, cannot surface in the kind of non-adjacent, rightward position that extraposition structures would require. Further, thanks to this dependence on the relevant lexical verbs, the P-V combinations are recognized by native-speakers as (separable) particle verbs of the transparent (rather than idiomatic; cf. Wurmbrand 2000) kind.

The second immediate consequence is that we can understand the unavailability of Afrikaans (and Dutch) postpositional PP-extraposition as another manifestation of a more widely observed pattern in terms of which only "full" structures are extraposable (cf. i.a. Wurmbrand 2001: 294, Hinterhölzl 2005: 15, Biberauer & Sheehan 2012: 32ff, and Sheehan & van der Wal 2015: 8–9 for different versions of this idea). In West Germanic and many other OV-systems, for example, we observe that full CP-complements surface in postverbal position (cf. again (4) above, and (45a) below), while reduced clausal complements necessarily appear to the left of the verb (45b):

(45) a. (German)
          Es scheint, [$_{CP}$ **dass** der Hans sich rasiert].
          it seems   that the John self shaves

          'It seems that John is shaving himself.'

      b. ... dass Hans [$_{TP}$ sich zu rasieren] schien.
              that Hans   self to shave   seemed

          '... that Hans seemed to shave himself.'

      c. * ... dass Hans schien [$_{TP}$ sich zu rasieren].
              that Hans seemed   self to shave

If, as we have argued above, postpositional (directional) Ps lack the full functional structure associated with prepositional Ps, – which are mostly, but not exclusively locative; cf. *na* in (43) – we expect prepositional PPs to be extraposable, while postpositional PPs are not. Further, we also expect the pattern in (46), which would be puzzling if extraposition simply rested on the presence versus absence of a preposition-containing PP:

---

[40]If P_{PATH} is to constitute a defective goal in Roberts' terms, it has to be assumed that its categorial status will not render it partially distinct from V_{DIR}. Precisely how the formal specification of "what it means to be a V" versus "what it means to be a P" is to be captured is not a matter on which there is currently any consensus. What is clear, however, is the empirical fact that certain P-elements, like certain predicative nominal elements, can incorporate into verbal elements; if Roberts (2010) is correct in analyzing incorporation as involving the presence of defective goals, we can use cases like those under discussion here to make progress on long-standing questions about the categorial make-up of P-elements.

(46)   a.   Hulle het **by/in die bos** in geloop.
            They have by/in the bush in walked

            'They walked into the bush.'

       b. * Hulle het   geloop **by/in die bos** in.
            they have walked by/in the bush in

       c.   Hulle het   **ingeloop by/in die bos.**[41]
            they have in.walked by/in the bush

            'They walked into the bush.'

Here we see that circumpositional directional PPs mirror the behaviour of their post-positional counterparts (35/44b) in resisting extraposition (46b), despite the presence of a preposition. Significantly, extraposition of the (locative) prepositional component of the structure becomes possible where the postposition is immediately left-adjacent to the verb (46c), i.e. where, in our terms, it has incorporated, via V_{DIR} (cf. 42 above), with the lexical verb and thus been licensed by it.[42] In this case, the prepositional PP, which is, as always, a complete phasal structure, may extrapose; in (46b), by contrast, extraposition is barred because postpositional *in*, located on top of the fully phasal prepositional PP, is defective, meaning the circumpositional structure as a whole is non-phasal and thus, by hypothesis, non-extraposable. An appealing way to think about what is at stake here is via Sheehan & van der Wal's (2015) Extend licensing mechanism, given in (47):

(47)   Extend: All categories must be part of a phase (where phases include vP, CP, nP, DP, pP, and its CP-/upper-phase counterpart – MTB).

In terms of this plausibly interface-imposed requirement, incorporation into V in cases like (46c) allows defective directional *in*, which lacks its own functional structure, to satisfy (47): via incorporation, it becomes part of the vP-phase. Because postpositional *in* is not part of a (complete) phase prior to incorporation with V, it is not extraposable along with the lower (prepositional) phase of the PP-structure it is first-merged with.

As registered in note 39, *na ... toe* circumpositions constitute an exception to the pattern illustrated in (46): a *na ... toe* circumposition can extrapose, unlike *by/in die bos in* in (46b). Strikingly, we also do not see incorporation of the type in (46c) with *na ... toe* circumpositions. This is shown in (48), which is interpretively equivalent to (43) above:

---

[41]Importantly, *Hulle het ingeloop in die bos* in (46c) means 'They walked into the bush', like (46a), and not 'They walked in the bush', like (34b), *Hulle het geloop in die bos.*

[42]Interestingly, this structure may at first sight seem to resemble the extraposition pattern predicted by Sheehan's (2013) FOFC analysis (see again §2 above). As it is very clearly the *post*position that precedes the verb, with the prepositional PP following it, this is not a possible analysis of the structure, however. This is demonstrated in (i), which shows the scattered-deletion operation that would be expected on this approach:

   (i)   Hulle het **by/in** ~~die bos in~~ geloop ~~by/in~~ die   bos in.
         they have by/in the   bush   in walked by/in the bush in

(48)   a. Hulle het **na die swembad**   **toe** gehardloop.
    they have to the swimming.pool to   run

    'They ran to the swimming pool.'

   b. Hulle het   gehardloop **na die swembad**   **toe**.
    they have run   to the swimming.pool to

    'They ran to the swimming pool.'

   c. *Hulle het   **toe**gehardloop na die swembad.
    they   have to.run   to the swimming.pool

An immediate difference between (46a) and (48a) is that the preposition in (48), *na*, is already inherently directional, i.e. DIR-bearing; postpositional *toe* thus simply echoes its directional meaning in a manner semantically, though not lexically, reminiscent of the so-called German *shadow Ps* discussed in Noonan (2010). Further *toe* is one of the alternating P-forms in Afrikaans: like *vir/voor* illustrated in (36–37) above, it consistently takes a different form (*toe*) when it surfaces postnominally to that which we see when it occurs prenominally (*tot*); *met/mee* ('with') is the final member of this trio. (49) illustrates the alternation between *tot* and *toe*.

(49)   a. Sy het **tot** [PP by die see] gehardloop (en   daarna   omgedraai).
    she has to   by the sea run   and there.after around.turned

    'She ran to the sea and then turned around.'

   b. Sy het see **toe** gehardloop.
    she has sea to   run

    'She ran to(wards) the sea.'

As noted above, Vos (2013) analyses this alternation as signifying a difference between agreeing (*voor/toe/mee*) and non-agreeing (*vir/tot/met*) prepositions. Building, on the one hand, on this insight and on the idea that agreement is a property of a non-defective phasal domain (cf. i.a. Chomsky 2001), and, on the other, on the observation that *toe* differs from *tot* in giving non-telic directional interpretations, we propose that *toe* differs from the (particle) postpositions discussed to date in (i) being part of a non-defective upper (i.e. directional) phasal domain, and (ii) selecting a defective *lower* (i.e. locative) phasal domain. More specifically, I propose that *toe* is a P_{PATH}-head which consistently selects a nominal headed by silent PLACE (cf. Kayne 2008); see (51b) below. This nominal and the overt nominal structure it introduces are then always available for probing (and, in keeping with phi-probing heads in Afrikaans more generally,[43] subsequent movement) by the agreement-bearing P_{PATH}-head that is ultimately spelled out as *toe*.

---

[43] v, T and C can all be viewed as phi-probes which raise the nominals they probe. Prepositional Ps would then be an exception to this generalization. Since agreeing Ps are crosslinguistically unusual, it is tempting to think that selection relations between Ps and their complements do not typically involve phi, with the cases where we do see agreement signifying a departure from this norm. This would, of course, require rethinking of P's role as a licensor, with Sheehan & van der Wal's (2015) approach presenting a possible way forward.

A simplified version of the proposed derivation is schematized in (50) (strikethrough signifies a non-spelled-out lower copy, as before; the probing P_{DIR}-phasehead remains unrealized in (49b), but see (51) below for the overt realization option, which represents an innovation in Afrikaans):

(50)   [$_{PDIRP}$ DIR... [$_{PPATHP}$ [$_{DP}$ PLACE [$_{NP}$ *see*]] PATH-*toe* [$_{DP}$ PLACE [$_{NP}$ *see*]]]]

Tot, by contrast, selects a non-defective locative complement, necessarily introduced by an overt preposition (e.g. *by* in (49a)[44]), and lacks the phi-probe associated with *toe*, a factor which does not, however, render it defective in phasal terms, as the extraposition facts clearly show (see note 43 on the relation between P and phi); *tot* instead appears to lexicalize both PATH and DIR, suggesting that it may be the spellout of a composite head, i.e. both PATH and DIR in (50) above.

Significantly, the analysis proposed here means that *toe* in structures like (48) does not in fact combine with a PP headed by *na*, i.e. *na ... toe* structures do not involve a FOFC-violating final-over-initial configuration and are actually very different from the superficially very similar identical doubling circumpositions discussed above. The difference is schematized in (51):

(51)   a.   (=42)

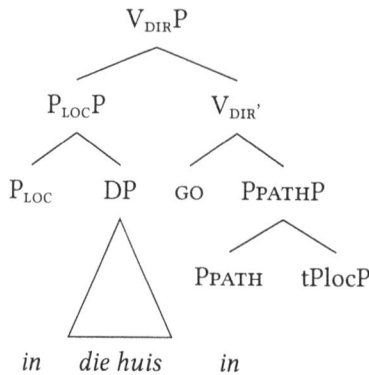

b.

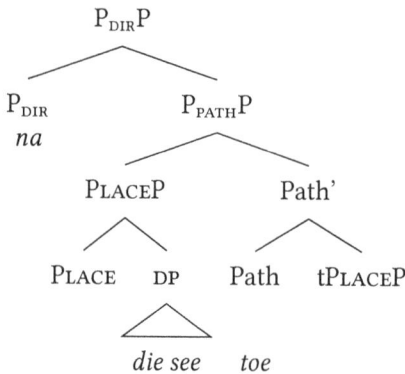

---

[44]Temporal *tot* – e.g. *tot Maandag*, 'until Monday' – is different, systematically selecting nominals.

The proposal for Afrikaans circumpositions, then, is that they come in two types. The first and most common type is that illustrated in (51a), in which the superficial postposition is not in fact part of a PP-structure, but is instead part of a particle-verb structure in which the directional component is contributed by silent V_{DIR} GO. Not expressing DIR itself, this defective P-element incorporates into V_{DIR} and, from there, into the lexical verb, which allows it to become part of a non-defective phasal domain (vP); the fact that it necessarily surfaces adjacent to the lexical verb and cannot be extraposed as part of a circumpositional structure thus follows. This type is also found in Dutch, mostly in the non-doubling form (e.g. *by die bos in* as in (46)), but also in some varieties in the doubling form found in Afrikaans (i.e. the *in die bos in*-variant of (46); cf. the Asse Dutch example in (40b)). The second type is an innovation in Afrikaans and involves a genuine circumpositional structure. This is, however, not a FOFC-violating structure either as head-initial *na* dominates head-final *toe*, as shown in (51b). The Ps in this structure are both non-defective, with the result that we expect it to be able to extrapose as in (48b); since the postpositional element is structurally too distant from the lexical verb to undergo incorporation, the ungrammaticality of (48c) above is also expected. Afrikaans, then, does not present any challenges to (6)-type FOFC.

4.2 A brief look at circumpositions beyond Afrikaans

We do not have the space to demonstrate this here, but it appears to be the case that Afrikaans' West Germanic relatives do not present additional FOFC challenges: the majority appear to feature only particle-type postpositions and, thus, lack genuine final-over-initial PP-structures as the structure in question is that illustrated in (42/51a). Worth noting, though, is the fact that the varieties of colloquial German that permit the shadow Ps analysed in Noonan (2010) and illustrated in (52) appear to mirror Afrikaans in featuring both (51a)- and (51b)-type circumpositional structures, with the shadow-containing circumpositions instantiating the latter type:

(52)   a. **in** der Kiste **drin**
           in the box   DR-in

           'inside the box' (=locative; Noonan 2010: 164)

   b. **um**   den Tisch **rum**
           round the table R-round

           'around the table' (=directional; Noonan 2010: 169)

The Gbe languages discussed in Aboh (2005; 2010), in turn, appear only to feature the (51b)-type, i.e. initial-over-final, inverse FOFC structures. In fact, this language family facilitates particularly clear insight into how different the P-elements in circumpositional structures can be. Consider (53):

(53)   a. Kɔjó zé àkwɛ **xlán** Kwésí. [Gungbe]
           Kojo take money P_1 Kwesi

           'Kojo sent money to Kwesi.'

   b. Kɔjó xɛ   távò lɔ **jí.**
      Kojo climb table DET P_2

     'Kojo climbed on top of the table.'

   c. Kpònɔn lɛ   nyì   àgbàn cè **xlán** gbó **jí.**
      police   NUM throw luggage POSS P_1 trash P_2

     'The policemen threw my luggage onto the dumpster.' (Aboh 2010: 227)

As Aboh demonstrates, the prepositional Ps (P_1) behave consistently differently from the postpositional Ps (P_2). The former evidently constitute a small closed class of 5 members all expressing direction/goal/path, all derive from verbs (possibly via serial constructions), seem to assign Case, and, rather unusually given the crosslinguistic trend, must necessarily be stranded. The latter, in turn, are all derived from nouns and closely resemble the elements Jackendoff (1996) originally designated *Axial Parts*;[45] there are about 30 of them, they do not assign Case, and they must be piedpiped. Following Svenonius's (2006) characterization of Ax(ial)PartP as a nominal-peripheral ('light noun') projection located below the P-layers expressing location and direction (54a), Gungbe circumpositions will be initial-over-final structures (54b), with the finality of the high nominal layer being unproblematic in view of Gungbe's head-final nominal system (54c):

(54)   a. *pP* > LocP > **AxPartP** > KP > DP

      b. *P_1P (direction/goal/path)* > **P_2P** (Aboh 2010)

      c. Mì fɔn   hàdòkpólɔ *sɔn* zàn lɔ jí!
         2PL stand immediately P_1 bed DET P_2

       'Get out of the bed immediately!' (Aboh 2010: 229)

Neither the West Germanic nor the Gbe languages, then, appear to constitute a challenge to FOFC as defined in (6). Interestingly, they do not challenge Richards's more restrictive phasal-domain-based definition either (see §2) as we have seen that none of the superficially problematic structures we have considered here involves a final head dominating an initial one that is located in the same spellout domain. What is striking about the adpositional facts discussed here, however, is the way in which Extended Projections repeatedly emerge as a relevant consideration in characterizing the structure of the observed phenomena: in some cases, postpositions can be shown to be defective, lacking the higher functional structure that would lead to their forming part of a complete phasal domain, with the result that they incorporate into another lexical category (here: V) and become part of a second Extended Projection (possibly, in line with Extend, as given in (47); this holds for particle-type postpositions as in 42/51a); in others, functional structure *below* the final element is defective, meaning that we again have a

---

[45]Jackendoff (1996: 14) clarifies the notion "Axial Part" as follows: 'The "axial parts" of an object – its top, bottom, front, back, sides, and ends – behave grammatically like parts of the object, but, unlike standard parts such as a handle or a leg, they have no distinctive shape. Rather, they are *regions* of the object (or its boundary) *determined by* their *relation to the object's axes*. The up-down axis determines top and bottom, the front-back axis determines front and back, and a complex set of criteria distinguishing horizontal axes determines sides and ends.' (my emphasis –TB)

defective Extended Projection (this holds for (51b)-type postpositions). That apparently FOFC-violating structures should repeatedly exhibit some kind of Extended Projection-related peculiarity is precisely what is expected on the restricted condition in (6), while it is unexplained on Richards' phasal-domain alternative.[46] The internal structure of apparently FOFC-violating PPs, we contend, therefore provides another argument in favour of this intermediate interpretation of FOFC's restrictiveness.

5 Conclusion

Our objective in this paper was to take a closer look at adpositional phrases in order to establish what kinds of insights these may add to our understanding of a by now much-discussed word-order condition, FOFC. Adpositions present numerous superficial challenges to FOFC, in both of its most familiar formulations, (1) and (6) above. Closer inspection of, on the one hand, the external distribution of PPs in OV-languages and, on the other, the internal make-up of post- and circumpositional PPs suggests that the latter, which crucially makes reference to Extended Projections, seems the most promising. The data we have considered reveals a range of ways in which postpositions and circumpositional structures can be unproblematic in the FOFC context. This is the same finding as that which has emerged from closer investigation of two other domains in which apparently FOFC-violating structures seem to abound, final particle-containing structures (Biberauer 2017), and 231 verb-clusters in West Germanic (Biberauer 2013). In each case, it has proven productive to investigate each apparently problematic structure independently as it has become clear that apparently FOFC-violating structures can arise from quite diverse underlying structures (hence also their (relatively) frequent attestation); and, in each case, it has emerged either that there are reasons to reject the possibility that the troublesome final elements examined form part of the same Extended Projection as lower head-initial elements, or that the underlying structure is in fact the inverse-FOFC (initial-over-final) one. Many cases still require detailed investigation, but, at this stage, the hypothesis that something like the restricted, crucially Extended Projection-based FOFC defined in (6) may indeed be universal remains promising.

If this is correct, FOFC is a 'deep' universal, constituting a condition on syntactic structure-building that has wide-ranging consequences for word order. This makes it, in the terms of Whitman (2008), both a cross-categorial generalization – i.e. 'one that references the internal properties of two or more categories, irrespective of their relationship in a particular structure' (233); Greenberg's Universal 3 is an example[47] – and a hierarchical generalization – i.e. 'one that describes the relative position of two or more

---

[46]It is worth noting that acknowledging the significance of defectivity in the FOFC context also seems like an important step in facilitating progress on the intriguing question of why VOC should be completely barred where C is a subordinating Complementizer of the kind considered in typological studies since Greenberg (1963; see again Dryer 2009 for overview discussion) while it seems extremely common where C is some kind of particle; and, similarly, why inflecting auxiliaries obey FOFC, while their particle counterparts do not. If the conforming elements contribute to Extended Projections, while particle elements do not, the discrepancy becomes less mysterious (see Biberauer 2017 for discussion).

[47]**Universal 3**: Languages with dominant VSO order are always prepositional (Greenberg 1963: 78).

categories in a single structure' (234); Greenberg's Universal 1 is an example.[48] For Whitman, cross-categorial and hierarchical generalizations are very different, with only the latter being 'deep' (in hierarchical terms, Universal 3 follows from the universal leftness of specifiers; cf. i.a. Kayne 1994, Ackema & Neeleman 2002, and Biberauer, Roberts & Sheehan 2014). FOFC, however, would seem to be a hybrid of two of the generalization-types identified by Whitman, a truly novel kind of syntactic universal, the existence of which was first registered by the linguist to whom this volume is dedicated, Anders Holmberg.

Abbreviations

Abbreviations used in this article follow the Leipzig Glossing Rules' instructions for word-by-word transcription, available at: https://www.eva.mpg.de/lingua/pdf/Glossing-Rules.pdf.

Acknowledgements

This paper is based on a presentation at the International Workshop on Adpositions, organized by Anders Holmberg and Sameerah Saheed and held at the University of Newcastle in June 2014. Thanks to the audience for their comments and suggestions, to Erin Pretorius for subsequent (and on-going) discussions of matters Afrikaans PP-related, and to Ian Roberts and two anonymous reviewers for input that has hopefully led to a sharpening of some of the ideas in this paper.

References

Abels, Klaus. 2003. *Successive cyclicity, anti-locality and adposition stranding*. University of Connecticut (Storrs) dissertation.

Abels, Klaus. 2012. The Italian left periphery: A view from locality. *Linguistic Inquiry* 43. 229–254.

Aboh, Enoch. 2005. The category P: The Kwa paradox. *Linguistic Analysis* (32). 615–646.

Aboh, Enoch. 2010. The P-route. In Cinque Guglielmo & Luigi Rizzi (eds.), *Mapping spatial PPs. The cartography of syntactic structures*, vol. 6, 225–260. New York: Oxford University Press.

Ackema, Peter & Ad Neeleman. 2002. Effects of short-term storage in processing rightward movement. In Sieb Nooteboom, Fred Weerman & Frank Wijnen (eds.), *Storage and computation in the language faculty*, 219–256. Dordrecht: Kluwer.

Aelbrecht, Lobke & Marcel den Dikken. 2013. Preposition doubling in Flemish dialects and its implications for the syntax of Dutch PPs. *Journal of Comparative Germanic Linguistics* 16. 33–68.

---

[48]**Universal 1:** In declarative sentences with nominal subject and object, the dominant order is always one in which the subject precedes the object.

Anderson, Torben. 1988. Ergativity in Päri, a Nilotic OVS language. *Lingua* 75. 289–324.

Arsenijević, Boban. 2009. Clausal complementation as relativization. *Lingua* 119. 39–50.

Baltin, Mark. 1989. Heads and projections. In Mark Baltin & Anthony S. Kroch (eds.), *Alternative conceptions of phrase structure*, 1–16. Chicago: UCP.

Bayer, Josef. 2001. Two grammars in one: Sentential complements and complementizers in Bengali and other South-Asian languages. In Peri Bhaskararao & Karumuri Venkata Subbarao (eds.), *The Yearbook of South Asian Languages 2001*, 11–36. New Delhi: Sage Publications.

Benson, Charlie. 2016. *Processing efficiency in flexible word order languages: An investigation into Hungarian*. BA dissertation, University of Cambridge.

Biberauer, Theresa. 2011. In defence of lexico-centric parametric variation: Two 3rd factor-constrained case studies. Paper presented at the Workshop on Formal Grammar and Syntactic Variation.

Biberauer, Theresa. 2013. Germanic verb clusters again – with Afrikaans centre-stage. Paper presented at the 28th Comparative Germanic Syntax Workshop (CGSW 29).

Biberauer, Theresa. 2017. Optional V2 in Modern Afrikaans: Probing a Germanic peculiarity. In Bettelou Los & Pieter de Haan (eds.), *Verb-Second languages: Essays in honour of Ans van Kemenade*. Amsterdam: John Benjamins.

Biberauer, Theresa, Anders Holmberg & Ian Roberts. 2014. A syntactic universal and its consequences. *Linguistic Inquiry* 45. 169–225.

Biberauer, Theresa, Glenda Newton & Michelle Sheehan. 2009. Limiting synchronic and diachronic variation and change: The Final-Over-Final Constraint. *Language and Linguistics* 10(4). 699–741.

Biberauer, Theresa & Johan Oosthuizen. 2011. More unbearably light elements? Silent verbs demanding overt complementizers in Afrikaans. *Snippets* 24. 5–6.

Biberauer, Theresa & Ian Roberts. 2010. Subjects, tense and verb-movement. In Theresa Biberauer, Anders Holmberg, Ian Roberts & Michelle Sheehan (eds.), *Parametric variation: Null subjects in minimalist theory*, 263–303. Cambridge: Cambridge University Press

Biberauer, Theresa & Ian Roberts. 2015. Rethinking formal hierarchies: A proposed unification. In James Chancharu, Xuhui Hu & Moreno Mitrović (eds.), *Rethinking formal hierarchies: A proposed unification*, vol. 7, 1–31. Cambridge: Cambridge Occasional Papers in Linguistics.

Biberauer, Theresa, Ian Roberts & Michelle Sheehan. 2014. No-choice parameters and the limits of syntactic variation. In Robert Santana-LaBarge (ed.), *Proceedings of the 31st West Coast Conference on Formal Linguistics (WCCFL 31)*, 46–55. Somerville, MA: Cascadilla Press.

Biberauer, Theresa & Michelle Sheehan. 2012. Disharmony, antisymmetry, and the Final-over-Final Constraint. In Valmala Elguea & Miriam Extebarria (eds.), *Ways of structure building*, 206–244. Oxford: Oxford University Press.

Biberauer, Theresa & Michelle Sheehan. 2013. Introduction. In Theresa Biberauer & Michelle Sheehan (eds.), *Theoretical approaches to disharmonic word order*, 1–46. Oxford: Oxford University Press.

Biberauer, Theresa, Michelle Sheehan & Glenda Newton. 2010. Impossible changes and impossible borrowings. In Anne Breitbarth, Christopher Lucas, Sheila Watts & David Willis (eds.), *Continuity and change in grammar*, 35–60. Amsterdam: John Benjamins.

Biggs, Alison. 2014. *Dissociating Case from Theta-Roles: A Comparative Investigation.* University of Cambridge. Ph.D. dissertation.

Bošković, Željko & Howard Lasnik. 2003. On the distribution of null complementizers. *Linguistic Inquiry* 34. 527–546.

Broekhuis, Hans. 2013. *Syntax of Dutch: Adpositions and adpositional phrases.* Amsterdam: Amsterdam University Press.

Bruening, Benjamin. 2009. Selectional asymmetries between CP and DP suggest that the DP Hypothesis is wrong. In Laurel MacKenzie (ed.), *U. Penn Working Papers in Linguistics 15.1 : Proceedings of the 32nd Annual Penn Linguistics Colloquium*, 26–35. Philadelphia: University of Pennsylvania. http://repository.upenn.edu/pwpl/vol15/iss1/. last accessed 2 June 2016.

Bruening, Benjamin, Xuyen Dinh & Lan Kim. 2015. *Selection, idioms, and the structure of nominal phrases with and without classifiers.* http://udel.edu/~bruening/Downloads/IdiomsClassifiers7.3.pdf, accessed 2016-6-2. Unpublished ms.

Carlson, Robert. 1994. *A grammar of Supyire.* Berlin: Mouton.

Cecchetto, Carlo. 2013. Backwards dependencies must be short: A unified account of the Final-over-Final and the Right Roof Constraints and its consequences for the syntax/morphology interface. In Theresa Biberauer & Ian Roberts (eds.), *Challenges to linearization*, 57–92. Berlin: Mouton de Gruyter.

Chocano, Gema. 2007. *Narrow syntax and phonological form: Scrambling in the Germanic languages.* Amsterdam: John Benjamins.

Chomsky, Noam. 1995. *The minimalist program.* Cambridge: MIT Press.

Chomsky, Noam. 2000. Minimalist inquiries: The framework. In Roger Martin, David Michaels & Juan Uriagereka (eds.), *Step by step: Essays on minimalist syntax in honor of Howard Lasnik*, 89–155. Cambridge: MIT Press.

Chomsky, Noam. 2001. Derivation by phase. In Michael Kenstowicz (ed.), *Ken Hale: A life in language*, 1–52. Cambridge: MIT Press.

Cognola, Federica. 2012. *Syntactic variation and verb second: A German dialect in Northern Italy.* Amsterdam: John Benjamins.

den Dikken, Marcel. 2010a. On the functional structure of locative and directional PPs. In Guglielmo Cinque & Luigi Rizzi (eds.), *Mapping spatial PPs*, 74–126. Oxford: Oxford University Press.

den Dikken, Marcel. 2010b. Directions from the GET-GO: On the syntax of manner-of-motion verbs in directional constructions. *Catalan Journal of Linguistics* 9. 25–55.

Douglas, Jamie. 2015. *Unifying that* that-*trace and anti-*that-*trace effects.* http://ling.auf.net/lingbuzz/002793, accessed 2016-12-15. Unpublished ms.

Dryer, Matthew. 1992. The Greenbergian word order correlations. *Language* 68. 81–138.

Dryer, Matthew. 2009. The branching direction theory revisited. In Sergio Scalise, Elisabetta Magni & Antonietta Bisetto (eds.), *Universals of language today*, 185–207. Berlin: Springer.

Etxepare, Ricardo & Bill Haddican. 2017. Repairing Final-Over-Final Condition violations: Evidence from Basque verb clusters. In Laura R. Bailey & Michelle Sheehan (eds.), *Order and structure in syntax: Word order and syntactic structure*, vol. I. Berlin: Language Science Press.

Fodor, Janet Dean. 1978. Parsing strategies and constraints on transformations. *Linguistic Inquiry* 9(3). 427–473.

Fowlie, Meaghan. 2014. Adjunction and minimalist grammars. In Glyn Morrill, Reinhard Muskens, Rainer Osswald & Frank Richter (eds.), *Proceedings of Formal Grammar 2014, Lecture Notes in Computer Science Vol. 8612*, 34–51. Dordrecht: Springer.

Franco, Ludovico. 2012. *Complementizers are not (demonstrative) pronouns and vice versa.* http://ling.auf.net/lingbuzz/001539. Unpublished ms.

Greenberg, Joseph H. 1963. Some universals of grammar with particular reference to the order of meaningful elements. *Universals of Language* 2. 73–113.

Grimshaw, Jane. 1991. *Extended Projection.* Unpublished ms. (Also appeared in J. Grimshaw (2005), Words and Structure, Stanford: CSLI).

Haider, Hubert. 2005. Mittelfeld phenomena: Scrambling in Germanic. In Martin Everaert & Henk van Riemsdijk (eds.), *The Blackwell companion to syntax*, vol. 3, 204–284. Oxford: Blackwell.

Haider, Hubert. 2013. *Symmetry breaking in syntax.* Cambridge: Cambridge University Press.

Hawkins, John A. 1990. A parsing theory of word order universals. *Linguistic Inquiry* 21. 223–262.

Hawkins, John A. 1994. *A performance theory of order and constituency.* Cambridge: Cambridge University Press.

Hawkins, John A. 2004. *Efficiency and complexity in grammar.* Oxford: Oxford University Press.

Hawkins, John A. 2008. An asymmetry between VO and OV language: The ordering of obliques. In Greville Corbett & Michael Noonan (eds.), *Case and grammatical relations: Essays in honour of Bernard Comrie*, 167–190. Amsterdam: John Benjamins.

Hawkins, John A. 2013. Disharmonic word orders from a processing efficiency perspective. In Theresa Biberauer & Michelle Sheehan (eds.), *Theoretical approaches to disharmonic word orders*, 391–406. Oxford: Oxford University Press.

Heath, Jeffrey. 1999. *A grammar of Koyraboro (Koroboro) senni.* Köln: Rüdiger Köppe.

Hinterhölzl, Roland. 2005. *Scrambling, remnant movement, and restructuring in West Germanic.* Oxford: Oxford University Press.

Holmberg, Anders. 2000. Deriving OV order in Finnish. In Peter Svenonius (ed.), *The derivation of VO and OV*, 123–152. Amsterdam: John Benjamins.

Jackendoff, Ray S. 1996. The architecture of the linguistic-spatial interface. In Paul Bloom, Mary Peterson, Lynn Nadel & Merrill Garrett (eds.), *Language and space*, 1–30. Cambridge, MA: MIT Press.

Jones, Michael Allan. 1988. *Sardinian syntax.* London: Routledge.

Kayne, Richard S. 1994. *The antisymmetry of syntax.* Cambridge: The MIT Press.

Kayne, Richard S. 2008. Expletives, datives, and the tension between morphology and syntax. In T. Biberauer (ed.), *The limits of syntactic variation*, 175–217. Amsterdam: John Benjamins.

Kayne, Richard S. 2010. *Movement and silence*. Oxford: Oxford University Press.

Koopman, Hilda J. 2000. Prepositions, postpositions, circumpositions, and particles: The structure of Dutch PPs. In Hilda J. Koopman (ed.), *The syntax of specifiers and heads: Collected essays of Hilda J. Koopman*, 204–260. London: Routledge.

Koopman, Hilda J. 2010. Prepositions, postpositions, circumpositions and particles. In Guglielmo Cinque & Luigi Rizzi (eds.), *Mapping spatial PPs. The Cartography of syntactic structures*, 26–73. Oxford: Oxford University Press.

Ledgeway, Adam. 2012. *From Latin to Romance: Morphosyntactic typology and change*. Oxford: Oxford University Press.

Lehmann, Christian. 1984. *Der Relativsatz*. Tübingen: Narr.

Mobbs, Ian. 2015. *Minimalism and the design of the language faculty*. University of Cambridge dissertation.

Moulton, Keir. 2009. *Natural selection and the syntax of clausal complementation*. University of Massachusetts, Amherst dissertation.

Moulton, Keir. 2013. Not moving clauses: Connectivity in clausal arguments. *Syntax* 16(3). 250–291.

Moulton, Keir. 2015. CP: Copies and compositionality. *Linguistic Inquiry* 46(2). 305–342.

Mous, Marten. 1993. *A grammar of Iraqw*. Hamburg: Buske.

Noonan, Michael. 2010. À to *zu*. In Guglielmo Cinque & Luigi Rizzi (eds.), *Mapping spatial PPs. The Cartography of syntactic structures*, vol. 6, 161–195. Oxford: Oxford University Press.

Nunes, Jairo. 2004. *Linearization of chains and sideward movement*. Cambridge, MA: MIT Press.

Oosthuizen, Helena. 2009. *Prepositions and verb particles in Afrikaans: Dialectal variation and developmental patterns*. University of Potsdam MA thesis.

Oosthuizen, Johan. 2000. Prepositions left and right in Afrikaans. *Stellenbosch Papers in Linguistics* 33. 67–90.

Payne, John. 1993. The headedness of Noun phrases: Slaying the nominal hydra. In Greville Corbett, Norman Fraser & Scott McGlashan (eds.), *Heads in grammatical theory*, 114–139. Cambridge: Cambridge University Press.

Pesetsky, David. 1995. *Zero syntax: Experiencers and cascades*. Cambridge, MA: The MIT Press.

Philip, Joy. 2013. (Dis)harmony, the Head-Proximate filter, and linkers. *Journal of Linguistics* 49(1). 165–213.

Pintzuk, Susan. 2005. Arguments against a universal base: Evidence from Old English. *English Language and Linguistics* 9. 115–138.

Pretorius, Erin. in preparation. *Adpositions and verbal particles in Afrikaans: A nanosyntactic analysis*. Utrecht & Stellenbosch Universities.

Pretorius, Erin. 2015. On the status of postpositions in Afrikaans. Paper presented at the 4th South African Microlinguistics Workshop.

Richards, Marc. 2004. *Object shift and scrambling in North and West Germanic: A case study in symmetrical syntax*. University of Cambridge dissertation.

Richards, Norvin. 2016. *Contiguity theory*. Cambridge, MA: MIT Press.

Roberts, Ian. 2010. *Agreement and head movement: Clitics, incorporation, and defective goals*. Cambridge, MA: The MIT Press.

Rochemont, Michael. 1992. Bounding rightward Ā-dependencies. In Helen Goodluck & Michael Rochemont (eds.), *Island constraints*, 373–397. Dordrecht: Kluwer.

Sheehan, Michelle. 2008. FOFC and phasal complements of V/v. Unpublished handout.

Sheehan, Michelle. 2013. Explaining the Final-over-Final Constraint: Formal and functional approaches. In Theresa Biberauer & Michelle Sheehan (eds.), *Theoretical approaches to disharmonic word orders*, 407–468. Oxford: Oxford University Press.

Sheehan, Michelle, Theresa Biberauer, Ian Roberts & Anders Holmberg (eds.). 2017. *The Final-over-Final condition*. Cambridge, MA: MIT Press.

Sheehan, Michelle & Jenneke van der Wal. 2015. Do we need abstract case? In Kyeongmin Kim, Pocholo Umbal, Trevor Block, Queenie Chan, Tanie Cheng, Kelli Finney, Mara Katz, Sophie Nickel-Thompson & Lisa Shorten (eds.), *Proceedings of WCCFL 33*, 351–360. Somerville, MA: Cascadilla Press.

Sportiche, Dominique. 2005. *Division of labor between Merge and Move: Strict locality of selection and apparent reconstruction paradoxes*. http://ling.auf.net/lingbuzz/000163, accessed 2016-6-2. Unpublished ms.

Starke, Michal. 2009. *Nanosyntax. A short primer to a new approach to language*. ling.auf.net/lingbuzz/001230/current.pdf, accessed 2016-6-2. Unpublished ms.

Stilo, Don. 2005. Iranian as buffer zone between the universal typologies of Turkic and Semitic. In Éva Ágnes Csató, Bo Isaksson & Carina Jahani (eds.), *Linguistic convergence and areal diffusion: Case studies from Iranian, Semitic and Turkic*, 35–63. London: Routledge/Curzon.

Svenonius, Peter. 2006. The emergence of axial parts. *Tromsø Working Papers in Language and Linguistics (Nordlyd)* 33(1). 49–77.

Svenonius, Peter. 2007. Adpositions, particles, and the arguments they introduce. In Eric Reuland, Tanmoy Bhattacharya & Giorgios Spathas (eds.), *Argument structure*, 63–103. Amsterdam: John Benjamins.

Svenonius, Peter. 2010. Spatial P in English. In Guglielmo Cinque & Luigi Rizzi (eds.), *Mapping spatial PPs. The cartography of syntactic structures*, vol. 6, 127–160. New York: Oxford University Press.

Svenonius, Peter. 2011. *Spanning*. Unpublished ms: University of Tromsø. http://ling.auf.net/lingBuzz/001501, accessed 2015-12-26.

Svenonius, Peter. 2016. Spans and words. In D. Siddiqi & Heidi Harley (eds.), *Morphological metatheory*, 201–222. Amsterdam: John Benjamins.

Uriagereka, Juan. 1999. Multiple spell-out. In Norbert Hornstein & Samuel David Epstein (eds.), *Working minimalism*, 251–282. Cambridge, MA: MIT Press.

Van Riemsdijk, Henk. 2002. The unbearable lightness of GOING. The projection parameter as a pure parameter governing the distribution of elliptic motion verbs in Germanic. *Journal of Comparative Germanic Linguistics* 5. 143–196.

Vos, M. De. 2013. Afrikaans mixed adposition orders as a PF-linearization effect. In Theresa Biberauer & Michelle Sheehan (eds.), *Theoretical approaches to disharmonic word order*, 333–357. Oxford: Oxford University Press.

Whitman, John. 2008. The classification of constituent order generalizations and diachronic explanation. In Jeff Good (ed.), *Linguistic universals and language change*, 233–252. Oxford: Oxford University Press.

Whitman, John. 2013. Diachronic interpretations of word order parameter cohesion. Paper presented at the 15th Diachronic Generative Syntax Conference (Ottawa).

Williams, Edwin. 2003. *Representation theory*. Cambridge, MA: MIT Press.

Wiltschko, Martina. 2014. *The universal structure of categories: Towards a formal typology*. Cambridge: Cambridge University Press.

Wivell, Richard. 1981. *Kairiru grammar*. University of Auckland MA thesis.

Wurmbrand, Susi. 2000. *The structure(s) of particle verbs*. http://web.mit.edu/susi/www/research/, accessed 2015-12-26. Unpublished ms.

Wurmbrand, Susi. 2001. *Infinitives: Restructuring and clause structure*. Berlin: Mouton.

Chapter 10

Nuclear stress and the life cycle of operators

Norvin Richards

MIT

I offer a new argument in this paper for the proposal that empty categories left by extraction of DP may be of different kinds, depending on the nature of the extraction (Perlmutter 1972; Cinque 1990; Postal 1994; 1998; 2001; O'Brien 2015; Stanton 2016, and much other work). The argument is based on Postal's (1994; 1998; 2001) discussion of the interaction of extraction with antipronominal contexts, together with Bresnan's (1971) observations about the effects of extraction on the position of nuclear stress.

1 Introduction

I will offer a new argument in this paper for the frequently defended proposal that empty categories left by extraction of DP may be of different kinds, depending on the nature of the extraction (Perlmutter 1972; Cinque 1990; Postal 1994; 1998; 2001; O'Brien 2015; Stanton 2016, and much other work). The argument will lean on two discoveries in previous work.

Postal (1994; 1998; 2001) (and following him, Stanton 2016 and O'Brien 2015) draws a distinction between two kinds of A-bar extraction. He notes that some kinds of extraction cannot take place out of positions that could not be occupied by an unstressed pronoun (Postal's *antipronominal contexts*), while other kinds of extraction can move DPs from such positions:

(1) a. That Porsche cost $50,000/*it.
     b. * $50,000, which that Porsche cost, (...is a lot of money.)
     c. What did that Porsche cost?

Postal, Stanton, and O'Brien all claim that extractions which are impossible out of antipronominal contexts leave something like a pronoun in the position of the gap, while other kinds of extractions leave some other kind of empty category behind. I will adopt and argue for this proposal.

Norvin Richards. 2017. Nuclear stress and the life cycle of operators. In Laura R. Bailey & Michelle Sheehan (eds.), *Order and structure in syntax I: Word order and syntactic structure*, 217–240. Berlin: Language Science Press. DOI:10.5281/zenodo.1117716

Bresnan (1971) also draws a distinction between two kinds of A-bar extraction. Her observations are about the interaction of extraction with the distribution of nuclear stress. We will see that Bresnan's distinction is the same as Postal's and Stanton's, and I will argue that it has the same explanation; extraction of a DP from a position of nuclear stress has different effects, depending on what kind of DP is left behind in the gap position. In the end, Bresnan's observation will allow for an explanation of the ban on certain kinds of extraction from antipronominal positions, which will be based on the principle that nuclear stress may not be assigned to phonologically null material. We will see that English uses various means of creating PF representations that avoid stress on phonologically null material, and that when these means fail, the structure is ill-formed. The account will rely on an approach to syntax and phonology, like the one in Bresnan (1971) and in Richards (2016), in which the narrow-syntactic computation is responsible for the creation of certain kinds of phonological representations; in particular, syntax will have to determine the position of nuclear stress.

Stanton (2016) proposes that some kinds of extraction involve the creation of an operator out of a pronoun via liberal use of Late Merge; such extractions, she claims, therefore leave a null pronoun behind in the extraction site, which is why they cannot take place out of antipronominal contexts. Similarly, Johnson (2012) and O'Brien (2015) argue that movement involves the creation of multidominance structures, which again effectively allow an operator to grow in size as it moves up the tree. Either of these approaches will be consistent with the facts to be discussed here. We will see that the proposal offers new support for something like Johnson's (2012) version of Fox's (2003) operation of Trace Conversion; the syntactic differences between the operator and its trace, rather than being created by a rule at LF, are present throughout the derivation.

The next section will describe some facts of English nuclear stress that will be important for the coming arguments. I will then review the data discussed by Postal (1994; 1998; 2001); Stanton (2016), and O'Brien (2015), and show how an account based on conditions on assignment of stress might capture them. We will then turn to Bresnan's (1971) observations about extraction and nuclear stress, and I will show that the categories of movement identified by Bresnan are the same as those identified by Postal, Stanton, and O'Brien. Finally, the paper will conclude with some observations about consequences of the proposal, and suggestions for possible future work.

It may also be worth directly pointing out several things I will not attempt to do in this paper. The account will rest on two ideas from previous work: that certain types of extraction leave behind null pronouns in the extraction site, and that there are positions in the sentence where a pronoun must, unusually, receive nuclear stress. Both of these ideas raise a host of interesting questions: what determines which types of extraction leave pronouns behind? Why must pronouns receive stress in certain positions, though not in others? I will offer some speculations about the answers to these questions, but will leave serious investigation of them for the future. For answers to the first question, in particular, see Stanton (2016) and O'Brien (2015).

2 English nuclear stress

In English, and possibly universally, nuclear stress in examples like (2) typically appears on the direct object (I will mark nuclear stress throughout with SMALL CAPITALS):

(2)   a. Bill saw a CAR.

      b. Mary bought a BOOK.

      c. I heard MUSIC.

There are various kinds of expressions that typically do not get nuclear stress, even in object position, including pronouns and words like *something, someone, anything, anyone*, which I will refer to here as 'simple indefinites'. When a direct object is a pronoun or a simple indefinite, nuclear stress appears on the verb:

(3)   a. Bill SAW me.

      b. Mary BOUGHT something.

      c. I don't HEAR anything.

Bresnan (1971) notes that DPs which are immediately anaphoric to a preceding DP, even if definite, exhibit the same behavior (Bresnan 1971: 258):

(4)   John knows a woman who excels at karate, and he AVOIDS the woman.

Pronouns, simple indefinites, and immediately anaphoric DPs, then, all avoid nuclear stress; in all of the examples just discussed, nuclear stress then shifts to the verb. I will review some other salient cases in the following section. In the section after that, we will turn to Postal's antipronominal contexts, where we will see the facts change.

2.1 Nuclear stress in PP

Objects of prepositions are a common locus of nuclear stress, and when the object cannot bear nuclear stress, stress is relocated, typically either to the preposition or to the verb. The main point of this section is simply to demonstrate that for most contexts, pronouns, simple indefinites, and anaphoric DPs are generally treated alike.

Many prepositions, apparently including both arguments and adjuncts, behave like verbs in accepting nuclear stress from their unstressable complements:

(5)   a. The car crashed INTO it/me/you...

      b. The car crashed INTO something.

      c. (John spent most of the race well away from the perimeter wall, but then...) he crashed INTO the wall.

(6)   a. The hikers climbed up the MOUNTAIN.

      b. The hikers climbed UP it.

c. The hikers climbed UP something.

d. (I spent my whole childhood admiring the mountain from afar, and today...) I climbed UP the mountain.

(7) a. Mary is walking beside the CAR.

b. Mary is walking BESIDE it/me/you...

c. Mary is walking BESIDE something.

d. (Mary ran up to the car at the head of the parade, and now...) she is walking BESIDE the car.

(8) a. The waves crashed against the ROCK.

b. The waves crashed AGAINST it.

c. The waves crashed AGAINST something.

d. (I threw a rock towards the ocean as I left, and turned to watch as...) the waves crashed AGAINST the rock.

The examples in (5–8) do not all have identical stress patterns; to my ear, the verbs in (7–8) have a secondary stress which the corresponding verbs in (5–6) lack, perhaps reflecting adjunct status for the PPs in (7–8).[1]

Another set of prepositions, all of which are plausibly arguments of some kind, pass nuclear stress to the verb when their object is incapable of bearing it:

(9) a. They're talking about the MOVIE.

b. They're TALKING about it/me/you...

c. They're TALKING about something.

d. (They just got back from a movie, and now...) they're TALKING about the movie.

(10) a. They're fighting over the FOOD.

b. They're FIGHTING over it/me/you...

c. They're FIGHTING over something.

d. (They bought a bunch of food to cook together, but now...) they're FIGHTING over the food.

(11) a. They're running from the PREDATOR.

b. They're RUNNING from it/me/you...

c. They're RUNNING from something.

d. (The ecologists came here to study a certain predator, but now...) they're RUNNING from the predator.

---

[1]We might imagine, for example, that these adjunct PPs represent a stress domain of their own, unlike argument PPs, and that the verb receives nuclear stress in its domain, while the object of the preposition receives sentence-level nuclear stress.

The facts in (5–11) suggest that the distribution of stress is at least partly relatable to the verb's argument structure; (9–11) involve verbs which are plausibly unergative, while the verbs in (5–6) may be unaccusative (and the PPs in (7–8) could be adjuncts). Some prepositions seem to vary in their behavior depending on whether a direction or location meaning is intended:[2]

(12)   a.   They're walking under the TREES. [location]

     b.   They're WALKING under them.

     c.   They're WALKING under something.

     d.   (There's a nice grove of trees behind my house, so whenever I need to take a break...) I WALK under the trees.

(13)   a.   They're walking under the AWNING. [direction]

     b.   They're walking UNDER it.

     c.   They're walking UNDER something.

     d.   (It was just starting to rain as they made it to the town square and saw an awning, so...) they walked UNDER the awning.

Some temporal PPs seem to me to be ill-formed with pronoun or indefinite objects:

(14)   a.   John has been sleeping since the PARTY.

     b.   * John has been SLEEPING since it.

     c.   * John has been SLEEPING since something.

On the other hand, immediately anaphoric DPs do not sound bad:

(15)   (Most of us really enjoyed the party, but John sort of overdid it, and...) he's been SLEEPING since the party.

---

[2] Compare Wagner's (2005: 231–232) observation about a contrast in stress placement in German:

(i)   a.   Sie hat im   Garten GETANZT.
      she has in.the.DAT garden danced
      'She danced in the garden.'

     b.   Sie ist in den   GARTEN getanzt.
      she is in the.ACC garden   danced
      'She danced into the garden.'

The version of the sentence with the location meaning, in (ia), has nuclear stress on the verb, while the directional meaning in (ib) gives nuclear stress on the object of the preposition. I find a corresponding contrast in English when the object of the preposition is a pronoun:

(ii)   a.   She DANCED in it.

     b.   She danced INTO it.

With this exception, the behavior of the various nuclear-stress-avoiding nominals seems to be more or less parallel in all of the above examples. In structures in which nuclear stress would ordinarily appear on a pronoun, a simple indefinite, or an immediately anaphoric DP, stress is shifted instead to a verb or a preposition. The choice between stress on a verb and stress on a preposition is apparently determined by a number of factors, possibly including argument/adjunct status of the PP and the argument structure of the verb.

Developing a predictive theory of these facts is, again, beyond the scope of this paper. Descriptively, just for these data, we could say that nuclear stress that is shifted from the object of a preposition is realized on the verb just when the PP is an argument and the verb is unergative, and is otherwise realized on the preposition.[3] An imaginable account of these facts might divide the VP into domains in which stress may be realized, with domain boundaries around adjunct PPs and the underlying position of subjects (perhaps because stress-shifting takes place before unaccusative subjects move out of the VP, or at least before the trace of such movement has been definitely determined to be phonologically null). The general principle would then be that stress is shifted as far left as possible within the domain to which stress would ordinarily be assigned:

(16) a. They're | TALKING about it. |

     b. The car | crashed | *the car* | INTO it. | [*unaccusative verb*]

     c. She's | walking | BESIDE it. || [*adjunct PP*]

For what follows, however, the only important point of this section will be that the various types of nominals that avoid nuclear stress are generally treated in the same way.

2.2 Nuclear stress and antipronominal contexts

There are contexts in which pronouns are treated differently from both simple indefinites and anaphoric DPs:

(17) a. Frank turned into a FROG (after drinking the potion).

     b. Frank turned into ME.

     c. Frank turned INTO something.

     d. (Frank's always been afraid of frogs, which is ironic, because today...) he turned INTO a frog.

The object of *into* in (17) is one of Postal's (1994; 1998; 2001) examples of what he calls an *antipronominal context,* by which he means a context in which unstressed pronouns cannot appear. Pronouns like *it,* which cannot bear stress unless focused, are impossible in such contexts; (18) is an odd response to a question like *Where did that frog come from?*:

---

[3]The account sketched below does not extend to the behavior of prepositions like *since* in (14). Perhaps this preposition, not unlike the pronoun *it,* is simply incapable of bearing stress.

(18)   * Frank turned into it.

As (17) shows, simple indefinites and anaphoric DPs are unlike pronouns in this context, in that they can appear without stress, with nuclear stress appearing, in this case, on the preposition.

The contrast in (17) seems to be general in Postal's antipronominal contexts (though in some of them, at least for me, the only pragmatically reasonable pronouns are inanimates that are incapable of bearing stress at all, yielding ungrammaticality rather than a stressed pronoun). Examples include:

(19)   a. Frank became a FROG.

b. Frank became ME.

c. Frank BECAME something.

d. (Frank's always been afraid of frogs, which is ironic, because today...) he BECAME a frog.

(20)   a. Frank is HAMLET.

b. Frank is ME (that is, I am a character in the play, and Frank plays me).

c. FRANK is somebody (that is, Frank has a part in the play).

d. (Frank has always wanted to play the murderer, and in this play,) Frank IS the murderer.[4]

(21)   a. The movie stars MADONNA.

b. The movie stars ME.

c. The movie doesn't STAR anyone.

d. (The director swore to the producers that he wouldn't cast his wife, but in the end,) the movie STARS his wife.

(22)   a. Those facts mean [that he is GUILTY].

b. * (These facts may not mean that he's guilty, but) those facts mean it.[5,6]

c. Those facts MEAN something.

d. (She's spent a decade fighting to avoid the end of the company, but in the end,) these facts MEAN the end of the company.

---

[4]Here stress is on the verb, rather than on the subject as in (20c), perhaps because the subject is also immediately anaphoric.

[5]Compare (i), with a different meaning for *mean*:

(i)   I MEAN it.

By (i), the speaker means something like "I was serious in what I just said."

[6]Note that the problem here is not just that *it* cannot refer to the clausal complement of *mean*:

(i)   Those facts mean that he's guilty, though he denies it.

(23) a. Those remarks betrayed disregard for human RIGHTS.

  b. * Those remarks betrayed it.[7]

  c. Those remarks BETRAYED something.

  d. (John has spent his whole life fighting against widespread disregard for human rights, but, actually, in the end...) his remarks BETRAYED disregard for human rights.

(24) a. The Porsche cost FIFTY THOUSAND DOLLARS.

  b. * The Porsche cost it.

  c. The Porsche COST something.

  d. (When he saw my car, he said he'd give half his fortune for it, and in the end,) the Porsche COST half his fortune.

I will not attempt to formally characterize the distribution of antipronominal contexts in this paper; see Stanton (2016), in particular, for one proposal. All of the examples above have subjects that are non-agentive, and in many cases inanimate, and several of the predicates are clearly unaccusative, some with transitive variants that have the same antipronominal positions as their intransitive versions:

(25) a. She turned John into a FROG.

  b. She turned John into ME/*it.

  c. She turned John INTO something.

At the end of §2.1 above I sketched an account of the behavior of stress shift that suggested that unaccusative subjects can block shift of nuclear stress from the object of a preposition to the verb:

(26) The car | crashed |*the car*| INTO it.|

On this view, examples like (18b-c) above might have relevant representations like those in (27):

(27) a. Frank | became | *Frank* | ME. |

  b. Frank | BECAME | *Frank* | something. |

---

[7]Postal (2001: 226) claims that this example would be well-formed with a stressed *them* as its object. The examples crucially involve *betray* with a meaning something like 'inadvertently reveal', and contrast with similar examples in which *betray* has a meaning more like 'treat treacherously', which are not antipronominal:

  (i) He betrayed his COUNTRY.

  (ii) He BETRAYED it/me...

  (iii) He BETRAYED someone.

Antipronominal status would then reflect the grammar's attempts to realize the nuclear stress that would ordinarily appear on the last object; the grammar must choose between stressing a stress-avoiding nominal (as it does with the pronoun in (27a)) and shifting stress across the base position of the subject (as in 27b). I have nothing insightful to say about why the grammar makes the choices that it does in this case. Moreover, this cannot be the whole story, not least because there are examples with the relevant argument structure which lack antipronominal properties; contrast (28) with (25):

(28)   a. She turned John against his COUNTRY.

      b. She turned John AGAINST me/it.

      c. She didn't turn John AGAINST anything.

The speculations of the last paragraph are logically separable from the rest of the account. All that will truly be relevant for our purposes is that antipronominal contexts have a special status with respect to nuclear stress. In general, as we saw in (3–15) above, nuclear stress is shifted from pronouns, simple indefinites, and anaphoric DPs to some preceding head, either a verb or a preposition in all the examples considered. Just in antipronominal contexts, we have now seen, this general pattern breaks down; simple indefinites and anaphoric DPs may shift stress away from themselves, but pronouns are obligatorily stressed (and if the pronoun is one which cannot receive stress, like *it*, the result is ungrammaticality).

2.3 Summary

The previous two sections have sketched the lay of the land. We have seen that in English, nuclear stress is generally retracted from pronouns, simple indefinites, and immediately anaphoric DPs, either to the verb or to a preposition (with the choice between verbs and prepositions conditioned by factors that I have not tried to explore in any depth). We have also seen that just in Postal's antipronominal contexts, this retraction of stress is blocked specifically for pronouns, which must receive stress.

The following sections will build on this understanding of the behavior of English nuclear stress. In section 3 below, we will review Postal's (1994; 1998; 2001) observation that some forms of A-bar movement are blocked out of anti-pronominal contexts: following much work, we can understand this as evidence that the forms of A-bar movement in question leave behind null pronominals at the extraction site, and that these null pronominals are incapable of receiving nuclear stress. §4 will turn to Bresnan's (1971) observations about the interactions of various forms of A-bar movement with the placement of nuclear stress. We will see that Bresnan's insights, just like Postal's, may be described as an observation that certain forms of A-bar movement, but not others, leave behind null pronominals, which behave like pronominals for purposes of nuclear stress placement. Moreover, we will see that Bresnan and Postal identify the same set of A-bar extractions as the ones that leave null pronominals at the extraction site.

3 Avoiding nuclear stress

Postal (1994; 1998; 2001) notes that some but not all forms of A-bar movement are blocked out of anti-pronominal contexts:

(29) a. What kind of frog did he turn into?   [*wh-movement*]

     b. Any frog that he turns into is going to be poisonous.   [*restrictive relative*]

     c. The best kind of frog to turn into is a poison dart frog.   [*infinitival relative*]

     d. When we were in wizard school together, you always disliked whatever kind of frog you turned into.   [*free relative*]

     e. * This frog, which John turned into, is ugly.   [*non-restrictive relative*]

     f. * Frogs, her victims always turn into.   [*topicalization*]

     g. * Not a single frog did any of her victims turn into.   [*negative inversion*]

     h. * What kind of frog did he eat before turning into?   [*parasitic gap*]

     i. * That kind of frog is too ugly to turn into.   [*gapped degree phrase*]

     j. * That kind of frog would be tough to turn into.   [*tough-movement*]

Postal refers to the types of extraction in (29a-d) as A-extractions, and the ones in (29e-j) as B-extractions. He proposes (and see Perlmutter 1972; Cinque 1990; O'Brien 2015, and Stanton 2016 for related proposals and important discussion) that the empty category left behind by B-extraction is a pronoun, and hence banned from appearing in antipronominal contexts.

Given the facts about nuclear stress reviewed in the last section, we can understand the ban on B-extraction out of antipronominal contexts as an consequence of some condition like (30):

(30) Phonologically null material may not receive nuclear stress.

Recall that what distinguishes antipronominal contexts from the other positions of nuclear stress that we considered is that in antipronominal contexts, pronouns must receive nuclear stress (though other nuclear stress-avoiding elements need not). B-extraction out of an antipronominal context, then, will leave a pronominal empty category behind in a necessarily stressed position, in violation of (30). A-extraction from an antipronominal context, by contrast, will leave behind some kind of empty category that is not a pronoun, and nuclear stress may safely be shifted away from the extraction site.

This way of thinking about the facts involves thinking of (30) as a filter imposed by the PF interface on a syntactic representation in which nuclear stress has been irrevocably assigned. We have seen that the position of nuclear stress is apparently sensitive to a number of syntactic and semantic notions; the preceding informal discussion has made reference to 'unaccusatives', to 'adjuncts', to 'indefinites', and so forth. In every case in which a phrase is unable to bear stress for these semantic and syntactic reasons, stress is shifted to another element. It is not hard to imagine a system in which (30) is enforced by shifting nuclear stress at PF away from phonologically null elements to which it might otherwise be assigned; such a system might treat phonologically null elements, for example, the way simple indefinites are treated. But if we are to use (30) to rule out B-extraction from antipronominal contexts, then it must not in fact be possible for the grammar to shift stress in this way. Rather, nuclear stress is assigned to a structure in which, perhaps, nothing is phonologically null, and PF then filters out structures in which nuclear stress has been assigned inappropriately. In other words, stress is apparently assigned to a structure that contains syntactic and semantic information ("unaccusative", "indefinite"), but not phonological information ("phonologically null"). For extraction from positions of nuclear stress to succeed, the phrases left behind by movement must be safely free of nuclear stress, not simply because they are phonologically null, but because they belong to the categories of elements that avoid nuclear stress when overt (pronouns, simple indefinites, anaphoric DPs). The ban on B-extraction from antipronominal contexts, on this view, represents a failure to avoid the effects of (30); B-extraction leaves behind a pronoun, which is ordinarily enough to avoid nuclear stress, but just in antipronominal contexts, nuclear stress is assigned to the null pronoun in the extraction site, violating (30). To the extent that the account outlined above is successful, it represents an argument for approaches to the interface between syntax and phonology in which the building of phonological representations begins during the narrow syntax (e.g., Bresnan 1971, Richards 2016).

4 Nuclear stress and movement

Bresnan (1971) also observes a difference between kinds of extraction, this one having to do with effects on nuclear stress. In particular, she points out that wh-movement and restrictive relative formation (both A-extractions) interact with nuclear stress differently from tough-movement (a B-extraction). Consider the wh-movement examples in (31) (Bresnan 1971, 259):

(31) a. What has Helen WRITTEN?

  b. What BOOKS has Helen written?

As Bresnan points out, the wh-phrases have effects on the position of nuclear stress like those of corresponding indefinites:

(32) a. Helen has WRITTEN something.

  b. Helen has written some BOOKS.

Bresnan concludes that the derivation of (31) involves assignment of nuclear stress prior to wh-movement. The simple wh-phrase in (31a), like the simple indefinite in (32a), triggers shift of nuclear stress to the verb, and the complex expressions in the (b) examples receive nuclear scope in the standard way for direct objects.

The relative clauses in (33), Bresnan suggests, can be given a similar analysis (Bresnan 1971: 259):

(33) a. George found someone he'd like you to MEET.

　　　 b. George found some FRIENDS he'd like you to meet.

Assuming a raising analysis of relative clauses, Bresnan proposes an account of the contrast in (33) which is essentially identical to the one developed for the parallel wh-movement facts in (31) above; nuclear stress is assigned before the head of the relative clause becomes external, and the contrast in (33) is to receive the same account as the one in (34):

(34) a. He'd like you to MEET someone.

　　　 b. He'd like you to meet some FRIENDS.

On the other hand, Bresnan claims that *tough*-movement behaves differently from wh-movement and relativization, never assigning nuclear stress to the *tough*-moved phrase (Bresnan 1971: 265):

(35) That theorem was tough to PROVE.

Bresnan assumes that *tough*-movement involves literal movement of the promoted subject (here, *that theorem*) from the gap site. On this assumption, the position of nuclear stress in (35) demonstrates that *tough*-movement, unlike wh-movement and relativization, bleeds assignment of nuclear stress.

We can contrast (35) with the examples in (36):

(36) a. What THEOREM did she prove?

　　　 b. George found a THEOREM he'd like you to prove.

The facts in (36) are familiar from the discussion of wh-movement and relativization above, and both involve, in Bresnan's terms, assignment of nuclear stress to a moved phrase prior to movement. In (35), by contrast, it is the verb that is stressed. Bresnan takes the (35–36) contrast as evidence that while wh-movement and relativization take place after assignment of nuclear stress, *tough*-movement precedes nuclear stress assignment.

Another approach to (35), given the observation that *tough*-movement, like other B-extractions, cannot take place out of antipronominal contexts, would be to follow Postal, O'Brien, and Stanton in claiming that the empty category left behind by *tough*-movement is a pronoun. The position of stress in (35), on this account, has the same explanation as the position of stress in (37):

(37) It's tough to PROVE it.

In both (37) and (35), the object of *prove* is a pronoun, and nuclear stress therefore appears on the verb. Antipronominal contexts, we have now seen, are just those contexts in which nuclear stress appears on pronouns, and B-extraction from such contexts is therefore ruled out by the general ban on nuclear stress on phonologically null material.

4.1 A-extractions, B-extractions, and nuclear stress

In this section I will outline an account of the effects of different types of extraction on stress. The account will be based on the following generalizations:

(38)   a. B-extractions leave null pronouns behind in the extraction site, which must not be stressed.

   b. A-extractions leave behind full DPs in the extraction site.

   c. Nuclear stress assigned to the tail of a movement chain may be realized on the head.

Let us consider kinds of extractions in turn, beginning with A-extraction. What type of empty category does A-extraction leave behind?

We have some reason to think that the answer to this question may vary depending on what is A-extracted. As we have seen, Bresnan observes that the position of nuclear stress in clauses with A-extractions depends on the nature of the moved phrase (Bresnan 1971: 259):

(39)   a. What has Helen WRITTEN?

   b. What BOOKS has Helen written?

This contrast is subject to two possibly related complications, which we will need to bear in mind as discussion proceeds. One has to do with an asymmetry in the judgments in (39). For me, at least, (39a) does indeed represent the only possible position of nuclear stress, unless some other constituent (like *Helen*) is being contrastively focused. The judgment in (39b), on the other hand, is not nearly as sharp; nuclear stress on the verb in (39b) is not obligatory, as it is in (39a), but for me at least it is certainly an option.

The other complication about the contrast in (39) has to do with the distance over which the contrast can be maintained. We can find instances of the contrast over a fairly large structural distance, I think:

(40)   a. What do you think Helen will claim she has WRITTEN?

   b. What BOOKS do you think Helen will claim she has written?

However, at least for me, the contrast vanishes if wh-movement takes place across any constituent that contains its own nuclear stress, like a complex subject:[8]

(41)   a. What has [every author with an interest in HISTORY] claimed to have WRITTEN?

   b. What BOOK has [every author with an interest in HISTORY] claimed to have WRITTEN?

---

[8]The facts are reminiscent of the suggestion in footnote 2 above, that nuclear stress shift from PP to the verb is blocked in unaccusatives, perhaps because the subject intervenes between the verb and the PP at the relevant level of representation. Perhaps nuclear stress can never be shifted across an intervening sentential stress.

Bearing these caveats in mind, let us consider the distribution of Bresnan's effect.

Bresnan notes that there are complex wh-phrases that do not attract nuclear stress. Her example is in (42) (Bresnan 1971: 259):

(42)   Which books has John READ?

Bresnan claims that "the interrogative *which* is inherently contrastive", and that (42) involves contrasting *read* with some other activity (such as *skim*). It is not clear to me that contrastive focus on the verb is necessary; (42) is a natural way to ask a question about a known list of books, for example. On the other hand, if there is no particular list of books under discussion, and I am asking just because I think finding out which books someone has read is a good way to learn about them, then (43) sounds better:

(43)   Which BOOKS has John read?

The key examples in (44) can be understood as having derivations that begin as in (45), with nuclear stress as marked:

(44)   a. What has Helen WRITTEN?
       b. What BOOKS has Helen written?
       c. Which books has John READ? [preestablished set of books]
       d. Which BOOKS has John read? [no preestablished set]

(45)   a. [$_{vP}$ Helen WRITE something]
       b. [$_{vP}$ Helen write some BOOKS]
       c. [$_{vP}$ John READ the books] [preestablished set of books]
       d. [$_{vP}$ John read the BOOKS] [no preestablished set]

Wh-movement will then create a new copy of the object at the edge of vP, simultaneously converting the object to a wh-phrase, perhaps via Late Merge as in Stanton (2016):

(46)   a. [$_{vP}$ what Helen WRITE something]
       b. [$_{vP}$ what BOOKS Helen write some books]
       c. [$_{vP}$ which books John READ the books] [preestablished set of books]
       d. [$_{vP}$ which BOOKS John read the books] [no preestablished set]

In (46a) and (46c), the direct object of the verb is unstressable as soon as it is introduced (by virtue of being a simple indefinite, in (46a), and anaphoric on preceding discourse, in (46c)), and nuclear stress therefore appears on the verb.

In (46b) and (46d), by contrast, the direct object receives stress, and this stress is realized on the head of the chain. Currently popular approaches to movement generally arrive at the conclusion that the moved element is effectively in two places at once. If movement involves, for example, the creation of a multidominance structure, then in an example like (46d) there is literally a single DP node with two mothers, one inside the VP and another inside the phrase *which book*. Similarly, on the copy theory of movement, movement in (46d) creates two instances of a single object *which book*, and we must understand phonology as being directed to pronounce the higher of these two instances. On either account, we can say that the factors that determine the pronounced position of the displaced element dictate, not only that the segments that make up the DP are to be pronounced near the beginning of the clause, but that the nuclear stress assigned to the DP by virtue of its position as an object is to be realized in its pronounced position.

Contrast the derivation for B-extractions like the ones in (47):

(47) a. Something was tough to PROVE.

     b. Some theorems were tough to PROVE.

     c. The theorems were tough to PROVE.

Derivations for all of these examples will begin with the *v*P in (48):

(48) [*v*P PRO PROVE it]

Since the object in (48) is a pronoun, nuclear stress appears on the verb. Subsequent movement might then convert the pronoun into one of the various kinds of subjects in (47), but will have no effect on nuclear stress; the object left behind by *tough*-movement has no stress that can be realized on the head of its chain, and nuclear stress will therefore invariably be on the verb, as desired.

These two types of derivations will have different consequences for extraction from an antipronominal position. A-extraction, as desired, will be able to shift stress away from the extraction site:

(49) a. What did that Porsche COST ?

     b. How much MONEY did that Porsche cost?

(50) a. That Porsche COST something.

     b. That Porsche cost some MONEY.

The A-extractions in (49) will have the underlying forms in (50), with stress being realized either on the verb or on the moved phrase, as desired. B-extraction, on the other hand, is correctly predicted to be impossible:

(51) a. * Fifty thousand dollars would be tough for that Porsche to cost.

     b. * It would be tough for that Porsche to cost IT.

(51a) will be doomed by the fact that its derivation must begin with (51b), in which the pronoun, by virtue of being in an antipronominal context, must receive stress.

Why is the stress on the null pronoun in the extraction site in (51a) not simply transferred to the head of the movement chain, as in an example like (49b)? Here I think we can take advantage of a difference between A-extraction and B-extraction. The nominal Merged in object position in (49b), by hypothesis, is something like *some money*, and nuclear stress is assigned in the usual way to *money*. Subsequent operations determine that *money* is to be pronounced, not in object position, but at the head of a movement chain, and we have seen that wherever it is pronounced, *money* retains the nuclear stress assigned to it at an earlier point in the derivation.

In (51a), by contrast, nuclear stress has been assigned, by hypothesis, to *it*. This pronoun will not be pronounced anywhere; no matter what we think about whether the head of the *tough*-movement chain in (51a) is *fifty thousand dollars* or a null operator in a structurally lower position, the pronoun is pronounced in neither of these positions. Consequently, the nuclear stress assigned to the pronoun also cannot be realized anywhere else; it must be realized on the null pronoun itself, leading to ungrammaticality.

The derivations sketched above allow us to capture both Postal's and Bresnan's observations about the different effects of different kinds of extraction. By claiming that B-extractions leave pronouns behind, we account both for the fact that they are banned out of antipronominal contexts and for the fact that they invariably leave nuclear stress on the verb. A-extractions, by contrast, leave behind non-pronominal DPs, which means both that extraction is licit out of antipronominal contexts and that the position of nuclear stress is more variable than it is for B-extractions.

4.2 Extending Bresnan's paradigm

Bresnan discusses a distinction between wh-movement and relativization, on the one hand, and *tough*-movement, on the other. Let us consider the other instances of A- and B-extraction.

4.2.1 A-extractions

We have already discussed wh-movement in some detail:

(52)   a. What has Helen WRITTEN?

        b. What BOOKS has Helen written?

Most of Bresnan's examples of relativization have no overt relativization operators, and the position of stress is determined by the head of the relative clause:

(53)   a. George found someone he'd like you to MEET.

        b. George found some FRIENDS he'd like you to meet.

These facts are consistent with the account offered above; Bresnan assumes a raising analysis of relative clauses, but a matching analysis could presumably also be made consistent with the facts, as long as 'matching' is understood as being relevantly like the pronunciation of the head of a movement chain, forcing the pronounced head of the relative clause to be phonologically identical to the moved operator.

Relative clauses with overt operators seem to me to also be consistent with the theory above:

(54) a. George found someone who he'd like you to MEET.
    b. George found someone whose MOTHER he'd like you to meet.
    c. George found some friends who he'd like you to MEET.
    d. George found some friends whose MOTHER he'd like you to meet.

The readings in (54) all follow from the proposal on offer. In particular, (54b) and (54d) have the option of not stressing the verb of the relative clause, regardless of the form of the head of the relative clause, presumably because of the form of the relative operator. Stress may also appear on the verb in these examples, as is standard for A-extractions (see section 4.1 above for discussion).

Infinitival relatives pattern with restrictive relatives (without overt operators):

(55) a. George found someone to TALK to.
    b. George found some FRIENDS to talk to.

Free relatives seem to me to invariably place nuclear stress outside the operator:

(56) a. He'll attack whatever I TALK about.
    b. He'll attack whatever theory I TALK about.

This is not because free relatives have been misclassified as A-extractions; they are compatible with extraction from antipronominal contexts:

(57) a. Whatever he becomes, I'll always love him.
    b. I'll pay whatever this Porsche costs.
    c. You won't have heard of whoever this movie stars.

I suspect that free relatives may have their own intonational cues that make them appear to be counterexamples. Fully understanding their intonation is well beyond the scope of this paper, but for me, there are at least two kinds of intonational 'tunes' that may go with free relatives. In one, which is more or less obligatory in examples like (57a), there is a high pitch that begins at the end of the relative operator and lasts until the end of the free relative clause, at which point pitch falls. The same intonation is possible for me in examples like (51b-c) in which the free relative appears in an argument position, as is an alternative featuring a high pitch on the matrix verb, and then a low and flat pitch for most of the relative clause, ending in another high pitch at the end of the relative. I conclude that these pitch excursions make the true position of nuclear stress in free relatives difficult to determine.

4.2.2 B-extractions

The B-extraction already discussed was *tough*-movement, which invariably has nuclear stress outside the moved element. This is true regardless of the properties of the mover:

(58) a. That theorem was tough to PROVE.

    b. What theorem was tough to PROVE?

    c. It was tough to PROVE.

    d. I consider some theorems tough to PROVE.

I have followed Postal, O'Brien, and Stanton in claiming that *tough*-movement leaves a null pronominal in the gap site; as a result, regardless of the identity of the moving phrase, nuclear stress will appear on the verb in examples like (58), just as it would if the object of the verb were an overt pronoun.

I have said nothing about why *tough*-movement differs from the A-extractions in invariably leaving a pronoun in the gap site (see Stanton 2016 for one proposal). I think it is fair to say that the syntax of *tough*-movement is still not completely clear. Bresnan (1971) assumed that the subjects of the examples in (58) begin the derivation at the gap site; another well-attested approach to *tough*-movement (Chomsky 1977 and much subsequent work) posits a null operator within the embedded clause, and we could imagine that this operator is a null pronoun.

Other B-extractions which reliably place nuclear stress outside the moved phrase include:

(59) a. That theorem, I won't TALK about. [*topicalization*⁹]

    b. Some theorems, I won't TALK about.

(60) Not a single theorem did she TALK about. [*negative inversion*]

(61) a. That theorem is too complicated to TALK about. [*gapped degree phrase*]

    b. Some theorems are too complicated to TALK about.

(62) a. Caligula, [who I've TALKED about], was a terrible emperor. [*non-restr. relative*]

    b. Caligula, [whose MOTHER I've TALKED about], was a terrible emperor.

Parasitic gaps, intriguingly, have the B-extraction pattern of stress both for the parasitic gap and for the main gap:

(63) What books has she PUBLISHED after WRITING?

And, as Postal (2001) observes, in parasitic gap constructions, both the parasitic gap and the main gap are sensitive to antipronominal contexts:

---

⁹Bresnan (1971) also notes that topicalization has this property (footnote 18, pp. 276–277); she excludes it from her discussion on the grounds that it has a distinctive intonation that may blur the relevant distinctions, much as I have done for free relatives above.

(64)   a. What color did she paint the house __?

        b. * What color did she paint the house __ [after discussing __ with Abigail]?

        c. * What color did she discuss __ with Abigail [after painting __ the house]?

Again, sensitivity to antipronominal contexts seems to coincide with the placement of nuclear stress.

O'Brien (2015) discusses another case in which forms of extraction which are ordinarily A-extractions take on the antipronominal-sensitivity of B-extraction. Extraction from islands, he points out, makes wh-movement and restrictive relativization sensitive to antipronominal contexts:

(65)   a. * Coppe painted his bike orange, and Ted painted his car **it**.

        b. That's the color that I think I'll paint my bike __.

        c. * That's the color that I don't know why [anyone would paint their bike __].

        d. ? That's the bike that I don't know why [anyone would paint __ that color].

(65a) reminds us that the color-denoting expression following a verb like *paint* is an antipronominal context. (65b) demonstrates that restrictive relativization is normally immune to antipronominal contexts. The contrast in (59c-d) shows that relativization out of a wh-island becomes impossible out of antipronominal contexts: (65c), which takes place out of an antipronominal position, is much worse than (65d), which is merely somewhat degraded. I refer interested readers to O'Brien (2015) for much further discussion of the pattern in (65), which seems to be general across a number of kinds of islands.

Extraction out of islands also appears to behave like B-extraction for purposes of stress placement, reliably placing stress on the verb:

(66)   a. ? What books are you wondering [why she would have WRITTEN __]?

        b. * What BOOKS are you wondering [why she would have written __]?

        c. ? What book should she have resigned [after WRITING __]?

        d. * What BOOK should she have resigned [after writing __]?

I have not offered an account of why extraction types that ordinarily pattern with A-extraction become B-extraction just under particular circumstances, and will not, for reasons of space; see O'Brien (2015) for an account of the island facts. The important observation, for purposes of this paper, is just that the properties of B-extraction seem to pattern together reliably.

4.3 Conclusion

It seems that Bresnan's observations divide types of extraction in the same way as Postal's. B-extractions leave null pronouns behind in the gap site, and this has consequences both for their distribution (they cannot take place out of antipronominal contexts) and for their effects on nuclear stress (stress is invariably retracted to a verb or preposition). A-extractions, by contrast, leave an anaphoric DP behind; this DP may be safely left in antipronominal contexts, where it can avoid receiving stress, and it will sometimes pass nuclear stress along to the head of the movement chain, and sometimes to a verb or preposition, depending on the nature of the moving phrase. The two types of properties—sensitivity to antipronominal contexts and effects on placement of nuclear stress—appear to pattern together reliably.

5 Some other consequences and conclusions

This paper has been an attempt to demonstrate that various people were right, and that their proposals support each other.

In fact, not only were Postal (1994; 1998; 2001); Stanton (2016); O'Brien (2015), and Bresnan (1971) right, but Fox (1999; 2003); Sauerland (1998; 2004), and Johnson (2012) were also right. Let us turn to this fact next.

Chomsky (1993) proposes the copy theory of movement, which claims that examples like (67a) should have a syntactic representation like that in (67b):

(67)   a. Which book did Mary read?
       b. [which book] did Mary read [which book]

As Chomsky notes, the structure in (67b) is difficult to interpret as an operator-variable construction. He posits a later operation altering (67b) to (68):

(68)   which$_x$ did Mary read book x

Fox (1999; 2003) and Sauerland (1998; 2004) posit versions of a process which Fox (2003) names *Trace Conversion*, which converts the lower of two copies of movement into a definite description, yielding something like (69) as an LF representation of (67a):

(69)   which book x did Mary read [**the book x**]

Chomsky, Fox, and Sauerland all assume that the syntax creates a structure with multiple copies of a moving operator, and that the lowest copy is converted to something else postsyntactically, for reasons having to do with interpretation. If the account developed here is right, the direct object of *read* in (67–69) has, not only the semantics of a definite description, but also some of the phonological properties of a definite description—in particular, it patterns with definite descriptions with respect to the placement of nuclear stress. If the gap site is a definite description both at LF and at PF, we should probably regard it as a definite description in the narrow syntax.

This is Johnson's (2012) suggestion, which O'Brien (2015) adopts and extends. They posit movement operations that create A-bar operators out of definite descriptions, ultimately creating multidominant representations like the one in (70b):

(70) a. Which story about her should no linguist forget?

b.

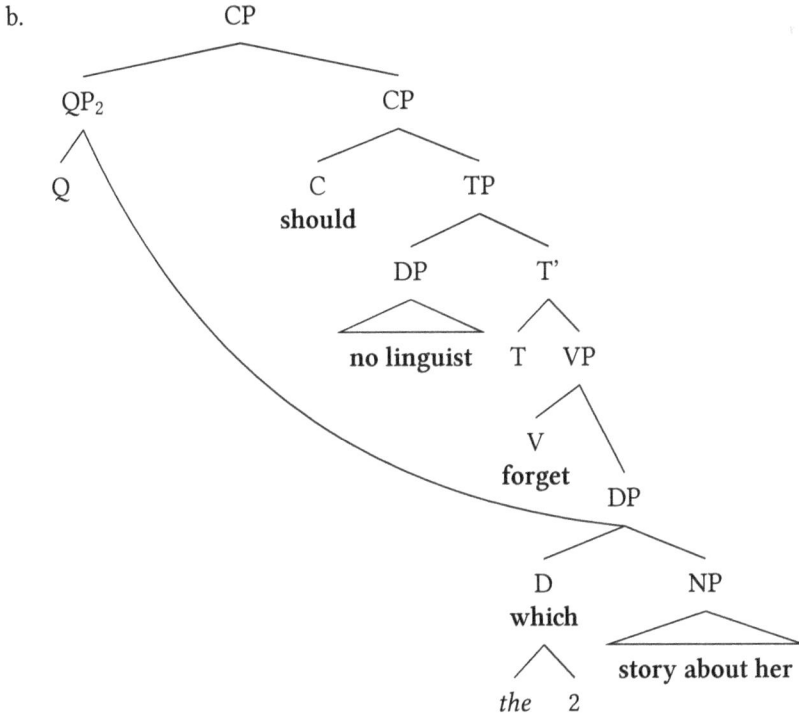

In (70b), QP and VP both immediately dominate the DP *which story about her*, and Q has converted the D *the* into *which* by Agreeing with it. Formally similar, though lacking Johnson's (2012) appeal to multidominance, is Stanton's (2016) use of Wholesale Late Merger, which creates operators for B-extraction out of pronouns (represented as instances of D) by Late Merging an NP to D.

Both of these mechanisms have the property, which I think is appealing, of preserving the original insight and virtues of Chomsky's Copy Theory; movement is just another instance of Merge. Where they depart from Chomsky is in identifying the repeatedly Merged phrase, not as an instance of the A-bar operator, but as a subpart of that operator, expanded on structurally in the course of the movement operation.

Let me end with three notes for future research.

The first has to do with covert movement. Fox (1999; 2003) and Sauerland (1998; 2004) intend Trace Conversion to apply, not only to overt movement, but to QR and wh-in-situ. I leave for future work the question of how the proposal here can be generalized to such cases; I hope that such work will shed further light on the syntax of covert movement.[10]

---

[10] The account developed here avoids a 'look-ahead' problem connected with wh-in-situ. Consider pairs like the one in (i-ii):

(i) Which book did the teacher say we should read?
(ii) Which teacher said we should read which book?

A second area of future research has to do with languages other than English. Languages vary in how they treat the kinds of phrases that avoid nuclear stress in English. Spanish, for example, assigns nuclear stress, when appropriate, to pronouns, simple indefinites, and immediately anaphoric DPs (Zubizarreta 1998; Hualde 2007; Nava & Zubizarreta 2009; 2011):

(71) Spanish (Karlos Arregi, p.c.; Hualde 2007: 61; Nava & Zubizarreta 2009: 179)

    a. He   hablado con **ella**.
       I.have talked   with her

       'I've talked with her.'

    b. Vi   **algo**.
       I.saw something

       'I saw something'.

    c. Por_qué compras ese sello tan viejo? — Porque colecciono SELLOS.
       why   you.buy that stamp so old   — because I.collect   stamps

       'Why are you buying that old stamp?' — 'Because I collect stamps.'

If the account developed here is correct, and if it is safe to regard Spanish nuclear stress and English nuclear stress as the same phenomenon, then Spanish cannot be using null pronouns for the tails of B-extractions. We might imagine, for example, that Spanish B-extraction chains have null clitic pronouns as their tails, since clitic pronouns do not bear nuclear stress in Spanish. This should have consequences for the distribution of B-extraction in Spanish (for instance, it should only be possible to B-extract DPs from positions of nuclear stress if they could in principle be clitic pronouns). Investigation of these consequences, and of similar facts in other languages, is a topic I will have to leave for the future.

Another topic for the future is the phonology of extraction of phrases other than DPs. AP extraction, for example, seems to me to be able to participate in alternations of nuclear stress position like those Bresnan (1971) identifies for A-extractions:

(72) a. How do you FEEL?

    b. How DIZZY do you feel?

An example like (72b), in particular, allows me to destress the verb, particularly if the topic of dizziness is not yet part of the discourse (imagine, for example, that I see you

---

In a bottom-up derivation, (i-ii) will have the same starting point, Merging *which book* as the object of *read*. On a certain set of assumptions, this poses a look-ahead problem: if movement is successive-cyclic, and if the decision about whether to perform overt successive-cyclic movement of *which book* must be made before the matrix subject is Merged, then it is difficult to see how this decision can be made without potentially crashing the derivation. There are various ways of avoiding the look-ahead problem, of course, some of which involve denying the assumptions just sketched (or being at peace with the idea that derivations can crash). But in the theory offered here, the problem does not arise; the matrix subject is invariably something like *the teacher*. If *which book* is successive-cyclically moving past it, the grammar must simply refrain from converting *the teacher* into *which teacher*, yielding (i) instead of (ii); if *which book* elects to remain in situ, then the grammar can convert *the teacher* into a wh-phrase, yielding (ii).

in some kind of distress and am trying to diagnose your problem; under these circumstances, (72b) seems like a natural way of saying the sentence).

Partly for reasons of space, I have had to leave these and many other mysteries largely unexplored. I have tried to demonstrate that Postal's division of A-bar movement types into A- and B-extractions is mirrored in Bresnan's observations about different effects of movement on nuclear stress. I have also argued that this parallelism represents an argument for something like Johnson's (2012) narrow-syntactic rendition of Trace Conversion; heads and tails of chains are different, not only in the semantic representation, but also in the phonological representation, and we should therefore posit a difference between them in the syntax.

6 Acknowledgements

Many thanks to Karlos Arregi, Juliet Stanton, David Pesetsky, audiences at MIT and the University of Pennsylvania, and two anonymous reviewers for comments on this work. I'm also very grateful to Anders Holmberg, for everything he's done for the field; it's a pleasure to be able to offer this paper in his honor. Responsibility for remaining errors is mine.

References

Bresnan, Joan. 1971. Sentence stress and syntactic transformations. *Language* 47. 257–281.

Chomsky, Noam. 1977. On wh-movement. In Peter Culicover, Thomas Wasow & Adrian Akmajian (eds.), *Formal syntax*, 77–132. New York: Academic Press.

Chomsky, Noam. 1993. A minimalist program for linguistic theory. In Kenneth L. Hale & Samuel Jay Keyser (eds.), *The view from building 20: Essays on linguistics in honor of Sylvain Bromberger*, 1–52. Cambridge, MA: MIT Press.

Cinque, Guglielmo. 1990. *Types of A'-dependencies*. Cambridge, MA: MIT Press.

Fox, Danny. 1999. Reconstruction, binding theory, and the interpretation of chains. *Linguistic Inquiry* 30. 157–196.

Fox, Danny. 2003. On logical form. In Randall Hendrick (ed.), *Minimalist syntax*, 82–123. Oxford: Blackwell.

Hualde, José I. 2007. Stress removal and stress addition in Spanish. *Journal of Portuguese Linguistics* 5. 59–89.

Johnson, Kyle. 2012. Towards deriving differences in how *wh* movement and QR are pronounced. *Lingua* 122. 529–553.

Nava, Emily & Maria Luisa Zubizarreta. 2009. Order of L2 acquisition of prosodic prominence patterns: Evidence from L1 Spanish/L2 English speech. In Jean Crawford, Koichi Otaki & Masahiko Takahashi (eds.), *Proceedings of the 3rd Conference on Generative Approaches to Language Acquisition North America (GALANA 2008)*, 175–187. Somerville, MA: Cascadilla Proceedings Project.

Nava, Emily & Maria Luisa Zubizarreta. 2011. Encoding discourse-based meaning: Prosody vs. Syntax. Implications for second language acquisition. *Lingua* 121. 652–669.

O'Brien, Chris. 2015. How to get off an island. Ms., MIT.

Perlmutter, David. 1972. Evidence for shadow pronouns in French relativization. In Paul Peranteau, Judith Levi & Gloria Phares (eds.), *The Chicago which hunt*, 73–105. University of Chicago: Chicago Linguistics Society.

Postal, Paul. 1994. Contrasting extraction types. *Journal of Linguistics* 30. 159–186.

Postal, Paul. 1998. *Three investigations of extraction*. Cambridge, MA: MIT Press.

Postal, Paul. 2001. Further lacunae in the English parasitic gap paradigm. In Peter Culicover & Paul Postal (eds.), *Parasitic gaps*, 223–250. Cambridge, MA: MIT Press.

Richards, Norvin. 2016. *Contiguity theory*. Cambridge, MA: MIT Press.

Sauerland, Uli. 1998. *The meaning of chains*. Cambridge, MA: MIT Doctoral dissertation.

Sauerland, Uli. 2004. The interpretation of traces. *Natural Language Semantics* 12. 63–127.

Stanton, Juliet. 2016. Wholesale late merger in A'-movement: Evidence from preposition stranding. *Linguistic Inquiry* 47. 89–126.

Wagner, Michael. 2005. *Prosody and recursion*. Cambridge, MA: MIT Doctoral dissertation.

Zubizarreta, Maria Luisa. 1998. *Prosody, focus, and word order*. Cambridge, MA: MIT Press.

Chapter 11

Response particles beyond answering

Martina Wiltschko
University of British Columbia

In recent years, response particles (*yes/no*) have received some attention in the formal syntactic and semantic literature. Most analyses focus on the use of response particles as answers to polar questions as well as (to a lesser extent) as responses to affirmations. In this paper I extend the empirical domain to explore the use of response markers as responses to other clause types including wh-questions, imperatives, and exclamatives. It is established that response particles can be used as (dis)agreement markers. Moreover it is shown that in German, response particles can also be used to mark the following utterance as a response. A unified analysis is developed according to which the difference in function of response markers is syntactically conditioned. Following recent work on the syntax of speech acts, an articulated speech act layer is utilized to derive these functions. The case is made for a more fine-grained typology of response markers than previously assumed.

1 Introduction

In his recent monograph (Holmberg 2015), Anders Holmberg extends the empirical domain for generative syntacticians by exploring the syntax of *yes* and *no* (henceforth *response particles, ResPrt*) as in (1) (see also Holmberg 2001; 2002; 2007; 2013; 2014).

(1) Q: Did you feed the dog?
     A: a. Yes. (= I fed the dog.)
         b. No. (= I didn't feed the dog.)

While *ResPrts* have been explored within other subfields of linguistics (e.g., conversation analysis) they have not been part of the core body of data generativists have typically taken into account (with the early exception of Pope 1976, and more recent studies such as Farkas & Bruce 2009; Kramer & Rawlins 2009, and Krifka 2013.) The absence of *ResPrt* from the syntactician's empirical domain may have to do with two factors. First, *ResPrts* are only found in conversations, while syntactic theory is typically concerned with sentences in isolation. Secondly, *ResPrts* – as the term *particle* suggests – are frequently morphologically simplex. That is, in many languages, neither positive

Martina Wiltschko. 2017. Response particles beyond answering. In Laura R. Bailey & Michelle Sheehan (eds.), *Order and structure in syntax I: Word order and syntactic structure*, 241–279. Berlin: Language Science Press. DOI:10.5281/zenodo.1117726

nor negative *ResPrts* display any surface complexity: they are mono-morphemic. If we consider syntax to be concerned with understanding the ways complex structures are derived, then *ResPrts* are not obviously an interesting object of exploration. However, modern syntactic theory is not only concerned with understanding word- or morpheme-order restrictions but it is a way to explore the relation between form and meaning. And in this respect, *ResPrts* are in fact interesting. Despite their morphological simplicity, they are able to convey a full fledged positive or negative proposition. So, the first question that is of interest to syntactic theory concerns the relation between the form of the *ResPrt* and its interpretation: how can we model the fact that a seemingly simplex form can convey a full proposition? And how is the content of this proposition determined? In §2, I review two current approaches to this question: Holmberg's ellipsis-based account and Krifka's (2013) pronominalization account. I then move on to the core empirical contribution of this paper. In particular, I explore other uses of *ResPrts* (§3) and whether they can be accounted for under current analyses. *ResPrts* serve as answers if they are used to respond to polar questions; but this is not their only function. Rather, I show that *ResPrts* can be used as responses to clause-types other than polar questions, in which case they function as agreement or disagreement markers, respectively. In §4, I propose an analysis for the (dis-)agreement function of *ResPrts*: they establish how the trigger of the response relates to the responder's set of beliefs. Furthermore, in §5, I introduce another use of *ResPrts*: in German *ResPrts* can be used to mark the utterance they precede as a response. In §6, I conclude.

For the purpose of this paper, I adopt the following terminological and representational conventions. It will be useful to distinguish between what the *ResPrt responds to* and what it *responds with*. I refer to the former as the TRIGGER (of response) and to the latter as the CONTENT (of response). This is exemplified in (1') for the example in (1). Here the TRIGGER of the response is the polar question (*Did you feed the dog?*), which (by virtue of containing an unvalued polarity variable) introduces a proposition and its negation (p (*B fed the dog*) $\vee\neg$p (*B didn't feed the dog*)). If the answer given is *yes*, the CONTENT of the response is the affirmation of the positive proposition (p: *B fed the dog.*). If the answer given is *no*, the CONTENT of the response is the negation of the proposition (¬p: *B didn't feed the dog*).[1]

(1') A: Did you feed the dog?   TRIGGER: polar question (p $\vee\neg$p)

　　　B:　　Yes. (= I fed the dog.)   CONTENT: affirming p (= p)

　　　　　　No. (= I didn't feed the dog.)   CONTENT: negating p (= ¬p)

Furthermore, I will use the term *responder* to refer to the speech-act participant who is responding; and I will use the term *respondee* to refer to the speech-act participant who the responder is responding to (i.e., the person who uttered the TRIGGER of the response).

---

[1]For a discussion of answers to negative questions see §2 below.

2 Holmberg's syntax of answers

Holmberg (2015) (following previous work of his) argues that *ResPrts* that are used to answer polar questions are best analyzed as combining with a full propositional structure the content of which depends on the preceding question. Their apparent simplicity stems from the fact that the propositional structure can be elided (i.e., remain unpronounced) as shown in (2), where strike-through indicates the elided constituent.

(2) Q: Did you feed the dog?
    A: Yes [~~I fed the dog~~].

This much accounts for the distributional properties of *ResPrts* – as we shall see – but what about their interpretation? How can they serve as answers to polar questions? Holmberg argues that polar questions introduce a polarity variable [±pol] inside the propositional structure (henceforth p-structure). In particular, as illustrated in (3), the polarity variable is analyzed as the head of a polarity phrase between CP and TP (though the position of PolP is assumed to be subject to cross-linguistic variation in Holmberg (2015); cf. also Laka (1990) for an early version of this idea).

(3) Did you feed the dog?

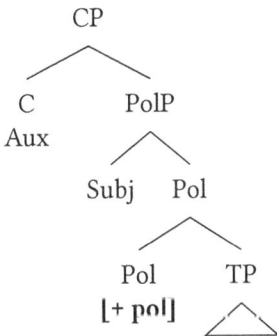

              CP
       ╱   ╲
    C   PolP
  Aux   ╱ ╲
       Subj   Pol
           ╱ ╲
       Pol   TP
      [+ pol]

Thus, according to Holmberg (2015: 4) the interpretation of a polar question is something like: *What is the value of* [±pol] *such that 'you fed* [±pol] *the dog' is true?.* The contribution of the *ResPrt* is to bind the polarity variable in the embedded p-structure. It does so from the specifier position of a focus phrase (FocP). If the answer is *yes*, the polarity variable is valued as [+pol], yielding the answer [*you* [+pol] *fed the dog*] as in (4a). In contrast, if the answer is *no*, the polarity variable is valued as [-pol] yielding the answer [*you* [-pol] *fed the dog*], as in (4b), which translates as '*You didn't feed the dog*'.

(4) The *ResPrt* binds the polarity variable

   a. the contribution of *yes*   b. the contribution of *no*

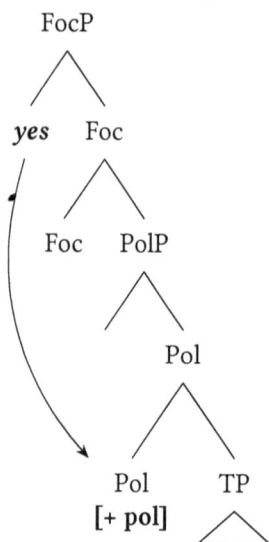

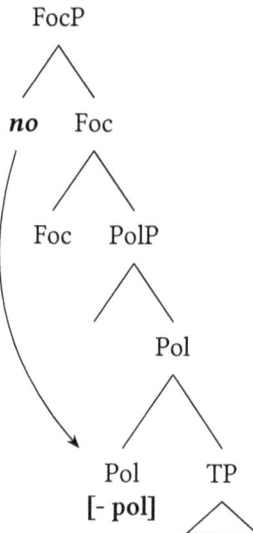

The reason that the constituent following the *ResPrt* (i.e., PolP) can be elided is that it is essentially identical to the propositional clause in the question it answers, i.e., it has an antecedent.

Since anaphoricity can be signalled via ellipsis or via pronominalization, it is not surprising that *ResPrts* have also been analyzed in terms of pronominalization. For example, Krifka 2013 argues that *ResPrts* can be viewed as *propositional anaphors*. As such, they are assumed to replace the entire p-structure, as illustrated in (5).[2]

(5) *ResPrt* as propositional anaphors

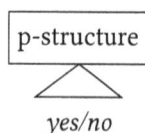

One empirical fact that speaks in favor of the ellipsis approach of the type developed by Holmberg (see also Kramer & Rawlins 2009 and Haegeman & Weir 2015) is the fact

---

[2]Replacing p-structure is however not the only possibility for response markers in Krifka's (2013) model. In particular, he assumes that p-structure is dominated by a speech act Structure (ActP) which, in turn, can also serve as the antecedent for a propositional anaphor. Depending on which layer of the clausal spine the propositional anaphor picks out, their interpretation differs. As we shall see the proposal developed here builds on this insight, but introduces a more fine-grained speech act structure.

that the proposition that serves as the antecedent for the *ResPrt* can be pronounced, as shown in (6).

(6)   A: Did you feed the dog?
　　　B: a. Yes, I fed the dog.
　　　　　 b. No, I didn't feed the dog.

The well-formedness of the complex answers in (6) is immediately predicted by the ellipsis analysis: the p-structure need not be elided since ellipsis is generally not obligatory. In contrast, the pronominal analysis, according to which *ResPrts* are propositional anaphors, will have to be augmented to accommodate the facts in (6).

Holmberg (2015: 2–6) discusses two more pieces of evidence for the syntactic complexity of *ResPrts*: one pertaining to their form and the other to their meaning.

Consider first variation in the *form* of polar responses. Not all languages make use of *ResPrts* to answer polar questions. Another cross-linguistically common strategy to answer polar questions is to repeat (echo) the verb (or auxiliary) of the question with the remainder of the proposition elided. This is exemplified in (7) on the basis of Finnish.

(7)   Finnish (Holmberg 2015: 3 (6))

　　　Q: Tul-i-vat-ko　　lapset　kotiin?
　　　　　come-PST-3PL-Q children home
　　　　　'Did the children come home?'

　　　A: Tul-i-vat.
　　　　　come-PST-3PL
　　　　　'Yes.'

This cross-linguistic pattern lends support to the ellipsis analysis of *ResPrts* as it allows for a unified analysis of polar responses.

The other piece of evidence Holmberg considers pertains to differences in the distribution and *interpretation* of *ResPrts*. There are essentially two types of patterns languages display. The two patterns are distinguishable based on responses to negative polar question. The first strategy is the so called *agree/disagree* system (cf. Kuno 1973; Pope 1976, and Sadock & Zwicky 1985) also known as the *truth-based* system (Jones 1999). This system is characterized by the fact that a positive response to a negative polar question indicates agreement with the respondee: both the respondee and the responder believe in the negative proposition. Hence, a positive answer is used to assert a [-pol] value for p. This is exemplified by the Cantonese data in (8).

(8)   Cantonese (Holmberg 2015: 4 (9))

　　　Q: John m　jam　gaafe?
　　　　　John not drink coffee
　　　　　'Does John not drink coffee?'

A: Hai.

yes

('John does not drink coffee.')

The second strategy is the *positive/negative system* also known as the *polarity-based system*. This system is characterized by the fact that a negative response to a negative polar question indicates that the polarity of the proposition is valued as [-pol]. Hence, unlike in the agree/disagree system, a negative answer is used to assert a [-pol] value for p. This is exemplified by the Swedish data in (9).

(9)   Swedish (Holmberg 2015: 4 (10))

Q: Dricker Johan inte kaffe?
      drinks Johan not coffee

'Does Johan not drink coffee?'

A: Nej.
      no

('He doesn't drink coffee.')

In sum, in a truth-based system, the use of a positive *ResPrt* results in an interpretation according to which the negative proposition is asserted to be true. In contrast, in a polarity based system the same effect is achieved by means of the negative *ResPrt*. According to Holmberg, the difference between the two systems reduces to a syntactic difference in negation. That is, Ladd (1981) observes that a negative polar question like (10) can have two readings (see also Büring & Gunlogson 2000; Romero & Han 2004; Asher & Reese 2007). The first reading (10-i) introduces a negative bias and is characterized by *low scope* of negation; hence this is known as the "inside negation reading". The second reading (10-ii) introduces a positive bias and is characterized by high scope of negation; hence it is known as the "outside negation reading".

(10)   Q: Doesn't John drink coffee?

A: i. Is it true that John does **not** drink coffee? [low NEG]

ii. Is it **not** the case that John drinks coffee? [high NEG]

To distinguish the two readings we can add the negative polarity item *either*, which forces the low negation reading (11i). Alternatively, we can add the positive polarity item *too*, which forces the high negation reading (11ii).

(11)   i. Doesn't he drink coffee either? [low NEG]
            = Is it also the case that **he does not drink coffee**?

ii. Doesn't he drink coffee too? [high NEG]
            = Is it **not** also the case that **he drinks coffee**?

The difference between high and low negation affects the syntax of *ResPrts*: if the elided proposition contains negation (as is the case with low negation), then a positive *ResPrt* is used to mean 'Yes it is the case that not p'; if the elided proposition does not contain negation (as is the case with high negation), then the negative *ResPrt* has to be used to achieve the same result because the positive *ResPrt* would have to be interpreted as 'Yes, it is not the case that p', which is not a well-formed answer. In other words, *yes*, has to agree in polarity with the assertion rather than with the proposition.

(12) Q: Doesn't John drink coffee
     A: i.   Yes.   (=He does drink coffee.)   CONTENT: p
                     (=He doesn't drink coffee.)   CONTENT: ¬p
       ii.   No.   (=He doesn't drink coffee.)   CONTENT: ¬p
                     (= He does drink coffee.)   CONTENT: p

To obtain a positive response in such contexts, some languages make use of a dedicated *ResPrt*, namely a polarity reversing particle. This is exemplified in (13) by German *doch* (Holmberg 2015: ch. 6; Krifka 2013).[3]

(13)   German

     Q: Trinkt Hans nicht Kaffee?
         drinks Hans not   coffee

         'Does Hans not drink coffee?'

     A: **Doch** (er trinkt Kaffee).
         yes

         ('He does drink coffee.')

In sum, what Holmberg's study establishes is that *ResPrts* are syntactically complex: they are sensitive to categories that are syntactically defined, namely the distinction between low and high negation.

In addition, the syntactic treatment of *ResPrts* has another advantage: it makes it possible to explore the cross-linguistic differences in a systematic way. And there are good reasons to explore this variation. The form and function of *ResPrts* is under-documented: existing grammars of individual languages do not often contain information about the strategies used to answer polar questions. Hence, exploring this question from a cross-linguistic point of view will contribute to our knowledge base, which in turn will inform the formal analyses of *ResPrts*.

The present paper contributes to the question regarding the range of variation. In particular, I explore other uses of *ResPrts*, hence extending the typological space within which to investigate them. That is, in addition to Holmberg's two questions (i) does a language make us of the *ResPrt* strategy and (ii) how do *ResPrts* pattern as answers to negative questions, we can also ask questions about the other functions of *ResPrts*. In particular, in what follows, I show that *ResPrts* can be used as markers of (dis)agreement (Sections 3–4) and as generalized response markers (§5).

---

[3]The Old English *ResPrt* system used to distinguish between two forms of positive *ResPrts*: *gae* was used to answer positive utterances while *gyse* was used to answer negative ones, mirroring the difference between German *ja* and *doch* (Wallage & van der Wurff 2013).

3 *Yes* and *no* as markers of (dis)agreement

The bulk of Holmberg's (2015) treatment of *ResPrts* is dedicated to their use as answers to polar questions (henceforth the **answering** *function*). This *answering* function of *ResPrts* comes about when the TRIGGER of the response is a polar question and the CONTENT is either affirmation or negation, as summarized in (14).

(14)　Conditions for the answering function of *ResPrts*

　　　　TRIGGER: polar question (p ∨¬p)

　　　　CONTENT of response:

　　　　i.　*yes:* affirming p (= p),

　　　　ii.　*no:* negating p (= ¬p)

However, *ResPrts* can be used in a variety of other contexts that go beyond the answering function.

3.1 TRIGGERS across clause-types

In this section, I explore the use of *ResPrts* following TRIGGERS other than polar questions. To make a systematic exploration possible, it is useful to make explicit some assumptions about the relation between utterance form (*clause type*) and utterance function (*speech act type*). I assume a (simplified) mapping between clause-type and speech act-type. In particular, I assume that declaratives map onto assertions; interrogatives map onto questions; imperatives map onto commands or requests; and exclamatives map onto exclamations. Thus, for the purpose of this paper, I abstract away from indirect speech acts and other forms of modifying speech acts. The mapping is summarized in 1.

Table 1: Mapping between utterance form and utterance function

Utterance form	Utterance function
Declarative	
	Assertion
Interrogative	
	Question
Imperative	Command/request
Exclamative	Exclamation

In what follows I explore the possibility of responding with a *ResPrt* to each of these utterance forms.

3.1.1 Responding to assertions

As discussed in Holmberg (2015), *ResPrts* can be used to respond to assertions (cf. also Farkas & Bruce 2009; Krifka 2013). In this use, they are sometimes referred to as *rejoinders* (Halliday & Hasan 1976) but I will refer to them as (dis)agreement markers. Consider the examples in (15–16). Assertions are encoded with declarative syntax and falling intonation (indicated by \\). Note that (dis)agreement markers, too, are associated with falling intonation.

(15)	A: John speaks French really well \\.	TRIGGER: assertion (p)
	B: i. *Yes* \\. (= p)	CONTENT: agreement w/p
	ii. *No* \\. (=¬p)[4]	CONTENT: disagreement w/p
	(adapted from Holmberg 2015: 211 (4))	

(16)	A: You stole the cookie \\.	TRIGGER: assertion (p)
	B: i. *Yes* \\. (= p)	CONTENT: agreement w/p
	ii. *No* \\. (=¬p)	CONTENT: disagreement w/p
	(adapted from Krifka 2013: 2 (2a))	

Despite the difference in the TRIGGER, *ResPrts* still express the same CONTENT as in their answering function: affirmation or negation. Nevertheless, the effect of the *ResPrt* is different. With a positive response to an assertion, the responder *agrees* with the previous utterance and conversely, with a negative response, the responder *disagrees* with the previous utterance (cf. Farkas & Bruce 2009).

This contrasts with *ResPrts* when used as answers to polar questions. In this case, there is nothing to agree with, because no statement is being made with which the responder could agree or disagree. Polar questions are used to shift the commitment to p from the speaker (S) to the addressee (A) (Gunlogson 2003), thereby requesting an answer from A. If the respondee is committed to the content of her utterance (as is the case with an assertion), it follows that the response will be interpreted as (dis)agreement. In contrast, if the respondee is not committed to the content of her utterance (as is the case with polar questions), it follows that the response is not interpreted as agreement or disagreement, but as an answer.

Within the syntactic analysis developed in Holmberg (2015), the difference between the answering function and the (dis)agreement function is as follows. As we saw above, *ResPrts* used as answers are analyzed as occupying SpecFocP c-commanding an embedded p-structure, which contains an unvalued polarity variable (the head of PolP). *Yes* values this variable as [+pol] while *no* values it as [-pol].

---

[4] According to Holmberg (2015), *no* cannot be used as a disagreement marker without adding more content to the response. According to my consultants, however, the short answer is well-formed though it comes across as confrontational. One might therefore reframe Holmberg's generalization as follows: a negative response is ill-formed only in polite conversations. Note also that there appears to be a special intonation associated with it. I tentatively identify this as the contradiction contour (Liberman & Sag 1974).

As for their (dis)agreement function, Holmberg (2015: 81) suggests that it does "not assign a value to a polarity variable, because there is no polarity variable in the preceding statement."

Holmberg (2015) doesn't offer an explicit syntactic analysis for the (dis)agreement function of *ResPrts*, but given his description of this phenomenon, we may conclude that the structure is something like in (17).[5]

(17)   a. yes

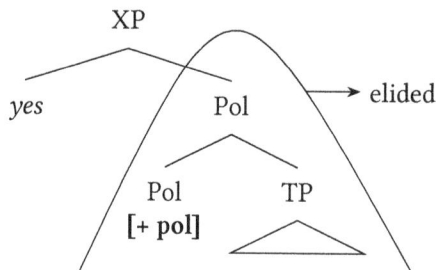

   b. no

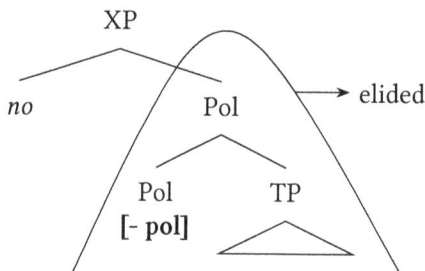

Like in their answering function, the (dis)agreement *ResPrts* combine with an elided p-structure, the CONTENT of which (including its polarity value) is determined by the TRIGGER of the response. This assumption is consistent with the fact that the CONTENT of the response can be overtly spelled out.

(18)   A: John speaks French really well \.

   B: i. Yes\. He {does\, speaks French really well\}.

   ii. No\. He {doesn't\, speak French really well\}.

(19)   A: You stole the cookie \.

---

[5]I have left the label for the structure dominating the *ResPrt* vague (X). This is because Holmberg (2015) suggests two possible analyses: one according to which the (dis)agreement function is instantiated by a different type of *yes/no*, one that is more akin to predicates like *true* or *false* which can take a valued proposition as their complement. The other option is that the (dis)agreement function is instantiated by the same lexical element as the answering function: it still is associated with a focus projection but it doesn't bind the polarity variable associated with PolP.

B: i. Yes\. {I did\, I stole the cookie\}.

   ii. No\. {I didn't\, I didn't steal the cookie\}.

This analysis raises the question as to what the contribution of the *ResPrt* is in this configuration. That is, if it doesn't serve to value the polarity variable, how does the positive *ResPrt* contribute to agreement and the negative *ResPrt* to disagreement with the TRIGGER? This is a particularly pressing problem with the negative answer (*no*), because there is no negative proposition available to serve as the antecedent for the embedded p-structure.

Holmberg's analysis correctly predicts that the answering function differs from the (dis)agreement function. Empirical support for this difference stems from the fact that other expressions of agreement (*true, right, that's right*) and disagreement (*false, wrong, that's wrong*) can be used as responses (20–21) but unlike *ResPrt*s, they cannot be used as answers, as shown in the examples in (22–23) (adapted from Holmberg 2015: 211 (5)).[6]

(20) A: John speaks French really well.   TRIGGER: assertion (p)

    B: i. Yes.   CONTENT: agreement w/p

       ii. True.   CONTENT: agreement w/p

       iii. Right.   CONTENT: agreement w/p

       iv. That's right.   CONTENT: agreement w/p

    (adapted from Holmberg 2015: 211 (4))

(21) A: John speaks French really well.   TRIGGER: assertion (p)

    B: i. No.   CONTENT: disagreement w/p

       ii. False.   CONTENT: disagreement w/p

       iii. Wrong.   CONTENT: disagreement w/p

       iv. That's wrong.   CONTENT: disagreement w/p

(22) A: Does John speak French?   TRIGGER: polar question (p ∨¬p)

    B: i. Yes.   CONTENT: affirming p

---

[6]The difference between *ResPrt* and other expressions of (dis)agreement has to be explored in more detail. An informal survey suggests that matters are complicated. While *true/false* can be used in response to assertions, they are less well-formed (though not fully ruled out) in response to rising declaratives (i) or tag questions (ii).

  (i) Q: You fed the dog?

     A: Yes./?True./?Correct.

  (ii) Q: You fed the dog, didn't you?

     A: Yes./?True./?Correct.

  (iii) Q: Did you feed the dog?

     A: Yes./*True./*Correct.

Before we can develop an analysis that captures these differences, it is necessary to properly establish the empirical facts. I will have to leave this as an avenue for future research however.

    ii. * True.

    iii. * Right.

    iv. * That's right.

(23) A: Does John speak French?   TRIGGER: polar question (p ∨¬p)

      B: i.   No.   CONTENT: negating p

          ii. * False.

          iii. * Wrong.

          iv. * That's wrong.

Thus, *ResPrts* have a wider distribution than other forms of agreement. This confirms Pope's (1976) insight that English is simultaneously an agreement-based system and a polarity-based system. When the TRIGGER is a polar question, *yes* shows up in its polarity guise: it values the polarity value. When the TRIGGER is an assertion it shows up in its agreement guise. This still leaves us with the question as to what *yes* and *no* contribute when they function as (dis)agreement markers. How is this function derived?

Suppose that as an agreement marker, *yes* asserts the truth of the preceding proposition while as a disagreement marker, *no* asserts that the preceding proposition is false, thereby establishing agreement or disagreement with the interlocutor, respectively. However, this potential analysis cannot be right, given what we find with negative assertions. First consider positive answers. Just as with negative questions, *yes* is ambiguous: it can be used to agree with the negated proposition or else it can be used to assert the truth of the proposition and hence reject the negation of the proposition (24). In this way, *yes* differs from the other predicates of agreement and hence cannot simply be analyzed as a predicate of agreement (like *true* or right).

(24) A: John doesn't speak French well.   TRIGGER: negative declarative ¬p

      B: i. Yes.   CONTENT: agreement w/¬p

                                        CONTENT: disagreement w/¬p

          ii. True.   CONTENT: agreement w/¬p

          iii. Right.   CONTENT: agreement w/¬p

          iv. That's right.   CONTENT: agreement w/¬p

Next consider the negative answers. Here *no* – unlike the other predicates of rejection – is ambiguous. It can be used to reject the negated proposition or else it can be used to agree with it. The other predicates of rejection, in contrast, can only be used to disagree with the negated proposition.

(25) A: John doesn't speak French well.   TRIGGER: negative declarative ¬p

      B: i. No.   CONTENT: disagreement w/¬p

                                           CONTENT: agreement w/¬p

          ii. False.   CONTENT: disagreement w/¬p

iii. Wrong.   CONTENT: disagreement w/¬p

iv. That's wrong.   CONTENT: disagreement w/¬p

This establishes that the contribution of *ResPrts* cannot simply be asserting or negating the truth of p. So we are still left with the question about the contribution of *ResPrts* when they function as (dis)agreement markers. Moreover, the data in (24-i) and (25-i) raise the additional question as to how interlocutors determine the contribution of the *ResPrts*, if both are ambiguous. Of course, this is the signature of a system that is simultaneously an agree-based system and a polarity based system. Goodhue & Wagner (2015), and Goodhue et al. (2013) show that the ambiguity of the *ResPrts* is resolved by means of intonation contours: speakers most frequently use the Contradiction Contour (Liberman & Sag 1974) when reversing, and they use declarative intonation when confirming, regardless of the particular *ResPrt* used.

We have also established that the agreement vs. polarity function of *ResPrts* does not correlate with the difference between binding the polarity value of the embedded proposition or not, because both functions are possible with answers to polar questions (where *ResPrts* bind the polarity value) and with responses to assertions (where there is no open polarity variable to be bound).

In the remainder of this section, I show that *ResPrts* have an even wider distribution than typically discussed. That is, they are not restricted to serve as responses to polar questions or assertions. Instead they can be used to respond to all kinds of speech acts – a fact that makes the question as to what their contribution is even more pressing.

3.1.2 Responding to wh-questions

Wh-questions differ from polar questions in that they require an answer to the open variable denoted by the wh-word in the question.[7]

(26) A: When did you feed the dog?
      B: i.   {At around eight\, After I had breakfast\,...}
          ii. * Yes\!
          iii. * No\!

(27) A: Why did you feed the dog?
      B: i.   {Because he was hungry\, Because you told me to\, ...}
          ii. * Yes\!
          iii. * No\!

The temporal wh-word in (26) requires the answer to give an indication of the time of feeding whereas the causal wh-word (*why*) in (27) requires the answer to give an indication of the reason for feeding, etc. Unsurprisingly, in these contexts, simplex *ResPrts* are ill-formed.

---

[7]Thus the meaning of a wh-question is not a proposition with a valued polarity variable. According to Hamblin's (1958; 1973) influential work, wh-questions denote sets of propositions (as indicated by {p_1, p_2, p_3...} in (32)).

Martina Wiltschko

However, there are contexts where *ResPrts* are possible as a response to a wh-question. Consider the examples in (28)–(30) from the corpus of American soap operas (SOAP; http://corpus.byu.edu/soap/).[8]

(28) Katie: Why would he do something like that?
      Brooke: **Yes**, I know. That is the question.
      BB-2012-05-23[9]

(29) Brady: Why is joining Basic Black so important to me?
      Madison: **Yes**, please tell me, Brady, because I really want to know.
      DAYS-2012-01-06

(30) Avery: How did that happen?
      Lauren: (Chuckles) yes.
      Michael: It happened because your amazing nephew convinced Daisy to move out of the building.
      YR-2012-05-17

      Bill: What do you want to bet?
      Liam: **No**, I am not playing this game with you.
      BB-2012-03-27

      Sami: Rafe, what are you doing here?
      Rafe: **No**, I'm sorry to drop by so late.
      DAYS-2012-02-10

These responses do not answer the wh-question TRIGGERS but they are still well-formed. With the use of the positive *ResPrts* the responders indicate that they have the same question as the respondee. In other words, the responder indicates agreement with the respondee in their evaluation of the situation as triggering a particular question. This is confirmed by the content of the statements following the *ResPrts*. Note that these statements are more or less obligatory in these contexts. They all suggest that the responder has no real answer to the preceding question precisely because s/he has the same question. Hence, we can conclude that *ResPrts* can be used to respond to wh-questions despite the fact that they do not serve as answers.

The question still remains, however, as to what exactly the *ResPrts* contributes and how. Ideally, an analysis of *ResPrts* should be able to account for all uses of *ResPrts*. The

---

[8]SOAP was chosen over other available corpora of spoken language for several reasons. While soap operas are in part scripted, they are not necessarily scripted in full detail (many discourse markers may not be found in the script; Thoma 2016). Moreover, the current exploration is ultimately one of competence. I assume that both the script writers as well as the actors will create conversations that do not violate their conversational competence. Finally, according to Jones & Horak's (2014) study, the spoken language used in a British Soap Opera (*EastEnders*) is similar to unscripted conversational language in other spoken language corpora. Our quantitative study is based on the episodes aired in 2012 which consists of 2.2 million words.
[9]Abbreviations underneath the SOAP examples are as follows: BB (Bold and Beautiful), (DAYS) Days of Our Lives, (GH) General Hospital, YR (Young and Restless). The 8-digit number following the abbreviation represents the release date for the episode from which the example is selected.

ellipsis-based analysis developed in Holmberg (2015) cannot straightforwardly account for *ResPrts* when used to respond to wh-questions. This is because the proposed structure has an embedded p-structure containing a valued polarity variable as in (31) repeated from (17) above. However, if the TRIGGER of the response is a wh-question, then the elided structure cannot be a p-structure with a valued polarity variable.

(31)   a. agreement w/assertion

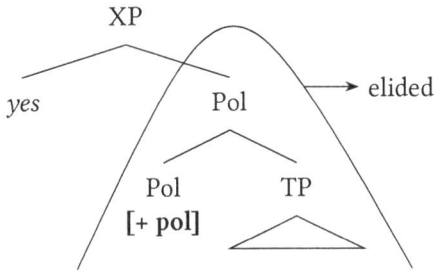

XP

yes   Pol   → elided

Pol   TP
[+ pol]

b. disagreement w/assertion

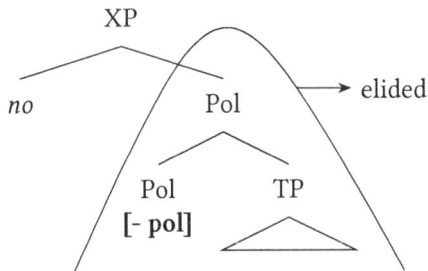

XP

no   Pol   → elided

Pol   TP
[- pol]

So the question remains as to the contribution of the *ResPrts*. Descriptively, the contribution of the positive *ResPrt* is to agree that the respondee's question is a valid question and the contribution of the negative *ResPrt* is to disagree that the respondee's question is a valid question, at least not from the responder's point of view. This is summarized in (32).

(32)   A: [Wh ...?]   TRIGGER: wh-question {p_1, p_2, p_3...}
       B: i. Yes ...   CONTENT: agreement with wh-question
            ii. No ...   CONTENT: disagreement with wh-question

But how does this (dis)agreement function come about?

3.1.3 Responding to imperatives

We now turn to imperatives, a clause-type that is used to express requests and commands. Unlike questions, imperatives do not explicitly solicit a response in the form of an answer from the addressee. However, we have already seen that *ResPrts* are not restricted to answering contexts. They can serve as more general response markers. Hence, we might expect that they can also be used to respond to imperatives. This is indeed the case, as exemplified by the data in (33)–(37), which are all from SOAP.

(33) Alison: So go back to the farmhouse and wait for us.
      Deacon: **Yes**, Ma'am.
      BB-2012-06-20

(34) Steffy: Treat me like one of your patients..
      Taylor: **Yes**, I will.
      BB-2012-06-29

(35) Michael: Breathe!
      Starr: Yes.
      GH-2012-03-29

(36) Tracy: Give it to me!
      Maxie: **No**!
      GH-2012-01-20

(37) Billy: Hey, open the door! Let me in!
      Chloe: **No**, I am not letting you in. Forget about it!
      YR-2009-03-16

The well-formedness of these examples indicate that *ResPrts* can be used to respond to imperatives. In this context they can roughly be paraphrased as *Yes, I will do what you requested of me* vs. *No, I won't do what you requested of me*.

Again, existing analyses of *ResPrts* cannot account for this use. This is because, like wh-questions, imperatives do not denote propositions, and hence do not make available a proposition to agree with nor a proposition whose polarity value has to be valued. Instead, an imperative is often analyzed as denoting a property that can only be true of the addressee (Portner 2004). So again, the question arises as to what the contribution of the *ResPrt* is when it is used to respond to an imperative. Descriptively, the contribution of the positive *ResPrt* is to agree with the respondee's evaluation of the situation that a command is in order (and hence the responder indicates that s/he will comply with it). In contrast, the contribution of the negative *ResPrts* is to disagree with the validity of the command in this situation (and hence the responder indicates that they refuse to comply with it). This is summarized in (32).

(38) A: [Imperative!]   TRIGGER: Imperative P
      B: i. Yes ...   CONTENT: agreement with command
          ii. No ...   CONTENT: disagreemen with command

3.1.4 Responding to exclamatives

Finally, we consider exclamatives. While some languages have dedicated exclamative clause-types, it is also the case that all kinds of utterances can be interpreted as exclamations, provided they have the right intonation and occur in the right context. What is crucial for our purpose is that responders can respond to commands with a *ResPrt*. This is exemplified by the data in (39)–(44). Note that none of the examples from the corpus are exclamations that are based on the dedicated exclamative clause-type. Nevertheless they still are instances of exclamations. Furthermore, the constructed example in (41) shows that the use of *ResPrts* as a response to dedicated exclamative clause-types is also well-formed.

(39) Steffy: Whoo-hoo.
 Liam: **Yes**!
 BB-2012-05-03

(40) Brooke: Steffy is leaving town.
 Hope: No way!
 Brooke: (Squeals) **Yes**! I shouldn't say "good" because she is Ridge's daughter, and I really shouldn't celebrate, but I am.
 BB-2012-03-19

(41) A: What a beautiful sunset.
 B: **Yes**, I know. Isn't it gorgeous.

(42) Anita: She found it at Victor's.
 Chelsea: Oh, my God!
 Anita: **No**, relax. It's Victor's problem.
 YR-2012-02-17

(43) Will: What a perfect time to lay low.
 Gabi: **No**, Will, look, I'm trying to find an agent.
 DAYS-2012-05-15

(44) Michael: What a lovely family tradition to hand on to your own niece.
 Avery: **No**, I got to know Daisy through all this.
 YR-2012-02-24

In this context *ResPrts* can roughly be paraphrased as follows. The positive *ResPrt* indicates that the responder agrees with the evaluation of the situation by the respondee (45i); the negative *ResPrt* indicates that the responder does not agree with the evaluation of the situation by the respondee (45ii).

(45) A: [Exclamative!]   TRIGGER: Exclamative $\{p_1, p_2, p_3,...\}$
 B: i. Yes ...   CONTENT: agreement w/exclamation
 ii. No ...   CONTENT: disagreement w/exclamation

Again, existing analyses of *ResPrts* cannot account for this use. This is because, like wh-questions and imperatives, exclamatives do not denote propositions, and hence do not make available a proposition to agree with nor a proposition whose polarity value has to be valued. Instead, as indicated in (45), an exclamative can be analyzed as denoting a set of alternative propositions (Zanuttini & Portner 2003). So again, the question arises as to how the (dis)agreement function of *ResPrt* is derived when they are used to respond to an exclamative.

3.2 The analytical challenge

We have now explored *ResPrt* as responses to all major clause-types and we have seen that they are not only used as answers to polar questions. In fact, a survey of 1013 tokens of positive *ResPrt* in SOAP reveals that the vast majority of instances of *yes* is used to respond to preceding assertions ($n = 654$), followed by responses to yes/no questions ($n = 279$). The other functions of *yes* are much less frequent, but nevertheless occur: response to exclamatives ($n = 44$); response to imperatives ($n = 36$); and response to wh-questions ($n = 9$). This is summarized in Figure 1.[10]

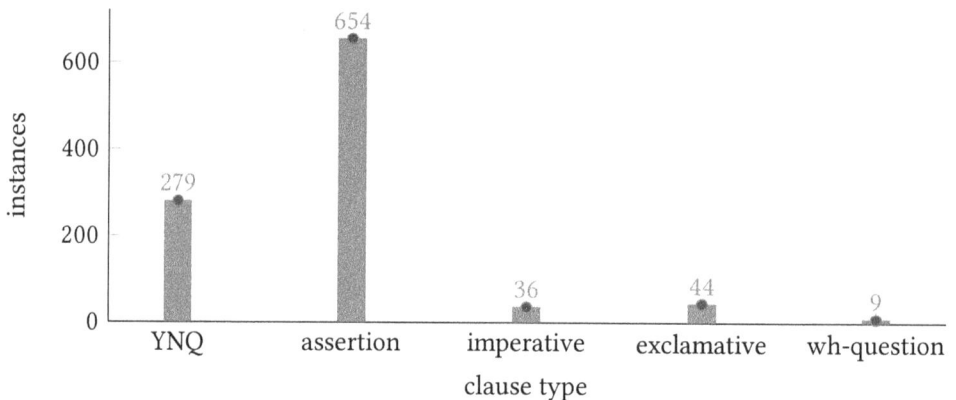

Figure 1: Distribution of *yes* across different TRIGGERS

As shown in Figure 2, the numbers are similar for *no*. The vast majority is used to respond to preceding assertions ($n = 1387$), followed by responses to yes/no questions ($n = 711$). The other functions of *no* are again much less frequent, but nevertheless occur: response to exclamatives ($n = 16$), response to imperative ($n = 172$), and response to wh-questions ($n=58$).

We have established above that the function of the *ResPrt* differs depending on the clause type of the TRIGGER, as summarized in Table 2.

---

[10]In this study, we looked at 1469 tokens of *yes* and 3093 tokens of *no*. Not all tokens are included in the quantitative analysis above. In particular, not included in the chart above are those tokens that respond to tag questions and rising declaratives, as well as echo-questions, addresses, and backchannels.

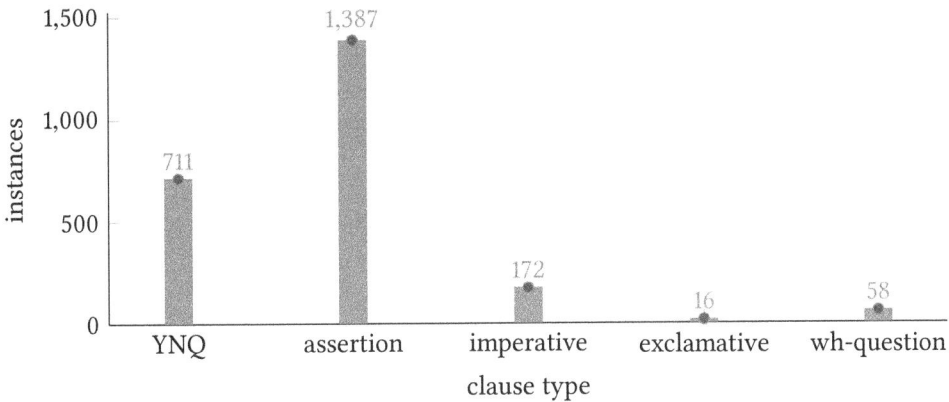

Figure 2: Distribution of *no* across different TRIGGERS

Table 2: Distribution and function of ResPRTs

TRIGGER of response		*yes*	FUNCTION	*no*	FUNCTION
Polar question	positive polar questions	✓	Answer: affirmative	✓	Answer: negative
	negative polar questions	✓	Answer: i) polarity-based ii) agreement-based	✓	Answer i) polarity-based ii) agreement-based
Declarative		✓	agreement w/assertion	✓	disagreement w/assertion
Interrogative		✓	agreement w/question	✓	disagreement w/question
Imperative		✓	agreement w/command	✓	disagreement w/command
Exclamative		✓	agreement w/exclamation	✓	disagreement w/exclamation

Note that *ResPrts* function as answers only if they serve to answer polar questions. In all other contexts they serve to express agreement or disagreement with the speech act of their TRIGGER. At first sight, the fact that *ResPrts* can be used to express agreement might not be surprising within a language that makes use of an agree/disagree-based system (referred to as *truth*-based in Holmberg 2015). But unfortunately, this is not sufficient to understand this pattern. First, we do not have a good understanding of what the contribution of *yes* and *no* is when they are used to mark agreement and disagreement. We have seen throughout the discussion that it is not immediately clear how to extend Holmberg's analysis to cover the full range of functions of *ResPrt*. Second, if the multifunctional profile of the type identified for English *ResPrt* is dependent on English having a polarity based system AND an agree/disagree based system in the sense of Kuno (1973), then we would expect that languages where answers are polarity-based will have a different profile, and that *ResPrts* could not be used as (dis)agreement markers following TRIGGERS other than polar questions. However, this prediction is not borne out, as I now show.

According to Holmberg (2015: Section 4.2), German does not have an agree/disagree-based system. Nevertheless, German *ResPrts* can be used with all of the TRIGGERS discussed for English *ResPrts* and with the same functions. This is shown below with examples from the Upper Austrian variety of German (henceforth UAG).[11]

Relative to the parameters explored in Holmberg (2015), UAG *ResPrts* have the following profile. The first thing to note is that *ResPrt* exist in this language. That is, in answering a polar question, UAG employs dedicated particles *jo* ('yes') and *na* ('no'). As shown in (46), both can be used in isolation or be followed by the CONTENT of the response (i.e., the proposition introduced in the TRIGGER of the response).

(46) Upper Austrian German

Q: Host du an Hund gfuattat?   TRIGGER: $p \lor \neg p$
    Have you DET dog   fed

    'Did you feed the dog?'

A: a. Jo. (I hob an Hund gfuattat.)   CONTENT: p
       Yes. I have DET dog   fed

    b. Na. (I hob an Hund net gfuattat.)   CONTENT: $\neg p$
       No. I have DET dog   NEG fed

Moreover, according to the criteria Holmberg (2015) adopts, UAG has a polarity-based system: negative questions cannot be answered with the positive *ResPrt* (47i). Like Standard German, UAG has a dedicated polarity reversing strategy: the positive *ResPrt* is prefixed with *oh* (47iii). With this strategy the CONTENT expressed by the response is p by virtue of reversing the negation of p ($\neg(\neg p)$).

---

[11]There are several reasons to use dialectal data for this discussion. First, conversations like those reported on here are a spoken language phenomenon and the status of Standard German as a spoken language is questionable (Weiß 2004; Auer 2004). In addition, in ongoing work on the form and function of response particles we find a staggering range of variation even among dialects of the same language (i.e., German).

(47)   Upper Austrian German

    Q: Trinkt da Hons net an   Kaffee?   TRIGGER: $\neg p \vee \neg(\neg p)$

        drinks DET Hans NEG DET coffee

        'Does Hans not drink coffee?'

    A: i. * Jo. (=He does drink coffee.)   *CONTENT: p

       ii.   Na. (= He doesn't drink coffee.)   CONTENT: $\neg p$

      iii.   Oh jo. (= He does drink coffee.)   CONTENT: $p = (\neg(\neg p))$

Now, if the possibility for *ResPrt* to be used as (dis)agreement markers were contingent on the answering system of the language being an agree/disagree based system, then we would predict that *ResPrt* in UAG cannot be used in this way. However, this prediction is not borne out. The same *ResPrts* that can be used as answers to polar questions can also be used to respond to assertions (48), wh-questions (49), commands (50), and exclamations (51).

(48)   Upper Austrian German

    A: Da Hons red-t   guat Französisch \.   TRIGGER: assertion (p)

        DET Hons speak-3SG well French

        'Hans speaks French well.'

    B: i. *Jo\.* (= p)   CONTENT: affirming p

       ii. *Na\.* (=$\neg p$)   CONTENT: negating p

(49)   Upper Austrian German

    A: Wonn foast   denn du jetzt eigentlich?   TRIGGER: wh-question

        When leave-2SG PRT you now PRT

        'When are you finally leaving?'

    B: i. **Jo**, des is a   guate frog.   CONTENT: agree w/Q

        Yes, DEM is INDF good question

        'Yes, that's a good question.'

      ii. **Na**, des deafst   me ned frogn.   CONTENT:disagree w/Q

        No, DEM may-2SG me NOT ask

        'No. You can't ask me that.'

(50)   Upper Austrian German

    A: Jetzt geh endlich ins   Bett.   TRIGGER: command

        Now go finally into.the bed

        'Go to bed now!'

    B: i. **Jo** i geh jo eh scho.   CONTENT: agree w/command

        yes I go PRT PRT PRT

        'but I'm going already.'

    ii. **Na** wirkli ned.   CONTENT: disagree w/command
       No really not

       'No way.'

(51)   Upper Austrian German

    A: Ma is des a   liaba Hund.   TRIGGER: exclamation
       PRT is DEM INDF cute dog

       'What a cute dog that is!'

    B: i. **Jo** wirkli woa, geu?   CONTENT: agree w/excl.
          yes really true, TAG?

          'Yeah, that's true, isn't it?'

      ii. **Na** owa wirkli ned.   CONTENT: disagree w/excl.
          no PRT really NEG

          'No, that's really not true.'

This establishes that the possibility for using *ResPrt* as responses to speech acts other than assertions is not contingent on the answering system being an agree/disagree based one. And, as indicated in the above examples, the general function of *ResPrt* in contexts where the TRIGGER is not an assertion is still agreement or disagreement with the TRIGGERING speech act. Thus we can conclude that the ability of *ResPrts* to express agreement or disagreement is not restricted to agree/disagree based answer systems.

But this still leaves us with the question as to how to analyse the (dis)agreement function of *ResPrt*.

4 The syntax of (dis-)agreement

To understand the difference between the answering function and the (dis)agreement function of *ResPrt* it is useful to compare their contribution with two TRIGGERS: polar questions vs. wh-questions. With polar questions, the *ResPrts* are used to affirm or negate the *proposition* (52) embedded in the question while with wh-questions, they are used to agree with or reject the *question* (53).

(52)   A: [y/n...?]   TRIGGER: polar question ($p \lor \neg p$)
     B: i. Yes ...   CONTENT: affirming p ($= p$)
        ii. No ...   CONTENT: negating p ($= \neg p$)

(53)   A: [Wh .....?]   TRIGGER: wh-question $\{p_1, p_2, p_3...\}$
     B: i. Yes ...   CONTENT: agreement w/wh-question
        ii. No ...   CONTENT: disagreement w/wh-question

Thus when responding to a wh-question, the CONTENT of the response is the same as the TRIGGER, namely the speech act of questioning itself. This contrasts with the answering function of *ResPrts* in response to polar questions. Here the CONTENT of the response is the proposition embedded in the polar question, and not the polar question itself. To account for this difference, let us begin by assuming that the analysis for *ResPrts* in their answering function is essentially as in Holmberg (2015): the *ResPrt* values the polarity value associated with the p-structure, as in (54), repeated from (4) above.

(54)   *ResPrts* bind the polarity variable

a. the contribution of *yes*

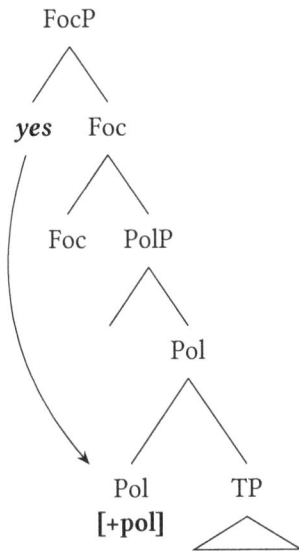

FocP

yes   Foc

Foc   PolP

Pol

Pol   TP
[+pol]

b. the contribution of *no*

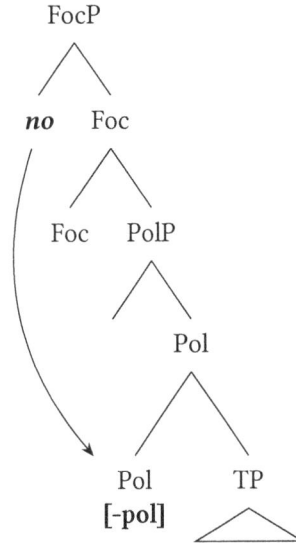

FocP

no   Foc

Foc   PolP

Pol

Pol   TP
[-pol]

However, as we have seen, *ResPrts* are not restricted to indicating the polarity value of a proposition. Hence this cannot be their intrinsic content. In fact, the association with polarity is, on this analysis, syntactically conditioned. *ResPrts* value an open polarity variable, but they do not themselves establish polarity *per se*.

So suppose that the core content of the *ResPrts* is to value an unvalued clausal feature as either positive (*yes*) or negative (*no*). Positive and negative values are themselves not restricted to propositional polarity. Instead, all types of features have been assumed to be bi-valent such that one value is positive and the other negative (Jakobson 1932; Trubetzkoy 1939). I propose that – when used to establish (dis)agreement – the contribution of *ResPrts* is to value an unvalued feature in the speech act structure. In particular, following Wiltschko (2017); Wiltschko & Heim (2016); Thoma (2016), I assume that speech act structure contains a *grounding* layer, which is responsible for encoding the commitment of S towards p. The label *GroundP* is meant to evoke Clark & Brennan's (1991) mechanism of *grounding* as well as the notion of the common ground (cf. Heim et al. (2014); Thoma (2016) and Wiltschko & Heim (2016) for discussion). In particular, GroundP takes the CP (typed p-structure) as a complement and an abstract argument referring to the

S's ground (Ground-S) in its specifier as in (55).[12]

(55) Speech act structure

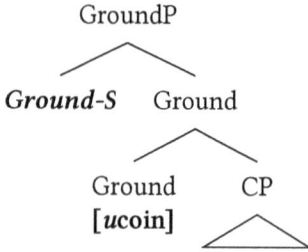

GroundP

    Ground-S   Ground

           Ground   CP
           [*ucoin*]

This structure follows the basic template for functional categories assumed in Wiltschko (2014): they are transitive heads which establish a relation between their complement and an abstract argument in their specifier. The relation is established via the unvalued coincidence feature [*ucoin*] which is universally associated with all clausal heads. This feature establishes whether or not the two arguments coincide and is independent of the dimension relative to which they coincide. That is, coincidence may be in time, place, participancy or belief states, among other things. That coincidence is a central universal characteristic of a variety of grammatical categories was first observed in Hale (1986) (see Wiltschko 2014 for detailed discussion).

On this analysis then, the contribution of *ResPrts* is to value the unvalued coincidence feature associated with Ground. So when the TRIGGER is a wh-question, the structure associated with the *ResPrt* is as in (56). The *ResPrt* attaches to GroundP, which in turn takes a CP as its complement. This CP corresponds to the TRIGGER and is typically elided but can also be spelled out, as shown in (57).[13]

(56) *ResPrt* values [*ucoin*] in Ground

    a. the contribution of *yes*

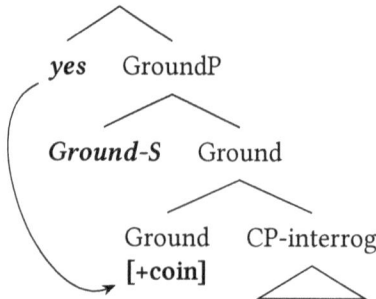

    yes GroundP

          Ground-S   Ground

              Ground   CP-interrog
              [+coin]

---

[12]For evidence that the speaker's ground (Ground-S) and the addressee's ground (Ground-A) are associated with two distinct layers in the structure, see Lam (2014); Heim et al. (2014); Thoma (2016). Since Ground-A plays no role in the analysis of the *ResPrts* discussed here, I will not discuss it here.

[13]In (56) the *ResPrt* is represented as attaching to GroundP in the same fashion as *ResPrts* are analysed in Holmberg (2015). It may be the case, however, that *ResPrts* are better analysed as heads associating directly with the Ground head. For the purpose of this discussion, the question whether *ResPrts* function as heads or phrases can be put aside.

b. the contribution of *no*

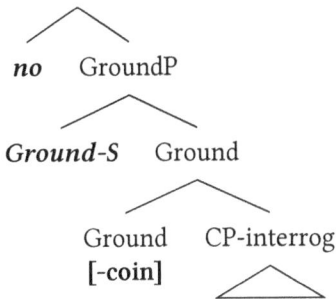

```
        /\
   no   GroundP
          /\
   Ground-S   Ground
              /\
         Ground   CP-interrog
         [-coin]    /\
```

(57) A: When are you leaving?
  B: i. Yes. (When am I leaving?) That's the question.
      ii. No! (When am I leaving?) You can't ask me that.

According to this analysis, *yes* values [*u*coin] associated with Ground as [+coin], thereby asserting that the wh-question is in the speaker's ground; in contrast, *no* values [*u*coin] as [-coin] thereby asserting that the question which serves as the TRIGGER is not in the speaker's ground. The assumption that questions can be part of someone's ground (in addition to propositions and discourse referents) has been independently established in Ginzburg (1995a; 1995) and Roberts (1996). They argue that the discourse component associated with wh-questions is a Question Set (a set of propositions). Evidence that this is so comes from the fact that a question may serve as a discourse referent, just like propositions do. Hence they can be anaphorically referenced, as in (57) by *that*.

According to this analysis, the multi-functionality of *ResPrts* derives from the fact that they can associate with the clausal spine in two different positions: i) immediately above p-structure and ii) above the speech act structure. In the former case, which is the one that Holmberg discusses, *ResPrts* serve to value an open polarity variable associated with the proposition. This derives their answering function because they provide the value for the open variable. Since by hypothesis, there is no polarity variable associated with wh-questions, this function is not available if the TRIGGER is a wh-question. The felicity of *ResPrts* in this context derives from the fact that the *ResPrts* can also associate with the spine above the speech-act structure. In this context, they serve to value the unvalued coincidence feature. This derives the (dis)agreement function of *ResPrts*. In particular, if the responder asserts that the TRIGGER question is in their ground it follows that they agree with the responder. By virtue of asking the question in the first place, the respondee makes it clear that this question is in their ground. If the same question is also in the respondee's ground, it follows that they agree on the felicity of the speech act. In this way, the proposed analysis can derive the fact that *ResPrts* can be used to respond to all clause-types. As just discussed, with assertions, the discourse component is a proposition; with wh-questions the discourse component is a Question Set. And following Portner (2004), we can assume that with imperatives, the discourse component is a *to do list.* Finally, for expository reasons I assume that with exclamatives, the discourse component is list of *exclaimables.*

Hence the agreement function is communicated without a dedicated agreement marker. The essence of this analysis is summarized in (58).

(58)   The agreement vs. answering function of *ResPrt*

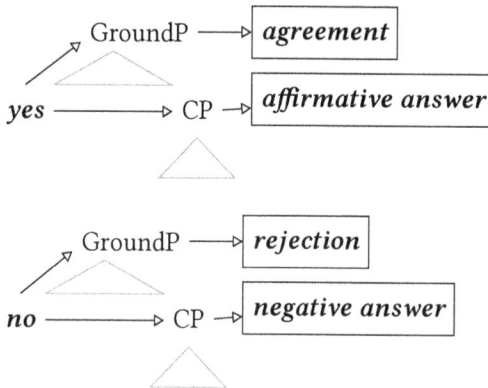

In the remainder of this section, I discuss two predictions of this analysis. First, I show that the (dis)agreement function does not interact with negation. This follows, because the agreement function arises by associating *ResPrt* with GroundP, and hence is too high to interact with negation within the propositional structure. Second, I show that the (dis)agreement function is also available with polar questions.

Evidence that the agreement function derives from a high position of the *ResPrts* comes from the fact that in this position they do not interact with negation in the same way as they do when they serve the answering function. Recall that in English, answers to negative questions are ambiguous between the polarity and the truth-based reading because the *ResPrts* may or may not take negation in their scope. The relevant data exemplifying this pattern are repeated below for convenience.

(59)   Q: Doesn't John drink coffee?
      A: i. Yes. (=He does drink coffee.)   CONTENT: p
                     (= He doesn't drink coffee.)   CONTENT: ¬p
         ii. No. (=He doesn't drink coffee.)   CONTENT: ¬p
                     (= He does drink coffee.)   CONTENT: p

If *ResPrts* in their (dis)agreement function associate with the spine above the speech act phrase we predict that they cannot interact with negation in the same way. This prediction is borne out. When a wh-question contains negation, the positive *ResPrt* agrees with the negated question (60i/ii) while the negative *ResPrt* has to disagree with the negated question (60iii/iv). Hence no ambiguity arises with *ResPrts* in this context and negated wh-questions behave just like their positive counterparts.

(60)   A: Why wouldn't he do something like that?
      B: i.   **Yes**. That is the question.
          ii. * **Yes**. That is not the question.
         iii. * **No**. That's the question.
         iv.   **No**. That's not the question.

Next we turn to another question that the analysis raises: Why does the function of the *ResPrt* correlate with the speech act of the TRIGGER? That is, up until now we have seen that as responses to polar questions *ResPrts* function as answers while as responses to wh-questions as well as other speech acts, they function as (dis)agreement markers. Everything else being equal, we might expect that *ResPrts* could be associated with the answering function and the agreement function with any speech act. However, everything else is not equal. First, answering requires there to be an open variable inside the p-structure of the TRIGGER. This is the case in polar questions, but not in other speech act types such as assertions, content questions, commands, and exclamations. However, there are other ways to ask questions: rising declaratives and tag questions. And indeed, *ResPrts* can serve the answering function when these questions are the TRIGGERS for the response.

(61)   A: You fed the dog/?
      B: i. **Yes**. I fed the dog.
         ii. **No**. I didn't feed the dog.

(62)   A: You fed the dog, didn't you?
      B: i. **Yes**. I fed the dog.
         ii. **No**. I didn't feed the dog.

But what about the (dis)agreement function? The analysis predicts that the agreement function should also be available when the TRIGGER is a polar question. This prediction is indeed borne out. *ResPrts* can be used to (dis)agree with polar questions as well. That is, they can serve not only to answer the polar question but also to agree with or disagree with its felicity. Note however, that this use of the *ResPrt* is much more marked. It seems to improve with an initial *hmmm*, which, I assume, marks the responder's evaluation of the question.

(63)   A: Did you feed the dog?
      B: i. (Hmm) **Yes**. Did I feed the dog? That's a good question.
         ii. (Hmm) **No**. Did I feed the dog? That's an unfair question.

In sum, I have argued that the two different functions of *ResPrts* we have identified are syntactically conditioned. The answering function arises if the *ResPrt* associates just above p-structure and values the open polarity value; the (dis)agreement function arises if the *ResPrt* associates above the speech-act structure and values [*ucoin*] to assert whether or not the embedded speech act is in the responder's ground.

Note that simple *ResPrts* cannot be felicitously used with all types of assertion TRIG-GERS. Specifically, agreement is only possible if the CONTENT of the response is already in the responder's ground at the time of the exchange. However, if the respondee reports on something that is new to the responder (as indicated by the initial phrase *guess what*), then a simple *ResPrt* is infelicitous; rather, the *ResPrt* has to be modified. In such cases, as shown in (64), in English the positive *ResPrt* is preceded by *oh*, which marks the newness of the TRIGGER while at the same time, *yes* indicates that there are no contradictory beliefs in the responder's ground. Hence, this modified *ResPrt* serves to indicate acceptance. Note also that there is a rising intonation on *yes*, which indicates that the responder is requesting confirmation that this proposition is really true. Thus, with the rising intonation the responder indicates that s/he accepts the interlocutor as the authority over the truth of the proposition. As shown in (65), UAG has a dedicated particle that serves the acceptance function: it simultaneously indicates the newness of the proposition in the responder's ground and its acceptance. Like in English, this particle is realized with a rising intonation.

(64) A: Guess what. My sister just gave birth to a baby\.
      B: i. * Yes\.
          ii. Oh, yes/?

(65) Upper Austrian German

      A: Stoe da voa. Mei Schwesta hot grod a   Kind kriagt\.
          Put 2SG PRT. my sister   AUX just DET child got.

          'Imagine that. My sister just had a baby.'
      B: i. * Jo\.
          ii. Aso/?[14]

This much establishes that languages can have special means to mark the status of a particular proposition relative to the responder's ground: in English and in German, special markers are available to mark the newness of the proposition in the common ground. This is akin to the marking of the novelty or familiarity of a given discourse referent (i.e., definiteness marking). Given that definiteness is not marked across all languages, we may expect that the marking of novel propositions too is also not universally available. Hence this is another potential source of cross-linguistic variation that should be tracked when developing a typology of *yes* and *no*.

5 Marking response

We have now seen that there are at least two different functions available for *ResPrts*. They can be used as answers to polar questions and they can be used as markers of (dis)agreement with the speech act. I have argued that the difference between these two

---

[14]The standard German version of this particle is *ach so*.

functions is syntactically conditioned: associating a *ResPrt* with the spine just above the p-structure results in the answering function, while associating it above the speech act structure (GroundP) results in the (dis)agreement function. The assumption that *ResPrts* can associate with different positions in the spine and that they can thereby acquire different functions raises the question as to whether there are any other positions that *ResPrts* can associate with and that would derive other functions for *ResPrts*. In this section I show that this is indeed the case.

In Wiltschko (2017), it is argued that the speech act structure consists not only of the GroundP but also contains an articulated response layer above GroundP. That is, many speech acts can be characterized not only by the commitment the speaker displays towards the proposition (encoded in GroundP) but also by a request for the addressee as to how to respond to the utterance. This is known as the *Call on Addressee* (henceforth CoA; Beyssade & Marandin 2006). In English, CoA can be encoded by the intonational contour associated with a given utterance. For example, rising intonation can be analysed as encoding a request to respond (Beyssade & Marandin 2006), and according to Wiltschko (2017) is associated with another layer in the speech act structure, namely RespP (see also Heim et al. 2014). This is schematized in (66).

(66) A fully articulated speech act structure

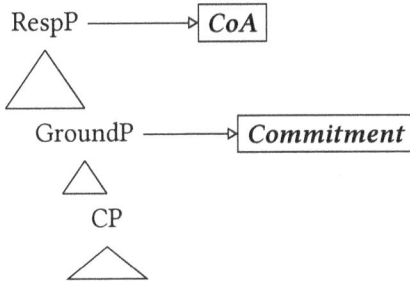

RespP ⟶ $\boxed{CoA}$

GroundP ⟶ $\boxed{Commitment}$

CP

Given the structure in (66), we might expect that *ResPrts* can also associate with RespP. There is indeed a use of *ResPrts* in UAG which is amenable to such an analysis. In particular, *ResPrts* can be used to mark the following utterance as a response. In this case the TRIGGER of the response can be an immediately preceding utterance as in (67) but also an immediately preceding (non-linguistic) situation as in (68)).

(67) Upper Austrian German
      Context. A and B work in the same cubicle. A usually leaves work at 4, but sometimes his schedule is a bit off. B wants to know if A is indeed planning to leave at 4 today.

      B: Gehst du heit   um 4 ham?
          Go-2SG you today at   4 home.
          'Are you going home at 4 today?'

> A: i. **Jo/Na** des was-st doch eh. I geh imma um 4 ham.
>   YES/NO that know-2SG PRT PRT I go always at 4 home.
> 'But you know that. I always go home at 4.'
>
> ii. **Jo/Na** des was-st leicht net?
>   YES/NO that know-2SG PRT NEG
> 'So you don't know that?'

(68) Upper Austrian German

Context. A and B are co-workers. Their working hours are fixed and they always go home at 4.30. Typically, they get ready to leave at 4.25 so they can be out the door by 4.30. Today B is not showing any signs of getting ready even at 4.25. A comments:

> a. **Jo/Na** wonn gehst denn du heit ham?
>   YES/NO when go-2SG PRT you today home
> 'So when are you leaving today?'
>
> b. **Jo/Na** geh-st du heit ned ham?
>   YES/NO go-2SG you today NEG home
> 'So aren't you going home today?'

In this use of the *ResPrt*, the CONTENT of the response is not established by the response marker itself, but instead by the following utterance. This has a number of consequences for the distribution of the *ResPrt* when used in this function. First, the following utterance cannot be elided. And second, the CONTENT of the response does not differ. depending on whether the positive or the negative *ResPrt* is used.[15] Finally, given that the TRIGGER can be a non-linguistic situation, we may expect there to be no restrictions on the type of linguistic TRIGGERS. This is indeed the case. All types of speech acts can serve as

---

[15] An anonymous reviewer points out that the interchangeability of the positive and negative *ResPrt* might indicate that at least in certain cases they might effectively be used expletively. To support this idea, the reviewer points out that in South African English there are certain uses of *no* that do not seem to mean *no* at all, as for example in i).

> (i) A: How are you today?
> B: **No**, I'm doing really well.

It is not clear that *no* is in fact meaningless here.

In particular, *ResPrts* do not only respond to propositional content and speech acts, but they may also respond to the mere fact that the TRIGGER expresses a belief on behalf of the speaker. So for example in ii) *yeah* and *no* co-occur without introducing a contradiction. In particular, *yeah* expresses that B accepts that A beliefs p, but *no* indicates that B does not agree (see Guntly 2016; Guntly & Wiltschko 2016 for further discussion).

> (ii) A: Yeah you don't know which is you don't know which is worse.
> B: **Yeah no** i know which is worse. (Switchboard Corpus 02078A)

In light of the data in ii), I hesitate to conclude that *no* in i) is really expletive. But to determine its function will have to await further research.

TRIGGERS for this use of the *ResPrt*. In (67), the trigger is a polar question, and in the data below we observe all other speech act types serving as TRIGGERS: WH-questions (69), assertions (70), commands (71), and exclamations (72).

(69) Upper Austrian German

    A: Wonn gehst denn du heit   ham?
        When go-2SG PRT   you today home.

        'When are you going home today?'

    B: **Jo/Na** des was-st   doch eh. I geh imma   um 4 ham.
        JA/NO that know-2SG PRT   PRT I go   always at   4 home.

        'You know that already. I always go home at 4.'

(70) Upper Austrian German

    A: I boag   ma gschwind dei   Auto aus.
        I borrow me quickly   your car   PRT

        'I'm going to quickly borrow your car.'

    B: **Jo/Na** des geht owa ned.
        YES/NO that goes but NEG

        'But that's not okay.'

(71) Upper Austrian German

    A: Jetzt geh endlich ins   Bett.
        Now go   finally into.the bed

        'Go to bed now!'

    B: **Jo/Na** i geh jo   eh scho.
        YES/NO I go   PRT PRT PRT

        'But I'm going already.'

(72) Upper Austrian German

    A: Ma a so a grossa Hund.
        PRT a so a big   dog

        'Gee, what a big dog!'

    B: **Jo/Na** ho-st   den no ned gsegn?
        YES/NO have-2SG DEM PRT NEG seen

        'Haven't you seen him before?'

I assume that the head of the response phrase (RespP) is associated with an unvalued coincidence feature [$u$coin], just as any other clausal projection. It relates the utterance to the interlocutor's response set. With the use of the positive *ResPrt*, [$u$coin] receives a positive value [+coin] and thus asserts that the utterance coincides with the responder's response set thereby marking it as a response, as in (73).

(73) Valuing [*u*coin] in Resp

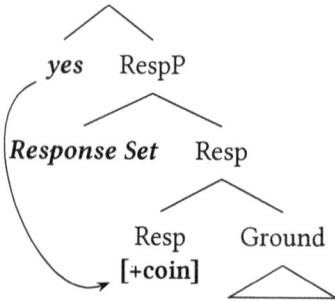

However, this raises the question as to why the negative *RePrt* can also be used in this context. Everything else being equal, we expect it to value [*u*coin] as [-coin] as in (74).

(74) Valuing [*u*coin] in Resp

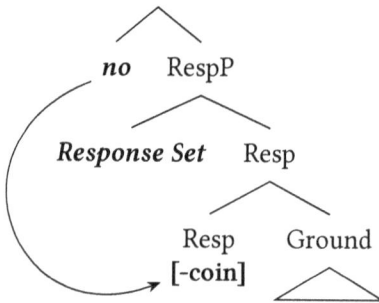

So why is it possible to express the same thing by valuing [*u*coin] as either positive or negative? I tentatively suggest that this may have to do with the timing of when the CONTENT of the response entered into the responder's response set. Specifically, with the positive *ReSPrt* the responder indicates that the content *is* in the response set *now* ([+coin]); in contrast, with the negative *ReSPrt* the responder indicates that the content *was not* in the response set prior to the time of utterance ([-coin]).[16] This is compatible with its being in the response set at the time of utterance. Hence, both the positive and the negative *ReSPrt* can express the same content, with a difference in perspective. If the negative *ReSPrt* is used, then the fact the response is now in the response set contrasts with the assertion that it wasn't in the response set prior to the time of utterance. Hence, the use of the negative *ReSPrt* focusses on the surprising nature of the response.

---

[16] This is reminiscent of the difference between languages with and without definiteness marking as analysed in Wiltschko (2014).

Note that the possibility for a *ResPrt* to mark the utterance as a response is subject to cross-linguistic variation. While in UAG this function is possible for *ResPrt*, it is not in English: neither the positive nor the negative *ResPrt* are well-formed in this context (75a); instead, the particle *so* is used (75b).

(75)   **Context.** A and B are co-workers. Their working hours are fixed and they always go home at 4.30. Typically, they get ready to leave at 4.25 so they can be out the door by 4.30. Today B is not showing any signs of getting ready even at 4.25. A comments:

    a.   * **Yes**/* **no**, when are you leaving today?

    b.   **So**, when are you leaving today?

It may be noted, though that UAG is not the only language where *ResPrts* can be used in this way. While relevant information about *ResPrts* is not easy to come by in grammars, I have found two candidates for *ResPrts* that serve to mark the utterance as a response, one in Macushi (Cariban) and the other in Cambodian. I briefly describe the relevant data in turn.

Consider first Macushi. Here the positive *ResPrt* (*inna*) can be used to answer polar questions as in (76) but it can also be used after questions of other types (i.e., wh-questions) as in (77), in which case it seems to express "*Yes I'm answering you.*" (Abbott 1991: 46–49).

(76)   Macushi (Abbott 1991: 46)

    A: attî pra nan?
        2.go NEG 2.be.Q
        'Didn't you go?'

    B: inna, uutî pra wai. Aminke man.
        Yes   1.go NEG 1.be far   3.be
        'Yes, I didn't go. It was far.'

(77)   Macushi (Abbott 1991: 49)

    A: î' warapo i-tî-pai-nîkon   nai?
        how:many ADV-go-DESID-COLL 3.BE.Q
        'How many are wanting to go?'

    B: inna, tamî'nawîrî anna   wîtî e'-pai   man.
        yes, all   1:EXCL go   be-DESID 3:be
        'Yes, we are all wanting to go.'

Thus, in Macushi, *ResPrt* can be used for answering as well as for marking the following utterance as a response.

A similar pattern is also found in Khmer (Cambodian), where affirmative responses to yes/no questions may consist of repeating the main verb in the question, or a full repetition of the question in affirmative form. Crucially, in polite speech, the echoed verb is usually preceded by a form of the response particle *baat* for men (78) and *caah* for women. In the examples below, the optional 'full' responses are shown in brackets.

(78)   Khmer (Huffman 1970: 24)

> A: Look   sok-səpbaay ciə   tee?
>   you(polite) well-well   well PRT
>
>   'Are you well?'
>
> B: Baat (kñom) sok-səpbaay (ciə   tee).
>   Yes   (I)   well-well   well PRT
>
>   'Yes, I'm quite well.'

Interestingly, negative responses to yes-no questions may consist solely of the negative particle *tee* which is often followed by the negative form of the main verb. Relevant for our purpose is the fact that in polite speech, *tee* may be preceded by the appropriate form of the positive *ResPrt* in which case it is followed by the full negative answer to the question. This is shown in (79).

(79)   Khmer (Huffman 1970: 24)

> A: look   sdap baan tee?
>   You(polite) listen can   Q
>
>   'Can you understand?'
>
> B: (baat) tee, (kñom) sdap min baan tee.
>   Yes   Q   I   listen NEG can   Q
>
>   '(Resp) no (I) don't understand.'

Given the profile of the *ResPrt* in Macushi and Khmer, I conclude that in these languages, *ResPrts* can be used to mark the host utterance as a response, just like in UAG, though a more thorough investigation will have to confirm that this analysis is indeed on the right track.

The use of *ResPrts* as markers of response is yet another source of cross-linguistic variation that will have to be tracked when developing a typology of *yes* and *no*.

6 Conclusion

In this paper I have shown that *ResPrts* are multi-functional: they can be used as answers to polar questions, as markers of (dis)agreement with preceding utterances no matter what their speech act type; and finally they can also be used to mark the utterance they precede as a response to some situation (linguistic or non-linguistic).[17] We have seen that there is considerable cross-linguistic variation. For example, in UAG simple positive

---

[17]There are still other uses of *ResPrt* that I haven't discussed here. These include backchannels (in the sense of Yngve 1970) and discourse particles.

ResPrts cannot be used to answer a negative polar question. On the other hand, in English, *ResPrts* cannot be used to mark a following utterance as a response. This is summarized in Table 3.

Table 3: Three functions of *ResPrts*

		English		UAG	
		yes	*no*	*jo*	*na*
Answering function	Positive question	✓	✓	✓	✓
	Negative question	✓	✓	✗	✓
Marker of (Dis)agreement		✓	✓	✓	✓
Marker of Response		✗	✗	✓	✓

In the analysis I have developed here, I have assumed (following Wiltschko 2014) that multi-functionality can be syntactically conditioned. A given unit of language may acquire different functions depending on its place of association with the syntactic spine. In addition, I have assumed an updated version of Ross' 1970 performative hypothesis according to which speech-act structure is part of the syntactic computation. With these assumptions we were able to develop a unified analysis for the three different functions of *ResPrts* we have discussed.

In this context, it is interesting to note that *ResPrts* can also grammaticalize.[18] In particular, *no*-elements are a common source of negative reinforcers and/or presupposition negation markers (Zanuttini 1997; Poletto 2008a,b; DeVos & van der Auwera 2013) while *yes*-type elements can grammaticalise as sentence-internal discourse particles in German (*Er hat **ja** gesagt, dass* ...). It will be interesting to explore whether there are any correlations between the types of responses *ResPrts* can be used for and their grammaticalization paths.

These findings highlight the importance of Holmberg's insight that i) *ResPrts* have a syntax, and ii) that the cross-linguistic patterns of *ResPrts* should be carefully studied. In fact, give the recent interest in the syntacticization of speech acts (Speas & Tenny 2003; Sigurðsson 2004; Giorgi 2010; 2015; Haegeman 2013; Haegeman & Hill 2013 a.o.) it seems that *ResPrts* will provide valuable insights into the articulation of speech act structure.

Acknowledgments

Research on this paper was financially supported by a SSHRC Insight grant ('*Towards a typology of confirmationals*') awarded to the author.

I wish to thank Strang Burton, Lisa Matthewson, Michael Rochemont and members of the *eh*-lab at UBC (http://syntaxofspeechacts.linguistics.ubc.ca) for useful discussion and help with data collection. In particular, Yifang Yang is responsible for the SOAP

---

[18]I am grateful to an anonymous reviewer to draw my attention to this fact.

corpus study and Jordan Chark for his help with the search for information on *ResPrts* in grammars. Furthermore, I thank the students in the seminar on the grammar of discourse held at UBC, audiences of the workshop on *Linguistic Variation in the Interaction between Internal and External Syntax* (Utrecht, February 2014) and the students in Leslie Saxon's seminar at the University of Victoria.

This paper is dedicated to Anders Holmberg, who - once again - has been a pioneer in extending the empirical base for generative syntacticians by studying the syntax of response particles.

References

Abbott, Miriam. 1991. Macushi. In Desmond Derbyshire & Geoffrey Pullum (eds.), *Handbook of Amazonian languages 3*, 23–160. Berlin: Mouton de Gruyter.

Asher, Nicholas & Brian Reese. 2007. Intonation and discourse: Biased questions. *Interdisciplinary Studies on Information Structure*. Working Papers of the SFB 632 8. 1–38.

Auer, Peter. 2004. Non-standard evidence in syntactic typology–methodological remarks on the use of dialect data vs spoken language data. In Bernd Kortmann (ed.), *Dialectology meets typology: Dialect grammar from a cross-linguistic perspective*, 69–92. Berlin: Mouton de Gruyter.

Beyssade, Claire & Jean-Marie Marandin. 2006. The speech act assignment problem revisited: Disentangling speaker's commitment from speaker's call on addressee. In *Selected papers of CSSP 2005*, 37–68. http://www.cssp.cnrs.fr/eiss6/index_en.html.

Büring, Daniel & Christine Gunlogson. 2000. Aren't positive and negative polar questions the same? Unpublished manuscript, University of California at Santa Cruz.

Clark, Herbert & Susan Brennan. 1991. Grounding in communication. In Lazren B. Resnick, John M. Levine & Stephanie D. Teasley (eds.), *Perspectives on socially shared cognition*, 127–149. Washington DC: American Psychological Association.

DeVos, Mark & Johan van der Auwera. 2013. Jespersen cycles in Bantu: Double and triple negation. *Journal of African Languages and Linguistics* 34. 205–274.

Farkas, Donka & Kim Bruce. 2009. On reacting to assertions and polar questions. *Journal of Semantics* 27. 81–118.

Ginzburg, Jonathan. 1995a. Resolving questions, part I. *Linguistics and Philosophy* 18. 459–527.

Ginzburg, Jonathan. 1995. Resolving questions, part II. *Linguistics and Philosophy* 18. 567–609.

Giorgi, Alessandra. 2010. *About the speaker: Towards a syntax of indexicality*. Oxford: Oxford University Press.

Giorgi, Alessandra. 2015. Discourse and the syntax of the left periphery: Clitic left dislocation and hanging topic. In Josef Bayer, Roland Hinterhölzl & Andreas Trotzke (eds.), *Discourse-oriented syntax*, vol. 226 (Linguistik Aktuell/Linguistics Today), 229–250. Amsterdam: John Benjamins.

Goodhue, Daniel, James Pickett & Michael Wagner. 2013. English reverse prosody in yes-no responses. In *Sem Dial 2013: Proceedings of the 17th Workshop on the Semantics and Pragmatics of Dialogue 2013*.

Goodhue, Daniel & Michael Wagner. 2015. It's not just what you say, it's how you say it: Intonation, yes and no. In *The Proceedings of the North East Linguistics Society (NELS) 45*. http://semanticsarchive.net/Archive/TRjYmNiN/GoodhueWagner_2015.pdf.

Gunlogson, Christine. 2003. *True to form: Rising and falling declaratives as questions in English*. New York: Routledge.

Guntly, Erin. 2016. *Yeah no. Response markers can tell you a lot*. Unpublished manuscript.

Guntly, Erin & Martina Wiltschko. 2016. Response markers in Ktunaxa. Poster given at Semantics of Understudied Languages of the Americas 2016.

Haegeman, Liliane. 2013. West Flemish verb-based discourse markers and the articulation of the speech act layer. *Studia Linguistica* 68. 116–39.

Haegeman, Liliane & Virginia Hill. 2013. The syntactization of discourse. In Raffaela Folli, Christina Sevdali & Robert Truswell (eds.), *Syntax and its limits* (Oxford Studies in Theoretical Linguistics), 370–390. Oxford: Oxford University Press.

Haegeman, Liliane & Andrew Weir. 2015. The cartography of yes and no in West Flemish. In Josef Bayer, Roland Hinterhölzl & Andreas Trotzke (eds.), *Discourse-oriented syntax*, vol. 226 (Linguistik Aktuell/Linguistics Today), 175–210. Amsterdam: John Benjamins.

Hale, Kenneth L. 1986. Notes on world view and semantic categories: Some Walpiri examples. In Pieter Muysken & Henk van Riemsdijk (eds.), *Features and projections*, 233–254. Dordrecht: Foris.

Halliday, M.A.K. & Ruqaiya Hasan. 1976. *Cohesion in English*. London: Longman.

Hamblin, Charles Leonard. 1958. Questions. *Australasian Journal of Philosophy* 36. 159–168.

Hamblin, Charles Leonard. 1973. Questions in Montague English. *Foundations of Language* 10. 41–53.

Heim, Johannes, Hermann Keupdjio, Zoe Wai Man Lam, Adriana Osa Gomez, Sonja Thoma & Martina Wiltschko. 2014. What to do with particles. In *Proceedings of CLA*. http://syntaxofspeechacts.linguistics.ubc.ca/wp-content/uploads/2014/02/heim-et-al-cla-2014-proceedings.pdf.

Holmberg, Anders. 2001. The syntax of yes and no in Finnish. *Studia Linguistica* 55. 141–174.

Holmberg, Anders. 2002. Expletives and agreement in Scandinavian passives. *Journal of Comparative Germanic Linguistics* 4. 85–128.

Holmberg, Anders. 2007. Null subjects and polarity focus. *Studia Linguistica* 61. 212–236.

Holmberg, Anders. 2013. The syntax of answers to polar questions in English and Swedish. *Lingua* 128. 31–50.

Holmberg, Anders. 2014. The syntax of the Finnish question particle. In Peter Svenonius (ed.), *Functional structure from top to toe*, 266–289. Oxford: Oxford University Press. http://www.ncl.ac.uk/elll/research/publication/177509.

Holmberg, Anders. 2015. *The syntax of yes and no*. Oxford: Oxford University Press.

Huffman, Franklin E. 1970. *Modern spoken Cambodian.* Ithaca, New York: Cornell University. reprinted in 1991.

Jakobson, Roman. 1932. *The structure of the Russian verb.* The Hague: Mouton. Reprinted in: Russian and Slavic Grammar Studies, 1931-1981, Mouton 1984.

Jones, Bob Morris. 1999. *The Welsh answering system.* Vol. 120 (Trends in Linguistics, Studies and Monographs). Berlin: Mouton de Gruyter.

Jones, Christian & Tania Horak. 2014. Leave it out! The use of soap operas as models of spoken discourse in the ELT classroom. *The Journal of Language Teaching and Learning* 4. 1–14.

Kramer, Ruth & Kyle Rawlins. 2009. Polarity particles: An ellipsis account. In. Amherst, MA: Graduate Student Linguistic Association.

Krifka, Manfred. 2013. Response particles as propositional anaphors. In *Proceedings of Semantics and Linguistic Theory (SALT) 23*, 1–18.

Kuno, Susumu. 1973. *The structure of the Japanese language.* Cambridge, MA: MIT Press.

Ladd, Robert D. 1981. A first look at the semantics and pragmatics of negative questions and tag questions. In *Papers from the 17th regional meeting of the Chicago Linguistic Society,* 164–171.

Laka, Itziar. 1990. *Negation in syntax, on the nature of functional categories and projections.* Massachusetts Institute of Technology, Dept. of Linguistics & Philosophy dissertation.

Lam, Zoe Wai-Man. 2014. A complex ForceP for speaker- and addressee-oriented discourse particles in Cantonese. *Studies in Chinese Linguistics* 35. 61–80.

Liberman, Mark & Ivan Sag. 1974. Prosodic form and discourse function. *Chicago Linguistic Society* 10. 416–427.

Poletto, Cecilia. 2008a. On negative doubling. *Quaderni di Lavoro ASIt* 8. 57–84.

Poletto, Cecilia. 2008b. The syntax of focus negation. *University of Venice Working Papers in Linguistics* 18. 181–202.

Pope, Emily Norwood. 1976. *Questions and answers in English.* The Hague: Mouton.

Portner, Paul P. 2004. The semantics of imperatives within a theory of clause types. *Semantics and Linguistic Theory* 14. 235–252.

Roberts, Craige. 1996. Information structure: Towards an integrated formal theory of pragmatics. In Andreas Kathol & Jae Hak Yoon (eds.), *OSU working papers in linguistics,* 91–136. Columbus, OH: Ohio State University Department of Linguistics.

Romero, Maribel & Chung-hye Han. 2004. On negative yes/no questions. *Linguistics and Philosophy* 27. 609–658.

Ross, John R. 1970. On declarative sentences. In Roderick Jacobs & Peter Rosenbaum (eds.), *Readings in English transformational grammar,* 222–272. Waltham, Mass.: Ginn & Co.

Sadock, Jerrold M. & Arnold Zwicky. 1985. Speech act distinctions in syntax. In Timothy Shopen (ed.), *Language typology and syntactic description,* 155–196. Cambridge: Cambridge University Press.

Sigurðsson, Halldór Ármann. 2004. The syntax of person, tense, and speech features. *Italian Journal of Linguistics* 16. 219–251. Special issue.

Speas, Peggy & Carol Tenny. 2003. Configurational properties of point of view roles. In Anna-Maria Di Sciullo (ed.), *Asymmetry in grammar*, 315–343. Amsterdam: John Benjamins.

Thoma, Sonja. 2016. *Discourse particles and the syntax of discourse. Evidence from Miesbach Bavarian*. University of British Columbia. Unpublished PhD dissertation.

Trubetzkoy, Nikolai Sergeevich. 1939. *Grundzüge der Phonologie*. Prague: Jednota ceskoslovenskych matematiku a fysiku.

Wallage, Philip & Wim van der Wurff. 2013. On saying 'yes' in early Anglo-Saxon England. *Anglo-Saxon England* 42. 183–215.

Weiß, Helmut. 2004. A question of relevance: Some remarks on standard languages. *Studies in language* 28. 648–674.

Wiltschko, Martina. 2014. *The universal structure of categories: Towards a formal typology*. Cambridge: Cambridge University Press.

Wiltschko, Martina. 2017. Ergative constellations in the structure of speech acts. In Jessica Coon, Diane Massam & Lisa Travis (eds.), *The Oxford handbook of ergativity*, 419–446. New York: Oxford University Press.

Wiltschko, Martina & Johannes Heim. 2016. The syntax of sentence peripheral discourse markers. A neo-performative analysis. In Gunther Kaltenböck, Evelien Keizer & Arne Lohmann (eds.), *Outside the clause: form and function of extra-clausal constituents*, 305–340. Amsterdam: John Benjamins.

Yngve, Victor. 1970. On getting a word in edgewise. *Chicago Linguistic Society* 6. 567–578.

Zanuttini, Raffaela. 1997. *Negation and clausal structure: A comparative study of Romance languages*. Oxford: Oxford University Press.

Zanuttini, Raffaela & Paul P. Portner. 2003. Exclamative clauses: At the syntax-semantics interface. *Language* 79(1). 39–81.

Chapter 12

The common syntax of deixis and affirmation

George Tsoulas

University of York

This paper pursues a formal analysis of the idea that affirmative answers to Yes/No questions correspond to a sort of propositional deixis whereby the relevant proposition is pointed at. The empirical case involves an analysis of the deictic particle *Nà* in Greek and a comparison of its syntax with that of the affirmative particle *Nè*. It is shown that both involve an extra head which in the case of the deictic particle is uniformly externalised as the pointing gesture. It is argued that gestural externalisation of syntactic structure should be considered on a par with phonetic externalisation (not only in sign languages). The grammar of the affirmative particle gives us also an account of the observed facts about Greek whereby both the truth and the polarity answering system appear to coexist.

1 Introduction

Holmberg (2015) begins thus: 'It is certainly not obvious that expressions like *Yes* and *No* have syntactic structure.' It is even less obvious that elements like *Yes* and *No* have *complex* internal syntactic and semantic structure. In the literature on the semantics of Yes/No questions an explicit semantics for *Yes* is rarely given. Groenendijk & Stokhof (1984) is one of these exceptions and their semantics is given in (1):

(1) $[\![yes]\!] = \lambda p\ p(a)$

Groenendijk & Stokhof's (1984) syntactic assumption is that *Yes* and *No* are sentential adverbs of type S/S. It would then seem that there is not much of interest that either the semantics or the implied syntax would give us. In this paper I will take Holmberg's stance and try to show that interesting insights and conclusions can follow from pursuing the non-obvious. Yes/No questions in Greek can receive either a verb-echo answer (2-b) or a particle answer (2-c):

(2)   a.   Petai o   gaidaros?
             flies the.NOM donkey
             'Do donkeys fly?'

Laura R. Bailey & Michelle Sheehan. 2017. Order and structure in syntax I. in Laura R. Bailey & Michelle Sheehan (eds.), *Order and structure in syntax I: Word order and syntactic structure*, 281–309. Berlin: Language Science Press. DOI:??

    b.   Petai
           flies
    c.   Ne
           Yes

Our focus in this paper will be on particle answers only and verb echo answers will not be considered. Holmberg's (2015) proposal for the particles *Yes* and *No* is that they are the spell-out values of a focused polarity variable. If this is so, and given that languages usually have small unanalysable particles for this function, it makes little sense to ask why these particles take the form that they do. They just do. But now imagine that there is a language where the affirmative particle is, if not immediately transparently complex, at least arguably so. Then it does make sense to ask why it is this, rather than a different complex form that has this meaning and function. Furthermore, if the particle is indeed complex, the question of its internal syntax and compositional semantics justifiably arises over and above that of its external distribution. This seems correct, but is there such a language? In this paper I will argue that Greek, at least concerning the affirmative particle *Nè* (Yes), corresponds quite precisely to the above description and, therefore, gives us a very good opportunity to formulate and explore questions that may lead to a better understanding of affirmation.

My ultimate goal here is to understand the affirmation particle *Nè* in Greek. Anecdotally, speakers of Indo-European languages are often surprised not only because the way to say *Yes* in Greek resembles more the way to say *No* in other languages but also that the language does not use the *-n-* element in negatives. Greek *n*-words have no /*n*/ in them.

To understand this particle, however, we will have to take a somewhat circuitous route starting from the properties and analysis of the deictic (or presentational) particle *Nà*. *Nà* and *Nè* share the initial element *N-* and the hypothesis that I will explore is that this is not an accident. In other words, deixis and affirmation have a common core. I contend here that understanding what I call *N-* deixis leads us to a particular understanding of affirmation as essentially a sub-case of deixis, namely propositional deixis. The paper is structured as follows. §2 begins with two apparently unrelated observations regarding, on the one hand, an intuitive understanding of what it means to answer a Yes/No question and, on the other, an observation regarding the (possible) origin of the word *Nè* in Greek. §3 consists of a short primer on Greek particles focusing mainly on an observation from Tsoulas (2015) on the meaning of the endings of two classes of particles (speaker and addressee oriented particles respectively). §4 is an analysis of the deictic particle *Nà* which relates its syntax and semantics directly to the required presence of a pointing gesture. An extension of the proposal to other gestural elements is also discussed. Having established the syntax and semantics of *Nà*, §6 applies the same principles to the affirmation particle *Nè* using the analysis of Holmberg (2015) as point of departure.

2 Two apparently unrelated observations

To make the argument that I want to make here, I will start with two seemingly unrelated observations. The first is a generally offered intuitive and informal description of what answering a Yes/No question amounts to. I will again borrow this intuitive description from Holmberg (2015) who writes:

(3)   [...] The answer provides a value for the variable in the question, and thereby indicates which of the two disjunctive propositions posed by the question the respondent **presents as being true** [Emphasis mine, GT].

The first part of the above quote will be important later on in this paper in §6. It is the emphasised part that I would like to draw attention to for now. Although it is an informal way of describing what answering a Yes/No question amounts to, it can be taken to express an important intuition regarding the formal relationship between *the respondent* and the relevant proposition.

The second observation is an etymological one. The Greek word for *Yes*, i.e. *Nè*, has a somewhat mysterious etymology. It is already found in Homer and is a very common marker of affirmation and agreement in Plato's dialogues as well as the major tragic poets of the 5th century BCE, and it is also found frequently in the New Testament and in Medieval texts. So it seems that this particle was part of Greek from the start though it is trickier to establish its origin with certainty. There is, however, general agreement between Indo-Europeanists that it incorporates the Proto-Indo-European element $*n$ whose function is deictic.[1] There is an obvious intuitive connection here: if answering a Yes/No question amounts to presenting or pointing at a proposition (or its truth-value) then it is not unexpected that elements with a deictic function appear in the formation of the Yes/No particles. In other words, the speech act that the speaker performs by answering a Yes/No question amounts to, or is at least related to, a kind of propositional deixis, as if in order to say *Yes* one had to point at the relevant proposition and state that it is true by providing the relevant polarity value (which, of course, is positive in the case of *Yes*). And this is what the Greek case shows more clearly. If the above connection remains merely an (informed) intuition it is not of great value. I contend here that it can be cashed out in formal structural and semantic terms. To see this we need to start with a short primer on Greek particles.

3 Greek particles: A primer

Greek has a large number of particles of different types and functions. Tsoulas's (2015) study of the higher field particles in Greek shows that so-called discourse particles in Greek, though small and monosyllabic, are consistently complex elements that are made up of (at least) two heads, one that encodes anchoring and perspective and another that

---

[1]There is a vast literature on deictic and demonstrative pronouns in (proto)-Indo-European and their uses as elements of inflection. Brugmann (1904; 1911) are classic references. Shields (1992) and references therein provide further context.

encodes attitude/evidentiality. The most relevant observation for the purposes of the present work is that the elements *E* and *A*, while particles in their own right, as in (4)–(5), also combine with other elements to create complex particles (6), (7)[2]:

(4) a. A, irthe   o Kostas
         PRT came.3rd.SG the Kostas
         'I see, Kostas has arrived.'

     b. A, o   giannis agorase aftokinito
         PRT the Giannis bought car
         'I see, Giannis bought a car.'

(5) a. E, irthe   o Kostas
         PRT came.3rd.SG the Kostas
         'As you know/would expect, Kostas has arrived.'

     b. E, agorase o   Giannis aftokinito
         PRT bought the Giannis car
         'As you know/would expect, Giannis bought a car.'

(6) E-series
     Re, De, Vre etc...

(7) A-series
     Na/Nà, δa, Ba etc...

The meanings of the particles in (6)–(7) are complex and difficult to describe.[3] Except for *Nà* (to which we return) they are not directly relevant to the present paper, and an illustration will be given shortly. The point to retain from this is the following:[4] the particles in the *E* series are what I will call addressee-anchored particles while those in the *A*-series are speaker-anchored ones. We will elaborate further on the notion of anchoring later on. Comparing the distribution of the different particles, Tsoulas (2015) observes that the complex particles of the *E*-series have a wider distribution than the bare particle *E*, which is restricted to the sentence initial and sentence final position.[5] In other words, complex *E*-particles can appear at various positions inside the sentence.[6] Interestingly, this is not true of the *A*-series particles, which remain restricted in their distribution to sentence initial position. From these facts, the conclusion is that the two series of particles have different syntactic structures. The *E*-series is headed by the evidential/attitudinal morpheme, which allows and accounts for their wider distribution, while the *A*-series is headed by what we called the *anchor*. The two structures are as follows:

---

[2]To avoid unnecessarily complicating the glosses, and when there is no possibility of confusion, I will simply gloss the particles PRT.

[3]Blakemore's (2002) term for the difficulty in formulating descriptively the meanings of discourse particles is *descriptive ineffability*. Speakers mostly provide contexts where the particles are felicitous in order to explain their meanings.

[4]See Tsoulas (2015) for more details.

[5]In fact, Tsoulas (2015) suggests that only the sentence initial position is available to these particles and the sentence final one results from slifting of the clausal complement of the particle.

[6]With some restrictions for some particles which can be derived from their meanings.

(8)   E-series

Evid/AttitudeP

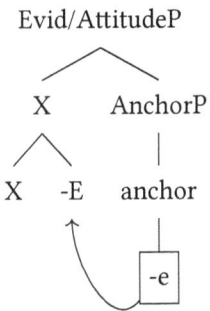

(9)   A-series[7]

AnchorP

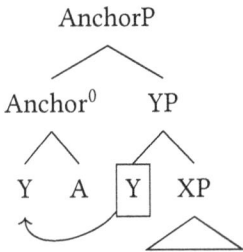

With this in mind, let us illustrate with one example from the list of particles in (7) the general approach. Consider the particle *De*. This particle only appears in sentence final position. Deriving this restriction would take us too far afield but the final structure will look similar to the following:[8]

(10)   AttitudeP

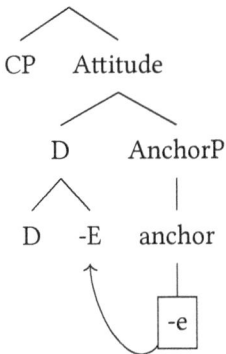

---

[7]We will return shortly to the nature of the element noted as Y in the structure.
[8]I also set aside here the question whether the CP has moved from a lower position.

The attitude head relates a proposition to an anchor. The semantic question, given that *e* is the anchor is the content of the attitude expressed by *D*. To formulate this the following examples will help:

(11)   a.   Graps-to De.
　　　　　write-it PRT
　　　　　'Write it (for goodness sake).'
　　　b.   To vlepo   De.
　　　　　it   see.1.SG PRT
　　　　　'I see it.'

As can be seen from the above example the particle can follow imperatives as well as declaratives – therefore the notion of *proposition* should be understood broadly. The attitude is one of exasperation. (11-a) is felicitous in a context where the addressee has perhaps been talking repeatedly about writing something but never does. (11-a) is then an expression of the speaker's exasperation with the addressee's failure to do the relevant writing. A similar description applies to (11-b) where the addressee has repeatedly drawn the attention of the speaker to a particular object. Although formalising precisely these notions remains to be done, this example can serve as a general illustration of the relevant types of meaning.

Now if the above is on the right track, it seems reasonable, or at least possible, to identify the *-e* ending of the *Yes* particle *Nè* with the addressee oriented element seen above. But what about the *N* part? It may be that there was a deictic element *N* in Proto-Indo-European but what is the evidence, if any, in the Modern version of Greek? In the next section I show that the evidence is rather strong and that the analysis leads us to unexpected considerations.

4 *N-* deixis in Greek

The particle that is of immediate interest here is the particle *Nà*. There are two versions of this particle, one that is a modal particle and marks the subjunctive (12), and one that is a deictic particle (13).

(12)   I　　　　Maria theli   na   fai.
　　　　The.NOM Maria wants SBJV eat
　　　　'Maria wants to eat.'

Although the two may be related and perhaps, ultimately the same particle[9] we will set aside for the purposes of this discussion the modal particle and concentrate on the deictic version. Deictic uses of *Nà* are accompanied by a pointing gesture:

---

[9]This is the claim made by Christidis (1990). We will return to his account, though not the issue of whether there is one or two different elements *Nà*, which is not directly relevant to our concerns here.

(13) *Nà* ☞ o   Giannis
      Nà ☞ the Giannis
      'There is Giannis'

The orientation of the deixis is always with respect to the speaker, since it is the speaker who actually gestures towards the thing that is pointed at. This is confirmed by the fact that this particle contains the speaker anchoring morpheme *-a* that we saw in the previous section. Let me set aside the question of the pointing gesture and return to it in §4.5. A closer look at the properties of the deictic particle *Nà* reveals an interesting set of properties and is necessary in order to substantiate the claim that particles have complex structure. I will focus here on three aspects of the grammar of this particle, namely the Case patterns of the DPs following the particle, ethical datives and Person Case Constraint effects, and the plural agreement that is manifested on the particle in some dialects.

4.1 Case patterns

To begin with, as Tzartzanos (1946/1953) has observed, the DP following the particle can surface in either nominative or accusative. Note, however, that in the case of the accusative, a clitic pronoun must accompany the particle:[10]

(14) *Nà* *(ton)   ton   Kosta.
      Nà him.ACC the.ACC Kosta.ACC
      'Here is Kostas.'

(15) *Nà* (tos)   o   Kostas.
      Nà he.NOM the.NOM Kostas.NOM
      'Here is Kostas.'

It is also possible that the DP following the accusative clitic is in the nominative:

(16) *Nà* ton   o   Kostas.
      Nà him.ACC the.NOM Kostas.NOM
      'Here is Kostas.'

The origin of the case marking here is unclear. An ellipsis-based account whereby the DP is the object or subject of some verb that has been deleted immediately suggests itself. Unfortunately, there appears to be little justification for postulating an elided sentence here. More importantly, sentences like (16) above seem to militate openly against such an account given that not only would there be no source for the nominative on the overt DP but even if we accepted that it surfaces in some sort of default case[11] as we eventually

---

[10]Joseph (1981) claims that (14) is grammatical without the clitic pronoun though he acknowledges that some speakers reject it. In my dialect *Nà* +accusative is completely ungrammatical. These judgements are shared by all those speakers I asked too. There may be dialects where *Nà* +Acc is grammatical. It is, however, unclear whether any significant conclusion can be drawn from that fact.

[11]And it seems appropriate to think that if there is a default case in Greek it would be the nominative.

might have to do, the problem is that the overt counterpart of (16) is generally ungrammatical. By generally, I mean that with some verbs, a nominative DP co-referential with the clitic can appear in the post-verbal position as an apposition after a markedly long pause, which suggests that these cases are indeed examples of elliptical constructions where a T level constituent has been omitted. It is significant that there should be a pause in these cases especially as the pause is not required in the cases with *Nà*:

(17) ??/*Kita ton, o   Kostas.
      Look him the.NOM Kostas.NOM
      'Look at him, Kostas.'

But with other verbs this is impossible:

(18) *Pare ton [...] o   ipologistis.
      Take him [...] the.NOM computer.NOM
      'Take the computer.'

Note that (18) with the deictic particle and an understood[12] *take* is perfectly fine in the ACC-NOM pattern:

(19) *Nà* ton o   ipologistis.
      here him the.NOM   ipologistis.NOM
      'Here is the computer.'

This suggests that if an ellipsis account were the right approach then there ought to be some way, grammatical or contextual, to ensure that the right verb is chosen. But there is no such way, at least none that I can think of. The content of the putative elided predicate cannot readily be recovered (though guesses can be made). Furthermore, there can be follow ups with further specification of the intended predicate which could not have been the origin of the elided material as the overt counterpart is ungrammatical, as in (20)-(21) respectively:

(20) *Nà* ton o ipologistis ...hrisimopiise/katharise/spase/kan' ton (oti thelis.)
      here him the.NOM computer.NOM ...use/clean/break/do him (what want-you)
      'Here is the computer, use it, clean it, break it do whatever you want to it.'

(21) *Hrisimopiise/etc ton o   ipologistis.
      Use   him the.NOM computer.NOM
      'Use the computer.'

It therefore appears that the ellipsis account is not *prima facie* at least a viable one.[13]

---

[12]By *Understood* I mean roughly accommodated. There is no suggestion here that there is a verb that has been deleted/left unpronounced.

[13]A significantly different variant of the ellipsis account is Joseph (1981). We return to his account in §4.4.

4.2 Ethical datives and Person-Case Constraint effects

Another interesting property of these constructions is that in certain contexts, mostly narrative, an ethical dative clitic (*su*) can appear before the DP or accusative clitic:

(22) Kai opos strivo stin Kalidromiu na su mia kluva me MAT
     And as turn.1SG in Kalidromiu here 2SG.DAT one bus with MAT
     'And as I turn into Kalidromiu street there is a bus full of riot police.'

Interestingly in the presence of the ethical dative the clitic cluster is subject to the Person Case Constraint (PCC). At least in my Greek these clitic clusters are subject to the strong version of the PCC (the one that bans all first/second person direct object clitics if any dative clitic is present):[14]

(23) a. *Nà su me
          Nà 2.DAT 1.ACC

      b. *Nà me su
          Nà 1.ACC 2.DAT

      c. *Nà se mu
          Nà 2.ACC 1.DAT

      d. *Nà mu se
          Nà 1.DAT 2.ACC

I take this as another indication of more complex covert structure.

4.3 Plural agreement

The final property of this particle that we will mention here is that in certain dialects of Greek the deictic particle *Nà* shows person and number agreement.[15] In the dialects that have it, the plural version of the particle is *Nàte*:

(24) *Nàte* ta pedia sas.
     Here.2PL the.PL children yours
     'Here are your children.'

(25) *Nàte* enan para ke min ton skotosete.
     Here.2PL one coin and not him kill
     'Here you all, take some money and don't kill him.'

---

[14]On ethical datives in Greek and more generally, see Michelioudakis & Kapogianni (2013) and references therein. It would be interesting to juxtapose the ideas in this paper with the analysis in Michelioudakis & Kapogianni (2013). Unfortunately, this will have to be left for another occasion.

[15]Although I have not been able to check in many dialects, the plural versions of the particle are certainly found in Cretan Greek and in North-Western dialects (Epirus). It can be found in texts and transcripts of folktales from Epirus and it is very common in Cretan Greek as well as – seemingly at least – other Island varieties. This form of the particle first appeared in Medieval Greek

In general, no other particles of this type show this sort of agreement. There is, however, another particle, *Ade*, meaning roughly *Go* when followed by a second person verb in the imperative:

(26)   a.   Ade na   vrite to Gianni.
              Go SBJV find the Gianni
              'Go find Gianni.'
        b.   Ade gamisou.
              Go fuck.yourself
              'Go fuck yourself.'

When followed by a first person verb the meaning is more complex. In certain cases it can mean roughly *Let's*:

(27)   Ade na   pigenoume.
        Let's SBJV go
        'Let's go.'

It also conveys the meaning that it is difficult (for whatever reason) to do what is described in the proposition:

(28)   Ade na   vroume trapezi tetia ora.
        PRT SBJV find   table   such hour
        'Go find a table at this hour.' (meaning: 'It is virtually impossible.')

(29)   Ade parkare sto   kentro.
        PRT park   in.the centre
        'Go find a parking place in the centre...' (meaning: 'It is virtually impossible.')

Now, in the same dialects as those that show a plural form of *Nà*, *Ade* also has a plural form *adeste*:[16]

(30)   Adeste tora pame.
        Adeste now   go.1PL
        'Come on now, let's go.'

Again, the origin of this agreement remains unclear. It would be difficult to incorporate it into an ellipsis account as it would require us to accept that while the whole verb has been elided the agreement ending would somehow stay and stick to the particle.

Having said that, accounting for the presence of agreement on these particles is not straightforward in the model presented here either. Assuming that the anchor head can optionally carry a [+PL] feature is descriptively adequate but no more. This idea is also generally in line with a suggestion made by an anonymous reviewer for this volume.

---

[16]The meaning of the plural here is somewhat unclear in the sense that judgements vary on whether the plurality in question includes the speaker or not. I want to thank Anna Roussou for giving me this example and also Evi Sifaki and Stella Gryllia for discussing their intuitions on the interpretation of these plurals.

The reviewer suggests that in these cases we may be dealing with something akin to allocutive agreement. If this is so, it makes the argument against an ellipsis account a little weaker as the agreement is not the one that is found on the verb. In other words while there is ellipsis, the agreement is independent from what we find on the verb. While this is an interesting possibility it does not rescue the ellipsis account from the earlier objections. This suggestion, of course, faces the same difficulties. There is no reason why this agreement would appear only with these particles. I will leave this issue open for further research at this point. More needs to be discovered about the agreement patterns in the relevant dialects before a more convincing account can be developed.

To summarise, we have seen that the deictic particle shows properties that would push us to associate it with a larger structure and yet as far as we can tell an account that is based on mere ellipsis of a larger, fully clausal, structure seems unwarranted and unsupported by the evidence.

4.4 Two earlier proposals

The issues surrounding the particle *Nà* have been the focus of some attention in the literature. Joseph (1981) and Christidis (1990) are the most complete accounts. The two accounts differ sharply but from the perspective pursued here, they both contain valid insights and intuitions. Both Joseph (1981) and Christidis (1990) are concerned with the proper categorisation of *Nà*. I will briefly present their accounts below.

Joseph's (1981) careful study considers a number of issues regarding the status of deictic *Nà*. His central claim is that *Nà* is a verb and more specifically a non-finite imperative form of a verb meaning roughly *look* or *take*. This analysis allows us to understand the presence of an accusative (in clitic form or bare, see footnote 10) after the particle as well as the fact that it does not appear before a verb. It also affords an understanding of the plural agreement that appears dialectally on the particle. At the same time, the analysis runs into problems (as Joseph himself observes) in the cases where the particle is followed by a nominative which would have no source. He offers a view according to which this is the result of reanalysis that is mainly due to the case ambiguity found in Greek with neuter nouns (where nominative and accusative are not differentiated). The result is that there is a finite version of the verb *Nà* which takes the nominative DP as its subject, deriving from an abstract underlying *Here comes DP$_{NOM}$*.

Although ultimately I disagree that *Nà* itself is a verb in the sense that it carries a category determining V feature, I think that Joseph's intuition that there are two types of deictic *Nà* and that the way to capture the difference is by appealing to something predicative is correct. My general implementation will differ greatly though.

Another aspect of Joseph (1981) is the discussion of the etymology of the particle. He discusses what he calls the generally accepted etymology (due to Hatzidakis 1907) and which he describes as follows:

(31)   [...] The Classical Greek form *ēnìde* 'see there!', composed of the interjection *ēn* 'see there' plus the imperatival form *íde* 'see!' was reanalyzed as *ēní* plus *de*, with the result that a new form *ēní* was abstracted from *ēníde*. Then by

the substitution of the final -*a* of adverbs [...] and other particles (as in δά [...]) for the *í*, along with the regular aphaeresis of the unstressed initial vowel *ē*-, the form *ná* arose. (Joseph 1981: p.141)

Quite rightly perhaps, Joseph notes that this is a rather involved etymology for a very simple word and that, most importantly 'It is not at all clear why a particle like *ēni* (or even *dé* for that matter) would be influenced by the form of adverbial elements like *kálista* 'very well', *katakéfala* 'on the head', *akóma* ['more'], and so forth'.

Instead, Joseph proposes that *Nà* is a borrowing from South Slavic where similar elements are found. What the ultimate truth about the etymology of deictic *Nà* is I don't know. However, if we assume that the *a* that was substituted for *í* is that of the speaker anchoring particle *a*, which is both independently found in the language and appropriate for the final nature of the particle, as in the structure in (9) then the accepted etymology becomes less problematic and more attractive than a borrowing from South Slavic. Having said that, not much really turns on the etymology anyway. I take it that, should it be the case that *Nà* is indeed a borrowing from South Slavic, Greek must have projected on it the morphosyntactic structures existing in the language.

The etymological issue notwithstanding, Joseph's (1981) account expresses some important insights as already mentioned.

Let me now turn briefly to the account offered by Christidis (1990), who, unlike Joseph, suggests that searching for a category to assign *Nà* to is futile and in the end misleading as the particle resists all categorisation attempts[17] simply because it is just not the sort of element that falls within any of the traditionally recognised categories. He suggests that this is natural if we assume (following Ross 1972) that categorial distinctions are elastic and are better understood as a continuum rather than a set of discrete points. He also rejects Zwicky's (1985) ban on acategorial words. His analysis of *Nà* makes it a *holophrase*. Holophrases are syntactically undifferentiated units that often express fully sentential meanings. To fully understand the idea it is best to quote at some length:

(32)   Holophrasis is a term meant to describe linguistic formations where, to use Halliday & Hasan's (1976: 26) terminology, the differentiation between the 'ideational' and the 'interpersonal' components of language is 'still' undifferentiated. The 'ideational' component [...] concerned with the expression of content [...] the interpersonal component [...] is concerned with expressing the speaker's angle. [...] The holophrastic nature of *Nà* is a manifestation of an archaic fusion of the interpersonal and ideational component (Christidis 1990: 67).

It must be said too that while Christidis does offer an account of *Nà*, his main objective is to argue against the views on categorisation championed by Zwicky (1985) and instantiated in a sense in Joseph's work. Nonetheless, and despite the fact that his account is couched in very different analytical and theoretical terms, it is clear that it

---

[17]He rightly also rejects the view held, albeit rather halfheartedly, by Householder et al. (1964) that *Nà* is a preposition.

contains important insights. Overall it seems that both Joseph and Christidis, despite their differences, see the elliptical or incomplete character of the particle as essential to understanding its nature.

The question of categorisation is rendered rather moot, however, if we adopt a view where traditional categories are mostly epiphenomenal and where labels on syntactic objects often include none of the traditional *categorial* features. This allows us to build a theory that preserves, and eventually analyses away, the important insights of apparent incompleteness, while circumventing the problems of the ellipsis view, whether one holds that the particle is a verb or something altogether different. I attempt this in the next section. The novelty of the account I develop is that I don't take, like Joseph (1981), Christidis (1990), and others who mention this particle in passing, the pointing gesture as a mere optional accompaniments to the particle, nor do I subscribe to Christidis' view that the particle is 'the linguistic substitute of the pointing gesture'. I think both these statements are wrong. The idea is that the gesture is a fully integrated part of the syntactic makeup of the particle.

4.5 The role of the gesture ☞

The proposal I will put forward here is that, as the evidence suggests, there is indeed invisible (or rather inaudible) structure involved in this particle but it is not structure that has been elided. Rather, the idea is that the central element of the structure that appears as the complement of the particle is the pointing gesture itself, notated for convenience simply as ☞.

Thinking about example (13), repeated here:

(33)   *Nà ☞o   Giannis*
          Nà ☞the Giannis
          'There is Giannis.'

It needs to be emphasised that the pointing gesture does not merely accompany the particle or vice versa in fact. Without the gesture itself the sentence is ungrammatical or at the very least completely uninterpretable. Note here that I use the word "gesture" in a general sense, not confined to hand pointings: it could be a head nod or an eye movement or something else altogether (we will see another example shortly). The crucial point is that it is not omissible. The relation of the gesture to the particle must, however, be elucidated. First of all, merely pointing at an object does achieve some effect, albeit a rather limited one: the object has been pointed at and that's about it. Clearly, the person perceiving the gesture might, and often will, extract some meaning from it but whatever that meaning is will be reached via the application of standard Gricean principles (i.e. if the person sitting across from me is winking at me he is either deranged or ..., where the [...] part can be filled with reasoning guided by the Cooperative principle). The point here is that while a gesture itself can be related to the overall meaning of the exchange this can only happen through global pragmatic principles rather than local compositional processes. As a result the object pointed at is not fully integrated in the discourse as a discourse referent. Lascarides & Stone (2009) claim that a gesture on its own is limited in what it can contribute to linguistic meaning through inference. They show that while gesturally introduced referents remain available for the interpretation of subsequent *gestures*, it is not the same for subsequent discourse. For example, merely pointing at an object does not suffice to create a discourse referent which would license subsequent pronominal anaphora. This is not surprising, as they point out, since pronominal anaphora require a linguistic antecedent. [18]

While the above is true for the gesture on its own, interestingly, the particle on its own does not have the required demonstrative effect either. The particle without a gesture is ungrammatical/uninterpretable. The composition of the two has the effect of making the thing that is being pointed at relevant to the current discourse, relating it to the epistemic state of the speaker, and adding it to the common ground. This may be in contrast to other deictic elements which are, apparently, interpretable without a pointing. Concerning the particle at hand, unsupported (gestural) uses lead to more than just infelicity or too much underspecification. These uses are as ungrammatical as a transitive verb missing its object. (34) corresponds to (36) and the status of (35) is analogous to that of (37):

(34) *Nà* ☞o Giannis.
      Nà ☞the Giannis
      'There is Giannis.'

(35) *Nà* o Giannis.
      Nà the Giannis
      'There is Giannis.'

(36) John admires Mary.

(37) John admires.

---

[18] A reviewer raises an interesting objection at this point, namely that in some pro-drop languages the gesture by itself does suffice to create a discourse referent that would be available for subsequent pronominal anaphora. It is clear that more research is needed in order to establish the extent to which this is true and the specific contexts where it applies, including the specific grammatical positions where anaphora may be licensed; it is for example conceivable that there is a difference between pronouns in subject and object position. But if we assume that the observation is correct, within the present analysis we may speculate that a pointing to a cup, which may license an utterance of *wash it*, where *it* refers to the cup, has the structure in (ii) rather than the one in (i):

(i)   ☞👆K

(ii) ☞pro$_K$

Given that the relevant languages certainly license *pro* it is not unreasonable to assume that they could take it as an argument.

Consider now a gesture together with a naming act[19] in a neutral context.[20] This amounts, I think, to a presentational statement, a thetic statement which has little effect on the discourse.[21] Again, it seems that it is the complex [Particle + Gesture + Naming Act] that foregrounds the relevance of the object referred to to the concerns of the participants. To clarify the position I am defending here: many proposals exist according to which speakers use both language and gesture in tandem to construct meaning and ultimately, a single semantic representation. Many, such as Mcneil (2005), Lascarides & Stone (2009), Kopp et al. (2004) among others, have suggested that gesture is fully integrated with speech. The position that I take here for the gestures following the particle under discussion is that they are more than just vaguely integrated or just semantically integrated. They are in fact the "pronunciation" of specific syntactic heads. In this I differ from some of the authors cited above in that although they assume that coverbal gesture is timed to align with prosodic units and that sometimes it fills a vacant grammatical slot, they do not assume, at least not overtly, that gestures have syntactic reality and syntactic effects. The strong position that I take in this paper concerning the syntax-semantics interface is that elements that contribute to meaning and are present in the semantic representation must have some kind of syntactic substance. This is true of intonation, which contributes to meaning but not, say, palatalisation or other phonetic processes that do not contribute to the construction of a semantic representation. This, it goes without saying, leaves completely open the possibility that such processes offer pragmatic clues that lead to additional "meaning" distinctions, sociolinguistic or other. I am not interested in those here. I think the deictic gestures accompanying the particles show that they do. So I would like to take Lascarides & Stone's (2009) idea that since gesture and language contribute to the construction of meaning, they should be represented in the same logical language one step further and suggest that at least for some gestures they should be represented in the same syntactic representation too. This is in exactly the same spirit as Jouitteau's (2004) proposal that gestures can be expletives filling the *EPP position* in Atlantic French. The basic claim here is that at least some gestures are fully grammatical elements. It would not be appropriate here to talk of grammaticalised gestures. Rather, certain syntactic heads have a gestural rather than an oral externalisation. It follows that, under this view, we should not be talking of PF as the relevant interface level but of EF, for *Externalization Form*, which will contain in most cases more than just phonetic information. I will briefly return to this discussion after showing more precisely the relevant structures.

---

[19] As a reviewer correctly points out, we should ensure that we make the distinction between an Austinian *naming act* (Austin 1962) which corresponds to the use of an example like (i) which provides a new name for something that was nameless prior to the relevant act:

(i)　　I name this ship the *Heart of Gold*

　　　　and the *naming act* as used in the text which amounts to supplying the pre-existing name to an entity that one points at and does amount to a presentational statement:

(ii)　　This is the Nostromo

[20] In this case by "neutral context" I mean specifically that this is not an answer to a question.

[21] Indeed these are difficult to integrate in a coherent discourse save for special cases.

5 The syntax of *Nà*

In this section my aim is to put some syntactic meat on these semantic bones. The proposal is that in the case of the deictic *Nà* the pointing gesture heads its own projection, ☞P. The gesture takes a DP as its argument and is in turn merged with the N element which is then merged with the speaker-anchoring particle A. Movement of N into A completes the derivation.[22] Schematically: [23]

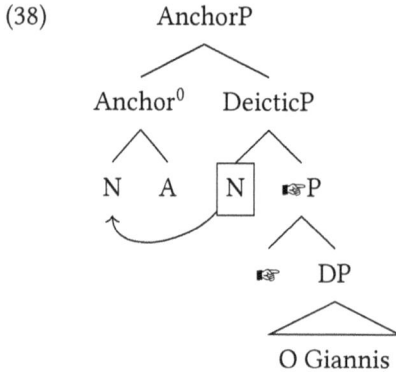

(38)

```
              AnchorP
             /       \
        Anchor⁰      DeicticP
         /  \        /     \
        N   A     ┌──┐     ☞P
        ↑_____│ N│     /  \
                  └──┘    ☞    DP
                               / \
                           O Giannis
```

The labels in the tree in (38) are chosen for ease of reference purposes. The N morpheme then can be understood as a relation between a pointing and an anchor. One might question the need for a special element to indicate this relation between the anchor and the pointing; usually the pointing instrument tends to be attached to the speaker's body, after all. This is true in most cases but in contexts of reported speech/gesture (at least in Greek) it is not the case that the anchor is the individual who actually makes the gesture while reporting:

(39) Otan bike   o   Giannis sto grafio girnai o   Kostas ke xoris   na   me
      When entered the Giannis into office turns the Kostas and without sbjv me
      proidopiisi mou lei na   ☞o   Giannis
      warn   to.me say there ☞the Giannis
      'When Giannis came into the office Kostas turned to me and without warning
      he said there ☞is Giannis.'

In this case the gesture is made by the reporting speaker but the anchor is the original one. There is no requirement that the pointing be at Giannis or at anything identifiable really. There has got to be a pointing though, this is the important requirement. One way to explain this is that gestures cannot be very easily embedded partly due their nature as an externalisation device, so (40), with an overt complementiser, is actually ungrammatical:

---

[22] The reason for the N-to-A movement is somewhat unclear.

[23] Clearly, the pointing can take many forms as we noted before depending on the context (a rather famous one involved a kiss) but the relation remains constant.

(40)   *O   Giannis ipe oti Nà   ☞ o   Alexis pou tha figi.
       The giannis said that here ☞ the Alexis who will leave
       'Giannis said that this is the Alexis who will leave.'

This suggests an incompatibility between the anchor -*a* and the complementiser. This is also true of other particles in the -*A* series. Consider the negative particle *Ba*:

(41)   *O   Kostas ipe oti ba   dhen tha erthi.
       The Kostas said that PRT NEG will come
       'Kostas said that he will not come.'

There is no incompatibility between the negative particle and sentential negation:

(42)   Ba, dhen tha ertho.
       PRT NEG will come
       'I will not come.'

Also, the notion of *Anchor* should not be understood in too limited a fashion. Although for the limited purposes of this paper I just link it to the speaker/addressee, it should be underlined that this linkage will interact with the rest of the discourse in complex ways which we have to set aside for now. In sum, the idea is that there is no reason to postulate elided clausal structure in order to understand the behaviour of the complex category that surfaces as the deictic/presentational particle *Nà* in Greek. The gesture that must accompany the particle is not a "parallel" yet independent act. It is part of the syntactic structure like any other morpheme might have been, say the agreement morpheme on a verb.

Before we turn to a more explicit formulation of the semantics we need to consider the case and agreement properties mentioned earlier in the light of the proposed structure.

5.0.1 Case and agreement

The pieces of the case puzzle are the following: The DP complement to the particle can be a single DP in the nominative or a complex [clitic+DP] where the following combinations are possible:

(43)   a. CL_{-ACC} DP_{-ACC}
       b. CL_{-ACC} DP_{NOM}
       c.   *CL_{NOM} DP_{-ACC}
       d. CL_{NOM} DP_{NOM}

Recall also that, *pace* Joseph (1981), an accusative DP without the clitic is ungrammatical. Note further that nominative clitics are very rare in Greek. In fact they only appear following deictic *Nà* and in the interrogative *Puntos/i/to*, 'where is he/she/it'. *Puntos* is a contracted form of *Pu* 'where', *n*, which is a reduced form of the copula (*Ine*) and the nominative clitic:

(44) a.   Puntos
            where.is.he
      b.   Natos
            here.he.is

Anticipating somewhat the evidence in §5.2 on *intransitive gestures* I would like to suggest that the solution to the case puzzle lies in the recognition that the gesture-head (☞) has two versions, one which is transitive and one which is unaccusative. This is not particularly strange since we take the gesture to be the externalisation of a linguistic morpheme. The cases where a clitic is present are cases of clitic doubling (which is independently found in Greek). When the gesturally expressed element is transitive it assigns accusative case to its object and nothing more needs to be said. When the DP associated with the clitic surfaces in the nominative it is attached in a higher position and surfaces in the default case, which is nominative. In the unaccusative case, there is no appropriate case assigner and the DP and clitic appear in nominative case.[24] Given how restricted nominative clitics are it seems correct to suggest that this is a realisation of default Case. What is impossible is for the clitic to appear in the nominative, which signals that the unaccusative version of the pointing is selected, and the associated DP to appear in the accusative. Given that nominative is the default, it is predicted that an accusative marked DP in the absence of a case assigner will lead to ungrammaticality. Why the clitic is obligatory with the accusative in many dialects is a question I have no answer to at present and will leave it for future work.

Turning now to the agreement issue involving the appearance of second person plural agreement on the particle, we should recognise that the gestural expression of the pointing, while, as I argued, fully integrated into the structure, differs from other lexical items in that it cannot act as host to other bound morphemes by its very nature. As a result, the agreement morpheme will attach to the next (only) available host which is the particle complex itself. Presumably this is not generally allowed since the agreeing version of the particle is only found in some dialects.

Let's now turn to the semantics of these structures.

5.1 The semantics of deictic *Nà*

In this section we turn to the compositional semantics of the structure in the (38). A pointing gesture can be understood broadly as an event. For maximal regularity in the semantics of different heads I will take the gesture head to have the semantics in (45)

(45) $[\![☞]\!] = \lambda x.\lambda e\ ☞(x), e$

In other words the gesture functions, at the relevant level of abstraction, unsurprisingly, as a demonstrative (event). Now clearly, a pointing entails a pointer. However, I want to propose that the pointing in itself is not syntactically a two place relation. Rather,

---

[24]The details of the analysis might slightly differ with respect to the view one takes of clitic doubling and nominative case but the central points will remain unchanged.

the anchor or subject of the pointing is introduced by the N morpheme, much like v introduces the external argument (which is the Anchor rather than the actual pointer). In this way N introduces a relation between an individual that was pointed at and the anchor of that pointing, simplifying somewhat:

(46) $[\![N]\!] = \lambda w \lambda y \lambda Z.\ Anchor(☞, y)\ in\ w$

To keep things simple, I will assume that the A particle introduces the relevant anchor as an individual.[25]

Once the Anchor argument has been introduced the result is:

(47) $\lambda w.\ Anchor(☞, x\ )\ in\ w$

It all really works in a manner parallel to the way vPs and nPs are built, a welcome result.

Before we turn to the case of *Yes (Ne)* I would like to show briefly how this approach generalises to other gestures with one example.

5.2 Generalising to other gestures

The approach sketched here also allows us to understand cases where the particle *Nà* is accompanied by a gesture but no naming act, in other words the use of intransitive gestures. One case in point is the rather notorious Greek *moutza*. This is a very commonplace insulting gesture in Greek which consists in the palm and fingers open wide pointed towards the addressee (in the same way that an English speaker might indicate the number five). Roughly like this:

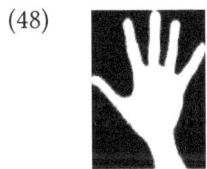

(48)

This gesture is made *towards* the addressee but crucially it does not point at the addressee. Using it to point at someone in a neutral situation would be roughly as felicitous as pointing to the next questioner during the question period after a presentation and identifying him as *the bastard in the second row*. A felicitous use of this gesture would be to another driver who has just moved at high speed across the path of your car almost causing an accident.

Given the framework adopted here which shares much of the underlying objectives and guiding principles of Lascarides & Stone's (2009)[26], especially the idea that linguistic discourse and at least co-speech gesture must be represented in the same logical and

---

[25] A different approach is possible which would keep more in line with the fact that A is not directly referring to an individual (the speaker). The ensuing complications are, however, not relevant to the points of this paper.

[26] Though my implementation of these ideas differs significantly from theirs.

syntactic language, I want to propose that the *moutza* functions much as a particle in Greek. More precisely, it can combine with *Nà*, by taking the place of ☞. There are two empirical arguments for this position. First, semantically, its meaning is qualitatively similar to that of particles in that it is *descriptively ineffable*, to use Blakemore's (2002) term. A speaker of Greek will have great trouble explaining what a *moutza* actually means, beyond the fact that it is an insult. As for the actual content of the insult, he or she will most likely resort to a series of contexts where the use is felicitous. The same is true of discourse particles. The second argument is that there are both coocurrence restrictions with other particles and ordering effects when used with more than one particle. The gesture can be used on its own, which suggests that in some cases the anchoring particle can remain silent, but when used in conjunction with other particles it must be simultaneous/immediately adjacent to *Nà*. Interestingly, it can never occur alone with an addressee oriented particle such as *Re*.[27] If used, an addressee oriented particle must follow the gesture. Consider the following examples:[28]

(49) a. *Nà* ✊

     b. **Re* ✊

     c. *Nà* ✊ *Re*

     d. **Nà Re* ✊

The proposal above that ✊ is merged as the complement of *N* predicts precisely these patterns. For the cases at hand (no pun intended) the structure will be as follows:

(50)

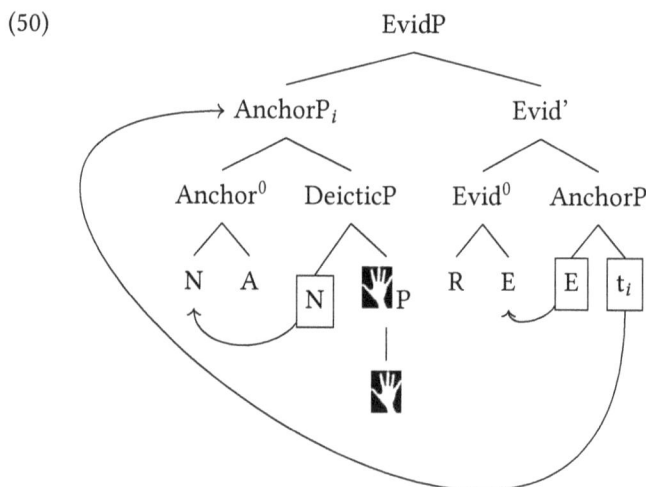

---

[27] On *Re*, see Tsoulas & Alexiadou (2006)

[28] This gesture has further characteristics, found in linguistic elements, that we cannot go into here in detail. For example, it can be reduplicated and this reduplication leads to two different meanings. If the hands overlap then a focus or emphatic reading is obtained. When the hands are further apart and do not overlap a distributive reading is favoured.

Semantically, given the contextual dependency of the gesture's meaning we can give the following general semantics:

(51)　　⟦ 🖐 ⟧= λsλk(🖐 ^{k} in s)

where the variable k indexes a contextual parameter which independently determines the nature and felicity of the insult in situation s and relates it causally to s.

My purpose in this section was to show that the idea of integrating gesture within both the syntactic and the semantic representation of the sentences with which they are co-temporaneous is a viable and perhaps illuminating option. We will turn now to the issue of the affirmative particle *Nè*.

6 The affirmative particle *Nè*

With this analysis of *Nà* in mind let us now turn to the affirmative particle *Nè*. This particle seems to combine deixis with what we called *addressee anchoring*. Intuitively, this does not seem quite right since in a question-answer situation the questioner asks (in a yes/no question) for the respondent to tell which of the two values of the proposition is the true one. Admittedly, this ought to be done from the point of view of the participant who provides the answer, *the respondent*. Anchoring to the addressee seems like an odd thing to do. I want to suggest here that we should take a closer look at the notion of anchoring in order to understand what is going on. The importance of the notion of anchoring in deixis is obvious especially given the analysis of *Nà* in the previous section. In the case of answers to questions, however, perhaps less so. However, anchoring is not the only notion that these speaker/addressee elements can express. Consider questions in general. There are many types of questions and many speech acts that may be performed using the interrogative form. However, when we restrict attention to open, non-confirmation, non-rhetorical questions, we can say that in a relatively standard setting uttering in good faith a question addressed to a particular addressee entails the following:[29]

(52)　a.　That there is a proposition p such that p is the answer to the question.
　　　b.　That knowledge of that proposition lies with the addressee.
　　　c.　That p is relevant to the questioner.

Setting (52-a) aside, we can identify (52-b) with Holmberg's (2015) *Q-force* operator (see (54)) equivalent to *Tell me which...* (an imperative which is clearly addressee-anchored) which is externalised in various way in different languages. Marking (52-c) in the answer is what we find in Greek. This idea can be formalised using Truckenbrodt's (2006) notion of *Context Index*. The following (53) are context indices for declaratives and interrogatives based on Truckenbrodt (2006):

---

[29]We also have to exclude the sort of question that may have no answer. Scientific questions are sometimes like that. The qualification *in good faith* in the text is meant to also exclude sarcasm, irony etc. For very relevant commentary and analysis on these issues see Fiengo (2007). I am indebted to an anonymous reviewer for comments on this point and for bringing the relevance of Fiengo's book to my attention.

(53) a. Declarative: $< \text{Deont}_S, A, < \text{Epist} >>$
'S wants from A that it is common ground that p.'
  b. Interrogative: $< \text{Deont}_S, A, < \text{Epist} >>$
'S wants from A that it is common ground whether p.'

The effects of these context indices are given in the paraphrases. In these cases, in Truckenbrodt's words, *S wants to change the world by changing the epistemic state of S or A*. So the intuition here is that the particle *Nè* in Greek encapsulates a deictic element that relates a proposition to that participant to whose epistemic state it is relevant. Clearly this participant is the addressee. It is therefore expected that the *E* particle will be part of this particle complex (*Nè*). To formalise this I introduce the notion of Anchor_REL(EVANCE) which encodes a relevance-related perspectival dependence as opposed to an *origo*-related one. In informal, intuitive terms this particle says: *This is the proposition that is of relevance to your belief/knowledge*.[30] Now let's turn to a more specific syntactic implementation. Holmberg's (2015) structure for Yes/No questions is (54), and for a *Yes* answer, (55):

(54)

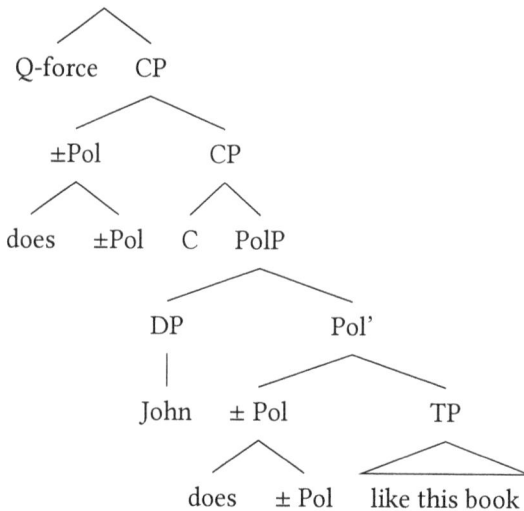

---

[30]This notion has implications for the analysis of indexicality and perspective (especially in the context of Giorgi (2010); Hinzen & Sheehan (2013)) as it implies that in particle answers the speaker is, if not absent, at least somewhat removed from the representation. Space and time constraints prevent me from delving deeper into these questions on this occasion.

(55)

```
            FocP
         ／      ＼
      +Pol        Foc'
       |        ／    ＼
      Yes    Foc      PolP
                   ／      ＼
                DP          Pol'
                 |        ／    ＼
               John    +Pol      TP
                               ◸      ◹
                            like this book
```

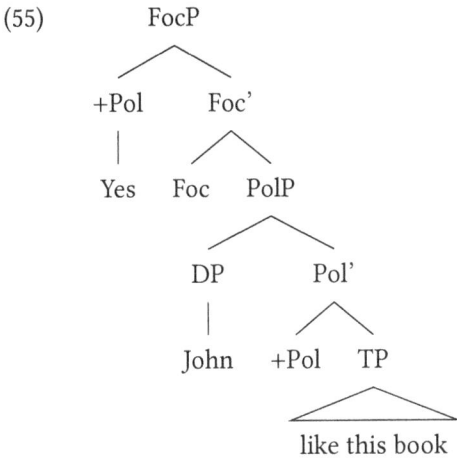

One thing that we should observe is that in face-to-face dialogue, saying *Yes* is also accompanied by a gesture (usually a head nod). It is, however, not the case that this gesture is as necessary as the deictic pointing discussed in the previous section. I assume that the reason for this is that the question provides enough context for the interpretation. At the same time, I also understand it to be evidence, beyond what was discussed up to now, that an account in parallel with the deictic particle is called for and may prove fruitful. I will therefore assume that the structure of the particle *Nè* is roughly equivalent to that of *Nà* except that the Anchor *A* will now be replaced with what I called Anchor$_{REL(EVANCE)}$. For maximum consistency with *Nà* (but hopefully avoiding potential confusion) I use the label *G* for the head which is the complement of *N-*. So the structure that we start with is (56):

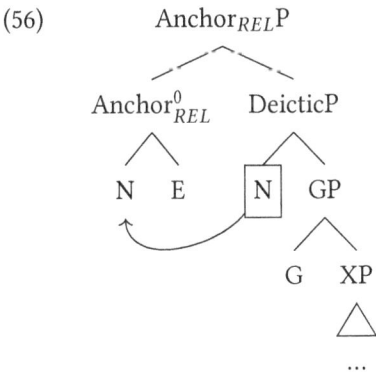

(56)

```
              Anchor_{REL}P
            ／          ＼
      Anchor^0_{REL}       DeicticP
          ／ ＼          ／    ＼
        N     E       N       GP
                            ／    ＼
                          G       XP
                                  △
                                  ...
```

Turning to the nature of the XP, I will assume that Greek Yes/No questions have, for the relevant part, a structure that is similar to the one proposed by Holmberg. Most importantly, I assume that there is a PolP, which is the highest functional head in the IP domain. I also assume, again following Holmberg, that the PolP is copied from the question with its Pol feature unvalued. Unvalued Pol can be valued in two ways: it can be valued by negation which is lower in the structure. It can also be valued by the G head. I propose that the G head is specified with two features. First, a selectional uPol feature. Technically, if selectional features are by definition uninterpretable then this feature should be a **uuPol**. In other words G selects for a PolP whose head Pol is specified for a uPol feature. Presumably, if the uPol feature is carried by a different element then that element can in principle be selected by G. The second feature for which G is specified is +Pol, which represents the effect that it has on the PolP. This is not contradictory, it is simply a way to express modification. Modifiers are of type <x,x>. Syntactically we need to express that they are also selective ("*a passionately car" is, after all, not a well formed expression), and this is what uPol expresses. +Pol tells us what the result of the composition is, i.e. a syntactic object of category Pol specified for +Pol. What happens next is relatively unremarkable: G values the uPol feature of PolP and the derivation proceeds in exactly the same way as with the deictic particle *Nà*. The deictic head N- merges with GP and licenses the introduction of the $Anchor_{REL}$ argument which this time is E. The final result is produced following head movement of N in $Anchor^0_{REL}$, which is pronounced *NE*. Ideally, nothing more would need to be said. However, a complication arises with negative questions to which we turn in the next section. To summarise, the account of the affirmative particle *Nè* stands as follows:

(57)   a.   There is a head G specified for uuPol and + Pol.
      b.   G merges with the PolP (with uPol) inherited from the question.
      c.   G values uPol as +.
      d.   Deictic N- merges with G and introduces the Anchor argument.
      e. $Anchor_{REL}$ E is merged.
      f.   N- moves to E.

Now for negative questions.

6.1 Negative polar questions

The approach that we have pursued up to this point brings the issue of negative polar questions into sharp focus. This is so in two related ways. First, assuming that uPol acts just like any other uninterpretable feature, then one expects it to act as a probe and find a matching goal in Neg^0 and will be valued -Pol. We could argue here that Neg is an inactive goal for the Pol probe. But this, together with the idea that saying *Yes* involves propositional deixis, makes the general prediction that Greek should pattern more like Chinese in that it would always be possible to answer *Yes* to a negative question and confirm the negative alternative. In other words Greek should have a truth-based answering system rather than a polarity based one. As it turns out, Greek seems to allow both. There seems to be two major dialects in Greek in this respect. It has been reported (Holton et al. 1997)[31] that Greek allows *Yes* answers to negative questions whereby the negative alternative is confirmed:[32]

---

[31]See also the data in SSWL (http://sswl.railsplayground.net/)
[32]Example (58) is adapted slightly from Holton et al. (1997: 414)

(58)   Dhen to pire to danio o   Giannis telika?
       NEG it took the loan the Giannis finally
       'In the end, didn't Giannis get the loan?'

(59)   Ne dhen to pire
       Yes NEG it took
       'Yes he didn't get it.'

Call this Dialect 1. Dialect 2[33] does not allow this type of confirmatory answer except in the presence of special elements to which we return. Observe, however, that the pattern above is *only* possible, in Dialect 1, if the answer contains an overtly realised copy of the PolP of the question. If the PolP is not overt the result is ungrammatical:

(60)   Dhen to pire to danio o   Giannis telika?
       NEG it took the loan the Giannis finally
       'In the end, didn't Giannis get the loan?'

(61)   *Nè
       Yes

How can we account for these patterns with the theory that we have so far? To begin with Dialect 1, the data suggest that there is a formal recoverability condition that must be met in order for ellipsis of the PolP to be licensed. We can formulate this condition as follows:

(62)   *Recoverability Condition for PolP*
       PolP can be elided if the valuer of uPol is overt.

This principle derives Dialect 1 directly. If Neg values Pol, then ellipsis of PolP is not licensed. Note that (62) is a formal condition and therefore immune to being circumvented pragmatically given that recovering the meaning of PolP is rather easy. It may be but it is not allowed. Note that in the case of a *No* answer ellipsis will be licensed since there is no way to distinguish which -Pol feature valued uPol of Pol⁰. So despite appearances, Dialect 1 seems to be a polarity-based system.

Let me turn now to Dialect 2. This dialect does not allow *Yes* confirmation answers to negative questions quite generally except when there is overt material between the affirmative particle and the PolP. The material in question is not just any material. As far as I can tell what is required is either certain particle clusters like *Re gamoto*, meaning roughly *bloody hell* or, more interestingly, elements like *siga* and *kala*. The literal meaning of *siga* is 'slowly' or 'quietly' and of *kala* is 'fine/OK'. Their meaning *qua* particles in this context is scalar and indicates that the proposition with the opposite polarity value of that of the PolP is, in fact, the most unlikely.[34] Note, also, that these elements

---

[33] As far as I know Dialect 1 and 2 are not geographically circumscribed.

[34] The proposition whose position at the scale is made salient through the particle can be made overt with the particle *siga* but not with *kala*. Offering a detailed analysis of the resulting patterns, including the appearance of expletive negation with *siga*, would take us too far afield and are set aside for future work.

are prosodically grouped with the affirmative particle rather than with what follows. Consider the following examples:

(63) Dhen to pire to danio o   Giannis telika?
NEG it took the loan   the Giannis finally
'In the end, didn't Giannis get the loan?'

(64) a. Ne [re gamoto] dhen to pire.
Yes PRT PRT   NEG it took

'Yes, bloody hell, he didn't get it.'

b. Ne kala, dhen to pire.
Yes PRT NEG it took

'Yes, how could he, he didn't get it.'

c. Ne siga, dhen to pire.
Yes PRT NEG it took

'Yes, how could he, he didn't get it.'

I believe that we can understand these patterns if we take seriously the idea that the syntax of the G head is really very closely aligned with the syntax of the ☞head in the case of the deictic particle *Nà*. Specifically, the pattern above is reminiscent of the cases of the deictic particle when it is followed by a clitic and a full DP. We can think of the complement of G as the Pol equivalent of the [clitic DP] doublet where the clitic element can be realised overtly by elements like *siga* or *kala*. As the intonational pattern suggests, just as in the case of the DPs, the PolP ends up higher in an extraposed position. Whether it moves there or it is base-generated in the higher position is an important question but one that can be safely set aside for now. The result, in either case, is that the PolP ends up outside the scope domain of the G-head. To capture this I want to propose that there is a second constraint alongside recoverability which can be formulated as follows:

(65) *G-Scope Constraint*
If G has a determinate feature specification (+ or -) it does not tolerate contradictory Pol values in its scope.

Perhaps (65) is ultimately formulable in terms of AGREE but there are complications as we saw earlier.

We could also draw a parallel with the Case patterns observed with *Nà* too. Recall that an accusative clitic could associate with a higher DP in the nominative while the opposite is impossible. Depending on the speaker's attitude to the fact that Giannis *did* get the loan or to *Giannis* himself, the following patterns are observed. Assuming NOM=+Pol and ACC=-Pol and that the particle complex in (66-a) corresponds to a negative value:

(66) a. *Ne [re gamoto] to pire.
Yes PRT PRT   it took
'Yes, bloody hell, he got it.'

b. Ne kala, to pire.
    Yes PRT it took
    'Yes, how couldn't he, he got it.'
c. Ne siga, to pire.
    Yes PRT it took
    'Yes, how couldn't he, he got it.'

At the same time, if the particle position in the [PRT PolP] doublet is filled by the element *pos* which is a polarity-reversing positive particle[35] a negative PolP is impossible:

(67) Ne pos to pire.
      Yes PRT it took
      'Yes, on the contrary, he got it.'

(68) *Ne pos, dhen to pire.
      Yes PRT NEG it took
      'Yes, on the contrary, he didn't get it.'

Intuitively the effect of this is to produce a two part answer, roughly: 'Correct, $(\neg)p$'. We can then think of the difference between the two dialects as involving the interplay of the two constraints:

(69) a. Recoverability
      b. G-Scope Constraint.

While Dialect 1 tolerates violations of (69-b), Dialect 2 does not. Neither tolerates violations of (69-a).

7 Conclusion

This paper explored the hypothesis that affirmation and deixis share a common core. Greek shows this common core overtly in the morphological composition of its deictic and affirmative particles. But looking at the details of the syntactic representations we observed very striking similarities. Most importantly the fact that there is a head that corresponds to a pointing, real or metaphorical, which is clearly part of the syntactic representation. Accepting this leads us to take at least a subset of gesture as an integral part of linguistic representations. The syntactic complexity of seemingly very simple words was also a surprising conclusion. Of course much work remains to be done. The role of focus and intonation deserves closer study than I have been able to offer here, the negative particle *óχι* 'No' was set aside (for good reason, as the morphology is far less transparent), and the cross-linguistic applicability of the account was not considered. I would expect that this account extends crosslinguistically quite widely although one

---

[35] Akin to French *Si*, although *Si* cannot coocur with *Oui*, unlike pos. There is another version of the particle *pos* which is scalar along the same lines of *siga/kala*. The claim here is for the polarity reversing one.

cannot expect that the morphology will be as transparent as what we saw in Greek (although there is suggestive evidence). This I leave for future work.

C. P. Cavafy wrote in a famous poem:[36]

> [...] It's clear at once who has the Yes
> ready within him; and saying it,
> he goes forward in honor and self-assurance.
> He who refuses does not repent. Asked again,
> he would still say no. Yet that no—the right no—
> undermines him all his life.

I am sure the poet is right, but if I am right too then saying *Yes* in Greek is no mean feat either.

Acknowledgments

It is with great pleasure that I dedicate this work to Anders on his birthday. Much of what is in here was prompted by his work on *Yes* and *No*. The influence of his work on the present paper is pervasive.

Parts of this paper have been presented at the 12th International Conference on Greek Linguistics in Berlin, and at seminars in York and Newcastle. I want to thank these audiences for many useful comments and suggestions. More specifically I would like to thank: Kook-Hee Gil, Stella Gryllia, Anders Holmberg, Shin-Sook Kim, Margarita Makri, Dimitris Michelioudakis, Moreno Mitrovic, Bernadette Plunkett, Anna Roussou, Peter Sells, Evi Sifaki, and Rebecca Woods for suggestions and comments. I would also like to thank the two anonymous reviewers for this volume for comments that led to a number of improvements. Finally, I would like to thank the editors, Laura Bailey and Michelle Sheehan, for giving me this opportunity and for being so patient.

References

Austin, John L. 1962. *How to do things with words*. Oxford: Oxford University Press.

Blakemore, Diane. 2002. *Relevance and linguistic meaning* (Cambridge Studies in Linguistics 99). Cambridge: Cambridge University Press.

Brugmann, Karl. 1904. *Die demonstrativpronomina der indogermanischen sprachen*. Leipzig: Teubner.

Brugmann, Karl. 1911. *Grundriss der vergleichenden grammatik der indoger manischen sprachen*. Vol. 2. Strassburg: Trübner.

Christidis, Anastasios-Phoebos. 1990. On the categorial status of particles: The case of holophrasis. *Lingua* 82(1). 53–82.

Fiengo, Robert. 2007. *Asking questions: Using meaningful structures to imply ignorance*. Oxford: Oxford University Press.

---

[36] *Che fece ...Il gran rifiuto*, which I quote in Edmund Keely's translation.

Giorgi, Alessandra. 2010. *About the speaker.* Oxford: Oxford University Press.

Groenendijk, Jeroen & Martin Stokhof. 1984. *Studies in the semantics of questions and the pragmatics of answers.* University of Amsterdam dissertation.

Halliday, M.A.K. & Ruqaiya Hasan. 1976. *Cohesion in English.* London: Longman.

Hatzidakis, G. 1907. *Meseonika ke nea elinika (medieval and modern Greek) 2 vols.* Athens: P.D. Sakelariou.

Hinzen, Wolfram & Michelle Sheehan. 2013. *The philosophy of Universal Grammar.* Oxford: Oxford University Press.

Holmberg, Anders. 2015. *The syntax of yes and no.* Oxford: Oxford University Press.

Holton, David, Peter Mackridge & Irene Philippaki-Warburton. 1997. *Greek: A comprehensive grammar of the modern language.* London: Routledge.

Householder, Fred, Kostas Kazazis & Andreas Koutsoudas. 1964. Reference grammar of Literary Dhimotiki. *International Journal of American Linguistics* 30(2). 1–187.

Joseph, Brian. 1981. On the synchrony and diachrony of Modern Greek NA. *Byzantine and Modern Greek Studies* 7. 139–154.

Jouitteau, Mélanie. 2004. Gestures as expletives: Multichannel syntax. In Gina Garding & Mimu Tsujimura (eds.), *Proceedings of WCCFL 23*, 101–114. Somerville, MA: Cascadilla Press.

Kopp, Stefan, Paul Tepper & Justine Cassell. 2004. Towards integrated microplanning of languages and iconic gesture for multimodal output. In *Proceedings of ICMI.* State College, PA.

Lascarides, Alex & Matthew Stone. 2009. A formal semantic analysis of gesture. *Journal of Semantics* 26(4). 393–449.

Mcneil, David. 2005. *Gesture and thought.* Chicago: Uiversity of Chicago Press.

Michelioudakis, Dimitris & Eleni Kapogianni. 2013. Ethical datives: A puzzle for syntax, semantics, pragmatics, and their interfaces. In Raffaella Folli, Christina Sevdali & Robert Truswell (eds.), *Syntax and its limits*, 345–369. Oxford: Oxford University Press.

Ross, John Robert. 1972. The category squish: Endstation hauptwort. In Judith N. Levi & Gloria C. Phares (eds.), *Papers from the 8th regional meeting.*

Shields, Kenneth. 1992. *A history of Indo-European verb morphology.* Amsterdam: John Benjamins.

Truckenbrodt, Hubert. 2006. On the semantic motivation of syntactic verb movement to C in German. *Theoretical Linguistics* 32. 257–306. DOI:10.1515/TL.2006.018

Tsoulas, George. 2015. Higher field particles in Greek. Ms. University of York.

Tsoulas, George & Artemis Alexiadou. 2006. On the grammar of the Greek particle *Re. Sprach und Datenverarbeitung: International Journal for Language Data Processing* 30(1). 47–56.

Tzartzanos, Achileas. 1946/1953. *Neoeliniki sintaxis (modern Greek syntax).* Thessaloniki: Ekdotikos ikos adelfon Kiriakidi.

Zwicky, Arnold. 1985. Clitics and particles. *Language* 61. 283–305.

Part II

Squibs

Chapter 13

V2 and cP/CP

Sten Vikner

Ken Ramshøj Christensen

Anne Mette Nyvad

Dept. of English, Aarhus University, Denmark

As in Nyvad et al. (2017), we will explore a particular derivation of (embedded) V2, in terms of a cP/CP-distinction, which may be seen as a version of the CP-recursion analysis (de Haan & Weerman 1986; Vikner 1995 and many others). The idea is that because embedded V2 clauses do not allow extraction, whereas other types of CP-recursion clauses do (Christensen et al. 2013a; 2013b; Christensen & Nyvad 2014), CP-recursion in embedded V2 is assumed to be fundamentally different from other kinds of CP-recursion, in that main clause V2 and embedded V2 involve a CP ("big CP"), whereas other clausal projections above IP are instances of cP ("little cP").

1 Introduction

Verb second (V2) has long been and continues to be a fascinating topic, as witnessed by articles and books all the way back to Wackernagel (1892) and Fourquct (1938) and up to Holmberg (2015).

This paper will briefly present an analysis of the CP-level in embedded clauses, including what is often seen as CP-recursion in cases of embedded V2. The analysis is discussed in much more detail in Nyvad et al. (2017).

We follow the suggestion in Chomsky (2000) that syntactic derivation proceeds in phases and that the syntactic categories *v*P and CP are phases. We also follow Chomsky (2005; 2006) in taking Internal Merge operations such as A-bar movement to be triggered by an edge feature on the phase head (in Chomsky 2000, this feature is called a P(eripheral)-feature, in Chomsky 2001 a generalised EPP-feature). Below, this feature will be referred to as an OCC ("occurrence") feature (following Chomsky 2005: 18), which provides an extra specifier position that does not require feature matching. OCC offers an escape hatch allowing an element to escape an embedded clause.

The availability of this generic edge feature OCC together with the availability of multiple specifier positions, however, in principle permits any element from within the

Sten Vikner, Ken Ramshøj Christensen & Anne Mette Nyvad. 2017. V2 and cP/CP. in Laura R. Bailey & Michelle Sheehan (eds.), *Order and structure in syntax I: Word order and syntactic structure*, 313–324. Berlin: Language Science Press. DOI:10.5281/zenodo.1117724

phase domain to move across a phase edge, and so island effects should not exist (as also observed by Boeckx 2012: 60–61).

If instead of multiple specifiers, CP-recursion is possible, the Danish data presented in the present paper may be captured in a uniform manner. We will explore a particular derivation of (embedded) V2, in terms of a cP/CP-distinction, which may be seen as a version of the CP-recursion analysis (de Haan & Weerman 1986; Vikner 1995; Bayer 2002; Walkden 2017, and many others). Because embedded V2 clauses do not allow extraction, whereas other types of CP-recursion clauses do (Christensen et al. 2013a; 2013b; Christensen & Nyvad 2014), CP-recursion in embedded V2 is assumed to be fundamentally different from other kinds of CP-recursion:

(1) a CP with   V2 (headed by a finite verb)   = **CP** ("big CP")
     a CP without V2 (headed by a functional element) = **cP** ("little cP")

The idea is to attempt a distinction parallel to the vP-VP distinction (Chomsky 1995: 347), with cP being above CP (cf. Koizumi 1995: 148 who posits a CP-PolP corresponding to our cP-CP, and de Cuba's (2007) independent proposal that non-factive verbs select a non-recursive cP headed by a semantic operator removing the responsibility for the truth of the embedded clause from the speaker).

c° like v° is a functional head, whereas C° like V° should be a lexical head. The latter admittedly only works partially, in that C° is only lexical to the extent that it must be occupied by a lexical category, i.e. a finite verb.

2 C°

(2)   cP

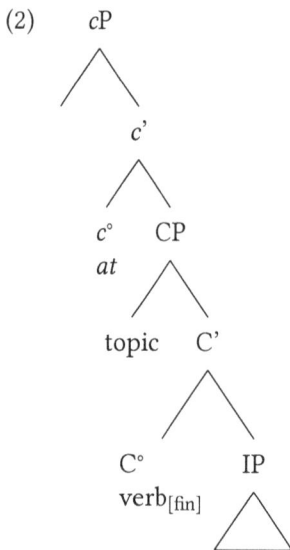

Although CP-spec is the specifier position that attracts topics, also in embedded clauses, its associated head, C°, does not have a topic-feature "in the ordinary way", because verb movement into C° would then erase that feature. The fact that C°'s topic feature is thus different from e.g. the way *c°* can have a feature like *wh* should be related to the fact that topicalisations are never selected for, i.e. there are verbs that select only embedded questions, but there are no verbs that select only embedded topicalisations (maybe not being selected is what allows verb movement into C°, whereas being selected prevents movement into $c°_{[\text{WH}]}$). The closest we get are verbs that allow embedded topicalisations, but even such verbs never require them, e.g. *vide* 'know', *tro* 'think', etc.

Where we thus say that the C° associated with the specifier that attracts topics is deficient/unusual in not really having a topic-feature, e.g. Julien (2015: 146) argues that the topic head is a normal head that may contain other things than finite verbs, e.g. *så* 'then' in contrastive left dislocations, (3a):

(3) Danish
    a. [Topic-sp Hvis man ikke kan sige noget pænt,] [Topic° så   ] [ForceP
    b. [cP-spec Hvis man ikke kan sige noget pænt,]   [CP   så
          If   one not can say smth. nice   (then)   (then)
    [Force° skal] man tie   stille.]]
    [C°   skal] man tie   stille.]]
          shall   one keep quiet

We take it that the fact that *så* also occurs in the first position in V2 clauses with no dislocation means that it is a rather unlikely head element. We also hesitate to draw conclusions about the syntax of embedded V2 from contrastive left dislocations, as they are also perfectly possible in non-V2 embedded clauses (although we have no account for why this is strongly degraded in Swedish and Norwegian, cf. Johannesen 2014: 407):

(4) Danish
    Det er en skam   at   den her artikel den aldrig er blevet udgivet.
    It   is a   shame that this here article it   never is been   published

As topicalisations are never selected for, it follows that a topicalisation-CP (i.c. with a topic in CP-spec and with a verb moving into C°) cannot be the highest level of an embedded clause (in most Germanic languages, e.g. Danish or English). Another level is necessary above CP, viz. a cP with *at/that* in *c°* (though see the discussion at the end of section 4 below). It is this higher *at/that* which prevents extraction from CP-spec (as a kind of *that*-trace violation, perhaps derived in terms of anti-locality as in Douglas 2015), i.e. (5d):

(5) Danish
    a. *   Sagde Andrea   Lego-filmen havde Kaj allerede set __?
    b.   Sagde Andrea at   Lego-filmen havde Kaj allerede set __?
    c. ˄ Lego-filmen sagde Andrea   _________ havde Kaj allerede set __.
    d. * Lego-filmen   sagde Andrea at   _________ havde Kaj allerede set __.
      (Lego-film.the) said   Andrea (that) (Lego-film.the) had   Kaj already seen

(Notice that (5c) is ungrammatical for the same reason as (5a): topicalisations cannot be selected, they must be inside a cP.)

This is supported by German, which for some reason allows embedded topicalisation without this higher *that*, (6a), and which allows extraction via CP-spec, (6c):

(6) German

    a.   Hat Andrea gesagt,   den Lego-Film hat Kai schon   — gesehen?

    b. *   Hat Andrea gesagt, dass den Lego-Film hat Kai schon   — gesehen?

    c. Den Lego-Film hat Andrea gesagt,   _____ hat Kai schon   — gesehen.

    d. * Den Lego-Film hat Andrea gesagt, dass   _____ hat Kai schon   — gesehen.

    e. (The Lego-film) has Andrea said   (that) (the Lego-film) has Kai already   seen

CP may thus be a phase in German, and also in Danish and English (where extractions via spec-CP are *that*-trace violations). From this, it would follow that CPs are strong islands (cf. Holmberg 1986: 111; Müller & Sternefeld 1993: 493ff; Sheehan & Hinzen 2011), provided there is no OCC escape hatch in CP, like the one suggested for *c*P in §3 below:

(7) Danish

    a.   Sagde Andrea at   måske havde Kaj allerede set Lego-filmen?

    b. * Lego-filmen   sagde Andrea at   måske havde Kaj allerede set __?

       (Lego-film.the) said   Andrea that maybe had   Kaj already seen (Lego-film.the)

(8) German

    a.   Hat Andrea gesagt, vielleicht hat Kai den Lego-Film schon gesehen?

    b. * Den Lego-Film hat Andrea gesagt, vielleicht hat Kai __   schon   gesehen.

       (The Lego-film) has Andrea said   maybe   has Kai (the Lego-film) already seen

A different approach that might explain the absence of an escape hatch could be to say that embedded V2 clauses are not really embedded at all, but instead there is a radical break/restart at the beginning of an embedded V2 clause, similar to what happens at the beginning of a new main clause (as argued e.g. by Petersson 2014). Then extraction out of an embedded V2 clause like (7b/8b) would correctly be ruled out, but this would also incorrectly rule out all other potential links across the edge of embedded V2 clauses (see also Julien 2015: 157-159), so that e.g. the following c-command difference should not exist, as co-reference should incorrectly be ruled out in both (9a) and (9b):

(9) Danish

    a. * Han$_1$ sagde at [$_{CP}$ den her bog ville   Lars$_1$ aldrig læse.]

    b. Hans$_1$ mor sagde at [$_{CP}$ den her bog ville   Lars$_1$ aldrig læse.]

       He/His mum said   that   this here book would Lars never read

Both (9a,b) would be expected to be just as impossible as such links across a main clause boundary:

(10) Danish

    a. * I går   mødte jeg ham$_1$ i bussen. [$_{CP}$ Lars$_1$ var lige blevet forfremmet.]

    b. * I går   mødte jeg hans$_1$ mor i bussen. [$_{CP}$ Lars$_1$ var lige blevet forfremmet.]

       Yesterday met   I   him/his mum in bus-the   Lars had just been promoted

3   *c*° with OCC

(11)   cP

$$
\text{cP} \;\begin{array}{c}\diagup\;\diagdown\end{array}\; \text{t} \quad c'
$$

t   c'

$c°_{[OCC]}$ cP/CP/IP

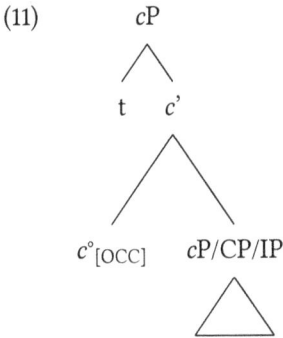

c° can have a feature that may cause movement to cP-spec, and such a feature can either be a so-called occurrence-feature or a slightly more standard type feature as e.g. a *wh*-feature. (As mentioned above, for some reason C° cannot have an OCC-feature.)

Chomsky (2005: 18–19) suggests an OCC ("occurrence") feature, which provides an extra specifier position "without feature matching", i.e. the XP moves into the specifier of $c°_{[occ]}$ without itself having an OCC-feature. A $c°_{[occ]}$ thus offers an escape hatch which allows an XP to escape an embedded clause. In fact only those XPs that move into a cP-spec because of OCC will be able to move on, because they are the only XPs whose feature make up has not been altered/valued/checked as a result of the movement into cP-spec.

$c°_{[occ]}$ may be above another cP, and then the cP-layer headed by a *c*° carrying an OCC-feature is transparent to selection in the same way as e.g. NegP is in constituent negation (e.g., *she ate not the bread but the cake*) or quantificational layers (as in *she ate all/half the cake*), cf. the notion of extended projections (Grimshaw 2005). However, $c°_{[occ]}$ may also be inside another cP, in which case nothing further needs to be said.

4   *c*° with other features, e.g. *wh*

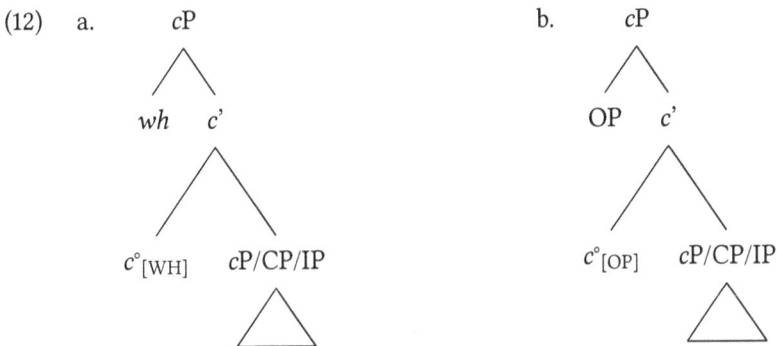

(12)   a.   cP   b.   cP

wh   c'   OP   c'

$c°_{[WH]}$ cP/CP/IP $c°_{[OP]}$ cP/CP/IP

We take the basic distinction between CP and cP to be whether or not there is verb movement into the head, but we want this to go hand in hand with other basic distinc-

tions between the two, e.g. that C° is the potential host of the topic feature, whereas c°
is the relevant/necessary head for the outside context, e.g. as the highest head of embedded questions or of relative clauses (= in the terms of Rizzi 1997: 283, cP is 'facing the
outside' whereas CP is 'facing the inside').

In other words, we want to link the difference c°/C° not just to individual features
(much like the difference between different heads in the C-domain is linked to features in
the cartographic approach, Rizzi 1997; Wiklund et al. 2007; Julien 2015; Holmberg 2015...)
– but we also want to link the difference to whether or not the head is the landing site
of verb movement.

Spec-cP$_{[WH]}$ in (12a) is where the *wh*-phrase in an embedded question occurs, and spec-
cP$_{[OP]}$ in (12b) is where we find the empty operator that may occur in e.g. *som*-relative
clauses in Danish (and in *that*-relative clauses in English).

It appears that a *wh*-element that has moved into such a specifier cannot move on
from here:

(13)   Danish

				Spurgte	Andrea	[$_{cP}$ hvilken	film	c°$_{[WH]}$	Kaj
b. *	Hvilken	film	spurgte	Andrea	[$_{cP}$ ___	___		c°$_{[WH]}$	Kaj
	(Which	film)	asked	Andrea	(which	film)			Kaj

allerede	havde	set]?
allerede	havde	set]?
already	had	seen

This may be because the embedded clause in (13b) with an empty specifier and an
empty c° can no longer be identified as a *wh*-clause, as is required of an object clause of
the verb *ask* (cf. clausal typing, Cheng 1991).

Following Rizzi & Roberts (1996: 20), Vikner (1995: 50), Grimshaw (1997: 412), the
reason why there can be no verb movement into c°$_{[WH]}$ is that this would change the
properties of the selected head (i.e. c°$_{[WH]}$), and therefore this head would no longer
satisfy the requirements of the selecting matrix expression. In fact, according to Mc-
Closkey (2006: 103), a head modified in this way (by movement into it) is not an item
that could possibly be selected by a higher lexical head (it is not part of the "syntactic
lexicon"), which would lead to the prediction that there could not be movement into
heads of complements of lexical heads (which may very well be too strong, cf. that it
would have consequences for many other cases, e.g. N°-to-D° movement in Scandinavian
would have to be something like N°-to-Num° movement).

If, on the other hand, there is a cP (with the declarative Complementizer *at* in c°) above
the CP in which V2 takes place, then this problem does not arise. The selected clause is
a cP, its head is a c° containing a complementiser, and the C° into which there is verb
movement is situated lower down inside the cP.

(Embedded topicalisations in German, embedded questions in Afrikaans, and embedded questions in some variants of English might be exceptions to the above in that they
seem to have embedded V2 into the highest selected complementiser head. In such cases,
an "invisible" cP above the embedded V2 CP have been suggested, e.g. in McCloskey

(2006: 101) and in Biberauer & Roberts (2015: 12–13). In fact, being inside such an "invisible" cP might even be a possible analysis for those Danish examples with embedded V2 but not preceded by *at*, which do occur sometimes, e.g. (ii) in Jensen & Christensen (2013: 55), although we find such examples ungrammatical.)

5 $c°$ without features

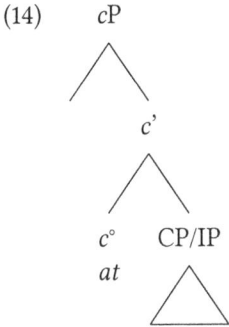

(14)   cP

c'

$c°$ CP/IP
at

It is also possible for a $c°$ not to have any features, in which case no movement will take place into spec-cP. This is possible both when such a $c°$ is the sister of an IP and the sister of a CP.

(15)   Danish
    a.   Sagde Andrea at   Kaj allerede havde set
    b.   Sagde Andrea at   Lego-filmen   havde Kaj allerede   set?
         Said   Andrea that (Lego film.the) (had)   Kaj already (had)   seen
    Lego-filmen?

    (Lego-film.the)

Because such an *at/that* has no special features, it may also occur below other complementisers, when these are selected from above, e.g. below a *wh-* or a relative cP-layer. As an extra complementiser, *at* is preferred over other complementisers, which have more content:

(16)   Danish (Tom Kristensen, *Livets Arabesk* (novel), 1921, cited in Hansen 1967: III:
    388; in Vikner 1995: 122, (149c); and in Nyvad 2016: 368, (10)).
    ... hvis at   det ikke havde været så sørgeligt.
        if   that it   not   had   been   so sad

6 Predictions concerning extraction

The above suggestions (especially the OCC escape hatch in cP) make the prediction that extraction is possible almost everywhere (i.e. except tòpic islands), which is much more general than usually assumed (including in Vikner 1995). However, it turns out that such unexpectedly acceptable examples are fairly widespread, including extractions from relative clauses:

(17) Danish (Christensen & Nyvad 2014: 35, (13c,d))

    a.   Pia har engang mødt en pensionist som havde sådan en hund.
           Pia has once met a pensioner that had such a dog

    b.   Sådan en hund₁ har Pia engang mødt [DP en [NP pensionist]
           Such a dog has Pia once met a pensioner

      [cP —₁ c°[occ] [cP OP₂ [c° som] [IP —₂ havde —₁.]]]]
                        that had

... and extractions from embedded questions (*wh*-islands):

(18) Danish (Christensen et al. 2013a: 63)

    a.   Hvilken båd₁ foreslog naboen   [cP —₁ c°[occ] [cP
           Which boat suggested neighbour.the

      hvor billigt₂ c°[WH] [IP vi skulle sælge —₁ —₂.]]]
      how cheaply we should sell

    b.   Hvor billigt₂ foreslog naboen   [cP —₂ c°[occ] [cP
           How cheaply suggested neighbour.the

      hvilken båd₁ c°[WH] [IP vi skulle sælge —₁ —₂.]]]
      which boat we should sell

(19) Danish (http://ordnet.dk/ddo/ordbog?query=stads, Hjorth & Kristensen 2003-2005)

    Om morgenen skulle jeg give dem medicinen, noget brunt
    In morning-the should I give them medicine-the, some brown

    stads, [cP OP₁ som [IP jeg ikke ved [cP —₁ c°[occ] [cP hvad₂ c°[WH]
    stuff, that I not know what

    [IP —₁ var —₂.]]]]]
          was

... as well as extractions from adverbial clauses:

(20) Danish (Knud Poulsen, 1918, cited in Hansen 1967, I: 110)

    ... men det₁ bliver han så vred [cP —₁ c°[occ] [cP OP [c° når]
        but that becomes he so angry when

    [IP man siger —₁.]]]
        one says

7 Conclusion

We have presented an analysis of the CP-level in embedded clauses, including what is often seen as CP-recursion in cases of embedded V2. The analysis, which is discussed in much more detail in Nyvad et al. (2017), attempts to unify a whole range of different phenomena related to extraction and embedding, while acknowledging that extraction in Danish is considerably less restricted than has often been assumed.

The CP-recursion that takes place in syntactic environments involving movement out of certain types of embedded clauses seems to be fundamentally different from that occurring in embedded V2 contexts, and hence, we propose a cP/CP distinction: The CP-recursion found in complementiser stacking and long extractions requiring an OCC-feature involves a recursion of cP, (21a), whereas the syntactic island constituted by embedded V2 involves the presence of a CP, (21b).

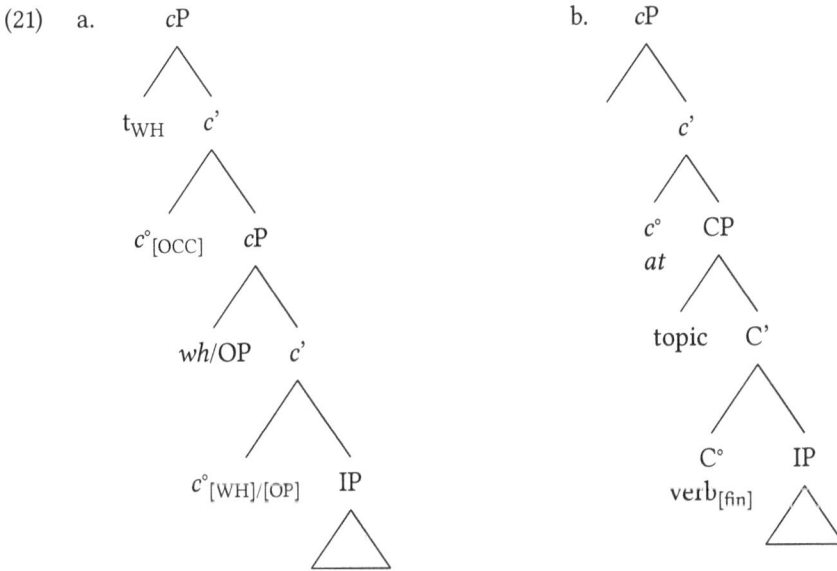

(21) a.

$$
\begin{array}{c}
cP \\
\diagup\diagdown \\
t_{WH} \quad c' \\
\phantom{t_{WH}}\diagup\diagdown \\
c^\circ_{[OCC]} \quad cP \\
\phantom{c^\circ_{[OCC]}}\diagup\diagdown \\
wh/OP \quad c' \\
\diagup\diagdown \\
c^\circ_{[WH]/[OP]} \quad IP
\end{array}
$$

b.

$$
\begin{array}{c}
cP \\
\diagup\diagdown \\
 c' \\
\diagup\diagdown \\
c^\circ \quad CP \\
at \\
\diagup\diagdown \\
topic \quad C' \\
\diagup\diagdown \\
C^\circ \quad IP \\
verb_{[fin]}
\end{array}
$$

The exact structure of CP-recursion may be subject to parametric variation: German does not seem to allow CP-recursion given that extraction from embedded *wh*-questions is ungrammatical irrespective of which function the extracted element has (unless it moves via spec-CP, (6c)), and that embedded V2 is in complementary distribution with the presence of an overt complementiser in C°.

Whether a cartographic approach to the structure of the CP-domain in the Scandinavian languages will turn out to be more appropriate than a CP-recursion analysis (e.g. Rizzi 1997; Wiklund et al. 2007; Julien 2015; Holmberg 2015), we will leave for future research to decide. Until we have data that support a fine-grained left periphery in the relevant structures in Danish, the version of CP-recursion as argued for here would appear promising, as it captures the data presented here while making perhaps slightly fewer stipulations than e.g. the cartographic approach or the multiple specifier analysis.

8 Acknowledgements

We are grateful to Laura Bailey, Theresa Biberauer, Constantin Freitag, Hans-Martin Gärtner, Johannes Kizach, Doug Saddy, Johanna Wood, and two anonymous reviewers for helpful comments and suggestions as well as to participants in the Grammar in Focus workshop series at the University of Lund, participants in the SyntaxLab talk series at the University of Cambridge, and participants in the DGfS conference in Konstanz, February 2016.

Special thanks to Anders Holmberg not just for being such a role model when it comes to creating worldwide interest in Scandinavian syntax, but also for his help and support from Trondheim 1984 to this very day.

The work presented here was partly supported by *Forskningsrådet for Kultur og Kommunikation* (Danish Research Council for Culture and Communication).

References

Bayer, Josef. 2002. *Decomposing the left periphery: Dialectal and cross-linguistic evidence.* Israeli Association of Theoretical Linguistics. http://linguistics.huji.ac.il/IATL/18/Bayer.pdf.

Biberauer, Theresa & Ian Roberts. 2015. Rethinking formal hierarchies: A proposed unification. *Cambridge Occasional Papers in Linguistics* 7. 1–31.

Boeckx, Cedric. 2012. *Syntactic islands.* Cambridge: Cambridge University Press.

Cheng, Lisa Lai-Shen. 1991. *On the typology of wh-questions.* Cambridge, MA: MIT (doctoral dissertation).

Chomsky, Noam. 1995. *The minimalist program.* Cambridge: MIT Press.

Chomsky, Noam. 2000. Minimalist inquiries: The framework. In Roger Martin, David Michaels & Juan Uriagereka (eds.), *Step by step: Essays on minimalist syntax in honor of Howard Lasnik*, 89–155. Cambridge: MIT Press.

Chomsky, Noam. 2001. Derivation by phase. In Michael Kenstowicz (ed.), *Ken Hale: A life in language*, 1–52. Cambridge: MIT Press.

Chomsky, Noam. 2005. Three factors in language design. *Linguistic Inquiry* 36(1). 1–22.

Chomsky, Noam. 2006. *Approaching UG from below.* Ms, MIT.

Christensen, Ken Ramshøj, Johannes Kizach & Anne Mette Nyvad. 2013a. Escape from the island: Grammaticality and (reduced) acceptability of wh-island violations in Danish. *Journal of Psycholinguistic Research* 42. 51–70.

Christensen, Ken Ramshøj, Johannes Kizach & Anne Mette Nyvad. 2013b. The processing of syntactic islands: An fMRI study. *Journal of Neurolinguistics* 26(2). 239–251.

Christensen, Ken Ramshøj & Anne Mette Nyvad. 2014. On the nature of escapable relative islands. *Nordic Journal of Linguistics* 37(1). 29–45.

de Cuba, Carlos. 2007. *On (non)factivity, clausal complementation and the CP-field.* Stony Brook: Stony Brook University (doctoral dissertation).

de Haan, Germen & Fred Weerman. 1986. Finiteness and verb fronting in Frisian. In Hubert Haider & Martin Prinzhorn (eds.), *Verb Second Phenomena in Germanic Languages*, 77–110. Dordrecht: Foris.

Douglas, Jamie. 2015. *The that-trace and anti- that-trace effects: Unification and theoretical implications.* http://linguistics.concordia.ca/nels46/wp-content/uploads/2015/10/nels_2015_talk_douglas.pdf. Hand-out from a talk at NELS 46, Concordia University, Montréal, 16.-18.10.2015.

Fourquet, Jean. 1938. *L'ordre des éléments de la phrase germanique ancien — études de syntaxe de position [The order of the elements in the Old Germanic clause – Studies in positional syntax].* Paris: Les Belles Lettres.

Grimshaw, Jane. 1997. Projections, heads, and optimality. *Linguistic Inquiry* 28. 373–422.

Grimshaw, Jane. 2005. *Words and structure.* Stanford: CSLI Publications.

Hansen, Aage. 1967. *Moderne dansk [Modern Danish].* Vol. 1–3. Copenhagen: Grafisk Forlag.

Hjorth, Ebba & Kjeld Kristensen. 2003-2005. *Den danske ordbog [the Danish dictionary].* Copenhagen: Gyldendal. http://ordnet.dk/ddo/.

Holmberg, Anders. 1986. *Word order and syntactic features in the Scandinavian languages and English.* Stockholm: Stockholm University dissertation.

Holmberg, Anders. 2015. Verb second. In Tibor Kiss & Artemis Alexiadou (eds.), *Syntax – Theory and analysis: An international handbook*, 2nd edn., 342–382. Berlin: de Gruyter.

Jensen, Torben Juel & Tanya Karoli Christensen. 2013. Promoting the demoted: The distribution and semantics of "main clause word order" in spoken Danish complement clauses. *Lingua* 137. 38–58.

Johannesen, Janne Bondi. 2014. Left dislocation in main and subordinate clauses. *Nordic Atlas of Language Structures Journal* 1. 406–414.

Julien, Marit. 2015. The force of V2 revisited. *Journal of Comparative Germanic Linguistics* 18(2). 139–181.

Koizumi, Masatoshi. 1995. *Phrase structure in minimalist syntax.* Cambridge, MA: MIT (doctoral dissertation).

McCloskey, James. 2006. Questions and questioning in a local English. In Raffaella Zanuttini, Hector Campos, Elena Herburger & Paul Portner (eds.), *Crosslinguistic research in syntax and semantics: Negation, tense, and clausal architecture*, 87–126. Washington, DC: Georgetown University Press.

Müller, Gereon & Wolfgang Sternefeld. 1993. Improper movement and unambiguous binding. *Linguistic Inquiry* 24(3). 461–507.

Nyvad, Anne Mette. 2016. Multiple complementizers in Modern Danish and Middle English. In Sten Vikner, Henrik Jørgensen & Elly van Gelderen (eds.), *Let us have articles betwixt us: Papers in historical and comparative linguistics in honour of Johanna L. Wood.* Aarhus: Dept. of English, Aarhus University. www.hum.au.dk/engelsk/engsv/papers/vikn16a.pdf.

Nyvad, Anne Mette, Ken Ramshøj Christensen & Sten Vikner. 2017. CP-Recursion in Danish: A cP/CP-Analysis. Forthcoming in *The Linguistic Review.* DOI:10.1515/tlr-2017-0008

Petersson, David. 2014. *The Highest Force Hypothesis: Subordination in Swedish*. Lund: University of Lund (doctoral dissertation).

Rizzi, Luigi. 1997. The fine structure of the left periphery. In Liliane Haegeman (ed.), *Elements of grammar: A handbook of generative syntax*, 281–337. Dordrecht: Kluwer.

Rizzi, Luigi & Ian Roberts. 1996. Complex inversion in French. In Adriana Belletti & Luigi Rizzi (eds.), *Parameters and Functional Heads*. 91–116. New York: Oxford University Press. (Reprinted from 1989, Probus 1(1), 1-30).

Sheehan, Michelle & Wolfram Hinzen. 2011. Moving towards the edge: The grammar of reference. *Linguistic Analysis* 37. 405–458.

Vikner, Sten. 1995. *Verb movement and expletive subjects in the Germanic languages*. Oxford: Oxford University Press.

Wackernagel, Jacob. 1892. Über ein gesetz der indogermanischen wortstellung [about a law for word order in Indoeuropean]. *Indogermanische Forschungen* 1. 333–436.

Walkden, George. 2017. Language contact and v3 in Germanic varieties new and old. *Journal of Comparative Germanic Linguistics* 20. 49–81.

Wiklund, Anna-Lena, Gunnar Hrafn Hrafnbjargarsson, Þorbjörg Hróarsdóttir & Kristine Bentzen. 2007. Rethinking Scandinavian verb movement. *Journal of Comparative Germanic Linguistics* 10. 203–233.

Chapter 14

Verb second not verb second in Syrian Arabic

Mais Sulaiman

Newcastle University

This paper discusses the obligatory verb second order in a non-verb second dialect, Syrian Arabic. It will be argued following Holmberg (2012) that the obligatory Wh-V-S order in Syrian Arabic is a consequence of a property on a functional head F in the left periphery similar to that on C in V2 languages. This head has another property that allows movement of one and only one constituent past its specifier. In cases where more than one XP precedes the verb, the first XP is externally merged. Unlike C, it does not have to attract a constituent to its Spec, so declarative clauses may have VS(O) order.

1 Verb second and residual verb second

In verb second (V2) languages, the finite verb must obligatorily be the second constituent in main clauses or in all finite clauses (den Besten 1977; Rizzi 1990b; Holmberg 2012). Some languages manifest V2 in specific constructions, as is the case with wh-questions in languages such as English and Italian illustrated in (1) and (2). A subject cannot intervene between the wh-element and the auxiliary in main questions. These languages are classified as residual verb second, a residue of a verb second system.

(1) English (Rizzi 1996: 63)

    a.   What has Mary said?

    b. * What Mary has said?

(2) Italian

    a.   Che cosa ha detto Maria?
         what   has said Maria

        'What has Mary said?'

    b. * Che cosa ha Maria detto?
         what   has Maria said

Mais Sulaiman. 2017. Verb second not verb second in Syrian Arabic. In Laura R. Bailey & Michelle Sheehan (eds.), *Order and structure in syntax I: Word order and syntactic structure*, 325–331. Berlin: Language Science Press. DOI:10.5281/zenodo.1117720

Similarly, some languages derive verb second order; however, they are not real V2 languages. This is the case in Standard Arabic:

(3)   Standard Arabic (Fassi Fehri 1993: 13)

    a. Kataba   Zayd-un   r-risaalat-a.
        wrote.3SG.M Zayd-NOM the-letter-ACC

       'Zaid wrote the letter.'

    b. Zaydun   kataba   r-risaalat-a.
        Zayd-NOM wrote.3SG.M the-letter-ACC

       'Zayd wrote the letter.'

Sentences like (3b) manifest a V2-like effect; however, Standard Arabic is different from V2 languages in that it allows a V-initial order as the unmarked order see Fassi Fehri (1993: 27ff).

In this paper, I argue that Syrian Arabic is not a residual V2 language, yet the subject cannot intervene between the wh-phrase and the verb in wh-questions. This order can be accounted for if we assume that there is a specific feature on a lower functional head in the left periphery that is in common with V2 languages.

2 Syrian Arabic: A non-residual V2-language

Syrian Arabic employs the VSO order, as is the case in Standard Arabic. V2 orders are forced in specific constructions, as in SVO declarative sentences and wh-questions. The Wh-V-S order is obligatory with most questions introduced by argumental wh-phrases.

(4)   Syrian Arabic (Sulaiman 2016: 32)

    a.   shw ħaka   basem?
         what said.3SG.M Basem

        'What did Bassel say?'

    b. * shw   basem ħaka?
         what Basem said.3SG.M

(5)   a.   miin shaf   Iyad?
         who saw.3SG.M Iyad

        'Who did Iyad see?'

    b. * miin Iyad shaf?
         who Iyad saw.3SG.M

However, the Wh-V-S can be optional with some questions introduced with certain adjuncts like *lesh* 'why'. Compare (6a) and (6b):

(6)   a. lesh mary tddayʔ-et?
        why Mary upsetted-3SG.F

        'What did upset Mary?'

      b. lesh tddayʔ-et   mary?
        why upsetted-3SG.F Mary

        'What did upset Mary?'

It is also possible to have a topic phrase preceding the wh-phrase in questions, as in (7):

(7)   a. bassel šw   ħaka?
        Bassel what said

        'What did Bassel say?'

      b. mama lesh ʕam tʕayeT?
        mom why PROG shouting

        'Why is mom shouting?'

An adverbial phrase can intervene between the wh-phrase and the verb see (8).

(8)   a. min hallaʔ ija?
        who now   come

        'Who has just arrived?'

      b. shw issa ʕam t-ʕml-i?
        what still PROG PRES.F-doing-2SG.F

        'What are you still doing?'

In contrast, movement of either an auxiliary or the support *do* to C is obligatory in English, leaving the adverb behind, as in (9a, b).

(9)   a. Who would you never offend with your actions?

      b. Which language does Pepita still study in her free time?

From what has been discussed, it can be concluded that Syrian Arabic is not a V2 or a residual V2 language, yet it manifests a V2 order in specific constructions derived by V movement to a lower functional head in the left periphery (see Benmamoun 2000; Aoun et al. 2010; Sulaiman 2016 for an overview). The obligatory restriction on the verb appearing in a second position in wh-questions can be explained following Holmberg's (2012) account of V2 languages.

3 Movement condition

Holmberg (2012) argues that V2 languages are characterised by two properties: There is a functional head in the left periphery, C1, which (a) attracts the finite verb, and (b) has an EPP feature that requires movement of a constituent to the Spec of C1. C1 has a third property as well: it prevents movement of any other constituent across it, apart from the one attracted by its EPP feature. The rationale for this property, in Holmberg (2012), who follows Roberts (2004), is the following: the EPP feature can attract any constituent (argument or adjunct or wh-phrase, with almost any features). This property blocks movement of any other category to a higher position than Spec of C1. This allows for the possibility, however, that categories are externally merged in the C-domain higher than Spec of C1. The two properties are independent, so in some languages C1 may have property (a) but not property (b), as is the case in certain VSO languages. It is also possible that a language may have a finiteness particle or a null C as C1 with the EPP with no verb movement to C1.

Following from these assumptions, it can be argued that in Syrian Arabic, there is a functional head in the left periphery marked with a feature that is in common with that of C1 in V2 languages. This head allows movement of only one constituent past its specifier, assuming Rizzi's (1997) fine structure of the left periphery. More than one constituent can appear before the verb if one of the constituents is externally merged. Unlike C1, it does not have to attract a constituent to its Spec, so declarative clauses may have the VS(O) order.

This analysis can thus explain sentences like (10), where more than one XP can appear before the verb.

(10)   a.   basem šw   ħaka?
           Basem what said.3SG.M
           'What did Bassel say?'

      b.   Mama lesh ʕam   t-ʕayeT?
           mom   why PROG PRES-shouting.3SG.F
           'Why is mom shouting?'

Basem in (10a) and *mama* in (10b) can be externally merged in the highest TopP position in the left periphery, only when the wh-phrase raises across C1.[1]

This analysis can also explain sentences like (8), in which an adverbial phrase intervenes between the verb and the wh-phrase, if we assume that the adverb is externally merged as an adjunct.

A subject can intervene between the wh-phrase and the verb in questions introduced with wh-phrases like *lesh* 'why', as illustrated in (11):

(11)   a.   lesh mary tdday?-et?
           why Mary upset-3SG.F
           'What upset Mary?'

      b.   lesh tdday?-et   mary?
           why upset-3SG.F Mary
           'What upset Mary?'

---

[1]For discussion on externally merged *aboutness topics* see Reinhart (1981); Lambrecht (1994), and Frascarelli & Hinterhölzl (2007).

It is well known since Rizzi (1991) that *why* questions are distinctive. Rizzi noted that while other wh-questions require inversion in Italian, this is not the case with *perché* 'why'.

(12) Italian (Rizzi 2001: 273)

    a.   Dove è andato Gianni?
           where went   Gianni

           'Where did Gianni go?'

    b. * Dove Gianni è andato?
           where Gianni went

Rizzi (1991) proposed that this is because *perché* 'why' is base-generated (i.e. externally merged) in the C-domain. Rizzi (2001) suggests that *perché* is externally merged in SpecINT, a position higher than the landing site of other, moved wh-phrases. INT is an interrogative head marked with an [uWh] feature. This feature is checked/valued by movement of the wh-phrase to SpecC1, or by an externally merged wh-phrase in SpecINTP like *lesh* 'why'. This can also be the case for *lesh* 'why'. If *lesh* 'why' is externally merged in the C-domain, the EPP feature on C1 can still attract a subject to its Spec, which explains subject intervention between the wh-phrase and the verb in (11a).

While V2 appears as a restrictive order in Germanic languages, V2 is only triggered in certain constructions like wh-questions in Syrian Arabic. V3 orders are possible in wh-questions provided that the first constituent is initially merged in that position as is the case with a topic preceding the wh-phrase, or a base generated wh-adjunct. This can be accounted for following Poletto's (2002) theory that languages can vary with regards to whether left-peripheral functional features are distributed over a hierarchy of distinct heads, each with its own Spec, assuming Rizzi's (2001) hierarchy of [Force, Focus, Topic, and Finiteness], and that only one Spec-position higher than the head hosting the finite verb can be filled by movement, which can be the case in Syrian Arabic, or whether they are encoded in one head, with one Spec-position.

4 Conclusion

The fact that the subject cannot intervene between a wh-phrase and the inflected verb in main questions renders Syrian Arabic similar to residual V2 languages; however, different facts prove Syrian Arabic not to be a V2 or a residual V2 language, yet this restrictive V2 order can best be accounted for following Holmberg's (2012) analysis of V2 languages. The assumption that a lower functional head in the left periphery is specified for a feature that attracts a finite verb, and an EPP feature that can attract a subject or a wh-phrase allowing movement of only one constituent past its specifier can justify this restrictive Wh-V-S order in most questions.

Acknowledgements

This work is dedicated to Anders Holmberg to express my gratitude for his support and feedback.

References

Aoun, Joseph, Elabbas Benmamoun & Lina Choueiri. 2010. *The syntax of Arabic*. Cambridge: Cambridge University Press.

Benmamoun, Elabbas. 2000. *The Feature Structure of Functional Categories: A Comparative Study of Arabic Dialects*. Oxford: Oxford University Press.

den Besten, Hans. 1977. On the interaction of root transformations and lexical deleave rules. In W. Abraham (ed.), *On the formal syntax of Westgermania*, 47–138. John Benjamins: Amsterdam.

Fassi Fehri, Abdelkader. 1993. *Issues in the structure of Arabic clauses and words*. Dordrecht: Kluwer Academic Publishers.

Frascarelli, Mara & Roland Hinterhölzl. 2007. Types of topics in German and Italian. In Kerstin Schwabe & Susanne Winkler (eds.), *On information structure, meaning and form*, 87–116. Amsterdam: John Benjamins.

Holmberg, Anders. 2012. Verb second. In Tibor Kiss & Artemis Alexiadou (eds.), *Syntax – an international handbook of contemporary syntactic research*, 343–384. Berlin: Walter de Gruyter Verlag.

Lambrecht, Knud. 1994. *Information structure and sentence form: Topic, focus, and the mental representation of discourse referents*. Cambridge: Cambridge University Press.

Poletto, Cecilia. 2002. The left-periphery of V2-Rhaetoromance dialects: A new view on V2 and V3. In Sjef Barbiers, Leonie Cornips & Susanne van der Kleij (eds.), *Syntactic microvariation*, 214–242. Amsterdam: Electronic publications of Meertens Instituut.

Reinhart, Tanya. 1981. Pragmatics and linguistics: An analysis of sentence topics in pragmatics and philosophy i. *Philosophica anc Studia Philosophica Gandensia Gent* 27. 53–94.

Rizzi, Luigi. 1990b. Speculations on verb-second. In Joan Mascaró & Marina Nespor (eds.), *Grammar in progress: Essays in honour of Henk van Riemsdijk*, 375–386. Groningen: Foris.

Rizzi, Luigi. 1991. Residual verb second and the Wh criterion. In *Technical reports in formal and computational linguistics* 2. Geneva: University of Geneva.

Rizzi, Luigi. 1996. Residual verb second and the wh-criterion. In Andriana Belletti & Luigi Rizzi (eds.), *Parameters and functional heads*, 63–90. Oxfort: Oxford University Press.

Rizzi, Luigi. 1997. The fine structure of the left periphery. In Liliane Haegeman (ed.), *Elements of grammar: A handbook of generative syntax*, 281–337. Dordrecht: Kluwer.

Rizzi, Luigi. 2001. On the position "Int(errogative)" in the left periphery of the clause. *Current studies in Italian syntax* 14. 267–296.

Roberts, Ian. 2004. The C-system in Brythonic Celtic languages, V2, and the EPP. In Luigi Rizzi (ed.), *The cartography of syntactic structures*, vol. 2, 297–327. New York & Oxford: Oxford University Press.

Sulaiman, Mais. 2016. *The syntax of Wh-questions in Syrian Arabic*. Newcastle University dissertation.

Chapter 15

Uniqueness of left peripheral focus, "further explanation", and Int.

Luigi Rizzi
University of Geneva, University of Siena

In this paper I would like to address the uniqueness of the focus position in the left periphery of the clause and the fixed order of focus with respect to Int, the left-peripheral position hosting interrogative complementizers corresponding to English *if*, Italian *se*, etc. (Rizzi 2001). Such properties may be amenable to "further explanations" in terms of principles applying at the interfaces of the syntactic component, or in terms of locality principles directly operating on syntactic computations. I will discuss the interplay between these two modes of explanation in the cases at issue, and will briefly explore the consequences of this analysis for ordering constraints involving focus and certain main-clause left peripheral particles such as Sicilian *chi* Bianchi & Cruschina (2016) and Finnish *-ko* Holmberg (2013; 2014).

1 Introduction

Cartographic research uncovers properties of functional sequences such as ordering and co-occurrence constraints. The observed generalizations are in need of "further explanations" in terms of more elementary ingredients of linguistic computations, or of principles ruling the interpretive processes at the interfaces with sound and meaning. In this short paper I would like to address certain properties of focus in the left periphery of the clause, such as the uniqueness of the focus position and the fixed order of focus with respect to Int, the left-peripheral position hosting interrogative complementizers corresponding to English *if*, Italian *se*, etc. (Rizzi 2001). Such properties may be amenable to "further explanations" in terms of principles applying at the interfaces of the syntactic component, or in terms of locality principles directly operating on syntactic computations. I will discuss the interplay between these two modes of explanation in the cases at issue, and will briefly explore the consequences of this analysis for ordering constraints involving focus and certain main-clause left peripheral particles such as Sicilian *chi* Bianchi & Cruschina 2016 and Finnish *–ko* (Holmberg 2013; 2014).

Luigi Rizzi. 2017. Uniqueness of left peripheral focus, "further explanation", and Int. In Laura R. Bailey & Michelle Sheehan (eds.), *Order and structure in syntax I: Word order and syntactic structure*, 333–343. Berlin: Language Science Press. DOI:10.5281/zenodo.1117718

2 Uniqueness of focus

A traditional observation in the study of the left periphery of the clause is that left peripheral focus is typically unique. This was observed, e.g. in Italian (Rizzi 1997; capitalization
is used to express the special prosody of focal constituents, on which see Bocci 2013):

(1) a. A MARIA devi dare il tuo libro __ (, non a Giulia).

'TO MARIA you should give your book, non to Giulia.'

   b. IL TUO LIBRO devi dare __ a Maria (non il disco).

'YOUR BOOK you should give to Maria, not the record.'

   c. * A MARIA(,) IL TUO LIBRO devi dare (non a Giulia, il disco).

'To Maria your book you should give, not to Giulia the record.'

   d. * IL TUO LIBRO(,) A MARIA devi dare (non il disco, a Giulia).

'Your book, to Maria you should give, not the record to Giulia.'

As the negative tag suggests, (1a) and (1b) are instances of corrective focus. If somebody says *I have to give my book to Giulia*, I can correct him/her by uttering (1a), and
similar felicity conditions are observed for (1b); but (1c–d), correctively focalizing both
the direct and indirect object, are ungrammatical, whatever order is selected.

The uniqueness requirement holds for corrective focus and for "mirative" focus, the
other major kind of focus which in Italian (and other Romance languages) licenses movement to the left periphery:

(2) Pensa un po'...

'Just think of it...'

   a. UNA FERRARI vogliono regalare a Mario! Che pazzia!

'A FERRARI they want to give to Mario! That's crazy!'

   b. A MARIO vogliono regalare una Ferrari! Che pazzia!

'TO MARIO they want to give a Ferrari! That's crazy!'

   c. * A MARIO(,) UNA FERRARI vogliono regalare! Che pazzia!

'TO MARIO A FERRARI they want to give! That's crazy!'

   d. * UNA FERRARI(,) A MARIO vogliono regalare! Che pazzia!

'A FERRARI TO MARIO they want to give! That's crazy!'

As pointed out by Bianchi et al. (2015), mirative focus differs from corrective focus
both in the pragmatic conditions for its felicitous use (it expresses surprise for a state of
affairs falling outside natural expectations, rather than correcting someone else's statement) and intonational contour. But it shares the uniqueness requirement with corrective focus. Both focal constructions were collapsed under the label "contrastive focus" in
Rizzi (1997); new information focus differs from these special focal constructions in that,
in Romance, it is expressed in a lower position, internal to the IP (Belletti 2004).

The special left peripheral focus constructions sharply contrast with topic constructions such as Clitic Left Dislocation, which is consistent with a proliferation of topics in any order:

(3)   a.   Il tuo libro, a Maria, glielo devi dare al più presto.

'Your book, to Mary, you should give it to her as soon as possible.'

    b.   A Maria, il tuo libro, glielo devi dare al più presto.

'To Maria, your book, you should give it to her as soon as possible.'

The uniqueness of left peripheral focus is not a quirk of Italian/Romance. A similar constraint has been observed in Finno-Ugric (Puskás 2000), West-African (Hager M'Boua 2014), and Jamaican Creole (Durrleman 2008). A principled explanation thus seems to be in order.

3 "Further explanation" of cartographic properties

Cartographic research has uncovered a variety of properties of functional elements occurring in specific zones of the clause, such as ordering and co-occurrence constraints. Some such properties are variable across languages, whereas other properties look cross-linguistically stable. These results raise the question of why one finds certain stable patterns rather than other imaginable alternative arrangements. As pointed out in Cinque & Rizzi (2010) it is unlikely that such patterns may be absolute syntactic primitives, to be stated in UG as unrelated to other requirements or constraints: why should natural language syntax have evolved to express such complex and apparently unmotivated primitives? It is more plausible that functional hierarchies and their properties (to the extent to which they are invariant) may be rooted elsewhere, hence be amenable to "further explanations". There are two major imaginable kinds of such explanations (here I follow the discussion in Rizzi (2013): they may invoke

- Interface principles: certain observed properties of the hierarchies may be derived from principles ruling the interfaces between syntax and the interpretive systems of sound and meaning;

- Formal syntactic principles: "further explanations" may also invoke formal principles internal to the syntactic box, for instance principles of locality (Abels 2012; Haegeman 2012) or labeling (Rizzi 2016).

For the case at issue, Rizzi (1997) proposed an explanation of the uniqueness of left-peripheral focus by invoking the routines that interpret discourse related "criterial" configurations at logical form. Suppose that the interpretive principle triggered by the Foc head is something like the following, in terms of a traditional terminology of, e.g., Jackendoff (1972):

(4)   [   ] Foc [   ]
          "Focus"   "Presupposition"

i.e., a Foc head goes with the instruction: "interpret my specifier as the focus (corrective or mirative), and my complement as the presupposed part".

So, let's suppose, counterfactually, that the Foc head could recursively occur in the left periphery, giving rise to a double focus. The derived representation would be something like the following:

(5)   * [[A MARIA] **Foc1** [[IL TUO LIBRO] **Foc2** [devi dare __ __]]].
      'TO MARIA YOUR BOOK (you) should give.'

Here IL TUO LIBRO should be interpreted as a focus of the relevant kind, being the Spec of Foc 2; but the whole sequence [[*IL TUO LIBRO*] [**Foc2** [*devi dare*]]] is the complement of Foc1, hence, under (4), it should be interpreted as the presupposed part. So, *il tuo libro* should at the same time be focus and presupposed; but presumably a clash arises between the two notions, hence Foc recursion in the left periphery never gives rise to a properly interpretable structure. The observed syntactic constraint is thus derived from a natural interpretive requirement.

I phrased the argument in terms of the traditional definition of the relevant articulation as Focus – Presupposition (Jackendoff 1972). If the articulation is more neutrally characterized as Focus – Background, as in much recent work, as far as I can tell the idea of the interpretive clash arising in configurations of double left-peripheral focus would remain unchanged: something cannot be simultaneously focus and background.

Now, there is a natural competitor to an interface explanation in this case. Abels (2012) argues that major ordering properties observed in the left periphery in Rizzi (1997; 2001) can be derived from the theory of locality and in particular from a featural characterization of Relativized Minimality (fRM) (as in Starke 2001; Rizzi 2004, building on Rizzi 1990).

Consider a representation like (5). When two foci are moved to the left periphery, one inevitably crosses over the other. So, in (5) the attempt to connect A MARIA to its variable would cross a featurally identical focus position filled by IL TUO LIBRO, a configuration which would be ruled out by fRM. So, the theory of locality seems to provide a competing "further explanation" for the uniqueness of left-peripheral focus.

There is, of course, another possibility: it could be the case that (5) is excluded by both orders of considerations. In general, a natural strategy of theory construction is to avoid redundancies, so that, if two paths of explanation compete, it is quite generally productive to try to eliminate the redundancy. Nevertheless, the elimination of redundancies is a useful research strategy, not a dogma: it is imaginable that two optimally stated principles may have areas of overlap, as well as areas of non-overlap in their respective empirical domains. Let us consider the case at issue by looking at other related but distinct effects.

4 Double focus exclusion without intervention

Consider the case of a complex sentence with a complement of the main verb and a complement of the embedded verb. Either one can be focused and moved to the left periphery of the clause immediately containing it, but they cannot be focalized simultaneously:

(6)   a.   Devi dire a Gianni che comprerai questo libro.

          'You should say to Gianni that you will buy this book.'

       b.   A GIANNI devi dire che comprerai questo libro (non a Piero).

           'To GIANNI you should say that you will buy this book (not to Piero).'

       c.   Devi dire a Gianni che QUESTO LIBRO comprerai (non quest'altro).

           'You should say to Gianni that THIS BOOK you will buy (not that one).'

       d. * A GIANNI devi dire che QUESTO LIBRO comprerai (non a Piero, quest'altro).

           'TO GIANNI you should say that THIS BOOK you will buy (not to Piero, that one).'

Sentence (6d) is sharply deviant, but in this case no crossing or intervention configuration arises because each focalized element is moved to the periphery of its own clause. So, this example is solely excluded by the interface considerations based on (4): even if the two FocP's are not adjacent and occur in different clauses, the presupposition of the higher focus still contains the lower focus, hence the interpretive clash arises here as well.

Other cases not amenable to locality considerations, but excluded by interface considerations, are those which involve clause initial adjuncts which plausibly are externally merged directly in the left periphery, such as "scene setting" adjuncts (Benincà & Poletto 2004):

(7)   a.   Nella foto di Gianni, Piero dà un bacio a Maria.

           'In Gianni's picture, Piero gives a kiss to Maria.'

       b.   NELLA FOTO DI GIANNI, Piero dà un bacio a Maria (non in quella di Giuseppe).

           'In GIANNI's picture, Piero gives a kiss to Maria (not in Giuseppe's picture).'

       c.   Nella foto di Gianni, A MARIA Piero dà un bacio (non a Giulia).

           'In Gianni's picture, TO MARIA Piero gives a kiss (not to Giulia).'

       d. * NELLA FOTO DI GIANNI, A MARIA Piero dà un bacio (non in quella di Giuseppe, a Giulia).

           'In GIANNI's picture, TO MARIA Piero gives kiss (not in Giuseppe's, to Giulia).'

In (7a) the PP *Nella foto di Gianni* is not a locative fronted from a lower position but an adverbial setting the scene for the following sentence; as such, it is plausibly externally merged directly in the periphery of the sentence (Reinhart 1981). It can be a corrective focus, as in (7b), but it cannot co-occur with another corrective focus, as in (7d). Again, there is no locality effect to be invoked here, whereas the interface explanation based on (4) correctly rules out the structure.

5 The strict ordering of Focus and Int

There are also cases that are naturally analyzable as involving intervention, whereas they don't seem to immediately fall under the effect of interface principles. Consider the relative ordering of Int, the position hosting yes-no interrogative complementizers like Italian *se* and English *if* (Rizzi 2001) in embedded questions, and Focus. The only possible order is Int Focus:

(8)   a.   Mi domando se IL TUO LIBRO abbiano comprato (non il mio).
      'I wonder if YOUR BOOK they bought (not mine).'

      b.   * Mi domando IL TUO LIBRO se abbiano comprato (non il mio).
      'I wonder YOUR BOOK if the bought (not mine).'

In this case, focus sharply contrasts with topic, which can both precede and follow Int:

(9)   a.   Mi domando se, il tuo libro, lo abbiano comprato.
      'I wonder if, you book, they bought it.'

      b.   Mi domando, il tuo libro, se lo abbiano comprato.
      'I wonder, your book, if they bought it.'

The ordering constraint illustrated by (8) is not straightforwardly amenable to an interface account of the kind ruling out a double focus, whereas it can be captured by a locality account à la Abels (2012): *se* presumably hosts a yes-no operator in its Spec (and, in any event, it is marked by a +Q feature, an operator feature). Hence, movement of an element plausibly involving an operator feature, like focus, determines a violation of Relativized Minimality, under the approach based on feature classes developed in Rizzi (2004). No violation is expected in the case of a topic construction like (9b), if such constructions in Italian/Romance do not involve any operator feature (Cinque 1990, Rizzi 2004). Putting together (8) and (6–7), we thus seem to reach the conclusion that both an interface approach and a locality approach are needed on independent grounds, and the two approaches may overlap in some cases, such as the exclusion of double focus constructions like (1–2).

There are additional elements of complexity, though. Callegari (2014) and Cinque & Krapova (2013) point out a problem for a simple locality account in cases analogous to (8b): long distance extraction of a focal element from an indirect question is more acceptable than local movement across *se*. In my judgement, there is a detectable difference of severity of ill-formedness: long distance focalization from an indirect question is only mildly deviant, and more acceptable than local focus movement across *if*, as in (8b):

(10)   ? IL TUO LIBRO mi domando se abbiano comprato, non il mio.
      'YOUR BOOK I wonder if they bought, not mine.'

The status of (10) suggests that movement of focus across *se* does indeed cause a locality violation, but the local movement in cases like (8b) must involves a mild locality violation, plus an aggravating factor. What could it be? Let us briefly reconsider the interface idea. (8b) would have, for the relevant part, the following representation:

(11)   ... IL TUO LIBRO Foc [se$_Q$ abbiano comprato]

'...YOUR BOOK if they bought'

We have seen that, according to (4), the complement of Foc must be interpreted as the presupposed part. We may speculate that a question (a clausal constituent headed and labeled by Q) is not the natural syntactic object expressing a presupposed part, whereas a FinP expressing a propositional content would be, as in the ordering in (8a) corresponding to the following configuration:

(12)   ... se$_Q$ ... IL TUO LIBRO Foc [$_{IntP}$ abbiano comprato]

'...if YOUR BOOK they bought'

If an interface analysis along these or similar lines can be made precise, it may well be that both factors play a role in the ill-formedness of (8b), with the mild locality violation observed in (10) getting "reinforced", as it were, by an interface factor in (8b). (For a compositional analysis requiring the order Q > Foc in the case of mirative focus, see Bianchi et al. 2015.)

6 Some comparative considerations

Main yes-no questions with left peripheral focus are also possible (Holmberg 2013; 2014 on Finnish; Bianchi & Cruschina 2016 on Italian and other Romance varieties), e.g.,

(13)   IL TUO LIBRO hanno comprato? (non volevano quello di Gianni?)

'YOUR BOOK they bought? (didn't they want Gianni's?)'

This case differs from the embedded question case in that the Int marker is null in main environments in Italian. Where does the structural position Int appear in main clauses? An extension of what was observed in embedded clauses suggests that the unpronounced Int of main clauses should be higher than Foc, much as the pronounced Int of embedded clauses: the opposite ordering Foc > Int would be ruled out both by locality and the interface requirement discussed in connection with the embedded environment.

When a given order is assumed in a certain language on the basis of abstract consideration, it is good practice to check if in other languages the assumed order is visibly manifested. In fact, Bianchi & Cruschina (2016) show that in Sicilian, which has a pronounced form of main Int (*chi*), the order is *chi* > Foc in main questions, as would be expected:

(14)   Chi a Maria salutasti?

'*Chi* to Maria (you) greeted? = Did you greet Maria?'

Belletti (p.c.) points out that in the colloquial variety of Italian spoken in Rome, main yes-no questions are introduced by the particle *che,* homophonous to the declarative Complementizer, which thus appears to be a plausible candidate for the overt lexicalization of Int in main clauses. As expected, *che* must precede a left-peripheral corrective focus:

(15)   a. Che MARIA hai salutato (e non Gianni)?

         'INT MARIA you greeted (and not Gianni)?'

      b. *MARIA che hai salutato (e non Gianni)?

         'Maria INT you greeted (and not Gianni)?'

Belletti also observes that in this variety topics differ from foci in that a clitic left-dislocated element can both precede and follow main clause Int:

(16)   a. Maria, che la conosci già?

         'Maria, Int (you) already know her?'

      b. Che Maria, la conosci già?

         'Int Maria, (you) already know her?'

The pattern is thus identical to the one visible only in embedded clauses is Standard Italian (as in 8–9): the sharply ungrammatical (15b) is ruled out both as a locality violation and, plausibly, as a violation of interface requirements, as per our previous discussion; neither kind of violation arises with a topic, as in (16a–b).

A potential problem arises in Finnish. Holmberg (2013; 2014) shows that in main environments in this language the question particle *–ko* occurs after a focalized element:

(17)   Pariisissa**ko** Matti on käynyt?

      'Paris Matti has visited?'

This order would be unexpected if *–ko* were to be analyzed as the Finnish equivalent of Int. But Holmberg argues in detail that (this instance of) *–ko* must be analyzed as affixed to the focused constituent, and then moved to the left periphery with it, rather than as a particle externally merged in the left peripheral spine (as Int is, under our analysis).

Other considerations support this analysis. For instance, Karoliina Lohiniva (p.c.) observes that, in her native Oulu dialect, *–ko* can be repeated after each conjunct in case of a coordination of focused DPs:

(18)   Isä-s-kö   ja   äiti-s-kö   se-n   auto-n ost-i?
      father-poss-Q and mother-poss-Q that-ACC car-ACC buy-3SG.past

      'Was it your father and your mother who bought that car?'

This is expected if *–ko* is affixed to the focal DP(s), whereas it is inconsistent with an analysis of *–ko* as a lexicalization of Int. Not surprisingly, a bona fide lexicalization of Int such as Roman *che* cannot be reduplicated in such cases (Belletti, p.c.):

(19)   Che MARIA e (*che) FRANCESCA hai salutato?
       'Int MARIA and (*Int) FRANCESCA (you) greeted?'

The observed ordering in Finnish thus is consistent, under Holmberg's analysis of –*ko*, with the general ordering constraint Int > Foc that we have discussed.

7 Conclusion

The necessity of seeking for "further explanations" of cartographic properties leads us to take into consideration the possible explanatory role of interpretive principles applying at the interfaces, and of locality principles applying within the syntactic box. In the attempt to study the interplay between these two orders of considerations, we have been led to look at the case of the exclusion of multiple left peripheral foci in Romance and other languages. Here, simple considerations on the functioning of interpretive principles of the scope-discourse articulations involving left peripheral focus may provide a straightforward analysis of the observed restriction: in cases of double left peripheral focus, the lower focalized element would inevitably end up in the presupposed, or background part, of the higher focus, giving rise to an interpretive clash. On the other hand, under minimal assumptions on the functioning of intervention, locality also marks cases of double focus movement as deviant, as one focalized constituent would necessarily be moved across the other. In the attempt to disentangle these two modes of further explanation, we have observed cases in which locality considerations are not (immediately) relevant, e.g. in ill-formed cases in which two focused elements come from different clauses and are moved to the respective immediate left peripheries: in such cases there is no crossing, and still the structures are deviant. So, such cases appear to be "pure" cases of violation of interface constraints. We have also looked at a potential case of "pure" locality violation: the case of the obligatory ordering Int > Foc in Romance. Here a violation of featural Relativized Minimality is certainly involved in the ordering Foc > Int, as the focal operator is crossing the Q-marked Complementizer particle, also a position marked by an operator feature. But the hypothesis that this is a pure case of locality violation has to face the problem of the different degree of deviance of local and long distance movement of a focal element across Int (as in 8b–10). The more severe violation of local movement suggests that some other consideration in addition to locality is operative here: this has led us to look again at the role of interface principles. Finally, comparative considerations on overt manifestations of the ordering phenomena in main clauses have lead us to assume, with Bianchi & Cruschina (2016), that Sicilian *chi* is a genuine Int marker, exhibiting the expected order Int > Foc also in main clauses, and to adopt Holmberg's (2013; 2014) analysis of Finnish –*ko* as an affix attached to the focused constituent, rather than as a manifestation of the Int head in the left peripheral sequence.

Acknowledgments

This paper is dedicated to Anders, who showed us the intricacies of the languages of the Northern countries, and their theoretical underpinning. I would like to thank Adriana Belletti, Valentina Bianchi and Karoliina Lohiniva for very helpful comments. This research was supported in part by the ERC Grant n. 340297 "SynCart".

References

Abels, Klaus. 2012. The Italian left periphery: A view from locality. *Linguistic Inquiry* 43. 229–254.

Belletti, Adriana. 2004. Aspects of the low IP area. In Luigi Rizzi (ed.), *The structure of CP and IP. The Cartography of syntactic structures*, vol. 2, 16–51. New York: Oxford University Press.

Benincà, Paola & Cecilia Poletto. 2004. Topic, focus and v2: Defining the CP sublayers. In Luigi Rizzi (ed.), *The structure of CP and ip*, 52–75. New York: Oxford University Press.

Bianchi, Valentina, Giuliano Bocci & Silvio Cruschina. 2015. Focus fronting, unexpectedness, and evaluative implicatures. *Semant. Pragmat.*

Bianchi, Valentina & Silvio Cruschina. 2016. The derivation and interpretation of polar questions with a fronted focus. *Lingua* 170. 47–68.

Bocci, Giuliano. 2013. *The Syntax-Prosody interface: A cartographic perspective with evidence from Italian*. Amsterdam: John Benjamins.

Callegari, Elena. 2014. Why Locality-Based Accounts of the Left Periphery Are Unfit To Account for its Variation. Paper presented at Variation in C: Macro- and microcomparative approaches to complementizers and the CP phase (Workshop). Venice, 21 – 22 October 2014.

Cinque, Guglielmo. 1990. *Types of A'-dependencies*. Cambridge, MA: MIT Press.

Cinque, Guglielmo & Iliyana Krapova. 2013. DP and CP: A Relativized Minimality approach to one of their non parallelisms. Paper presented at Congrès International des Linguistes, Geneva. July 2013.

Cinque, Guglielmo & Luigi Rizzi. 2010. The cartography of syntactic structures. In Bernd Heine & Heiko Narrog (eds.), *The Oxford handbook of linguistic analysis*. New York: Oxford University Press.

Durrleman, Stephanie. 2008. *The syntax of Jamaican Creole*. Amsterdam: John Benjamins.

Haegeman, Liliane. 2012. *Adverbial clauses, main clause phenomena, and composition of the left periphery* (The Cartography of Syntactic Structures 8). New York: Oxford University Press.

Hager M'Boua, Clarisse. 2014. *Structure de la phrase en Abidji*. University of Geneva dissertation.

Holmberg, Anders. 2013. The syntax of answers to polar questions in English and Swedish. *Lingua* 128. 31–50.

Holmberg, Anders. 2014. The syntax of the Finnish question particle. In Peter Svenonius (ed.), *Functional structure from top to toe*, 266–289. Oxford: Oxford University Press. http://www.ncl.ac.uk/elll/research/publication/177509.

Jackendoff, Ray S. 1972. *Semantic interpretation in generative grammar*. Cambridge, MA: The MIT Press.

Puskás, Genoveva. 2000. *Word Order in Hungarian: The Syntax of Ā-positions*. Amsterdam: John Benjamins.

Reinhart, Tanya. 1981. Pragmatics and linguistics: An analysis of sentence topics in pragmatics and philosophy i. *Philosophica anc Studia Philosophica Gandensia Gent* 27. 53–94.

Rizzi, Luigi. 1990. *Relativized minimality*. Cambridge, MA: MIT Press.

Rizzi, Luigi. 1997. The fine structure of the left periphery. In Liliane Haegeman (ed.), *Elements of grammar: A handbook of generative syntax*, 281–337. Dordrecht: Kluwer.

Rizzi, Luigi. 2001. On the position "Int(errogative)" in the left periphery of the clause. *Current studies in Italian syntax* 14. 267–296.

Rizzi, Luigi. 2004. Locality and left periphery. In Adriana Belletti (ed.), *Structures and beyond: The cartography of syntactic structures*, 223–251. New York: Oxford University Press.

Rizzi, Luigi. 2013. Notes on Cartography and further explanation. *Probus* 25.1.

Rizzi, Luigi. 2016. Labeling, maximality, and the head-phrase distinction. *The Linguistic Review*.

Starke, Michal. 2001. *Move dissolves into Merge, a theory of locality*. Université de Genève dissertation.

Chapter 16

Swedish wh-root-infinitives

Christer Platzack

Lund University

The purpose of this short paper is to present a minimalist account of the syntax of the Swedish Wh-Root-infinitives, trying to characterize the syntax of this generally neglected main clause equivalent while comparing its syntax to the syntax of finite root clauses. See (i) and (ii):

(i) Swedish
Varför sälj-a   huset?
why   sell-INF house.the
'Why sell the house?'

(ii) Swedish
Varför sälj-er   ni   huset?
why   sell-PRES you house.the
'Why do you sell the house?'

My account is based on the hypothesis that C minimally probes the sentence type features finite, imperative or infinitive, present in the inflection of the verb. More precisely, I will show that the Swedish facts, like corresponding facts in English, German and Icelandic, follow from a grammar driven by an asymmetry with respect to feature values (see Chomsky 2007: 6 and subsequent papers), and that all unvalued features must be eliminated before syntax can zip together form and meaning.

1 Root infinitives

In the Germanic languages, the overwhelming majority of independent sentences are finite, with a verb inflected at least for tense. Occasionally, however, we find independent sentences with an infinitival verb, as in the English examples in (1). These are usually introduced by *why* or *how*:

Christer Platzack. 2017. Swedish wh-root-infinitives. In Laura R. Bailey & Michelle Sheehan (eds.), *Order and structure in syntax I: Word order and syntactic structure*, 345–361. Berlin: Language Science Press. DOI 10.5281/zenodo.1117712

(1) English (Huddleston & Pullum 2003: 874)

    a. Why be so soft with them?

    b. Why not accept his offer?

    c. How to persuade her to forgive him?

In this paper I will discuss the syntax of Swedish independent infinitive sentences or Root-infinitives, introduced by a wh-word (Wh-RIs). This is a minor and mainly neglected sentence type, classified by *The Swedish Academy Grammar* (Teleman et al. 1999: IV: 826–827) as a kind of main clause equivalent. Some Swedish examples are presented in (2); as in English, Swedish mainly prefers root infinitives introduced by a wh-adverb *varför* 'why' or *hur* 'how':

(2) Swedish (# indicates that the example is not fully productive)

    a. #Vad göra?
       what do.INF

       'What to do?'

    b. #Vart vända sig?
       where turn.INF REFL

       'Where to turn?'

    c. Varför inte gå på bio?
       why not go.INF to movie

       'Why don't you go to the movie?'

    d. Varför sälja huset?
       why sell.INF house.the

       'Why sell the house?'

    e. Hur få personalen att förstå?
       how get.INF staff.the to understand

       'How to get the staff to understand?' (Teleman et al. 1999: IV: 826–828)

German accepts both wh-arguments and wh-adverbs (including *warum* 'why'), as shown by the examples in (3), mainly from Reis (2003).

(3) German

    a. Was tun?
       what do.INF

       'What to do?' Reis (2003), example (37a)

    b. Wohin sich wenden?
       where.to REFL turn

       'Where to turn?' Reis (2003), example (37b)

   c. Warum nicht ins   Kino   gehen?
       why   not to.the movies go.INF

       'Why not go to the movies?' Reis (2003), example (38b)

   d. Warum das Haus verkaufen?
       why   the house sell.INF

       'Why did you sell your house?'

Icelandic, finally, according to Halldór Sigurðsson p.c., seems to accept only Wh-RIs with *hvers vegna* 'why', preferably together with the infinitival marker *að*, see (4c,d).

(4)   Icelandic

   a. *Hvað (að) gera?
       what to   do.INF

       'What to do?' (Halldór Sigurðsson p.c.)

   b. *Hvert (að) snúa   sér?
       where to   turn.INF REFL

       'Where to turn?' (Halldór Sigurðsson p.c.)

   c. Hvers vegna ekki (að) fara   í bíó?
       why   not to go.INF to movie

       'Why don't go to the movie?' (Halldór Sigurðsson p.c.)

   d. ?Hvers vegna (að) selja   húsið?
       why   to   sell.INF house.the

       'Why sell the house? (Halldór Sigurðsson p.c.)

None of the other languages investigated seem to accept an infinitive Complementizer (English *to*, German *zu*, Swedish *att*) in Wh-RIs. Swedish and German (see Reis 2003: 156 for German) never use the infinitival marker in Wh-RIs. English, according to Huddleston & Pullum (2003: 875), has two types of Wh-RIs, one without infinitival *to* (5c,d), and one with infinitival *to* that accepts more options, as shown in (5a,b):

(5)   English

   a. *Where go? Where to go?

   b. *What do next? What to do next?

   c. Why be so soft with them?

   d. Why not accept his offer?

In short, of the four Germanic languages discussed above, German seems to be less restricted with respect to which Wh-RIs that are possible (both argumental and adverbial wh-words, e.g.). Swedish, Icelandic and English mainly allow Wh-RIs introduced by *why* (English) and its Swedish and Icelandic counterparts *varför* and *hvers vegna*. English Wh-RIs with *to* also accept other adverbial wh-words.

In this paper I will take a closer look at Swedish Wh-RIs, claming that Wh-RIs belong to an independent infinitival sentence type and arguing for an analysis that expands Reis' account of German Wh-RIs (2003). Reis' analysis is in its turn inspired by Platzack & Rosengren's (1997) account of the imperative sentence type, launched within the Minimalist program (Chomsky 1995 and subsequent work).

The paper is organized in the following way. §2 gives a brief introduction to those parts of the Minimalist program that are vital for understanding my account, and §3 outlines the analysis of the ordinary finite sentence type. §4 presents the non-finite sentence type Wh-RIs and comppares its syntax with the syntax of finite sentences. A short conclusion and discussion follows in §5.

2 A short presentation of the theoretical framework

In this section I will present some central assumptions of the feature-driven version of the minimalist program that I use for my analysis of Wh-RIs in Swedish. In general, I will stay close to Chomsky (2007; 2008) and Pesetsky & Torrego (2001; 2004; 2007). The assumption that there are three types of independent sentence types, finite, infinite and imperative, corresponding to the same three types of basic verbal inflection, is outlined in more detail in Platzack & Rosengren (2017).

2.1 Morphology Lexicon and Features

Following a recent discussion in Cecchetto & Donati (2015) I have chosen a version of the minimalist program where words are created in an autonomous morphological module. Hence a word can be seen as an atomic element from the point of view of syntax. Each word is, according to Chomsky (2007: 6), "a structured array of properties (*features*) to which Merge and other operations apply to form expressions."

Features enter the syntactic computation either as valued or unvalued; the purpose of the computation is to build structure so that all unvalued features become valued.

2.2 Merge, EPP and the operation Agree

The central player of the Minimalist syntactic derivation is the operation Merge that builds structure. Merge operates on (bundles of) features (valued or unvalued) that provide the building material for syntactic structure. Merge takes a feature bundle and adds it to another feature bundle, creating a minimal structure, see (6):

(6) Pick the feature bundle A and merge it to an available feature bundle B:

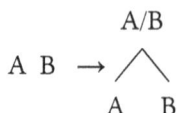

$$
\text{A B} \rightarrow \underset{\text{A} \quad \text{B}}{\overset{\text{A/B}}{\bigwedge}}
$$

The result of merging A and B is labeled either A or B. Merge can now take a new feature bundle X from the lexicon and merge it to the root of the structure, illustrated in (7), or it may take the feature bundle B, already present in the derivation, and remerge it to the root of the structure, yielding (8); this operation is also called "Move":

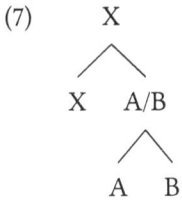

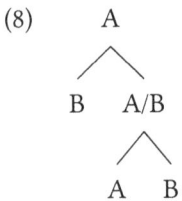

(7)   X
       / \
      X   A/B
         / \
        A   B

(8)   A
       / \
      B   A/B
         / \
        A   B

The operation Agree, see Chomsky (2001: 31ff.) and below, establishes a connection between an unvalued and a valued instance of a feature, valuing the unvalued one, see (9). The derivation will crash if there is any unvalued feature left at the semantic interface.

(9)   *The operation Agree*

   Step 1:   Select a **probe** i.e. a head with at least one unvalued feature [¬F], where [F] is a variable over features.

   Step 2:   Search the c-command domain of the probe for the closest **goal** with a valued instance of the same feature, [F].

   Step 3:   Value the unvalued feature of the probe in accordance with the value of the goal.

Agree may be accompanied by movement of the bearer of the valued feature to the bearer of the unvalued feature. This operation presupposes the presence of what I here call "EPP" which is associated with an unvalued feature, [¬F^{EPP}], saying that the agree-relation must be visible.

2.3 The Morpho-Syntactic interface

Following Cecchetto & Donati (2015: 14), I assume that "[a] word which is delivered by morphology to syntax, is intrinsically endowned with a category feature". For verbs, I assume the verbal feature [v], for nouns the nominal feature [n] and for adjectives the adjectival feature [a]. In addition to the categorial feature, morphology also provides inflectional features. With Platzack & Rosengren (2017), I assume three kinds of inflectional features in Germanic verbs, listed in (10) and exemplified in (11) with Swedish independent main clauses:

(10) a. **The finite inflection**, introducing the feature [fin] and expressed by the tense suffix in Swedish.

   b. **The imperative inflection**, introducing the feature [imp] and expressed by the verbal stem in Swedish.

   c. **The infinitival inflection**, introducing the feature [inf] and expressed by the infinitive suffix -*a* in Swedish.

(11) Swedish

   a. Johan läs-te   en roman.
       Johan read-TNS a   novel

       'Johan read a novel.'

   b. Läs en roman!
       read a   novel

       'Read a novel!'

   c. Varför läs-a   en roman!?
       why   read-INF a   novel

       'Why read a novel!?'

Simplifying, the first step in the derivation of a sentence like Swedish (11a) or its German counterpart, *Johann las einen Roman*, is to pick the verb *läste* / *las* 'read.PAST' from the lexicon and merge it with a DP *en roman* / *ein Roman* 'a novel' bearing an internal theta-role in relation to the verb. The Swedish case is outlined in (12) and the German one in (13), the main difference being that the Swedish vP structure is VO, the German one OV.

(12) Swedish
      [_{vP} Johan [läste en roman]]

(12) Swedish
      [vP Johan [läste en roman]]

(13) German
      [vP Johan [ein Roman] las]

Like all DPs, both the external argument *Johan* in Spec,vP and the object *en roman* / *ein Roman* in the complement of v carry a valued φ-feature. In addition, v carries a valued [fin] feature. The different order between v and DP in Swedish and German is mandatory to capture the syntactic differences between VO languages and OV languages, see Haider (2010: 5–43) for a detailed presentation. Among other things, this difference plays a role in accounting for the fact that Swedish but not German displays subject–object asymmetries, see Haider (2010: 79ff). Since the VO/OV distinction is not in focus here, I will mainly give structures where the head governs to the right, as in English, Icelandic and Swedish.

3 The derivation of the Swedish finite sentence type

In this section, I will illustrate the functional parts TP (called Finite Phrase in Rizzi 1997) and CP (called Force Phrase in Rizzi 1997).

In the absence of sentence adverbs and auxiliaries, which are supposed to be adjoined to vP, the next step after vP is assembled is to pick T from the lexicon and merge it to vP. The result is depicted in (14), assuming T to carry both unvalued phi-features and an unvalued fin-feature:

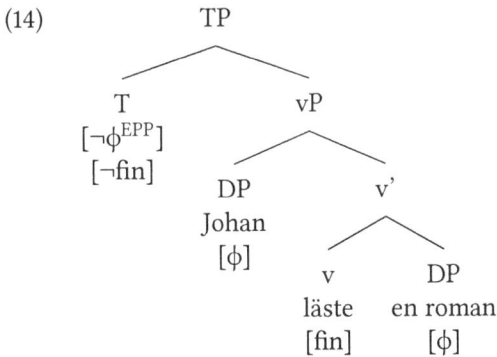

(14)

```
                     TP
              ┌───────────────┐
              T               vP
         [¬φ^EPP]        ┌──────────┐
          [¬fin]        DP          v'
                       Johan    ┌───────┐
                        [φ]     v       DP
                              läste  en roman
                              [fin]    [φ]
```

In Swedish, as in the Germanic languages in general, the subject is visible in Spec,TP, indicating the presence of an EPP feature. The presence of a visible subject is accounted for by postulating that EPP is attached to the unvalued $[\varphi]$-features in T, hence the proper formulation of this feature will be $[\neg\varphi^{EPP}]$. This forces the closest c-commanded DP, i.e. *Johan*, to move to Spec,TP.

The derivation of TP as illustrated in (14) is not complete. T contains an unvalued finiteness feature that must be valued. Acting as a probe, T with feature [¬fin] will establish an Agree relation with [fin] in little v and thereby the finite feature in T is valued. There is no reason to assume that the verb moves from v to T in Swedish; if so, we would, contrary to facts, have expected the finite verb to appear in front of the negation in an embedded clause, taking for granted that the negation is adjoined to vP and thus to the right of a verb that has moved to T.

The highest phase in the derivation of a sentence is the C-projection with an unvalued finiteness feature in C, which is valued by merging C to TP. In most Germanic languages the tensed verb is moved to C, due to EPP associated with [¬fin] in C. Among other things, this gives rise to verb second. Spec,CP may be filled by the subject or object, by an adverb phrase, prepositional phrase and various other elements. Since the main part of this paper discusses the adverb *varför* 'why' I will here show how a finite clause introduced by *varför* is derived. Being a wh-adverb, *varför* must move to Spec,CP. See Shlonsky & Soare (2011) for a partly different account.

I will assume that a TP containing *varför* 'why' merges with C that carries the features [¬fin] and [¬wh], both with EPP. This will force the closest wh-phrase to move to Spec. CP

This is illustrated with the Swedish sentence in (15) where both the unvalued features in C are marked EPP. The structure when C has merged is given in (16):

(15)   Swedish
       Varför läs-te   Johan en roman?
       why   read-PAST Johan a   novel
       'Why did Johan read a novel?'

(16)

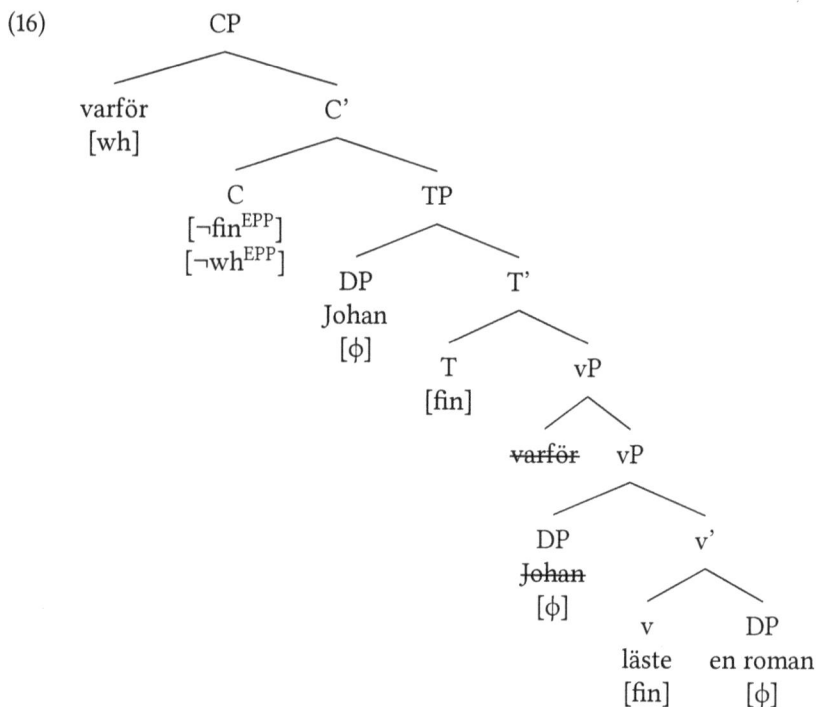

Let us start with the unvalued finiteness feature in C. When Agree is applied, C will probe its c-command domain for a goal with valued finiteness feature, which it finds in T. Due to EPP, the finiteness feature [fin] will be pronounced in C, a prerequisite for verb second.

As seen in (16), C hosts a second unvalued feature with EPP, viz. [¬wh^{EPP}]. This feature probes wh-words, *varför* 'why', in our example. In line with Shlonsky & Soare (2011: 667), *why* (and, I assume, Swedish *varför*) is first merged in Spec,ReasonP, here simplified as a high adjunction to vP. In particular, ReasonP is assumed to be to the left of the negation, which is adjoined to (a low) vP.

Starting from the structure in (16), I will in the next section compare the syntactic properties of the independent Swedish Wh-RIs with the properties of the independent Swedish finite sentence.

4 The syntax of the independent Swedish wh-root-infinitive

4.1 Structural analysis

In this section I will present an analysis of the independent Swedish root infinitive introduced by a wh-phrase, arguing for a structure that differs from the finite structure (cf. (16)) mainly in lacking a T-projection between C and v. This idea, which is taken from Reis (2003), is compatible with the fact that the infinitive verb is not inflected for tense and lacks a (visible) subject. See also Platzack & Rosengren (2017).

In short, I will assume that there is no TP in root infinitives. The Wh-RI in (17) will thus get the structure in (18) when all unvalued features are valued.

(17) Swedish
Varför läs-a   bok-en?
why   read-INF book-the

'Why read the book?'

(18)

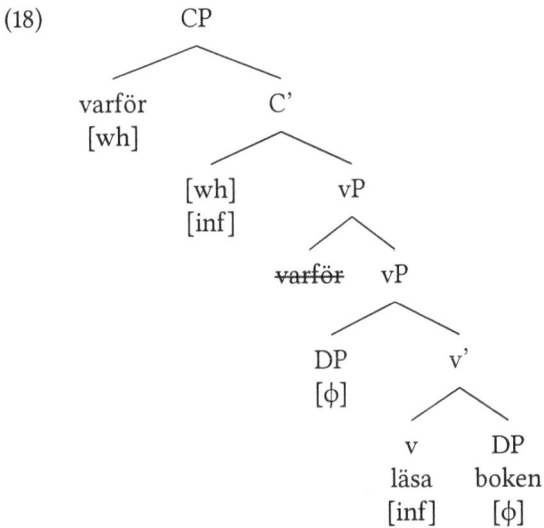

As will be shown below, the analysis proposed accounts for the main syntactic differences between Wh-RIs and the finite sentence type. §4.2 compares the finite and infinitival sentences with respect to word order, section 4.3 points out similarities and differences with respect to the external argument in Spec.vP, and section 4.4 briefly discusses A-bar movement of *varför* 'why' in the two sentence types. I will argue that the syntactic similarities and differences between Wh-RIs and Wh-finite clauses follow from the structural differences and similarities of (16) and (18).

4.2 Word order

As seen above, both the finite sentence and the root infinitive may be introduced by a wh-phrase with an adverbial function:

(19) Swedish

    a. Varför stäng-er Lisa dörr-en?
        why   shut-PRES Lisa door-the

        'Why does Lisa shut the door?'

    b. Varför stäng-a dörren?
        why   shut-INF door-the

        'Why shut the door?'

Only finite sentences may be productively introduced by an argumental wh-phrase:

(20) Swedish

    a. Vem välj-er   vi denna gång?
        who vote-PRES we this   time

        'Who do we vote for this time?'

    b. #Vem välj-a   denna gång?
        who vote-INF this   time

        'Who vote for this time?' (Teleman et al. 1999: IV: 827)

The finite verb precedes sentence adverbs and the negation, the infinitival verb follows sentence adverbs and the negation:

(21) Swedish

    a. Varför stäng-er Lisa inte dörr-en?
        why   shut-PRES Lisa not door-the

        'Why doesn't Lisa shut the door?'

    b. *Varför stäng-a inte dörr-en?
        why   shut-INF not door-the

        'Why not shut the door?'

    c. Varför inte stänga   dörr-en?
        why   not shut-INF door-the

        'Why not shut the door?'

The differences and similarities listed in (19–21) are all related to the C-domain. Comparing with the analysis of the finite main clause in section 3, the presence of a wh-phrase in first position, more precisely in Spec,CP, is accounted for by the presence of an unvalued wh-feature in C, $[\neg wh^{EPP}]$, which forces a wh-phrase to take first position. Since also the wh-infinitive begins with a wh-phrase, the feature $[\neg wh^{EPP}]$ is supposed to be present in the infinitival C as well as in the finite C. The specific mechanism that in the absence of a wh-word allows almost any phrase to be fronted in Swedish finite main clauses (verb second) is not present in Swedish root infinitives, however.

In Wh-RIs, as we see in (20b), the choice of initial wh-phrase is restricted in wh-infinitives but not in finite main clauses. Descriptively, we can account for this restriction if we limit the range of the feature wh in C in wh-infinitives to be only sentence adverbials, roughly adverbials being first merged as a high adjunct to vP. This is more or less the area that Cinque (1999) claims consists of functional projections hierarchically ordered in the same way in all of the world's languages. I will use the notation wh_{vP} to remind the reader of this limitation, claiming that C in wh-infinitives is merged with the feature bundle $[\neg wh_{vP}{}^{EPP}]$ and that the agree-relation that is established, see (9), will probe the closest goal in vP, supposed to be *varför* 'why'.

Whereas the wh-feature in C has an EPP feature both in finite main clauses and in wh-infinitives, there is a difference with respect to the other features in C. In §3 we concluded that the C of the tensed main clause in Swedish hosts an unvalued finiteness feature with EPP, $[\neg fin^{EPP}]$, forcing V2. There is no finiteness feature associated with wh-infinitives, but an infinitival feature is associated with the infinitive inflection in little v, see (21c).

As (21b,c) indicate, the infinitival verb does not seem to move away from little v, as the finite verb does, hence there is no indication of an EPP feature associated with the infinitival feature. In other respects the two inflectional features [fin] and [inf] are syntactically used in the same way: they are, for example both merged in v as valued, and in C as unvalued. The unvalued versions of the feature for the two cases are summarized in (22):

(22)   a. C in the finite sentence type contains the unvalued feature $[\neg fin^{EPP}]$

        b. C in the infinitive sentence type contains the unvalued feature $[\neg inf]]$

Both finite and infinite C will probe its c-command domain, valuing the feature in C. Like the finite sentence type, we conclude that the Wh.-RIs contain both CP and vP. The main difference is the absence of a T-projection between C and v.

4.3 The external argument

The external argument, less precisely the subject argument, is visible in Swedish finite sentences, but not in infinitive sentences.

(23)   Swedish

        a. Varför stäng-er   han fönstr-et?
             why   shut-PRES he window-the

           'Why does he shut the window?'

        b. Varför stäng-a (*han) fönstr-et?
             why   shut-INF he   window-the

           'Why shut the window?'

In the finite sentence type introduced by *varför* 'why', the subject appears in Spec,TP, after the finite verb in C. See the analysis in (16). The subject is visible in this position, due to EPP associated with the Agree relation between the unvalued [φ]-feature in T and the valued [φ]-feature in Spec,vP. The absence of a visible DP in the infinitive case indicates that there is no TP present to establish an agree relation between T and the external argument in this sentence type, as I argued above.

An alternative possibility would be to assume that no DP is merged to vP, but there is indirect evidence against such an analysis and in favour of the analysis which assumes the presence of an invisible DP in Spec,vP of the infinitive sentence, with the same theta-role as the visible subject in the finite sentence. As the examples in (24) and (25) show, the invisible DP in (24), like the visible counterpart in (25), may bind an anaphoric pronoun, or the possessive reflexive *sin*, and it agrees with a predicative adjective:

(24)   Swedish infinitive clauses

      a. Varför gömm-a sig   under säng-en?
          why   hide-INF REFL under bed-the

          'Why hide under the bed?'

      b. Varför gömm-a sin   bok   under sängen?
          why   hide-INF REFL book under bed-the

          'Why hide his book under the bed?'

      c. Varför komm-a full-ø   / full-a   till fest-en?
          why   come-INF drunk-SG / drunk-PL to party-the

          'Why come drunk to the party?'

(25)   Swedish finite clauses

      a. Varför gömm-er han sig   under säng-en?
          why   hide-PRES he REFL under bed-the

          'Why does he hide under the bed?'

      b. Varför gömm-er han sin   bok unde säng-en?
          why   hide-PRES he POSS.REFL book under bed-the

          'Why hide his book under the bed?'

      c. Varför komm-er han full-ø   / de   full-a   till fest-en?
          why   come-PRES he drunk-SG / they drunk-PL to party-the

          'Why does he / they come drunk to the party?'

Hence the binding and predicative agreement facts support the analysis that there is an invisible DP in Spec.vP.

From a syntactic point of view there seems to be no reason to expect anything else than a symmetrical distribution of *varför* in both finite and infinitival clauses. Thus, if we find a well-formed infinitive sentence introduced by *varför* 'why', we predict the existence of a corresponding finite sentence introduced by *varför* 'why', and vice versa.

So far, none of the Swedish examples given seems to violate this prediction; here I give another two examples of the same kind.

(26) Swedish

    a. Varför frukta-r   hon hundar?
       why   fear-PRES she dogs

       'Why does she fear dogs?'

    b. Varför frukt-a hundar?
       why   fear-INF dogs

       'Why fear dogs?'

(27) Swedish

    a. Varför sprang   Erik till affär-en?
       why   run.PAST Erik to shop-the

       'Why did Erik run to the shop?'

    b. Varför spring-a till affär-en?!
       why   run-INF to shop-the

       'Why run to the shop?'

So far, the prediction seems to hold. However, notice that the invisible subject cannot be some arbitrary 3rd person feminine in (26) or invisible *Erik* in (27), but must represent the person spoken to (an invisible *you*). Thus, there is an interpretative difference between the finite and the infinitival sentence types. As can be seen, this interpretative difference also shows up in cases like (28) and (29), where the "spoken-to" interpretation of the invisible DP in Spec.vP is not available, and hence there is no infinitival correspondence:

(28) Swedish

    a. Varför dog   han efter operation-en?
       why   die.PAST he after operation-the

       'Why did he die after the operation?'

    b. *Varför dö   efter operation-en!?
       why   die.INF after operation-the

(29) a. Varför sjönk   fartyg-et snabbt?
       why   sink.PAST ship-the fast

       'Why did the ship sink fast?'

    b. *Varför sjunk-a snabbt?!
       why   sink-INF fast

To understand why there is no well-formed infinitival correspondent to the well formed finite sentences in the a-examples in (28) and (29), and why there is an interpretation restriction in (26) and (27), I will turn to an observation by Reis (2003: 186). Reis notices with respect to the subject of Wh-RIs, that "[n]o matter how we represent the silent subject argument in RIs in syntax, whether by PRO or nothing (that is, by just suppressing the respective argument variable), one thing is clear: In order for RIs to receive a sensible utterance interpretation, the subject reference must be specified." As Reis (2003: 186) notices "[t]he possible candidates [---] are limited to the participants in the utterance situation: speaker(s) and addressees." A closer look at the ungrammatical b-examples in (28–29), reveals that in these cases, the subject reference cannot be a participant in the utterance situation, whereas in all the well formed cases it can.

4.4 A-bar movement of *varför* 'why'

As we saw in the last section, Wh.-RIs do not seem to allow A-movement, whereas finite sentences do. A-bar movement, on the other hand, is found in both sentence types, in the infinitive one only in form of Wh-movement. Consider the finite sentence in (30).

(30) Swedish
    Varför sa   du att Johan skrev   brev-et?
    why   say.PAST you that Johan write.PAST letter-the
    'Why did you say that Johan wrote the letter?'

    This sentence is ambiguous: the speaker is either asking why the subject of the main clause said something (the matrix reading), or why the subject of the embedded clause wrote the letter (the embedded reading). See Shlonsky & Soare (2011) and Simik (2006). Since the wh-word is in the same position in both cases, we must assume that *varför* has moved from its position in the embedded clause to the edge of the matrix clause (Spec,CP), supporting the analysis in §3 above. Notice that *varför* in this case is first merged in a finite domain and has moved to a position within a finite domain (Spec,CP of the matrix).

    The corresponding Wh-RI is (31):

(31) Varför säga   att Johan skrev brev-et?!
    why   say.INF that Johan wrote letter-the
    'Why say that Johan wrote the letter?!'

    Contrary to the finite clause in (30), example (31) only displays the matrix reading; hence in both the finite sentence matrix and the infinitival one, one option is that *varför* is merged to matrix vP and moved to matrix Spec,CP of the infinitive sentence. With regard to the embedded reading, *varför* is first merged to a high Spec,vP inside a finite domain, i.e. the embedded *att*-clause. Obviously, movement out of this domain to a position in the matrix infinitive domain is not allowed. In the sentence with an infinitive matrix, *varför*, when extracted, must move out of a finite domain and into an infinitive domain, which presumably is not allowed. There is no corresponding switch of domains in finite sentences like (30), hence extraction of *varför* from an embedded clause to the matrix one is only possible in finite sentences.

5 Summary and conclusion

As mentioned in the introduction, the purpose of my paper has been to present a narrow syntactic account of the Swedish Wh-Root-infinitives, trying to characterize this often neglected main clause equivalent while comparing it with finite root clauses. My account is based on the hypotheses that C minimally hosts the sentence type features finite, imperative and infinitive, in addition to an edge feature (Chomsky 2007: 11 f). More precisely, I have tried to show that the Swedish facts follow nicely from a grammar driven by an asymmetry with respect to features, which come in two guises, valued and unvalued, and that all unvalued features must be eliminated before the semantic and pragmatic interfaces are reached.

Working mainly with one language might be seen as a drawback: after all, our understanding of syntax has improved tremendously over the last 30 years, much as a result of us having a theory that may take variation (especially on a macro-level) into account. However, it may also be a problem for our field of research that we are always ready to take other languages into consideration before we are confident that the machinery we have at our disposal can handle at least one human language. Thirty years of studying macro-variation have taught us that the beautiful generalizations we found initially (the parameters), see e.g. Holmberg & Platzack (1995), usually fade away under a closer study. And we should not forget that each natural language is a possible outcome of Universal Grammar. Therefore, what I have presented in this paper can be seen as the basis for comparative syntactic studies. The outcome of a detailed study of a certain part of a single language will result in lists of properties, which, when used in the computation, predicts particular properties of the language studied. Any change that we are forced to make with respect to the theoretical apparatus that is motivated by a careful description of a single language when we are describing another language from the same perspective must be evaluated both with respect to the basic account of the data and possible accounts we have of other languages.

Acknowledgements

Thanks to two anonymous referees for a number of helpful and ingenious comments, only a handful of which it has been possible for me to take into consideration. I am also grateful to the editors Laura Bailey and Michelle Sheehan for additional help. A special thank you to professor emerita Inger Rosengren; without her enthusiasm and encouragement, I would never have thought about Wh-RIs in the first place. Thanks also to Halldór Sigurðsson for providing me with some Icelandic facts. I take full responsibility for all remaining faults and shortcomings.

References

Cecchetto, Carlo & Caterina Donati. 2015. *(re)labeling*. Cambridge, MA & London, England: The MIT Press.

Chomsky, Noam. 1995. *The minimalist program*. Cambridge: MIT Press.

Chomsky, Noam. 2001. Derivation by phase. In Michael Kenstowicz (ed.), *Ken Hale: A life in language*, 1–52. Cambridge: MIT Press.

Chomsky, Noam. 2007. Approaching UG from below. In Uli Sauerland & Hans-Martin Gärtner (eds.), *Interfaces + recursion = language?: Chomsky's minimalism and the view from Syntax-Semantics*, 1–29. Berlin: Mouton de Gruyter.

Chomsky, Noam. 2008. On phases. In Robert Freidin, Carlos P. Otero & Maria Luisa Zubizarreta (eds.), *Foundational issues in linguistic theory: Essays in honor of Jean-Roger vergnaud*, 133–166. Cambridge, MA, London: MIT.

Cinque, Guglielmo. 1999. *Adverbs and functional heads: A cross-linguistic perspective*. Oxford: Oxford University Press.

Haider, Hubert. 2010. *The syntax of German*. Cambridge: Cambridge University Press.

Holmberg, Anders & Christer Platzack. 1995. *The role of inflection in Scandinavian syntax*. Oxford: Oxford University Press.

Huddleston, Rodney & Geoffrey K. Pullum. 2003. *The Cambridge grammar of the English language*. Cambridge: Cambridge University Press.

Pesetsky, David & Esther Torrego. 2001. Tense-to-C Movement. Causes and Consequences. In Michael Kenstowicz (ed.), *Ken Hale: A life in linguistics*, 355–426. Cambridge, MA: The MIT Press.

Pesetsky, David & Esther Torrego. 2004. Tense, case, and the nature of syntactic categories. In Jacqueline Guéron & Jacqueline Lecarme (eds.), *The syntax of time*, 495–537. Cambridge, MA: The MIT Press.

Pesetsky, David & Esther Torrego. 2007. The syntax of valuation and the interpretability of features. In Simin Karimi, Vida Samiian & Wendy K. Wilkins (eds.), *Phrasal and clausal architecture: Syntactic derivation and interpretation*, 262–294. Amsterdam: John Benjamins.

Platzack, Christer & Inger Rosengren. 1997. On the subject of imperatives: A minimalist account of the imperative clause. *Journal of Comparative Germanic Linguistics* 1. 177–224.

Platzack, Christer & Inger Rosengren. 2017. What makes the imperative clause type autonomous? A comparative study in a modular perspective. *Working Papers in Scandinavian Syntax* 98. 1–82.

Reis, Marga. 2003. On the form and interpretation of German *Wh*-infinitives. *Journal of Germanic Linguistics* 15. 155–201.

Rizzi, Luigi. 1997. The fine structure of the left periphery. In Liliane Haegeman (ed.), *Elements of grammar: A handbook of generative syntax*, 281–337. Dordrecht: Kluwer.

Shlonsky, Ur & Gabriella Soare. 2011. Where's 'why'? *Linguistic Inquiry* 42. 651–669.

Simik, Radek. 2006. Why the hell what? A remark on the syntax and semantics of 'why' and 'what' in Czech. Paper presented at Syntaktisches Kolloquium in Leipzig 01/12/2006.

Teleman, Ulf, Erik Andersson & Staffan Hellberg. 1999. *Svenska akademiens grammatik.* Stockholm: Norstedts.

Chapter 17

A note on some even more unusual relative clauses

Richard S. Kayne

New York University

> Relative clauses can be found that contain a relative pronoun whose antecedent is not the head of the relative. The familiar relation between the head of a relative and the relative pronoun can thus be seen as a special case of a more general relation between a relative pronoun (a stranded determiner) and its antecedent (whose movement has stranded that determiner). The piece of relative clause syntax that is the antecedent-relative pronoun relation is less specific to relative clauses that it might have seemed.

1 Some general points on relative clauses

In the spirit of Chomsky (1970) on 'passive', the notion 'relative clause' is unlikely to be a primitive of the language faculty. This was explicitly recognized in Chomsky (1977), to the extent that the wh-movement operation that plays a role in the derivation of relative clauses also plays a role elsewhere (e.g in interrogatives). Rizzi (1997) might be interpreted as backtracking from this position insofar as the landing site for wh-movement in relatives is different (Spec,ForceP) from the landing site in interrogatives (Spec,FocP/IntP).

The difference in landing site, though, could be factored out from the common movement operation, and taken instead as something to be explained. The following proposal is based on the fact that the wh-phrase in headed relatives is in a relation to the 'head' of the relative in a way that has no exact counterpart in interrogatives, which lack a comparable 'head':

(1) Wh-movement in relatives cannot (normally) land below ForceP (or TopP[1]) because of locality requirements holding between the 'head' of the relative and the wh-phrase.

---

[1]Cf. Cinque (1982) on links with topicalization.

Richard S. Kayne. 2017. A note on some even more unusual relative clauses. In Laura R. Bailey & Michelle Sheehan (eds.), *Order and structure in syntax I: Word order and syntactic structure*, 363–371. Berlin: Language Science Press. DOI:10.5281/zenodo.1117708

The informal formulation in (1) abstracts away from the question of the correctness of the raising analysis of relatives.[2] In what follows, I will assume the raising approach (perhaps not crucially).

In addition to wh-movement, a second, related aspect of relative clauses that is not specific to them is the very presence of overt wh-words. A proposal expressing this non-specificity would be (cf. Postma 1994):

(2)　a.　The *which* of English (headed) relatives is identical to the *which* of English interrogatives (and to the *which* of *every which way*).

　　　b.　The *where* of English relatives is identical to the *where* of English interrogatives, as well as to the *where* of *somewhere, nowhere, anywhere, everywhere, elsewhere.*

　　　c.　and similarly for other wh-words in whatever language.

Needless to say, the surrounding syntactic environment must be at least partially different in relatives, interrogatives and indefinites.[3]

Note that (2) does not state that the sets of wh-words occurring in relatives and interrogatives and indefinites have to match perfectly. In English *where* occurs in all three, but *who* occurs only in relatives and interrogatives. In Italian *quale* ('which') occurs in both relatives and interrogatives, but *cui* ('who/what')[4] occurs only in relatives and *chi* ('who') occurs only in interrogatives (and free relatives).

This point about wh-words not being specific to relative clauses carries over to those relative pronouns that are clearly related to demonstratives (such as German relative *d*-words). If Kayne (2010a) is correct, this point also holds for English *that*, which occurs both as a relative pronoun and as an ordinary demonstrative.

The proposal in (2) can be understood as a particular case of a more general approach that is also illustrated by English numerals.[5] Consider:

(3)　They have seven children.

(4)　Their youngest child has just turned seven.

---

[2]See Brame 1976: 125, Schachter 1973; Vergnaud 1974; 1985; Kayne 1994: chap. 9; Bianchi 1999; and Kato & Nunes 2009. Headless relatives may be hidden instances of (adjunct) interrogatives, thinking of the similarity between:

(i)　We'll buy whatever you suggest.

and

(ii)　No matter what you suggest, we'll buy it.

For a suggestion along such lines, see Lin (1996).

[3]It is not essential to this discussion whether *everywhere* is a true indefinite – Beghelli & Stowell (1997).

[4]Italian *cui* is arguably an oblique form of *che*, i.e. *ch-+-ui*, with oblique (possibly bimorphemic - cf. Martín (2012)) *-ui* lacking in Spanish (and similarly for Italian *lui, altrui*). (Note that non-oblique *che* does occur in interrogatives in Italian.)

[5]Cf. Kayne (2016) on English *there* and more generally on anti-homophony.

(5) It'll be exactly seven in a couple of minutes.

Example (3) shows an ordinary instance of the numeral *seven*. In (4) and (5), a bare *seven* appears to be interpreted as an age and as a time of day, respectively. Kayne (2003) argued that cases like (4) and (5) are best analyzed in terms of the presence of silent nouns, with (4) containing (at least) the noun YEAR (capitalization indicates silence) and (5) containing (at least) HOUR.[6]

2 Unusual relative clauses (with more than one relative pronoun)

Like interrogatives, relatives can sometimes to some extent contain more than one wh-word:

(6) (?)Mary Smith, whose husband's love for whom knows no bounds, is a famous linguist.

(7) ?The only woman whose husband's love for whom knows no bounds is Mary Smith.

In (6) and (7), both of the wh-words/relative pronouns are related to the head of the relative. It may be that *whose husband's love for whom* in (6) and (7) has been pied-piped by the initial *who(se)*, rather than by *whom*. This *whom* appears in any case to be 'in situ' within the larger wh-phrase. Yet there is evidence that this *whom* is involved in a movement relation, perhaps of the parasitic gap sort.[7] This is suggested by the existence of ECP-like effects, as in:[8]

(8) ?Mary Smith, whose husband's desire for me to paint a picture of whom is perfectly understandable, is a very famous linguist.

(9) *Mary Smith, whose husband's desire for whom to paint a picture of me is perfectly understandable, is a very famous linguist.

---

[6]This approach, in which interpretations are constrained by the availability of silent elements, looks likely to be more restrictive that the allosemy-based approach of Marantz (2010) and Wood & Marantz (2017). This will be especially clear if the language faculty disallows elements that would be consistently silent in all languages.

[7]For some discussion, see Kayne (1983: 239ff).

[8]On the Empty Category Principle, see Chomsky (1981).

3 Even more unusual relative clauses

There also exist relative clauses containing two relative pronouns such that only one of them is related to the head of the relative.[9] These are for me somewhat more marginal than the preceding, but are still surprisingly close to acceptability (in the English of some speakers). An example is:[10]

(10)　?That car over there belongs to my old friend John Smith, whose long-standing attachment to which is well-known to all his friends.

Here, *who(se)* is related to the head of the relative *my old friend John Smith*, but *which* is not; rather, *which* is related to the subject of the matrix sentence, *that car over there*.

As in (8)-(9), sentences like (10) show ECP-like effects. These can be detected by comparing the following two examples. The first is:

(11)　??That car over there belongs to my old friend John Smith, whose long-standing desire for me to buy which is well-known to all his friends.

Although more marginal than (10), (11) nonetheless contrasts sharply with:

(12)　*That car over there belongs to my old friend John Smith, whose long-standing desire for which to be sold quickly is well-known to all his friends.

Replacing the embedded infinitive following *desire* with a finite sentence results in an appreciable drop in acceptability, but the contrast remains clear:

(13)　???That car over there belongs to my old friend John Smith, whose long-standing desire that I buy which is well-known to all his friends.

(14)　**That car over there belongs to my old friend John Smith, whose long-standing desire that which be sold quickly is well-known to all his friends.

It seems clear that the extra deviance of (12) and (14), as compared with (11) and (13), is akin to the greater difficulty that holds in a general way for extraction of or from within subjects as compared with extraction of or from within objects.

---

[9] There is a point of similarity here with Stowell's (1985) discussion of parasitic gap examples such as:

　(i)　Who did your stories about amuse?

which for some speakers (but not me, in this case) allow an interpretation in which two distinct individuals are at issue.

　It remains to be understood what underlies the variation in speaker judgments, both in the case of (i) and in the case of the unusual relatives discussed in the text.

[10] Another is:

　(i)　?That car over there just ran into my old friend John Smith, whose inability to get a good view of which was a determining factor in the accident.

This kind of relative is more difficult as a restrictive:

　(ii)　???That car over there belongs to the very person whose attachment to which is so well-known.

4 Steps toward an analysis

The raising approach to ordinary relative clauses, when extended to cover relative pronouns, leads one to take what we call relative pronouns to come about as the result of stranding a particular kind of determiner.[11] For example, a head + relative clause structure such as:

(15) books which I've read

will have a derivation that looks like:[12]

(16) I've read which books → wh-movement
      which books I've read <which books> → raising of NP to 'head' position,
      stranding the relative determiner *which*
      books which <books> I've read <which books>

The convenient informal term 'relative pronoun', then, is usually to be understood as short for 'determiner occuring within a relative clause and stranded by movement of its associated NP to the position of the 'head' of the relative'.[13] Let me call the movement operation that strands *which* in the last pair of lines in (16) 'relative pronoun stranding', henceforth abbreviated as RPS.

It seems natural, however, to also take the *which* of (10–14) to be a relative pronoun (in almost exactly the same sense), despite the unusual position of its antecedent. This is supported by the fact that it is also possible to find examples of such unusual relatives in which the unusual relative pronoun is *who(m)*:

(17) ?My old friend Mary Jones is still unaware of yesterday's discovery, the capacity of which to surprise whom cannot be exaggerated.

In (17), *which* is related to the nearby 'head' *yesterday's discovery* in a familiar way, whereas *whom* is related not to that head, but rather to the matrix subject *my old friend Mary Jones*.

To say that the *which* of (10–14) and the *whom* of (17) are relative pronouns is to say, then, that they have been stranded by RPS, despite the fact that the antecedent in question is not the head of the relative. Put another way, in (10–14) and in (17) RPS has moved the NP associated with *which* and *whom* to the position of matrix subject, hence out of the relative clause entirely.

---

[11] Various details are discussed in Kayne (2008a; 2010a).

[12] I abstract away from questions concerning the "outside" determiner, for example *the* in:

    (i) the books which I've read

For relevant discussion, see Leu (2014).

[13] Alongside relative *who* there is no **who person*. Possibly, *who = wh- + -o*, with the latter a noun, thinking of Bernstein (1993) on Spanish *uno*. Alternatively, *who* is a determiner and there is a link to **mine book* (cf. Bernstein & Tortora (2005)) and/or to French *Lequel (*livre) veux-tu?* ('the-which (book) want-you) (cf. Kayne 2008b) and other cases of the same sort.

That RPS can apply out of a relative clause might seem surprising, but the difficulty of extraction out of a relative clause is often exaggerated. For a detailed survey, see Cinque (2010). To his examples of extractions leaving a gap might well be added, thinking back to Ross (1967),[14] examples in which the extraction leaves behind a resumptive pronoun.

For all of (10–14) and (17) the question arises as to what precisely has been moved. RPS may perhaps be moving a full DP in such examples, rather than a NP. Alternatively, RPS may be moving just NP, in a more familiar way, if sideways movement is allowed.[15]

That the *which* of (10–14) and the *whom* of (17) are relative pronouns (and not just pronouns) is also suggested by the following considerations. Sentences like (10–14) and (17) require that *which* or *whom* be pied-piped as part of a phrase containing the other (ordinary) relative pronoun. This is shown by the contrast between (17), for example, and the unacceptable:

(18)   *My old friend Mary Jones is still unaware of yesterday's discovery, which will definitely surprise who(m).

The pied-piping in (17) now recalls the pied-piping of ordinary relative pronouns seen in:

(19)   the book the first chapter of which is being widely discussed.

That the *which* of (10–14) and the *whom* of (17) are not just ordinary pronouns is shown by:

(20)   *My old friend Mary Jones is still unaware of yesterday's discovery, even though it's very likely to surprise who(m).

As a final point to this squib, we can note that the 'head' of the relative cannot be 'skipped' entirely (even if the relative contains a resumptive pronoun linked to it):

(21)   **That car over there belongs to my old friend John Smith, a picture of which shows how tall he is.

This may be due to a requirement that the head of a relative clause must in all cases originate together with some relative pronoun (and that in (21) there is no option for a silent relative pronoun).

5 Conclusion

Relative clauses can be found that contain a relative pronoun whose antecedent is not the head of the relative. The familiar relation between the head of a relative and the

---

[14]Cf. Boeckx (2001; 2003). Kayne (2002) extends this tradition to all pronouns, even those with antecedents in A-positions.

That (resumptive) pronouns may reflect movement is not taken into account by Bošković (2015).
[15]On sideways movement, see Bobaljik & Brown (1997) and Nunes (2001).

relative pronoun can thus be seen as a special (even if overwhelmingly frequent[16]) case of a more general relation between a relative pronoun (a stranded determiner) and its antecedent (whose movement has stranded that determiner). The piece of relative clause syntax that is the antecedent–relative pronoun relation is less specific to relative clauses that it might have seemed.

Acknowledgments

An earlier version of this squib was presented (as part of a longer talk on relative pronouns) in June, 2010 at the Comparative Germanic Syntax Workshop, University of Tromsø and at the Workshop: 'Adjectives and Relative Clauses: Syntax and Semantics', University of Venice; in October 2010 at Rencontres d'Automne en Linguistique Formelle: Langage, Langues et Cognition, University of Paris 8; in May, 2011 at the University of Poitiers, at the Linguistics Institute, Academy of Sciences, Budapest, and at the University of Bucharest; in June, 2011 at the University of Vienna; and in October, 2011 at Leiden University. I am grateful to all those audiences, as well as to two anonymous reviewers of an earlier version of this paper, for useful questions and comments.

References

Beghelli, Filippo & Tim Stowell. 1997. Distributivity and negation: The syntax of *Each* and *Every*. In A. Szabolcsi (ed.), *Ways of scope taking*, 71–107. Dordrecht: Kluwer.

Bernstein, Judy. 1993. The syntactic role of word markers in null nominal constructions. *Probus* 5. 5–38.

Bernstein, Judy & Christina Tortora. 2005. Two types of possessive forms in English. *Lingua* 115. 1221–1242.

Bianchi, Valentina. 1999. *Consequences of antisymmetry. Headed relative clauses* (Studies in Generative Grammar [SGG] 46). Berlin: Mouton de Gruyter.

Bobaljik, Jonathan David & Samuel Brown. 1997. Interarboreal operations: Head movement and the extension requirement. *Linguistic Inquiry* 28. 345–356.

Boeckx, Cedric. 2001. Resumptive Pronouns as Derivational Residues. WCCFL, University of Southern California.

Boeckx, Cedric. 2003. *Islands and chains: Resumption as stranding*. Amsterdam: John Benjamins.

Bošković, Željko. 2015. From the complex NP constraint to everything: On deep extractions across categories. *The Linguistic Review* 32. 603–669.

Brame, Michael K. 1976. *Conjectures and refutations in syntax and semantics*. New York & Amsterdam: North-Holland.

---

[16] In languages that have relative pronouns. For a proposal on why prenominal relatives lack relative pronouns, see Kayne (1994: chap. 9).

Chomsky, Noam. 1970. Remarks on nominalization. In Roderick A. Jacobs & Peter S. Rosenbaum (eds.), *Readings in English Transformational Grammar*, 184–221. Waltham, MA: Ginn.

Chomsky, Noam. 1977. On wh-movement. In Peter Culicover, Thomas Wasow & Adrian Akmajian (eds.), *Formal syntax*, 77–132. New York: Academic Press.

Chomsky, Noam. 1981. *Lectures on government and binding*. Dordrecht: Foris.

Cinque, Guglielmo. 1982. On the theory of relative clauses and markedness. *The Linguistic Review* 1. 247–294.

Cinque, Guglielmo. 2010. On a selective "violation" of the Complex NP Constraint. In Jan-Wouter Zwart & Mark de Vries (eds.), *Structure preserved studies in syntax for Jan Koster*, 81–90. Amsterdam: John Benjamins.

Kato, Mary A. & Jairo Nunes. 2009. A uniform raising analysis for standard and nonstandard relative clauses in Brazilian Portuguese. In Jairo Nunes (ed.), *Minimalist essays on Brazilian Portuguese syntax*, 93–120.

Kayne, Richard S. 1983. Connectedness. *Linguistic Inquiry* 14. 223–249. Reprinted in Kayne (1984).

Kayne, Richard S. 1984. *Connectedness and binary branching*. Dordrecht: Foris.

Kayne, Richard S. 1994. *The antisymmetry of syntax*. Cambridge: The MIT Press.

Kayne, Richard S. 2002. Pronouns and their antecedents. In Samuel Epstein & Daniel Seely (eds.), *Derivation and explanation in the minimalist program*, 133–166. Malden, MA: Blackwell. Reprinted in Kayne (2005).

Kayne, Richard S. 2003. Silent years, silent hours. In Lars-Olof Delsing, Cecilia Falk, Gunlög Josefsson & Halldór Á. Sigurðsson (eds.), *Grammar in focus. Festschrift for Christer Platzack*, vol. 2, 209–226. Lund: Wallin & Dalholm. Reprinted in Kayne (2005).

Kayne, Richard S. 2005. *Movement and silence*. New York: Oxford University Press.

Kayne, Richard S. 2008a. Antisymmetry and the lexicon. *Linguistic Variation Yearbook* 8. 1–31. Also in Anna Maria di Sciullo and Cedric Boeckx (eds.) *The Biolinguistic Enterprise: New Perspectives on the Evolution and Nature of the Human Language Faculty*, Oxford University Press, London, 329-353, 2011. Reprinted in Kayne (2010b).

Kayne, Richard S. 2008b. Some preliminary comparative remarks on French and Italian definite articles. In Robert Freidin, Carlos P. Otero & Maria Luisa Zubizarreta (eds.), *Foundational issues in linguistic theory. essays in honor of Jean-Roger Vergnaud*, 291–321. Cambridge, MA: MIT Press. Reprinted in Kayne (2010b).

Kayne, Richard S. 2010a. Why isn't *this* a complementizer? In *Comparisons and contrasts*. New York: Oxford University Press.

Kayne, Richard S. 2010b. *Comparisons and contrasts*. New York: Oxford University Press.

Kayne, Richard S. 2016. *The Unicity of There and the Definiteness Effect*. Ms., New York University.

Leu, Thomas. 2014. *The architecture of determiners*. New York: Oxford University Press.

Lin, Jo-Wang. 1996. *Polarity licensing and Wh-phrase quantification in Chinese*. University of Massachussets, Amherst dissertation.

Marantz, Alec. 2010. Locality Domains for Contextual Allosemy in Words. Handout, New York University.

Martín, F.J. 2012. *Deconstructing Catalan object clitics.* New York University dissertation.

Nunes, Jairo. 2001. Sideward movement. *Linguistic Inquiry* 32. 303–344.

Postma, Gertjan. 1994. The indefinite reading of WH. In Reineke Bok-Bennema & Crit Cremers (eds.), *Linguistics in the Netherlands 1994*, 187–198. Amsterdam: John Benjamins.

Rizzi, Luigi. 1997. The fine structure of the left periphery. In Liliane Haegeman (ed.), *Elements of grammar: A handbook of generative syntax*, 281–337. Dordrecht: Kluwer.

Ross, John Robert. 1967. *Constraints on variables in syntax.* M.I.T dissertation.

Schachter, Paul. 1973. Focus and relativization. *Language* 49. 19–46.

Stowell, Tim. 1985. Licensing conditions on null operators. In J. Goldberg, S. MacKaye & M. Westcoat (eds.), *Proceedings of the west coast conference on formal linguistics vol. 4* (WCCFL 4), 314–326.

Vergnaud, Jean-Roger. 1974. *French relative clauses.* M.I.T. dissertation.

Vergnaud, Jean-Roger. 1985. *Dépendances et niveaux de représentation en syntaxe.* Amsterdam: John Benjamins.

Wood, Jim & Alec Marantz. 2017. The interpretation of external arguments. In Roberta D'Alessandro, Irene Franco & Ángel J. Gallego (eds.), *The verbal domain*, 255–278. Oxford: Oxford University Press.

Chapter 18

Theoretical limits on borrowing through contact; not everything goes

Joseph Emonds

Palacky University, Olomouc

The traditional derivation of Middle English (ME) from Old English (OE) is highly problematic.

- Essentially no Scandinavian borrowing in OE (Baugh & Cable 2002; Strang 1970).

- In a short period (1130–1200) when English wasn't written, most OE vocabulary was lost.

- The earliest ME texts (from 1200, *Ormulum*) are the first to contain numerous daily life Scandinavian "borrowings".

- Roughly *half of the ME grammatical lexicon* is cognate with Old Norse.

- ME syntax shares with North Germanic (NG) over 20 syntactic properties that West Germanic (WG) lacks (Emonds & Faarlund 2014).

From these facts, these authors conclude that ME is an NG language "Anglicized Norse" (AN) with many OE borrowings rather than the other way around. This paper proposes to strengthen this hypothesis by arguing on theoretical grounds that *several NG syntactic properties of ME could not have been borrowed from NG*. They must have resulted from internal developments in AN. That is, the paper justifies a hypothesis that limits the type of morpho-syntax that can be borrowed via language contact.

1 Introduction

The traditional derivation of Middle English (ME) from Old English (OE) is highly problematic.

- Essentially no Scandinavian borrowing in OE (Baugh & Cable 2002; Strang 1970).

Joseph Emonds. 2017. Theoretical limits on borrowing through contact; not everything goes. In Laura R. Bailey & Michelle Sheehan (eds.), *Order and structure in syntax I: Word order and syntactic structure*, 373–384. Berlin: Language Science Press. DOI:10.5281/zenodo.1117698

- In a short period (1130–1200) when English wasn't written, most OE vocabulary was lost.

- The earliest ME texts (from 1200, *Ormulum*) are the first to contain numerous daily life Scandinavian "borrowings".

- Roughly *half of the ME grammatical lexicon* is cognate with Old Norse.

- ME syntax shares with North Germanic (NG) over 20 syntactic properties that West Germanic (WG) lacks (Emonds & Faarlund 2014).

From these facts, these authors conclude that ME is an NG language "Anglicized Norse" (AN) with many OE borrowings rather than the other way around. This paper proposes to strengthen this hypothesis by arguing on theoretical grounds that *several NG syntactic properties of ME could not have been borrowed from NG*. They must have resulted from internal developments in AN. That is, the paper justifies a hypothesis that limits the type of morpho-syntax that can be borrowed via language contact.

Emonds & Faarlund (2014) discuss several NG constructions in ME that are not instances of single lexical items. The first four below are well attested in earliest Mainland NG and ME.

(a) A full system of *post-verbal directional and aspectual particles*, contrasted with WG pre-verbal separable prefixes.

(b) *Preposition stranding*, including in sluicing (*who with, what about*, etc.)

(c) Unmarked *head-initial word order in VPs*, in both main and dependent clauses.

(d) *Subject and object raising*, absent in in both OE and WG generally.

(e) *Parasitic gaps*, freely formed only in NG; restricted or absent in WG.

(f) *Tag questions*, based on syntactic copies of Subjects and Tense in NG but not in WG.

It is difficult to see how these properties, taken as changes from OE to ME, could be "borrowings" of lexical items via language contact of OE with Norse in England. Whole classes of verbs and prepositions would have to be borrowed *en masse*. The properties in italics satisfy no independent sense of "lexical item." Though these all are properties particular to NG (none seem to be Indo-European), there is no clear evidence that any have ever been borrowed by contact into or from neighbouring Germanic, Romance, or Slavic languages. At one time in the past, these constructions have developed, *internal to NG*. Consequently, properties (a-f) could not have entered ME through simple contact with Scandinavian even in a rapidly evolving OE language. Properties (a-f) rather testify to an unchanging NG character of ME.

2 A-theoretical perspectives on language contact

Middle English (ME), in contrast to Old English (OE), has many words of Scandinavian origin, conventionally attributed to language contact and borrowing. However, recourse to such an account doesn't stand up to even moderate scrutiny. Traditional scholarship, e.g. Campbell (1959) and Strang (1970), locates the great bulk of this borrowing from c. 1170 onwards, starting with the ME period, while in the OE period, hardly any Scandinavian words were borrowed (Baugh & Cable 2002: 99). Yet, the Scandinavian language in England, of which there are no records in the OE period, is taken to have died out by 1150 (Thomason 2016; Baugh & Cable 2002: 96), before serious borrowing from it even started. Hence this borrowing can't be ascribed to contact, at least contact with the living.

This inconsistent dating has been a fertile source for creative sociolinguistic scenarios, although no facts actually confirm these speculations in the contact literature.[1] A centre piece in such thinking is often some kind of "spoken Old English" (there are no texts) which must have borrowed extensively from the English variant of Scandinavian before the latter died out. Subsequently, these extensive borrowings, including much daily life vocabulary, suddenly came to light in written Early ME.

Moreover, this (allegedly borrowed) Scandinavian vocabulary was not limited to content words, counter to normal contact situations, as was the massive influx of French words into Late ME when French speakers in England all switched to English as their first language (14th c.). The fact is, not only did hundreds of daily life terms in ME have a known Scandinavian origin, so also did roughly half of its grammatical lexicon (For more on how this component differs from the open class lexicon, consult Ouhalla 1991 and Emonds 2000: Chs. 3 and 4). Something other than "borrowing through contact" must have transpired, not only because of dating but also because of the types of "borrowed" words and morphemes.

3 The importance of Middle English syntax

Another discrepancy between OE and ME is the key to understanding all these puzzles. If one assembles the data patterns of ME syntax, the language groups typologically with North Germanic (NG), while OE has unmistakable West Germanic (WG) syntax (Gianollo et al. 2008: 133). On the basis of such patterns, Emonds & Faarlund (2014) argue that ME

---

[1]One variant (Thomason & Kaufman 1988: 286–287) proposes that when in the 10th c. Norse died out in various areas, Anglo Saxon speakers introduced numerous aspects of Norse grammar and phonology into (unattested) OE dialects such as "East Mercian" and "East Saxon". These "packets" of dozens of "Norse grammatical elements" then spread southward and westward to the whole country, ultimately resulting in "Norsified English" (i.e. Early ME). The authors devise this *sui generis* scenario of contact to account for why, a century or more later, these diverse Norsification features first appear as a group in written ME: "These features of Simplification and Norsification ... did not appear gradually; *they appear in the earliest Middle English documents of the Danelaw.*" (op. cit. 278–279, my emphasis). In place of elaborate contact scenarios, Emonds & Faarlund (2014) claim that ME but not OE was a development of North Germanic Norse, eventually learned as a second and then first language by all Anglo-Saxons. Consequently, much ME grammatical vocabulary and morphophonology was Norse.

shares with Mainland Scandinavian more than 20 syntactic properties that OE and other WG languages lack. They conclude (1):

(1) **English as North Germanic.** Middle English was a direct descendent of the Mainland Norse spoken by Scandinavian settlers in England.

The presence in ME of Norse morphophonology and daily life and grammatical vocabulary is thus explained. The familiar facts that this hypothesis now makes strange are the daily life and grammatical vocabulary of OE found in ME; because of this factor, Emonds and Faarlund call Early ME by the name "Anglicized Norse". Under this view, in the realm of syntax there is basically nothing to explain, since, they argue, ME *shares no syntax or morpho-syntax with OE* that is not common to Germanic languages in general.

According to this study's guiding hypothesis (1), ME continues Mainland Norse and not Icelandic. I continue to follow Emonds & Faarlund (2014: Ch.1, p.127), who exclude any particularities of Icelandic, because all known or plausible Scandinavian immigration into the Danelaw was directly from Denmark and Norway, and also because Icelandic centrally differs from both Mainland Scandinavian and ME in maintaining productive proto-Germanic morphological case.[2]

In the new perspective that ME is basically the written down form of Anglicized Norse, there remains no reason why the earliest ME texts must follow the last OE texts. Indeed, a British Library webpage concludes that the first text in ME, a translation of a Latin homily, dates from c. 1150.[3] This dating is suspiciously late (possibly to reconcile its language with the notion that it must post-date OE texts), since Ralph d'Escures's original must have pre-dated his debilitating stroke in 1119 (d. 1122).[4] Though traditional histories of English don't acknowledge any dating overlap, works arguably in OE, e.g. the poem *The Owl and the Nightingale,* were written at least until close to 1200.[5]

When Anglicized Norse began to be written extensively around 1200 (e.g. the text *Ormulum*), it was considered to be a version of English, what is now called the East Midlands dialect of ME. Uncontroversially this dialect is the forerunner of Modern English, which therefore descends from Norse, not from OE. The latter became the Southern and Western dialects of ME, which eventually ceased being written or spoken.

This paper proposes to strengthen the hypothesis (1) by arguing on theoretical grounds that *several NG syntactic properties of ME could not have entered ME by borrowing.* They must have resulted from internal developments in Anglicized Norse. That is, the paper puts forward a claim that limits the *type* of morpho-syntax that can be borrowed via

---

[2] A reviewer objects that because the latter's texts are older, arguments about ME must be primarily based on Icelandic. This logic comes down to a version of *post hoc ergo propter hoc*: "if the texts of X are older than the texts of a related language Y, the a third related language Z must descend from X not Y." To see the fallacy, take X to be the oldest Italian texts, Y to be medieval French, and Z to be any dialects of Quebec French.

[3] http://www.bl.uk/learning/timeline/item126539.html

[4] https://en.wikipedia.org/wiki/Ralph_d'Escures

[5] This poem is said to be in the ME "southern dialect", again to preserve the idea that OE "changed" diachronically into ME in a short period around 1150. Historians of English allude to a long hiatus in written English to allow for this "development", but the hiatus was no more than 50 years; the two different written languages may have even co-existed for a short time.

language contact. It is of course not disputed that changes are sometimes simply internal to a language (e.g. in Modern English, the sharply differing syntax of modals and lexical verbs, the development of the progressive). My proposal here is that several Early ME syntactic properties must have developed this way. If these properties are moreover typical of NG, it must be that Early ME is also.[6]

Before continuing, I should acknowledge an extensive attempted refutation of hypothesis (1), the review of Bech & Walkden (2015). About a quarter of it consists of a section on method,[7] and the rest proposes different interpretations of mostly well-known patterns. Space limitation obviously precludes an evaluation of their 20 page work in this study, which focuses on presenting another type of argument for (1). I can indicate, however, that one syntactic argument which they stress (their Sect. 3.3.1) concerns their claim that ME and Scandinavian "verb-second" systems are different, and that the former continues at least one salient OE pattern, allowing scene-setting PPs in pre-subject position. Emonds & Faarlund (2016) argues that a better account of this ME construction is available in terms of Universal Grammar, and is unrelated to a language-particular continuation of OE.

4 Borrowable syntax: The lexical entries of Borer's Conjecture

Emonds & Faarlund (2014) discuss over 20 morpho-syntactic properties that indicate that ME has NG syntax. Some 15 of these can be formally expressed, without much difficulty, as single entries in its Grammatical Lexicon. According to Borer's Conjecture (Borer 1984: 29), now widely adopted in generative studies, such entries are the essence of language-particular grammars.

As a result, it is possible in principle that a rapidly evolving OE could have borrowed (or lost) such properties/entries through contact with Scandinavian speakers. Nonetheless, as Emonds and Faarlund argue, the sheer number of these entries and the short interval in which they were borrowed or disappeared (leaving aside speculations about a distinct "spoken OE"), constitutes a strong argument in favour of the Anglicized Norse Hypothesis (1).[8] Here is a list of the changes that can be associated with individual grammatical morphemes: The last two (2p–q) have been brought to my attention after publication of Emonds & Faarlund (2014).

---

[6]Rephrasing, if Early ME simply continues WG OE, and yet displays the NG properties discussed in §4, ME would have had to acquire them by borrowing. I will argue that certain such borrowings are impossible (contrary to the literature of language contact, which essentially holds that under contact "anything can happen".)

[7]That section takes issue with the decision of Emonds & Faarlund (2014) to argue on the basis of syntax and morpho-syntax, leaving aside studies of DNA, whether the bilingualism of the time was social or individual, sound change, etc.

[8]The traditional view (OE → ME) must locate this avalanche of changes and several others inside a single century.

(2) **Single entries in the ME Grammatical Lexicon** (attributable to Norse)[9]

(a) As in NG, certain modals start to express the future tense in ME. In contrast, OE uses present tense and Modern WG uses non-modal (agreeing) auxiliary verbs.

(b) The ME infinitival *to* is a free morpheme like Old Norse *at*; both can be split from V. WG uses only bound prefixes (Dutch *te*, German *zu*), and this includes OE *to* (Susan Pintzuk, pers. comm.).

(c) No passive/past participle prefix is the general rule in Old Norse and ME. But in OE and German the prefix *ge-/y-* is frequent and sometimes obligatory. (*Ge-* was also lost in some WG dialects bordering on NG areas, but these were not sources of ME.)

(d) The NG languages including ME have a perfect infinitive *to have V+en*. OE does not (Fischer 1992: 336–337).[10]

(e) Like NG, ME expresses sentence negation with free morphemes that are initial in VP (Norse *ikke*, ME *naht*). OE uses a pre-verbal bound morpheme *ne-*.[11]

(f) As in Old Norse, ME *that* appears in complex subordinators like *now that, if that, before that, in that, etc.* while OE and WG typically don't use general subordinators (*þe, dass*) in this way (Emonds & Faarlund 2014: 143–144; Fischer 1992: 295).

(g) The OE "correlative adverbs" *swa...swa, tha...tha,* etc. are unknown in Mainland Scandinavia and disappear in ME.

(h) Early ME loses OE relative pronouns that display case or gender (*se þe*; Mitchell & Robinson 1992). As in Old Scandinavian, Early ME relativizers are invariant.

(i) ME, like NG, grades long adjectives analytically (*more, most*). OE does not.

---

[9]These constructions are all discussed separately in Emonds & Faarlund (2014: Chs 3-6). I don't formalize these entries here because specific notations might be controversial and/or difficult to grasp at a glance. It is unfortunate that three decades of lip service to Borer's Conjecture have produced so few actual proposals for formalizing these entries, now the sine qua non for truly generative grammars. Cf Emonds (2000) for extensive arguments favouring syntax-based formalized lexical entries.

[10]A reviewer observes that the modern "West Germanic languages Dutch and German also have a perfect infinitive." But even so, no one suggests that these languages influenced the change from OE to ME, so this observation is beside the point. The only issue here is then whether the OE lack of a perfect infinitive was typical of WG or was somewhat special.

[11]Early ME puts together the OE prefix *ne-* and the post-verbal free morpheme *noht* (i.e. 'double negation'), but eventually drops *ne-*, and so syntactically adopts the NG pattern. Three reviewers bring up "Jespersen's cycle", a descriptive name for the preceding process, combined with the possibility that free negation morphemes can also become bound (Modern English *not* → *n't*). As always, the issue is, can we explain such replacements? Emonds & Faarlund (2014: Sect. 7.2.6) argue that the free morpheme in ME is simply a part of Anglicized Norse replacing West Saxon. One reviewer, after commenting that this "similarity of ME and NG is indeed striking," cites Breitbarth (2009) to the effect that negation developed similarly in Dutch, German and Frisian. If so, the question is again, which of Norse and these WG languages were in contact with Early ME, so that one of them could have either influenced OE (the traditional view) or replaced it (the view of this essay). Under either view, the historical facts point unambiguously to Norse.

(j) As in Mainland Scandinavian, the ME subjunctive is no longer used to mark indirect speech, as it could in OE (Fischer 1992: 314).

(k) Subject pronouns could be pro-clitics on second position Vs in OE, but not in NG languages. ME came to resemble NG in this regard (Kroch et al. 2000).

(l) The copula selects infinitive complements in both ME and NG, but not in OE (Fischer 1992: 336–337).

(m) The derived nominal suffix in OE is *–ung* (like German). NG also allows *–ing*, and in ME the latter form is the only possibility.

(n) The general patronymic suffix in NG for new families is *–son;* it replaces OE *–ing* throughout England in c. 1200 (Strang 1970).

(o) OE genitive case appears on the head *and* pre-modifiers in a possessive phrase. But in both ME and NG a single enclitic *–s* follows a possessive phrase, whether its head is final or not.

(p) In WG (OE and German), some intransitive verbs, with meanings "of movement and change of state" form the perfect with *be* (Denison 1993). But in *the earliest Norse texts,* the *perfect auxiliary* was uniformly *hafa* 'have' (J. T. Faarlund, pers. comm.) Similarly in England, the change to uniform use of *have* (ME) rather than *be* (OE) with motion verbs begins just after the Conquest (Denison 1993: 350–355).

(q) Mainland Scandinavian and Modern English (bur not Icelandic) share the possibility of a null Complementizer in a range of finite clauses (Holmberg 2016), It is difficult to search for null items in corpora, so this may be a medieval NP property or a more recent shared innovation.

On point (o) of (2), a reviewer asks if it isn't "very unlikely that the version of Norse that was spoke in the British Isles only marked genitive by adding *–s* at the end of the entire NP"? As there are no texts prior to ME, one can only note that this device, unknown in OE and WG generally, is restricted to and yet general in Mainland Scandinavian *throughout the ME period.* Chalupová & Chavratová (in preparation) give numerous examples, including these from Kroch & Taylor (2000).

(3) Middle English

ani ancre Iesu cristes spuse	(*Ancrene Riwle*, II.98.1173) (1215–1222)
Q hermit Jesus Criste-s spouse	
sein gregories wordes	(*Ancrene Riwle*, II.61.632) (1215–1222)
Saint George-s word.PL	
te holy gostes helpe	(*Ayenbite of Inwyt*, 98.1923) (1250–1350)
the Holy Ghost-s help	
þe dome of godes spelle	(*Ayenbite of Inwyt*, 11.125) (1250–1350)
the judgment of god-s story	

These authors further point out what most corpus dating obscures: mature authors are presumably using grammar acquired as children, often easily thirty years earlier than the date of a text. In particular, they report the last two examples as penned by a 70-year old born between 1180 and 1280. Hence these examples of phrasal -*s* no doubt reflect the spoken language of 1185–1285.

The question that emerges from such data is: where else could this highly unusual type of case-marking (a phrasal suffix in an otherwise analytic head-initial language) have come from, if not from a Norse continuously spoken in England throughout this period? We expect odd borrowings only into contracting or dying languages (the reviewer exemplifies with Prince Edward Island French), but ME was not dying out.

For purposes of discussion I grant that, at least singly, the Norse features of Early ME in (2) could have been borrowed through contact. Individually they all conform to Borer's Conjecture, and plausibly, changes in particular grammars involve borrowing or deleting single entries in Grammatical Lexicons.

Thus, looking through the list (2) one by one, *no single one of these properties is in itself implausible* as "contact borrowing in syntax" from Norse into an evolving OE.[12] A rather transparent interpretation of Borer's Conjecture is thus that changes in particular grammars are simply changes in the lexical entries of individual functional category morphemes, and as such, they can be borrowed through contact.[13]

5 Language-particular architecture: Syntax which cannot be borrowed

In addition to the constructions in (2), Emonds & Faarlund (2014) discuss six NG constructions in ME that *cannot be expressed as lexical entries for single morphemes*. That is, these constructions are generalizations that lexical entries may reflect, but the entries themselves do not suffice for expressing them in single statements. Because of their more general nature, I call them ARCHITECTURAL rather than lexical properties. The first four in the list (4) are well attested in earliest Mainland NG as well as ME; the last two are easily found only in the modern period. Discussion and references for each property are given in the sections indicated below from Emonds & Faarlund (2014).

These generalizations that describe these language-particular configurations cannot be adequately expressed formally by single lexical entries, e.g. P-stranding is not a property that different Ps accidentally have in common. To maintain an adequate model, either Borer's Conjecture or the notion of lexical entry will have to be modified in some

---

[12]But taken together, as noted above, it is completely implausible that the long list in (2) could be borrowings effected within a century. And sociologically, why would monolingual Anglo-Saxon speakers borrow so copiously from the supposedly dying language of their former adversaries?

[13]One reviewer provides a sequence of alternative scenarios for many of the points in (2). There is no unified pattern in these disparate and sometimes complex suggestions; it is simply a list of separate diachronic events which must be postulated to counter the unified explanation of (1), namely that in the syntactic development of early ME, nothing happened. In a few instances, the reviewer supports suggestions with evidence. Thus, there are ME remnants *y-* of the WG participial prefix *ge-*. I suggest this *-y* was due to bilingual Saxons, and predictably disappeared after a few generations. In other instances, data seems misinterpreted. E.g. ME and Norse both uniformly use *have* in the perfect tense, unlike the WG and Romance languages cited by the reviewer, where *have* and *be* alternate.

way. However this is to be accomplished, the content in (5) below of "lexical specifications of only single functional category items" should remain unchanged.

(4) **North Germanic architectural properties of** ME, not part of OE:

  (a) *Head-initial word order within* VPs is unmarked, in both main and dependent clauses (Emonds & Faarlund 2014: 3.1).[14]

  (b) A system of *post-verbal directional and aspectual free morpheme particles*, contrasted with WG systems of pre-verbal separable prefixes (3.2). This change may be facilitated by (4a), but the two properties are definitely not the same (Emonds & Faarlund 2016).

  (c) *Preposition stranding*, at first in relative clauses and eventually even in sluicing constructions (*who with, what for*, etc. Emonds & Faarlund 2014: 3.7–3.8.)

  (d) *Subject raising*, both into subject and object position after epistemic verbs. These are absent in both OE and WG generally (Denison 1993: 221; Hawkins 1986: 82; Emonds & Faarlund 2014: 3.3–3.4).

  (e) Freely formed *parasitic gaps;* these appear freely only in NG, and are restricted or absent in WG languages (for German, see Kathol 2001; for Dutch, see Bennis & Hoekstra 1985; Emonds & Faarlund 2014: 6.4).[15]

  (f) *Tag questions* based on syntactic copies of the Subject and Tense in NG but not in WG (Emonds & Faarlund 2014: 6.5).

These constructions all seem to be language-particular properties of NG languages. For example, there is no widely accepted evidence that any of them are Indo-European. This suggests that all must have developed *internally* in NG languages during the Germanic phase of their history. There is no evidence outside the issue at hand (the relation of OE to ME) that any of the six constructions in (4) have ever been borrowed by contact *either into or from* neighbouring West Germanic, Celtic or Slavic languages.

There are 72 ways one of these six properties could have been borrowed from one of these four language families into another.[16] While I cannot categorically state that none

---

[14] A reviewer feels that Norse could have changed English word order by contact. Keeping in mind that Norse was dying out under this traditional scenario, this is as likely as French shifting to vso order in the face of Breton dying out. The reviewer also claims that the IE shift away from verb-final orders was "arrested" in Indo-Aryan by contact with Turkic and Dravidian. But arrested change is no change and requires no convoluted contact explanations. This reviewer also repeats a widespread assumption that "Southern Semitic languages have shifted to head-final orders ... due to contact with Nilotic" [sic; presumably Cushitic, JE]. For a carefully argued alternative to this scenario in terms of diglossia, see Ouhalla (2015).

[15] As a reviewer notes, these sources indicate that the basic ov character of West Germanic seems to preclude many parasitic gaps that exist in English. A more complete future understanding of them may lead to deriving property (4e) from (4a). This does not affect this study's conclusion; it simply would mean that of the six architectural properties listed here, only five are independent.

[16] Given four families A, B, C, D, possible borrowings for each property are A→B, B→A, A→C, C→A, A→D, D→A, B→C, C→B, B→D, D→B, C→D, D→C, 12 total. There are six properties, so the total conceivable borrowings are 72 in all. Even if the source family for these properties is taken as certain, there are still 18 possible but unattested borrowings.

have ever occurred, the number of such borrowings is minuscule compared to the implication of traditional histories of English. These contend that contact with dying Norse (or pure accident) caused Middle and Modern English to acquire all six NG architectural properties, four in the space of at most 200 years.[17]

Given these considerations, I wish to strengthen the hypothesis that ME is Anglicized Norse (1), by proposing that *the NG syntactic properties in* (4), or at least most of them, could not in principle have been borrowed into late OE from NG. They must have resulted from internal developments in Norse, most of which we know predated or were simultaneous with Scandinavian settlement in England. That is, I suggest a restrictive and historically justified hypothesis that limits what aspects of morpho-syntax can be borrowed via language contact. Under this hypothesis, the NG syntax of ME cannot in principle be due to "OE + contact with Norse speakers".

To formulate this hypothesis, the morpho-syntactic properties that distinguish ME from OE (and group it with NG) have been divided into two types. As explained above, I coin the contrasting labels "lexical" and "architectural" for language-particular properties, according to which the second group has properties that cannot be reduced in a trivial way to the first, i.e. to the format required by Borer's Conjecture.

(5) **Restricted Borrowing Hypothesis.**
Under language contact, a living language L_1 can borrow from L_2 lexical specifications of *only single functional category items.*

That is, lexical properties can be (sparingly) borrowed under contact, but architectural properties cannot be.

It follows that properties (4a–f) could not have entered ME even in a rapidly evolving OE (a fortiori, essentially simultaneously) through language contact of OE with Scandinavian. The ME properties (4a–f) testify rather to *an unchanging NG character of ME.* That is, changes in patterns that we here call the syntactic "architecture" of a particular language can only arise through internal developments, not through simple contact of adjacent languages.

I note in conclusion how strongly this view contrasts with the traditional claim that OE → ME, and hence that all the properties in (4) developed in a very short time, at least four of them in the 12th and 13th c., via language contact with a language which had already died out (c. 1150) before the evidence of borrowing is attested (after 1170). The traditional view of the genesis of Early ME, when one reflects on its actual claims, violates not only the canons of a restrictive diachronic theory, but also those of common sense.

---

[17]There is one problematic instance that might require some revision in (5). Current research may point to a relation between Celtic and NG languages in the syntax of tag questions. When the import of this research becomes clearer, we can re-assess its relation to (5).

Abbreviations

AN	Anglicized Norse	OV	Object-Verb
DNA	Derived Nominal Agreement	P	Preposition
IE	Indo-European	PP	Prepositional Phrase
ME	Middle English	V	Verb
NG	North Germanic	VP	Verb Phrase
NP	Noun Phrase	VSO	Verb-Subject-Object
OE	Old English	WG	West Germanic

Acknowledgements

I have enjoyed and greatly profited from many linguistic conversations over three decades with Anders Holmberg, in many different venues throughout Europe. I am especially appreciative of his encouragement regarding this work relating Modern English to its syntactic and morphological Scandinavian roots, and for his suggestions of points to follow up on. I thank two reviewers and the editors for helpful suggestions and encouragement.

References

Ancrene Riwle. N.d. https://www.ling.upenn.edu/hist-corpora/PPCME2-RELEASE-4/info/cmancriw-m1.html. The Penn-Helsinki Parsed Corpus of Middle English (PPCME2).

Ayenbite of Inwyt. N.d. https://www.ling.upenn.edu/hist-corpora/PPCME2-RELEASE-4/info/cmayenbi-m2.html. The Penn-Helsinki Parsed Corpus of Middle English (PPCME2).

Baugh, Albert C. & Thomas. Cable. 2002. *A History of English (th edition).* London: Routledge & Kegan Paul.

Bech, Kristin & George Walkden. 2015. English is (still) a west germanic language. *Nordic Journal of Linguistics* 21. 559–571.

Bennis, Hans & Teun Hoekstra. 1985. Gaps and parasitic gaps. *The Linguistic Review* 4. 29–87.

Borer, Hagit. 1984. *Parametric syntax.* Dordrecht: Foris.

Breitbarth, Anne. 2009. A hybrid approach to Jespersen's cycle in west germanic. *The Journal of Comparative Germanic Linguistics* 12. 81–114.

Campbell, Alistair. 1959. *Old English Grammar.* Oxford: the Clarendon Press.

Chalupová, Anya & Petra Chavratová. in preparation. *The Phrasal Host of the Germanic Genitive in English. The Norse Origins.*

Denison, David. 1993. *English Historical Syntax: Verbal Constructions.* London: Longman.

Emonds, Joseph. 2000. *Lexicon and grammar: the English syntacticon.* Berlin: Mouton de Gruyter.

Emonds, Joseph & Jan Terje Faarlund. 2014. *English: The language of the Vikings*. Olomouc: Palacky University Press.

Emonds, Joseph & Jan Terje Faarlund. 2016. Anglicized Norse, or anything goes? *Language Dynamics and Change* 6.1. 49–66.

Fischer, Olga. 1992. Syntax. Middle English. In Norman Blake (ed.), *The Cambridge history of the english language*, vol. 2, 207–408. Cambridge: Cambridge University Press.

Gianollo, Chiara, Cristina Guardiano & Giuseppe Longobardi. 2008. Three fundamental issues in parametric linguistics. In Theresa Biberauer (ed.), *The Limits of Syntactic Variation*, 109–142. Amsterdam: John Benjamins.

Hawkins, John A. 1986. *A comparative typology of English and German: Unifying the contrasts*. London: Croom Helm.

Holmberg, Anders. 2016. Norse against old English. *Language Dynamics and Change* 6.1. 21–23.

Kathol, Andreas. 2001. On the nonexistence of true parasitic gaps in standard German. In Culicover Peter W. & Paul Postal (eds.), *Parasitic gaps*, 315–338. Cambridge, MA: MIT Press.

Kroch, Anthony S. & Ann Taylor. 2000. *The Penn-Helsinki Parsed Corpus of Middle English (PPCME2)*. CD-ROM, second edition, release 4.

Kroch, Anthony S., Ann Taylor & Donald Ringe. 2000. The Middle English Verb-Second Constraint: A Case Study in Language Contact and Language Change. In Susan Herring, van Pieter Reenen & Lene Schøsler (eds.), *Textual parameters in older languages*, 353–91. Amsterdam: John Benjamins.

Mitchell, Bruce & Fred C. Robinson. 1992. *A Guide to Old English*. 5th edn. Oxford: Blackwell.

Ouhalla, Jamal. 1991. *Functional Categories and Parametric Variation*. London: Routledge.

Ouhalla, Jamal. 2015. The origins of Andalusi-Moroccan Arabic and the role of diglossia. *Brill's Journal of Afroasiatic Languages and Linguistics* 7. 157–195.

Strang, Barbara. 1970. *A History of English*. London: Routledge.

Thomason, Sarah G. 2016. Middle English: English, not norse. *Language Dynamics and Change* 6.1. 42–45.

Thomason, Sarah G. & Terrence Kaufman. 1988. *Language Contact, Creolization, and Genetic Linguistics*. Berkeley: University of California Press.

Name index

Language index

Subject index

www.ingramcontent.com/pod-product-compliance
Lightning Source LLC
Chambersburg PA
CBHW080917100426
42812CB00007B/2309